TVA

Fifty Years of Grass-roots Bureaucracy

TVA

FIFTY YEARS OF GRASS-ROOTS BUREAUCRACY

Edited by

Erwin C. Hargrove

and

Paul K. Conkin

University of Illinois Press
Urbana and Chicago

Library of Congress Cataloging in Publication Data

Main entry under title:

TVA, fifty years of grass-roots bureaucracy.

   Based on a symposium held at Vanderbilt Institute for
Public Policy Studies during Dec. 1981.
   Includes index.
   Contents: Intellectual and political roots/Paul Conkin—
The TVA, 1933–45/Richard Lowitt—The TVA, 1945–80/
Wilmon H. Droze—[etc.]
   1. Tennessee Valley Authority—Congresses.   2. Elec-
tric utilities—Tennessee River Valley—Congresses.
3. Electric power—Tennessee River Valley—Con-
gresses.   4. Water resources development—Tennessee
River Valley—Congresses.   I. Hargrove, Erwin C.
II. Conkin, Paul Keith.   III. Vanderbilt Institute for Public
Policy Studies.   IV. Title. T.V.A., fifty years of grass-roots
bureaucracy.
HD9685.U7T37   1983   353.0082′3′09768   83-6475
ISBN 0-252-01086-8

PREFACE

The chapters in this book are the fruits of a research project carried out through the Vanderbilt Institute for Public Policy Studies in 1981 and 1982. Financial support from the Ford and Rockefeller foundations and the National Endowment for the Humanities made this possible.

In December, 1981, a symposium—"The Tennessee Valley Authority: An Experiment in American Government"—was held at Vanderbilt, with the support of the Rockefeller Foundation. At that time most of the papers that were to form this book were delivered to a scholarly and public audience.

We thank the following scholars who served as discussants at the symposium for their thoughtful suggestions and criticisms: William E. Leuchtenburg, professor of history, University of North Carolina, Chapel Hill, formerly of Columbia University; John Thomas, professor of history, Brown University; Francis E. Rourke, professor of political science, Johns Hopkins University; Jameson Doig, professor at the Woodrow Wilson School of Public and International Affairs, Princeton University; James Branscome, journalist, Sevierville, Tennessee; Otis Graham, professor of history, University of North Carolina, Chapel Hill; George Tindall, professor of history, University of North Carolina, Chapel Hill; and Philip Selznick, professor of sociology, University of California at Berkeley.

We wish to thank Scarlett Graham for organizing the symposium, Lottie Strupp for administering all budgetary aspects of both the symposium and the research that preceded it, and Janice Jones for typing and retyping manuscripts. Richard Westbrook, University of Tennessee at Knoxville, was an excellent research assistant.

Finally, we thank Richard Wentworth, director of the University of Illinois Press, for his sharp eye for what makes a good book, Bonnie Depp for superb copyediting, and Elizabeth Dulany for efficient management of the entire process.

ERWIN C. HARGROVE
PAUL K. CONKIN
Nashville, Tennessee
May, 1983

CONTENTS

PART FOUR: TVA AND AMERICAN DEMOCRACY

INTRODUCTION

Erwin C. Hargrove

THE Tennessee Valley Authority was fifty years old on May 18, 1983. Today the TVA faces uncertainties about the future that can only be explained in terms of the past. The essays in this book thus present a composite concern with the legacies of history. We have sought neither to idealize the institution nor to denigrate it but to understand it in terms of the intellectual, political, and economic forces that have shaped it. The book is organized according to four themes: the origins of the TVA idea and the development of established and stable organizational purposes and structures; the manner in which TVA has been led and has come to terms with other bodies of government; the time of troubles of the 1970s and 1980s, in which TVA has been criticized as much as praised, often by people who celebrated its early ideals; and, finally, an assessment of the TVA experience for what one might learn about politics and government in the United States.

Origins and Growth

The TVA ideal far exceeds the actual capacities of the organization to act. The ideal is that of a body designed for tasks of regional development in which the greatest possible efficiency and expertise are to be combined with responsiveness to citizens at the "grass roots." Paul Conkin describes the gap between ideal and reality in his comparison of Franklin D. Roosevelt's grandiose rhetoric about the TVA with the actual statutory powers of the agency. FDR emphasized planning and regional development in one of the most impoverished regions of the

South, with particular attention to the conservation and development of agricultural, water, and forest resources. But the actual powers of the corporation, as given in the TVA Act, are very specific, calling for the creation of dams for flood control, navigation, and electric power generation and the manufacture of fertilizer for the improvement of agriculture. Section 22 permits the preparation of plans for the region but provides no authority to carry them out. Conkin explains the TVA Act as a pragmatic response to political demands in the mid-South that the potentialities of the Muscle Shoals nitrate plants be developed on behalf of southern agriculture and that the turbulent Tennessee River and its tributaries be tamed and its power harnessed. But the halo effect of Roosevelt's rhetoric has continued to this day, not only as a protective "myth" invoked by the leaders of TVA to justify its existence but also as a strong element in the expectations for TVA by many of its adherents. The TVA has been presumed to be a grand experiment, a moral force and a beacon to the nation. Thus when Rex Tugwell wrote in 1950 that "from 1936 on the TVA should have been called the Tennessee Valley Power Production and Flood Control Corporation," he voiced the disappointment of many early believers.[1] Conkin would not share such disillusionment because he has no illusions.

Richard Lowitt's essay illustrates the power of the original TVA ideal, not only in his interpretation of the formative years but in his description of the actual force of such ideals in practice from 1933 to World War II. Lowitt describes TVA's many tangible achievements in the face of intense legal and political opposition from the private power companies. While it was fighting for its life, TVA built beautiful high dams, mastered the river, brought cheap electric power to country people, towns, and cities, and set about transforming Valley agriculture from the self-defeating cycle of corn and cotton to pasture and livestock. He tells how TVA encouraged the states to develop public parks, how malaria was eradicated around TVA reservoir lakes, and how in many other ways TVA was a catalyst for "modernization" in the Valley. But, when all is said and done, the picture is one not of comprehensive regional development according to plans but of practical actions to improve specific areas of life. Yet the spirit of action was utopian and TVA employees seemed possessed of a special dedication.

Wilmon Droze completes the story of institutional development by describing how the manufacture and distribution of electric power increasingly became the most important TVA mission, with subtle consequences for the character of the organization. Many of the other purposes of a multipurpose authority had been achieved by 1945, and TVA had won the political fight to be the power monopoly of the region. The great contribution of TVA electric power to the aluminum industry and the Oak Ridge laboratory during the war and to the Atomic Energy Commission in the postwar period strengthened this mission. Droze describes the transition from hydro to steam power and the political fights in Washington between TVA defenders and opponents, the Dixon-Yates controversy being the most dramatic. The 1959 compromise in which Congress permitted TVA to market bonds to finance its power operations introduced a new period of TVA history. The power service area had been delimited and private competitors were no longer threatened. Congress and presidents exercised little oversight over TVA expansion. Hardly anything was said about the transition to nuclear power in the mid-1960s. The TVA had ceased to be a body with a national mission and was now the power company for the Valley, with additional tasks of agricultural and natural resource development. The central commitment of TVA was to provide electric power for the citizens of the Valley at the lowest possible cost. So long as power was cheap and other costs were negligible, there were no political controversies. Droze leaves the story as such controversies were developing.

Leadership and Accountability

The very political insecurity of TVA has caused it to be inventive. Erwin Hargrove argues that the central task of leadership shared by successive TVA chairmen and their board colleagues has been to discern the most appropriate "technology" for the period ahead and create political support for that position in Washington and the Valley. Thus Lilienthal recognized that the fight against the private power companies could be dramatized as a contest in which the people of the Valley had a stake, and he cleverly tied that cause to Franklin Roosevelt and the New Deal. In subsequent periods TVA has been unable to proceed with adaptations in technology unless political support was present. Thus the transition to steam plants began under the postwar leadership of Gordon Clapp but was unable to continue until Herbert Vogel, Clapp's successor, engineered the self-financing compromise. Aubrey Wagner did not have to make a case for nuclear plants at a time when costs were moderate and growth seemed assured, but the failure to create a political coalition on behalf of continued technological development haunted his successor, S. David Freeman, in a period when costs were rising and growth diminishing. The central conclusion is that while TVA is a semi-independent government corporation, its capacity to carry out its mission depends upon political support.

As a government corporation, TVA is more autonomous in its operations than the federal departments. It is also an organization dominated by professionals, engineers in particular. Finally, it is suspended at a mid-point between the national government in Washington and state and local governments. It is the responsibility of the TVA board to interpret the act in terms of their understanding of present and future necessities and possibilities. The board is not accountable, in the short run, for its decisions. There is always the danger in such a situation that technological or professional imperatives will supersede political considerations. Avery Leiserson contends that it is a misreading of the act to assume that TVA should be pulled short at every turn by Congress, president, or public opinion. If autonomy were not present, the capacity of the organization to plan for the future would atrophy and responsibilities under the act could not be discharged. However, Leiserson would not press his case if he believed that TVA had blatantly disregarded political and public sentiments, as many critics charge. Rather, he concludes that TVA, as a bureaucracy, has been sensitive to changing currents of opinion and that this adaptability has been the key to its survival. The record of TVA in this regard is open to interpretation, as later authors suggest.

Vernon Ruttan concludes that TVA has been most effective in those missions for which it had special technological expertise such as electric power and fertilizer development. These also happen to be the areas in which the strongest statutory authority exists. Ruttan discusses the efforts of the S. David Freeman board to revive the nonpower programs, with particular attention to community development, and concludes that the organization lacks both professional capacities and institutional leverage. There are too many competitors, TVA has no special knowledge, and the problems are not amenable to the TVA technological approach.

Policies in Conflict

The era of good feeling lasted from 1959 to the early 1970s, when changes in the environment and in public values presented TVA with three large areas of challenge and controversy. First, the environmental movement came to the Tennessee Valley to charge TVA with fostering strip mining with its massive coal purchases and polluting the air with its smokestacks. The TVA and the Environmental Protection Agency engaged in a prolonged and bitter fight. The second area of controversy was about water. The TVA continued to press its mission to develop water resources, but projects such as the Land Between the Lakes and the Tellico and Normandy dams stimulated fierce disputes within the Valley. Finally, the cost of electric power increased greatly after the energy shocks of 1973 but TVA continued to project trends of economic growth, thus justifying an extensive program of construction of nuclear power units. The question of the safety of nuclear power was not a major public controversy in the Valley. Rather, the issue was whether ratepayers should be asked to bear the costs of present construction development that would benefit future citizens. The question became even more complicated in 1982 as new TVA projections indicated that the agency was building beyond the range of future needs and the credibility of TVA planning was called into question.

The one theme that is implicitly present in these three areas of controversy is whether TVA's virtues had become its faults. The commitment to provision of power at the lowest possible cost may help explain the struggle of the power division within TVA to ignore questions of environmental damage.[2] The strong ethic of TVA as a multipurpose organization could help account for the invention of new water projects that were not as obviously valuable as the first generation of achievements. The postwar drive to anticipate the needs of the Valley for electric power as a basis for growth may have made it very difficult for TVA to abandon the goal of growth, especially when it was free to set its rates and was not curbed in its development by regulatory bodies.

Dean Hill Rivkin tells the story of the environmental controversies by focusing on the development of new kinds of "public interest" advocates in the Valley who took TVA to court on behalf of environmental causes. Rivkin suggests that a new form of political accountability was invented by such groups in their insistence that TVA be required by judges to obey the law. The verdict was uncertain and the cases were mixed, but these legal challenges are most important as political challenges with which TVA eventually complied when S. David Freeman arranged a settlement with EPA in 1978.

The Tellico Dam controversy was ostensibly about the snail darter, a fish two inches in size which was at that time thought to be able to survive only in the river beneath the dam site and was therefore protected by the Endangered Species Act. As Michael McDonald and Bruce Wheeler make clear, Tellico and other episodes of its kind were, in fact, a manifestation of larger controversies over the appropriate uses of land

and water. Tellico would flood acres of valued farmland. The dam would not generate power but would promote the economic development of the area around the reservoir through recreation and new settlement. Arcane cost-benefit controversies raged between proponents and opponents, within the Valley, inside TVA, and in the Congress.

As these controversies emerged in the 1970s, popular support for TVA began to dwindle, as Richard Couto explains. The TVA was a victim of its own propaganda: it had preached the virtues of cheap power for so long that higher rates were a shock to the people of the Valley. They had been spoiled but TVA had done the spoiling. A beneficent force was now malevolent. Couto describes how TVA was gradually thrown back on the support of the one constituency that really existed at the grass roots, the power distributors. The distributors were hostile to the environmental movement, unenthusiastic about new departures in community development, anxious for growth in electric power capacity, but very unhappy about rate increases. The S. David Freeman board was unable to create a coalition in the Valley on behalf of environmental protection, community development programs, and power conservation. The people at large and the distributors appeared to want cheap power above all. Yet costs kept going up. Couto tells the story of how Freeman lost his chairmanship as a result.

By May, 1982, TVA seemed to have settled on a steady course of retrenchment. Eight nuclear reactors had been retired since 1979. The organization motto appeared to be "steady as you go." The effort to achieve a fresh synthesis of missions under new circumstances of decline in economic growth failed. The TVA had been responsive to external political forces but the old creativity was absent.

Assessment

Franklin Roosevelt had intended TVA to be the first of many regional authorities. Although the Columbia and Missouri Valley authorities were to be decentralized, like TVA, there was an implicit commitment among advocates of authorities to the ideal of national planning, through the National Resources Planning Board, with the regional authorities as the implementing agents. The NRPB's death at Congress's hands in 1943 symbolized the demise of an ideal. Craufurd Goodwin describes the skepticism of Truman administration officials about the valley authority idea after they had taken a good, hard look at TVA. They concluded that TVA had been shaped by administrative conceptions and that no economic theory of development was to be found in its inception or practice. At that time another piece of magic was in the wind, the belief that prosperity could be achieved through the central mechanisms of fiscal and monetary policy guided by macroeconomic theory. The appeal of regionalism was stale. Of course, the federal agencies in competition with TVA were determined that it would never happen again, and this time they were ready to do battle. Perhaps even more important, regional bodies with real authority are not compatible with federalism. The state governments of the mid-South were weak when TVA was created, but few regions or states would permit such authorities in their areas today. Subsequent regional bodies have been either weak coordinators or creatures of the states altogether, such as the Appalachian Regional Commission.[3] Goodwin's analysis leads to the conclusion that regional bodies serve purposes of national policy only when national political leaders create and define them in terms of national goals. Roosevelt did this for TVA, but the interest of subsequent presidents dwindled. S. David Freeman hoped that Jimmy Carter would make TVA the "energy laboratory" for the nation, but the words were not followed by action.

William Havard traces the history of rhetoric about TVA and finds two polar conceptions that have conflicted from the beginning. The first, best captured in David Lilienthal's *TVA: Democracy on the March*, is an idealized picture of harmonious material progress achieved by a happy combination of technology and "grass-roots democracy." The second, articulated by the skeptical Vanderbilt critic Donald Davidson in his book on the Tennessee River, depicts the TVA as a juggernaut beyond control that forces society to conform to its technological imperatives. Contemporary controversies about nuclear power, environmental damage, and disruptive effects of technology on human communities are restatements of the original dichotomy. Havard concludes that the dichotomy has been overdrawn but finds it to be useful as a context within which to analyze perennial questions about the accountability of TVA to the society and the polity.

Dewey Grantham draws together the themes of these essays and the comments of the scholars who served as discussants at the conference at which these ideas were first presented. He finds several persistent themes that match his own understanding of TVA's place among American reform movements. Like the New Deal itself, the TVA was less than it might have been but still a mighty force. The goals and methods of its advocates and leaders were pragmatic and ad hoc, and any conception of a grand design soon evaporated. It was also characteristic of southern reform in its emphasis on tangible material benefits. After all, fertilizer for farmers was the original reason for completing the development of the Muscle Shoals plants. One wonders if the more grandiose language about TVA was supplied by northerners. Certainly, the early TVA was populated by earnest midwestern engineers who saw themselves as agents of modernization in a backward South. It is not clear that the residents of the Valley ever thought of it this way or, if they did, that they resented being at the receiving end of a missionary enterprise.

Grantham's concluding essay gives rise to the thought that the retrospective assessment of reform can claim too much or too little. The TVA achieved a great deal but never lived up to the utopian language attending its birth. One might say the same of the New Deal or the Great Society. Scholarship that seeks to evaluate the achievements of these reforms suffers from the ambivalence of not knowing whether the cup is half-full or half-empty.

This book says nothing about the future of TVA because that future is very much in question. The power company will stay in business. Congress will provide modest appropriations for resource conservation and development. A new era of creativity could occur if the capacities of TVA match new national needs, but that union is not yet apparent. In any event, new departures would benefit from the lessons about the conditions for effective achievement that are contained in these essays.

Theory and Generalization

The social science literature on TVA has been descriptive rather than theoretical with the notable exception of Selznick's *TVA and the Grass Roots: A Study in the Sociology of Formal Organization.*[4] Selznick concluded that it had been necessary for TVA to give the implementation of its agricultural programs to the state agricultural colleges and county extension services in order for those programs to survive politically in the valley. He developed a theory of "co-optation" out of these circumstances in which it was argued that public institutions are dependent on the dominant groups in their environment and, therefore, must incorporate elements from those groups into the institutional leadership.

This book does not directly address Selznick's thesis. We have written analytical history rather than theory. In addition, we have followed the dominant line of historical development, which has been the power program. Agricultural programs have been only a small part of TVA. The story of the power program would appear to contradict Selznick's thesis, since organizational and technological dominance, rather than "co-optation," are the central theme of that mission.

One might join these contrary patterns by a single proposition about TVA. It has been most effective as a bureaucratic organization in those areas in which it could assert its autonomy. Thus, there have been two predominant ways for TVA to carry out its mission. The first has been through its autonomy—power generation and distribution, fertilizer manufacture, and navigation. The second has been technical assistance in the jurisdictions of other organizations—agricultural guidance to farmers, forestry, tributary area development. In the first sphere, TVA could dominate others. In the second sphere, TVA was dependent on the good will of others.[5]

The autonomy of TVA has limits. The essays in this book reveal that popular support for TVA in the valley has been crucial to the success of its mission. When that support has diminished, particularly in recent years, neither organizational nor technological autonomy has sufficed to permit TVA to be effective. The patterns of "co-optation" Selznick discovered are important for understanding other areas of TVA. But the central theme that emerges in the perspective of time is not "co-optation" of TVA by interest groups, but the tension between a strong, autonomous bureaucracy and the shifting tides of public opinion.

NOTES

1. Rexford G. Tugwell and E. C. Banfield, "Grass Roots Democracy—Myth or Reality," *Public Administration Review*, 10 (Winter, 1950):47–55.

2. Marc J. Roberts and Jeremy S. Blum, "The Tennessee Valley Authority," in *The Choices of Power: Utilities Face the Environmental Challenge* (Cambridge, Mass.: Harvard University Press, 1981).

3. Martha Derthick, *Between State and Nation: Regional Organizations of the United States* (Washington, D.C.: Brookings Institution, 1974).

4. Philip Selznick, *TVA and the Grass Roots: A Study in the Sociology of Formal Organization* (New York: Harper and Row, 1966).

5. Selznick recognizes these two forms of "co-optation" in his book and acknowledges the primacy of the power program over grass-roots institutions, such as local municipal power boards. But the book, as a whole, does not develop these theoretical implications.

PART ONE

The Formative Years

1

Paul K. Conkin

Intellectual and Political Roots

THE Tennessee Valley Authority, like a human infant, only slowly gained its own identity. At its birth in 1933, no one could have ever begun to predict how the new government corporation would mature. Even in genesis it had a mixed heritage, a heritage reflected in the complex legislation that brought it into existence. As it grew, unanticipated events and conflicting personalities helped mold an agency, and a program, that represented, at best, only some of the numerous options permitted by the Tennessee Valley Authority Act. Later a few TVA proponents would celebrate a "TVA idea," but they neither clarified the content of such a purported "idea" nor showed how "it" unified the disparate and changing TVA programs.

The problem of identity haunts any search for intellectual roots. Without some sense of what TVA now is, or at least was at some time in the past, one cannot pose clear questions about origins. Beyond dispute, TVA is a federally owned corporation, chartered by law to fulfill several itemized objectives. In two interactive characteristics—its mix of so many loosely coordinated programs, and its largely regional focus —it remains anomalous among federal agencies or even among the more limited number of government-owned corporations. It is not unique in any one of its programs. It simply supplemented, or supplanted, services normally rendered by other federal agencies.

Quite early TVA came to have an identity that went well beyond its particular programs. The Authority excelled in public relations. It carefully nourished a reputation for successful, even almost magical, achievement. Through annual reports, directors' speeches, and numer-

3

ous press releases, the Authority advertised its various programs and continually suggested, often by examples, the profound and beneficial effect of its efforts for the people of the region. It gained international fame and inspired imitations in several countries. By World War II TVA had gained such widespread plaudits that it seemed one of the few unalloyed successes of the early New Deal. It also won broad acceptance and praise in the Valley. Its directors and other high officials exuded a contagious idealism. Morale in the Authority was high, the early work performance efficient. The very magnitude of the dams, and the novelty of such a government institution, gained the attention and praise of numerous journalists and academic intellectuals. In all these ways the early TVA was a success story. Its enviable reputation lives on in part even to this day. Yet to note such claims of success is not to establish their accuracy. It is almost impossible to measure the actual impact of TVA on the people of the Valley, or even to demonstrate any differential impact at all (that is, effects that other government agencies did not achieve in other parts of the nation). And even if TVA had some hard-to-measure and distinctive impact upon the people of the Valley, this impact is only a prelude to the evaluative issue: have the effects been beneficial? To answer that is to invoke some framework of preferences or values.

Many threads of development came together in 1933 in the Tennessee Valley Authority Act. The oldest, and perhaps least controversial, was federal support for improved navigation on the Tennessee River. The Tennessee River, so named only from the confluence just above Knoxville of its two largest sources—the Holston and the French Broad—drains the highest rainfall area of the eastern United States. Thus, although just over 600 miles long, the main river has a water volume comparable to much longer rivers, such as the Ohio, and for most of the year it is larger than the Missouri. Such a volume normally suggests profitable navigation. But the Tennessee suffered from an intimidating obstacle at its midpoint in northern Alabama, the sharp drop and rapid waters known as Muscle Shoals. Only in the highest water of springtime, and then at great hazards, could river steamboats traverse the shoals and get to either Chattanooga or Knoxville.

The earliest local petitions for federal aid to conquer Muscle Shoals go back to 1809. In 1827 Congress appropriated $200 for a survey, and in 1828 deeded 400,000 acres of federal land to Alabama to help the state construct a bypassing canal. The inadequate state-owned canal opened for traffic in 1836 but soon fell into ruin. In the Rivers and Harbors Act of 1871 Congress authorized new surveys and a new canal, which the

Army Corps of Engineers completed in 1890 after an expense of over $3 million and which operated until the corps began construction in 1918 on Wilson Dam. Such pork-barrel aids to navigation were an accepted federal function; even diehard opponents of internal improvements expected such water projects from their constitutional caveats. Thus no significant policy controversies marked this early federal role in the Tennessee Valley.[1]

By the 1880s other issues joined at Muscle Shoals. The early commercial development of electricity slowly converted a great liability into a potential asset. The large volume and sharp drop of the Tennessee at Muscle Shoals constituted a usable hydroelectric potential second in value only to that of Niagara in the whole eastern United States. The Army Corps of Engineers soon appreciated the power potential not only of Muscle Shoals but of other dam sites on the upper Tennessee and its tributaries. But no one, it seems, much less the Army officers who supervised corps projects, believed that the federal government had the constitutional right, let alone the political inclination, to develop this potential. Thus by 1890 the corps increasingly took power into account in what became a series of detailed engineering surveys of the Tennessee watershed, but hoped only to integrate its navigational goals with dams constructed either by privately owned utilities or, more unlikely, by state governments.

While the great policy battles over Muscle Shoals's hydroelectricity occupied the limelight, the Army Corps continued its efforts to improve navigation. When completed in 1925, Wilson Dam and its locks finally conquered the one largest obstacle but still left multiple problems for successful year-round navigation, since it provided slack waters for only a few miles. Badly needed was a lower dam upriver (the later Wheeler Dam). Because of low water in the late summer and fall, year-round navigation for boats or barges drawing even six feet required either of three alternatives, or various combinations of them—numerous, inexpensive, low navigation dams; several multipurpose high dams; or enough upriver holding dams to facilitate a more even year-round flow. During the 1920s the corps developed several alternatives for the river, completing its most extensive survey in 1928. This would provide much of the needed engineering data for the later TVA. In fact, one 1928 map from the survey, which shows all the most likely dam sites, bears a remarkable resemblance to later maps of the completed TVA dam system.[2]

By 1928 the corps was ready to implement a more costly high-dam system of navigation in conjunction with power producers, whether private companies, the states, or a federally owned Muscle Shoals corporation. But on its own, tied as it was to the constitutional purpose of improved navigation, the corps had no realistic chance of securing appropriations for a contemplated and needed series of seven high dams, at least not under the Republican administrations of the 1920s. Corps engineers recognized some quite distinct advantages of high dams. They offered not only equal or better navigation (a much disputed issue) but also effective flood control and electrical generation. Negatively, they cost more, inundated large areas of good farmland, and required the difficult relocation of populations. By 1930, heavily supported by shipping interests and other boosters within the Valley, the corps was able to win congressional approval for its most innocuous and inexpensive navigational scheme—a nine-foot navigational channel to Knoxville secured by a series of thirty-two low dams. The Rivers and Harbors Act of 1930 authorized a $74,709,000 project, a sum increased by $17,500,000 in 1931. Congress appropriated $5,000,000 in 1930 for early work, which was underway by 1933.[3]

Since the corps plan allowed the substitution of power-producing high dams for low ones whenever outside agencies undertook such dams, nothing in the original Tennessee Valley Authority Act threatened the corps's navigational scheme. The act simply committed TVA to incorporate navigational facilities into its dams. But its slow progress on mainstream dams threatened an indefinite postponement of the corps plan for a nine-foot channel. This aroused intense political pressures in the Valley on behalf of an early completion of the required seven high dams, and by 1935 TVA welcomed the political and constitutional support it could gain from a more aggressive navigation policy. Thus the 1935 amendment to the TVA Act incorporated the old 1930 mandate of a nine-foot channel to Knoxville. The TVA became the responsible outside agency to take over the building of the high dams envisioned in the most utopian corps plans. The TVA in a sense gave the corps all the beneficial locks and the placid expanses of deep water that still allow the barges to get up to Knoxville. But the corps retained responsibility for navigation on the river; it designed the locks for TVA dams and continued to operate them.[4]

Public power issues dominated policy controversies about Muscle Shoals from 1897 to 1933. The first phase of an extended debate ended in 1916, with the passage of the National Defense Act of that year and the subsequent commitment to use Muscle Shoals waterpower to produce nitrates. The second began at the end of World War I and involved the extended impasse over the disposition of the wartime project. This controversy ended only with passage of the TVA Act.

In 1897 a fledgling Muscle Shoals Power Company first petitioned Congress for a franchise on the Tennessee River. A successful 1899 bill, authored by Congressman Joseph Wheeler, allowed the company to construct and operate canals and power stations at the shoals. Even this early, a few congressmen protested the potential giveaway of public resources and demanded stringent terms for private lessees. The small company never began construction. To the surprise of most congressmen, President Theodore Roosevelt vetoed a second such franchise bill in 1903. He argued that the government should not give away the potential power of Muscle Shoals, or of other such sites, unless lessees paid for all river improvements. The debate resumed in 1906 over a third Muscle Shoals bill. By then the majority of congressmen had accepted the Roosevelt principle—at the very least, power-leasing agreements should cover the cost of navigation facilities. Since the 1906 bill included such a trade-off, Roosevelt signed it. This was only the first of a series of such bills pushed by the small Muscle Shoals Company, which was never able to launch any construction. But beginning in 1907 the Alabama Power Company, a large and well-financed utility, pushed more grandiose schemes. It proposed three dams, and a six- or nine-foot navigational channel, to be jointly financed by the company and the federal government.

By 1907 a loose coalition of people expressed deep concerns about federal resource policies. Theodore Roosevelt spoke for this coalition. It included a reasonably coherent conservation movement and several politicians suspicious of the self-serving motives of large or monopolistic utilities. Organized agitation for the conservation of valuable, publicly owned resources began in the 1880s. Soon Gifford Pinchot, from a wealthy Pennsylvania family, became the leading spokesman for conservation as well as for professional forestry. He studied in Germany, and became chief of the Forestry Bureau in 1898. He helped get the Forest Service established in the Department of Agriculture in 1905, and was a close friend and mentor of Theodore Roosevelt. Pinchot was one of the first public officials in America to relate forestry to rivers, and to stress the unity of river basins and the need for their unified or multipurpose development. He wanted both to preserve waterpower sites and to keep electrical production under public ownership.[5]

Other committed conservationists served in the Bureau of Reclamation, which as an incidental product of its dams first began the sale of government-produced electricity. In Congress such men as Francis Newlands of Nevada and Theodore Burton of Ohio led early fights against the giveaway of public resources. Such conservationists had a very positive conception of government as a tool for achieving collective goals, and emphasized the necessary federal role, as against states, in the control of natural resources. The sources of such a conception of a central government are numerous, stretching back as far as the Puritans, to several leading Federalists in the early republic, to John Quincy Adams, and to the American System of Henry Clay. Such an openness to new government programs gained support in the late nineteenth century from European, particularly German, examples of a more active state involvement in economic regulation and resource development; from German-trained, historically and institutionally oriented economists; and from a spectrum of church leaders who wanted to legislate several new forms of public righteousness. Each of these trends converged in the struggle for an overt, articulated federal policy toward all major resources, with waterways perhaps only third or fourth in perceived significance (as compared to land, forests, and minerals).[6]

This early conservation effort, as it related to waterpower sites, climaxed in 1907 and 1908. In 1907 Theodore Roosevelt convened an Inland Waterways Commission and enlisted in its support a diversity of interests. The participants, in their prepared papers or lectures, touched upon the whole gamut of issues later incorporated in the TVA Act—problems of flood control and improved navigation, improved forests and watersheds, and the relationship of waterways to all other resources. The commission gave way, in 1908, to Roosevelt's much publicized Conservation Congress, which included the first gathering of state governors, plus a range of experts and representatives of different interest groups. The disparate delegates agreed on generalities, even in the area of waterways—the need to conserve water resources, to avoid monopoly, to use streams for multiple purposes, to use waterpower in the interest of the people—but reached no agreement on who was to develop the rivers, whether governments or regulated private firms, or whether state or federal governments would take the lead in resource development. This congress began a series of annual conservation congresses, or what soon became in effect the annual conventions of a National Conservation Association. Roosevelt followed his successful national effort with a North American congress in 1909 and even considered a world congress. As he left office, he also withdrew from entry all waterpower sites on public land.[7]

Conservationists fought from 1908 until the passage of the Water Power Act of 1920 to establish more detailed federal control over waterpower sites. The dramatic growth of electrical consumption triggered a new, entrepreneurial scramble as new power companies struggled to lease the best sites. After 1913 the Congress annually debated complex waterpower bills, but a predictable impasse resulted. The conservationists, again led by Pinchot and his followers, wanted to halt all gifts, grants, or sales of waterpower sites. Generally, the House favored public control of power sites; the Senate was more responsive to the claims of private utilities. In a prolonged debate, prefiguring the Muscle Shoals controversy of the twenties, Congress wrangled from 1914 to 1920 over the exact terms of a waterpower act. The bills pushed by conservationists were tough; they affirmed full federal ownership of hydroelectric sites on navigable streams, proposed carefully regulated leases of such sites with preference given to municipal bodies, proposed a Federal Power Commission to determine reasonable charges for the leased streams, and backed provisions that allowed the government to develop such sites on its own initiative. A few western mavericks, such as William E. Borah of Idaho, opposed any leasing at all and pushed for full federal development. The National Water Power Act of 1920 was a compromise. It affirmed federal ownership, permitted fifty-year leases, and established the Federal Power Commission. It allowed federal construction of dams and generating equipment and included a preferential clause on behalf of public or municipal agencies. But to the despair of conservationists, the bill based leasing rates on government costs, not on the value of power generated. The bill also contained many qualifications or short-term exceptions favorable to private development.[8]

Back at Muscle Shoals, the extended impasse over a federal waterpower act helped prevent private development. Already Muscle Shoals was a test case for conservationists. They faced formidable opponents. A process of consolidation led to politically powerful utilities and utility-holding companies. Alabama Power, a growing regional company, absorbed the small Muscle Shoals Company in 1912. It pushed hard for a joint company-corps project up to 1916, and in 1913 gained the endorsement of corps engineers for its more ambitious plans, which at one time included four dams. A new Tennessee River Improvement Association rallied local support for private development and for all the advertised progress this seemed to promise for the Valley. But in 1914, and again in 1916, authorizing bills lost in Congress, at first because of conservationist concerns and finally because of the near certainty that President Wilson would choose Muscle Shoals as the site of a vast defense plant to manufacture nitrates. As if a warm-up for the Muscle Shoals controversy of the twenties, public power congressmen loaded down Muscle Shoals bills with qualifying amendments and resorted to a successful filibuster in 1914–15. Even without congressional approval of any lease, the corps began preliminary borings and other work at the shoals.[9]

The National Defense Act of 1916 did not mention Muscle Shoals or the Tennessee River. Yet, in a backhanded sort of way, this was the first Tennessee Valley act. The Defense Act was a complex, comprehensive bill, aimed at American readiness for possible involvement in the European war. One aspect of such readiness was an adequate domestic munitions industry. Munitions then meant gunpowder, and gunpowder meant nitrates. The old saltpeter deposits of earlier wars were no longer adequate, while plentiful natural nitrates had to come all the way from Chile and thus were vulnerable in transport to blockades or submarine attacks. New synthetic processes, perfected in Germany, seemed to offer a promising new source of nitrates not only for explosives but for fertilizers in peacetime. Thus a section of the first draft of the National Defense Act provided for nitrate plants, as part of a cooperative plan worked out by the American Cyanamid Corporation. The government was to provide the power, the company to produce the nitrates. After a long debate the House deleted the nitrate provision. Since Muscle Shoals was the likely (also the best) site for such a joint venture, and since this again raised the old public-private issue, the House debate echoed earlier ones on Muscle Shoals.

Meantime, Senator Ellison D. Smith of South Carolina introduced a separate bill providing for government production of nitrates, both for defense and fertilizers. His bill did not specify the location for government plants, but again Muscle Shoals was the likely choice, since his bill authorized construction and operation of hydroelectric dams and provided for the improvement of navigation. Smith spoke for a new constituency in the long Muscle Shoals epic—that of beleaguered southern farmers anxiously looking for federal aid. Expectations of cheap fertilizer became irresistible bait for such farmers and for many farm organizations. Because Smith proposed, and defended, full government operation of his plant, debate on his defense and farm relief bill also bogged down on the explosive public versus private issue. One side charged socialism; the other protested any private profits realized on a wartime effort. By amendment, the Senate in effect incorporated Smith's nitrate bill into the final version of the National Defense Act, as Section 124. It eventually passed in this form. Thus the advocates of complete government ownership and control won an important battle; Section 124 specifically forbade any participation by private capital.[10]

President Woodrow Wilson quickly implemented Section 124 of the National Defense Act. After committee investigations, he authorized experiments with both feasible methods of synthetic nitrate production—synthetic ammonia and cyanamide. This decision was critical for the Tennessee Valley, for the older, less efficient, but better-understood cyanamide process required enormous quantities of electricity. Thus, after earlier consideration of a Virginia site, Wilson in September, 1917, selected Sheffield, Alabama, as the site of Nitrate Plant no. 1. Although this small, experimental plant would utilize the new ammonia (or Haber) process, and required no large new supply of electricity, its location next to Muscle Shoals made clear the likely location of the cyanamide experiment. In December, 1917, the War Department contracted with the American Cyanamid Company to construct a power-hungry cyanamide plant (Nitrate no. 2) at Muscle Shoals. Completed and tested just at war's end, this successful but expensive plant soon became the object of farmers' dreams of cheap fertilizer. For construction and the planned early operation of this plant, the War Department had to purchase power from the Alabama Power Company and, in negotiating such a contract, agreed to subsidize the extended facilities needed by the company (a typical wartime expedient). The War Department would also construct its own steam plant at Muscle Shoals in 1918.

In February, 1918, Wilson took the final, contemplated step as provided in Section 124. He authorized the corps to begin the construction of a large dam at Muscle Shoals (the Wilson Dam), or a dam that the corps had already largely planned in cooperation with Alabama Power. When the war ended, this dam was well underway; Nitrate no. 1 was an all-but-worthless attempt (because of its limited, noncommercial scope and the inexperience of its developers, not because of any limitations in the Haber process); Nitrate no. 2 was ready to produce nitrates, although apparently at higher than competitive costs; and the War Department had its own completed steam plant plus a shared interest in another steam plant built by Alabama Power at Gorgas, Alabama. Incidental property included land, transmission lines, worker homes, and even a small railroad. Equally important, southern farmers now waited expectantly for their cheap fertilizer, local businessmen looked forward to plentiful electricity and new industrial development, river shippers in Chattanooga and Knoxville patiently waited for barges that would negotiate the new navigational locks at the dam, and, nationally, conservationists and public power advocates prepared to defend this hard-fought-for exhibit against all the "private monopolists" who would now try to steal it.[11]

All the early tributaries of belief and preference that fed into the TVA Act had to flow through the tangled swamp that was the Muscle Shoals controversy. Here contended the opponents and proponents of public generation or distribution of electricity and of carefully regulated resource development. Here wandered various boosters of southern progress, from those who placed their hopes on the benefits of cheap fertilizer and improved agriculture to those still trying to attract northern capital and new manufacturing ventures. The constituencies were varied and tied to geography as well as to ideology or economic need. The boosters at Muscle Shoals, or in northern Alabama, cherished dreams of a great industrial center, whereas southerners more distant from the shoals opposed such intense development because they wanted their share of cheap power. Some commercially oriented Tennesseans pushed for upriver storage dams tied in with Muscle Shoals, for they yearned above all for navigation of the upper river, while others vehemently opposed the draining away of local power and the loss of its stimulus to industrial development.

At war's end, and well into the twenties, the nitrate or fertilizer issue dominated the public understanding of Muscle Shoals. The unfinished dam seemed only a convenient source of power for the nitrate plants, although with certain incidental benefits to navigation. But such public impressions were misguided. The great potential of Muscle Shoals lay in cheap hydroelectric power; both corps engineers and power company executives appreciated this, as did the proponents of public power. The original Muscle Shoals dam site, even though on a large and broad river, nonetheless allowed a dam with a head of almost 100 feet (comparable in height to dams on narrow streams) and a generating potential of 500,000 kilowatts (still by far the largest for any TVA dam). In addition, the Muscle Shoals project included plans for a second dam (not begun by 1918) only fifteen miles upstream. This dam (eventually named Wheeler when completed by the TVA) provided not only 40 percent additional generating capacity but an additional sixty-five—mile navigational channel. But in 1918 no market existed for such huge quantities of electricity, and few politicians seemed to appreciate the future importance of such a resource.

For maximum, sustained power production, the Muscle Shoals site had only one severe limitation—terribly uneven seasonal flows. These ranged from a potential of over 1,000,000 kilowatts in spring floods to a fall flow that, in some years, generated less than 100,000 kilowatts. Viewed as a power project, the Wilson Dam required upriver reservoirs to capture and slowly release the winter and spring floods, and this in turn meant better flood control. By good fortune, the very reliable rainfall patterns in the Valley (peak rainfall in winter and spring, low water in fall) meant that efforts to maximize flood control, or to maintain a navigable channel, usually came close to maximizing power production. Thus even before 1918 the corps had already identified the best single site for such a reservoir—at Cove Creek on the Clinch River (the later site of Norris Dam). By the early twenties those most interested in the power potential of Muscle Shoals, including advocates of both private and public development, began to add authorizations for upriver dams to their legislative proposals.

In 1919 the War Department and the Wilson administration opted to continue work on Wilson Dam and to convert Nitrate Plant no. 2 to fertilizer production, thus trying to get some benefit from the $68 million already invested. After the administrator at Muscle Shoals failed to locate any interested private bidders, Secretary of War Newton D. Baker decided to seek congressional approval, not for lease or sale but for a federally operated nitrate fertilizer program. James W. Wadsworth, chairman of the Senate Military Affairs Committee, introduced an administration bill to this effect, although he personally opposed public operation. This bill provided for a U.S. Fixed Nitrogen Corporation, with all stock owned by the government and an appointed board (the original bill provided for their appointment by the secretary of war, but later amendments assigned their appointment to the president). The use of the corporate device followed naturally upon the proven efficiency and independence of government corporations, first in the operation of the Panama Railroad Company after 1907, and then of several such corporations during World War I. This proposed corporation was to operate the nitrate plant, producing nitrates for sale to farmers or to fertilizer companies, while keeping the plant ready for munitions production. It was to sell at the switchboard any surplus power later generated by the two completed dams. Southern farm organizations led the support for this bill. It passed in the Senate but not in a more resistant House. Justified doubts about the efficiency of the cyanamide process, effective lobbying by fertilizer companies, and ideological objections to public ownership in peacetime all hurt its chances in the dying days of the Wilson administration. But the early decision to use the corporate device was crucial for the later TVA. Soon no one even thought of any other mode of government operation.[12]

In 1921 the new Harding administration opted for completion of the Muscle Shoals project in order better to lease or sell it. Involved in this decision was a partisan attack on past government mistakes at the shoals. Since any shift to private operation violated provisions of the 1916 National Defense Act, since many of the facilities had nothing to do with waterpower, and since the administration proved willing to offer terms somewhat more generous than those allowed by the new National Water Power Act, Harding had to seek special congressional approval for his plans. This ensured a partisan fight. In March, 1921, the secretary of war began privately soliciting prospective bids for the project. At first no one seemed interested, not even the power companies. But in July a much-publicized leasing letter from Henry Ford suddenly elevated Muscle Shoals to one of the most visible and controversial issues of the twenties.

An amended version of Ford's original offer remained before Congress for nearly three years. In brief, Ford tried to win full control of the enormous power capacity of Muscle Shoals, using the alluring promise of cheap fertilizer as his bait. In his original offer he asked the government to complete both dams at Muscle Shoals and then lease them to a newly formed company (presumably fully owned by Ford) for 100 years. Ford was to pay, as rent, 6 percent a year on the remaining cost of the dams, and also a small yearly payment (under $50,000) to amortize, over 100 years, the earlier government investment. He offered $5 million (a fraction of their cost of approximately $90 million, but possibly close to the market value) for the two nitrate plants, the valuable steam plant, and a wide range of other properties. His lure was his promise to operate the cyanamide plant (no. 2), to experiment in lower-cost fertilizer, and actually to produce fertilizer for sale to farmers. This meant that he would also keep the plant in readiness for munitions production. Although he placed an 8 percent limit on fertilizer profits, and invited farm organizations to monitor the accounts of his company, Ford never made an unambiguous offer to produce fertilizer if this meant a loss to the company. Not part of the offer, but a vital ingredient in the fervent local support, was Ford's well-publicized talk of other manufacturing enterprises at Muscle Shoals to absorb all the surplus power. A local real estate boom, fed by dreams of a huge, new industrial city, testified to the miracle-worker image that Ford then enjoyed.

The Ford offer won an enthusiastic early endorsement throughout the South. Southern congressmen pushed legislation enabling the secretary of war to accept Ford's terms. But Ford never met the terms demanded by Secretary of War John W. Weeks, and continuously confronted a degree of administration reluctance. This crucial foot-dragging by the Harding administration helped Ford's two major antagonists—the electrical utilities of the South, now fearful of losing any of the Muscle Shoals power, and the conservationists, who fought to maintain public ownership.[13]

Ford's offer triggered an alternative leasing offer from power companies. In 1922 the Alabama Power Company offered to complete the two dams at its own expense, buy the government equipment, and then lease the waterpower under the terms of the 1920 Water Power Act. This offer, which promised larger returns to the government, was favored by Secretary Weeks. But since it contained no fertilizer provision, the greatest lure of the Ford offer, it had little chance of congressional approval. Eventually a group of three power companies, including Alabama Power, did add a relatively firm fertilizer provision to a 1924 offer, but farmers doubted the sincerity of their commitment. Yet by 1924 outlying southern support for Ford had begun to erode, since he threatened to use all the available power and prevent its wider distribution.

Ford, and many in a coalition of supporters that cut across all normal political alignments, continually exploited existing class antagonisms in their opposition to the bids of power companies. They not only joined conservationists in indicting a monopolistic power trust but found a Wall Street conspiracy behind the utility bids. Ford, a self-conscious maverick among large manufacturers, not only exploited his hatred of Wall Street, of large publicly owned corporate enterprise, or of large bankers but on occasion gave vent to a growing anti-Semitism. Despite increasing doubts about the rather vague terms offered by Ford, the House approved his bid in March, 1924, leading to premature celebrations in northern Alabama, where people held on to their dreams of a new Detroit. A comparable Senate bill mired down in committee in the summer of 1924 but still had some slight chance of passage. Then, in October, Ford suddenly withdrew his offer, which he had always defended as a noble effort to relieve the government of a headache and to help the South. Typically, he blamed all the delays, and his final withdrawal, on the capitalists of Wall Street.[14]

Ironies abound in the Muscle Shoals controversy. One such involves the Senate committee assignment of the bills authorizing the Ford lease. In the House these bills, like earlier Muscle Shoals issues, went to the Military Affairs Committee. But because of the fertilizer angle, the Senate referred its bill to the Agriculture and Forestry Committee, then chaired by Senator George W. Norris, a maverick Republican from Nebraska and a long-time defender of public ownership of Muscle Shoals (he had fought against private leases at least since 1913). Norris would have been fervently involved in the Muscle Shoals controversy even had he not been on the appropriate committee, but its chairmanship gave him added leverage. Had he not been chairman, it is likely that the power facilities at Muscle Shoals would have ended up in private hands. This would have meant no TVA, for better or for worse.

Norris took the lead in publicizing the vagueness of Ford's offer. Ford promised to pay precious little for access to an immense quantity of increasingly valuable energy. After investigation, the majority of Norris's committee voted against recommending the Ford bill. Swayed by Norris, the majority also rejected the power company offer as a possible alternative. As a defensive ploy Norris introduced his own bill on behalf of continued government ownership and operation. Norris would keep amended versions of this bill before Congress through 1926. This first Norris bill revealed his most ambitious, if not most realistic, hopes for Muscle Shoals.

Norris had to emphasize fertilizer in 1922, for this was the then politically powerful issue in the South. His bill provided for a Federal Chemical Corporation headed by a three-member, presidentially appointed board of directors. The board was to appoint other officials solely on the basis of merit, without a political test of any kind. The corporation was to manage all completed dams, take over all the Muscle Shoals facilities, and remodel both nitrate plants in order to manufacture fertilizers. But the bill placed its greatest emphasis upon fertilizer experiments and gave the board the authority to establish other laboratories or experimental plants. It could also establish agencies anywhere in the United States for the sale of its products, "in order to prevent a monopoly of the fertilizer business or the undue and unreasonable advance in the price of fertilizers."

Almost coyly, Norris's bill provided for the sale of any surplus power developed at the dams, with preference to public agencies. The corporation had the right to regulate charges to consumers for all power sold to privately owned firms. The most revealing section of the bill came first, in the form of directives to the secretary of war. He was ordered not only to have the corps complete both dams (Wilson and Wheeler) as provided in Section 124 of the National Defense Act but also to survey the upper Tennessee River and its tributaries in order to locate storage reservoirs. It further authorized him, given reasonable costs, to buy such sites and build new dams. He was also to assess appropriate charges to any existing, or any future, private downriver dams for the added power gained from such storage reservoirs. In this first bill Norris envisioned nothing less than the full development of the Tennessee River basin above Muscle Shoals. The bill did not mention navigation or flood control, but these were already mandated considerations for the corps. Norris, in defending his bill, emphasized flood control on the Ohio and Mississippi, as well as the issue most prominent during the Ford battle—new economic development in the Valley. Norris talked glowingly of the most "complete and modern economic development" of the power of any river in the world, leading to cheaper electricity for the people and to new manufacturing throughout the Valley and the South: the "transformation to a great extent of a large portion of the United States. . . ." In summary, as early as 1922 Norris proposed a multipurpose corporation with powers remarkably close to those enjoyed by the later TVA.[15]

By 1924 Norris believed that the nitrate plants at Muscle Shoals were obsolete, useful only for fertilizer experiments. Thus in a 1924 version of his bill he first tried to separate power and fertilizer. His unsuccessful bill simply turned the fertilizer plants over to the secretary of agriculture, who was to operate a fixed-nitrate research laboratory. The laboratory would have experimentation as its primary purpose, but could produce fertilizer for sale in order to prevent private monopolies or to lower unreasonably high prices. Most of his bill pertained to power. Perhaps significantly, it began with an updated provision for new upriver dams to be built by the Army Corps of Engineers. A Federal Power Corporation was to control all the power facilities at such dams, while the corps was to use the dams and locks for navigational and flood control purposes. The corporation had an obligation to provide up to 100,000 horsepower of electricity to the fertilizer plant, but was to sell all the surplus, with preference to public bodies, through limited, carefully regulated contracts. It had the authority to swap power with private utilities in order to make up an efficient grid system. It also had the significant authority to build or lease its own transmission lines, a seeming necessity if it were to sell power competitively but also the one issue that most threatened private power companies in the region. This corporation was to accumulate an operating capital of $25 million from its power sales but, beyond that, return any profits to the federal treasury.[16]

By 1925 it seemed that Congress would be unable to find any acceptable solution for Muscle Shoals. From then until 1931 it considered several compromise bills, none very innovative. Norris pushed his comprehensive plan until 1927, but even after major concessions on fertilizer production he could never gain majority support. Beginning in 1925, the Coolidge administration sponsored a new, complex leasing bill, one which, short of any acceptable offer, provided for eventual government operation. One such bill (called the Underwood bill) passed the House early in 1925 and seemed to have excellent chances in the Senate. But Norris was able to stall the bill in conference committee until near the end of the session and then thwart it by a threatened filibuster. Even as Congress debated, the Army Corps completed Wilson Dam in 1925 and soon began selling electricity to the highest (and only feasible) bidder, Alabama Power Company.

Stymied on any early leases, the Coolidge administration turned to a study commission. Against Norris's opposition, it easily gained congressional authority for such an inquiry. In late 1925 a three-to-two majority of the commission recommended another effort to lease the entire project, with the power leased under the terms of the Water Power Act. Failing a lease, it also recommended government operation of the defense and fertilizer plants, with the sale of all surplus power. The minority of the commission adamantly opposed any government operation at all, wanted separate leases for the fertilizer and power facilities, and stressed the power potential of the project. Thus the minority argued for completion of the later Wheeler Dam and for a new dam at Cove Creek. Against Norris's protest, both houses of Congress authorized negotiations for leasing the entire project. The new legislation not only contained some complicating amendments but soon invited a tug-of-war between power and chemical companies. The only two serious leasing offers came from a power consortium, which reluctantly added commitments for fertilizer production, and from American Cyanamid Corporation, which sought cheap electricity not only for fertilizer but for other envisioned chemical plants (an offer that resembled Ford's earlier one but which included a dam at Cove Creek and access to other dam sites on the upper Tennessee). In fact, in the whole history of Muscle Shoals, no private companies ever offered bids that met all the stated criteria of either the War Department or separate commissions.[17]

Norris, clearly defeated in all his more ambitious plans, had to assume a more defensive role. Above all, he wanted to avoid a near giveaway of the immense power potential of the Tennessee River. He used his committee to expose and challenge bills that favored either the power companies or American Cyanamid. The power companies were at an increased disadvantage because of a series of exposures of monopolistic practices among the larger utilities, as well as a major Federal Trade Commission investigation that began in 1925. Its findings gave substance to the charges, by Ford as well as by Norris, of a giant, interlocking power trust. By 1925 all bidders recognized the pitfalls facing any profitable fertilizer operations and thus hedged their commitments, to the distress of southern agricultural interests. Although the Cyanamid bid had strong Farm Bureau support and seemed most likely to produce fertilizer, it threatened once again to deprive outlying parts of the South of Muscle Shoals electricity. Slowly, despite the effective lobbying of farm organizations, even the larger public came to view electrical power as the dominant issue at stake at Muscle Shoals.

As a final strategy to prevent leasing, Norris in 1927 considerably trimmed down his own bill. Instead of a more comprehensive development, he now sought a public answer only for the Muscle Shoals facilities (his new bill did not even include plans for Wheeler Dam, although amendments did add authority for a Cove Creek dam). In the sale of power, a Muscle Shoals Corporation was to give preference to public bodies and could build its own transmission lines. From its power profits it was to subsidize fertilizer research by the Department of Agriculture in a new, more efficient plant. But, in conference, Norris failed to maintain the clear separation of fertilizer and power. The final bill (S.J.R. 46) assigned the fertilizer experiments, and some actual production, to the corporation, which was to use experiment stations or demonstration farms to distribute its fertilizers. This bill listed, among its purposes, agricultural and industrial development, navigation, and flood control. By 1928 the Norris compromise became the only bill with any chance of passage in Congress. The declining support for actual fertilizer production, and the huge giveaway of power, doomed the Cyanamid bill, while the growing exposure of private utility pyramids and financing chicanery practically doomed any lease to the power companies. Thus both houses passed S.J.R. 46, but so near the end of the session that Coolidge pocket-vetoed it.[18]

Although Norris kept his bills on the legislative calendar until the spring of 1933, his last serious effort on behalf of his Muscle Shoals Corporation came in late 1930 and early 1931. His revised bill (S.J.R. 49) revealed a very conciliatory Norris, one open to any successful political compromise. This bill remained close to the one vetoed by Coolidge. It retained provisions for Cove Creek and a qualified provision for building transmission lines away from Wilson Dam. To appease local interests in Alabama and Tennessee, it included payments in lieu of taxes from the power revenues. It also provided for equal distribution of power among the states within transmitting distance. Norris remained vehement in his attack on private utilities (they were an excellent but discredited target in 1930) but tried to downgrade the power role of his proposed corporation. Disingenuously, he stressed that his was a navigation and flood control measure, and said that he would not advocate Cove Creek construction merely for its power (east Tennessee politicians had fought against Cove Creek and its contemplated hookup with Wilson Dam). Moreover, he now stressed how much Cove Creek would increase the power potential of existing, or future, private dams on the Tennessee—the clearest mark of how far Norris was willing to sacrifice the provisions of his 1922–26 bills, or his dream of a comprehensive public development of the whole upper Tennessee watershed. This bill again passed both houses.[19]

President Hoover, as expected, vetoed this Muscle Shoals bill in March, 1931. His brief message involved two issues—practicality and principle. He first analyzed the cost of what he saw as a power bill and little else. The value of existing facilities, plus all the new costs, would create a government facility worth over $100 million. After adding the new construction cost to the existing value of the properties, the corps would have to sell primary power at almost 1 cent per kilowatt, or much above existing rates, to amortize its cost. Thus, on its face, the prospect seemed to be a very poor investment. But much more important to Hoover, governmental production and sale of electricity, in competition with private firms and by what he called bartering in the marketplace, violated the whole purpose of government—the promotion of justice and equal opportunity. He believed that the proper role of government toward utilities or other natural monopolies was effective regulation to protect the larger public. He also saw the proposed corporation as an unwanted federal intrusion in the Valley, a type of bureaucratic tyranny. Such a large power corporation would also preclude any further private power development in the area. Yet, Hoover acknowledged the desires of the people in the Valley to gain some useful disposition for the properties, and even argued that the federal government should indeed construct the Cove Creek dam, but only when it could contract the power to local users at a price that would repay the government for its cost. Typically, Hoover recommended another commission, with members chosen by Alabama and Tennessee, plus a single representative each from farm organizations and the Corps of Engineers. He also asked Congress to give the commission power to lease Muscle Shoals fertilizer plants.[20]

The legislative juggling over Muscle Shoals confused normal ideological and economic alignments. By 1928 most southern congressmen supported the Norris bill, often not because of any commitment to the principle of public power but as the only feasible means of stimulating economic development in the South. The real ideological standoff always involved fervent advocates of public power, made up of some northern, urban Democrats but even more of western and midwestern Republicans who had earlier supported the Progressive party, as against a firm block of largely northeastern Republicans who opposed on principle any government competition with private capital. But the diehard opponents of public power made up a shrinking and even more futile minority by 1932. Leasing arrangements might still appeal to ideological principles but were clearly unrealistic in a deepening depression.

The election of Franklin D. Roosevelt in 1932 assured the passage of a Muscle Shoals bill that reflected the priorities of Senator Norris. In fact, any of the likely Democratic nominees would have signed a bill similar to the one Hoover vetoed in 1930. But of all potential candidates, Roosevelt was clearly the most sympathetic to public power. His interest and commitment had deep roots—in his emulation of Theodore Roosevelt, in his love of the outdoors, and in his emotional commitment to conservation. As New York governor he exploited public hostility to the large power companies, launched an investigation of their rates, and sought and won tougher regulation. In establishing a St. Lawrence Commission, and then a New York Power Authority, he pushed, unsuccessfully as it turned out, for a St. Lawrence River project. In New York he frequently appealed to a public yardstick as a guide to effective regulation, an elusive tactic exploited or abused by the later TVA. Because of his long-time involvement with utility regulation, Roosevelt had a rather detailed and technical grasp of power issues, a competence he so often lacked in other areas of public policy. In March, 1932, Judson King, an aide of Senator Norris, published a survey of all potential presidential candidates, ranking them on how they had defended the "public interest" against the "power trust." Roosevelt far outranked all the rest. Thirty-seven congressmen, including Norris, endorsed the survey.[21]

Muscle Shoals was not a major campaign issue in 1932. In his highly general acceptance speech Roosevelt promised only the rigid regulation of public utility-holding companies. The Democratic platform, which as early as 1924 had endorsed public ownership of Muscle Shoals, only asked for the "conservation, development, and use of the nation's water power in the public interest." In his only major public power campaign speech, at Portland, Oregon, on September 21, Roosevelt denied any commitment to full public ownership of utilities. Most should properly remain under private control or be owned by municipalities. The one major exception were hydro sites already owned by the government.

Here the government had the right not only to generate power but to transmit and distribute such whenever necessary to assure reasonable and good service, and also as a yardstick of fair rates. He specifically referred to four great government power developments as regional yardsticks—St. Lawrence, Muscle Shoals, Boulder Dam, and the Columbia River. These could prevent extortions against the public and encourage a wider use of electricity, that great servant of the people. In this speech, as elsewhere, Roosevelt reflected the widespread enthusiasm for all the wonders of a new electrical age.[22]

After the election the earlier Muscle Shoals bills matured into what seemed, at least on the surface, a whole new approach to the Tennessee Valley. Indispensable in this change was the New York connection: the role of Roosevelt and his personal advisers. In the busy interregnum Roosevelt apparently first turned his full attention to the Tennessee Valley in January, probably with a degree of relief. Here no great divisive issues had to be fought out. Here he faced no contending advisers, since he had a more compelling personal interest in Muscle Shoals than any of the political and academic staff who worked so hard to develop a legislative program. Roosevelt could play a free hand and work effectively with interested congressmen.

Thus, as part of a circuitous trip to Warm Springs in January, 1933, Roosevelt stopped by Wilson Dam on the morning of January 21. With him was a typical entourage of about seventy-five, including Norris, area congressmen, and power experts or technicians drawn from around the country. Norris was clearly the key person, and talked not only then but in subsequent sessions back in Washington, about the details of a new Muscle Shoals bill. Roosevelt spoke extemporaneously, and somewhat innocuously, at the dam, but in the evening at Montgomery, Alabama, he gave his earliest hint as to the type of Muscle Shoals legislation he wanted. The big innovation at this point was breadth. With typical exuberance Roosevelt asked that Muscle Shoals become part of a much greater development of the whole Tennessee River basin, from the mountains of Virginia to the Ohio and even the Gulf. The great new project would benefit many states and even the whole nation. It would become an example of planning for generations to come, tying together agriculture, forestry, and flood prevention.[23]

Like a boy with a new toy, Roosevelt became briefly absorbed with his Tennessee Valley proposal. His visit to Muscle Shoals, and his Montgomery speech, created almost as much excitement as Ford's original offer. Roosevelt basked in the attention and in the mostly favorable, even awed, response from the press. At Warm Springs on February 2, in a fireside conversation with reporters, he indulged his most daring and far-reaching hopes, or perhaps his wildest fantasies, about the Tennessee Valley project. He now described it as the largest such experiment ever conducted by a government, an experiment that would give employment to 200,000 men in the Valley. Of these, 50,000–70,000 would work to reforest the hillsides within the watershed, and this new forest would join new dams, such as the one at Cove Creek, in controlling floods. He also stressed cheap power as a means of decentralizing industry. Only his geography was suspect; he listed Ohio as one of the Valley states and left out both Georgia and Kentucky. He estimated the project would cost about $300 million and take ten to twelve years to complete. He took pride in the fact that this project would fulfill the goals of Pinchot and Theodore Roosevelt, particularly in reforestation, the subject he dwelt on at greatest length. He also saw the project as related to the Depression back-to-the-land movement, and as an application of the principles of city planning to larger areas. Finally, and most expansively, he described the Tennessee project as only a beginning, a test of a new approach that would end unemployment and decentralize industry in all major watersheds. In subsequent remarks he even suggested the Arkansas River Valley for the second such project.[24]

In the perspective of the actual program carried out by the later TVA, Roosevelt's most crucial contribution to the TVA Act was his stress not upon new programs or objectives but upon a Valley-wide project. He embraced all the upper river development envisioned by Norris back in 1922, and added to it the lower river. But in early 1933 this was not at all clear. Then all the drama lay in the new and exciting purposes Roosevelt assigned to a new government corporation. Everyone seemed tired of the Muscle Shoals controversy and of the interminable debates over fertilizer and public power. Roosevelt dropped all local images for the project and talked always of a vast watershed. By practically dropping fertilizer from his vocabulary, and emphasizing reforestation, flood control, industrial decentralization, rural planning, and massive re-employment, he seemed to launch a brand-new legislative effort. This was not to be the sequel to an old story but a brand-new departure. Thus Roosevelt gained for himself much of the credit for creating a TVA, not just politically but intellectually. This exaggerated view lived on in the early New Deal. Such key people as Director David Lilienthal, who shamelessly flattered Roosevelt at every opportunity, always attributed to Roosevelt the insight and vision that made TVA possible. Actually, Roosevelt's contribution proved to be as much rhetorical as substantive. His major emphasis was upon conservation and planning.

His concern for forestry or the proper use of submarginal lands would end up in the title of the TVA Act but led to an important forestry program only during the first years of the Authority. His frequent appeal to planning, a word as hopelessly ambiguous in the thirties as it is today, found expression in a tantalizing Section 22 of the TVA Act but had very limited impact even on the early programs carried out by the TVA.

By 1932 Roosevelt loved the word "planning." It joined other of his enthusiasms—for preserving scarce resources, for moving as many people as possible back onto the land, for making cities as orderly and as countrylike as possible, for making farming more profitable and fulfilling. Planning, of some sort, seemed the means to further these goals, goals embedded in Roosevelt's own sense of identity, in preferences that stretched back to his childhood. By 1931 Roosevelt particularly emphasized "regional planning." He had long known and sympathized with the efforts of professional city planners, such as his admired uncle, Frederic Delano. The work of city planners ran the gamut from bold plats of new towns or suburban communities to the nitty-gritty of remedial zoning or code regulation. The largest scope for American city planners had been broad, advisory, regional plans, such as the one that his uncle had helped develop for Chicago as far back as 1909, and the prodigious Regional Plan for New York City and Its Environs, completed only in 1931, again with the involvement of Delano. Here the word "regional" meant a city and its suburbs, while planning still encompassed only advisory blueprints for future growth, based on as many surveys and as much technical information as the trained planners could amass. Only politicians had the power to implement such advisory plans, although the planners encouraged the creation of special, transjurisdictional planning or operative agencies, such as the Port Authority of New York and New Jersey, that bore some comparison to the later TVA.

In the 1920s a group of architects, housing experts, city planners, and social critics joined in a loosely organized Regional Planning Association of America (RPAA). The group never numbered more than twenty or so people, but the quality of its members made up for its limited size. Its architects and housing experts, such as Clarence Stein and Henry Wright, departed from most American city planners in their wholehearted support of new town development. They drew their inspiration from the English garden-city movement. For them, a region encompassed a town or city and its immediate surroundings; in practice, this meant a greenbelt of parks or farms around new towns. Such experts helped procure, and then staff, a 1923 New York State Commission for Housing and Regional Planning, appointed by a sympathetic Governor Al Smith. The work of these men also led directly to the greenbelt towns launched by the Resettlement Administration during the New Deal. Other members of the RPAA, such as Lewis Mumford, Stuart Chase, and Benton MacKaye, had much larger policy goals. Influenced by French regional theorists, Mumford wanted planners to focus on true regions, those tied together as a functional unit by geography and cultural commonalities. Chase, an economist, also talked of broader regional development and would later do advisory work for TVA. MacKaye, a professional forester and a disciple of Pinchot, celebrated community development in terms very close to those of Arthur Morgan, the first TVA chairman. These three visionaries all stressed decentralized manufacturing. Drawing from European and Canadian examples, they advocated large, publicly owned electrical power stations as the key to decentralization and a new form of regional economic integration. These regional planners did not contribute to the TVA Act, except possibly indirectly through Roosevelt, who knew several of them and addressed the last conference held by the RPAA at the University of Virginia in 1932.[25]

With the Depression, Roosevelt's more idealistic hopes centered on rural America. He never relished large cities. Thus, without much clarification, he talked of rural planning. In 1931 he spoke before the fourteenth Country Life Conference, with all its reminders of Theodore Roosevelt. Here he entitled his address "A New Rural Planning," and utilized the same themes in an extemporaneous address on regional planning in New York City on December 11, 1931. Neither of these speeches touched on Muscle Shoals or clearly anticipated the TVA. He acknowledged his Uncle Frederic, talked about the importance of proper land use, and celebrated the advantages of rural life. He suggested tantalizingly, but not very precisely, that regional planning meant only the extension of city planning techniques to rural areas. His goal at this time was self-sufficient new rural communities, an enthusiasm of his, and of Eleanor Roosevelt's, that fed later into the Divison of Subsistence Homesteads. Roosevelt apparently shared some of this thinking with Arthur Morgan, and in a limited sense it may have influenced the little town of Norris as constructed by the early TVA (Morgan had hoped to direct the subsistence homesteads effort, perhaps as part of TVA). In a 1932 Survey article, "Growing Up by Plan," undoubtedly ghosted but consistent with Roosevelt's concerns, he again endorsed almost all forms of advisory planning. By 1932 he conveniently appealed to planning whenever possible, particularly on issues involving natural resources. It is thus no surprise that Roosevelt perceived an anticipated TVA so much in terms of resources and conservation, or that he described it as an example of regional planning, a phrase so loose and imprecise that it could fit almost any program, yet so elusive that it involved few specific commitments.[26]

"Region" is almost as elusive a word as "planning." Presumably, a region is a geographical area defined by certain common and distinguishing characteristics. But so generally defined, the word is too elastic to be of much use. Even so, it is still difficult to classify the watershed of the Tennessee River as a region, for the area involved was enormously diverse in geography, climate, economic resources, racial ratios, and cultural patterns. Only the river was common and distinctive. By 1932 the unique aspects of local regions had long engaged the interest of novelists, gained by the late twenties a distinctive rationalization among a group of writers at Vanderbilt University, and was beginning to receive increased study from sociologists and political scientists. In this sense, regionalism came into vogue by the thirties, a vogue comparable to ethnicity in the seventies. A more scholarly interest in southern regions flourished at the University of North Carolina, and in the North Carolina Institute for Research in the Social Sciences, long headed by Howard Odum. Odum and a colleague, Rupert Vance, stressed the distinct problems and characteristics of regions, and advocated what they called social planning for varied regions of the South. After the birth of the TVA, Odum published a notable book, *Southern Regions of the United States* (1936). But none of those intellectual streams seemed to flow directly into the TVA Act. Some of the Fugitives or Southern Agrarians at Vanderbilt feared the very type of economic development promised by the TVA. Odum was enthusiastic about the early TVA, spoke widely in its defense, and lent members of his institute to its early planning work, but the intellectual exchange remained slight, while Odum never received any of the research grants he hoped to pry out of TVA.[27]

In retrospect, what is remarkable is not how such diverse intellectual currents flowed into TVA but how tangential they all were to the policy negotiations that led to the TVA Act. Except for the older conservation movement, it is much easier to find intellectual parallels than direct lines of influence. Neither the legislative architects of TVA nor its early directors reflected any single or even any very coherent conception of the agency. It gained the title of "Authority" almost by accident, not from any self-conscious choice to model it on earlier regional authorities. Because Roosevelt loved the word "planning" and tried to ex-

ploit the grandiose expectations it suggested, Norris and his staff duti-
fully grafted some new language onto their older, virtually unchanged
bill. No one seemed to have a clear idea what the planning sections
mandated or allowed. No organized or coherent group of intellectuals
ever made the Muscle Shoals issue an object of special concern or incorporated their vision of its possibilities into any developed theory. No
important social theorists, no major economists, ever claimed it as their
own, at least not until TVA gained its own working identity in the thirties. Intellectually, Muscle Shoals remained a quite idiosyncratic child
of the twenties.

Roosevelt's Muscle Shoals trip launched work on new legislation.
Norris and his staff developed a substantially new Muscle Shoals bill in
the month before the inauguration. This bill (S.J.R. 4), introduced on
March 9, already embodied an early version of Section 22 on planning
(enabling the president to make surveys respecting reforestation, the
proper use of marginal lands, for locating dams for flood control and
navigation, and for improving agriculture and directing the proper use
of land in the Tennessee Valley) and Section 23, providing for proposed
new legislation to implement such plans. This bill also had reforestation and the proper use of marginal land in its title. But old habits die
hard. Norris still planned a "Muscle Shoals" corporation, and the major
sections on fertilizer and power remained close to his previous bills.
The earliest House bill did not reflect even this much administration
influence. Introduced on March 9 by John J. McSwain of South Carolina, chairman of the House Military Affairs Committee, this brief bill
(H.R. 1672) provided for a Tennessee Development Authority (the shift
from corporation to authority proved prophetic). This proposed authority could originally sell surplus electricity only at the switchboard,
but could build transmission lines when it needed increased revenues.
This bill was stronger than Norris's in one respect only—it not only
specified the Cove Creek dam but gave the authority the explicit right to
build such other dams as were wise and proper and authorized by the
president. McSwain's bill included a limited forestry program (projects
within twenty-five miles of the river and subject to state permission),
provided for the optional leasing of the fertilizer plants, and emphasized the recruitment of new manufacturing for the Valley.[28]

Roosevelt probably had no direct input into the language of Norris's
March 9 bill. After his trip to Warm Springs he had too many other
pressing responsibilities. Yet he and his staff devoted some time to the
Tennessee Valley project. Rexford Tugwell, in his *Diary*, notes that
much of the staff work on the TVA bill was complete before the inaugu-

ration. On February 26 he found Roosevelt enjoying, at Hyde Park, some confidential letters on Muscle Shoals dating from the time of Ford's offer. Almost as soon as the inauguration and emergency banking measures were out of the way, Roosevelt took out time for his Tennessee Valley project. On March 13 he asked Norris to come to the White House to talk about Muscle Shoals and to ready an appropriate bill. McSwain, representing the House Military Affairs Committee, contacted Roosevelt on March 14, sending along his March 9 version. The perfecting of the final bills took place over the next three weeks. On April 1 Roosevelt met for two hours to go over drafts with Norris and McSwain (the appropriate committee chairmen), plus Congressman Lister Hill. Congressman Almon, from the Muscle Shoals district, was too ill to attend. A week later Roosevelt again went over bill drafts with McSwain and Hill, and talked at least briefly with Almon. Yet, despite these four hours of conferences, Roosevelt was not able to arbitrate every detail of a complex bill, thereby leaving some leeway for variance between the House and Senate versions.[29]

With the outlines of a bill clearly in place, Roosevelt sent his brief message to Congress on April 10, recommending the creation of a TVA. In his message Roosevelt reiterated the purposes soon to be listed in the title of both Senate and House bills, but was not content to stop with legislative details. As at Warm Springs in February, he tried to elevate the significance of the project, for it led "logically to national planning for a complete river watershed," and touched and gave life to "all forms of human concern." He included a brief sermon on the failures of planning in the past, as well as words from Norris's Section 22 in charting the planning purposes of the TVA. He appealed to the spirit of the pioneers and predicted that, if successful, TVA would lead to a similar development of other territorial units.[30]

Coincident with Roosevelt's message, Norris and the three most involved Congressmen all introduced appropriate bills. McSwain, Hill, and Almon each submitted an identical bill, and then became jealous over which would be taken up by the House. Hill won this clash of egoes, and his bill (H.R. 5081), as amended, became the Tennessee Valley Authority Act of 1933. Norris introduced a bill (S. 1272), but one not very different from S.J.R. 4 of March 9. Among other changes, it now referred to a Tennessee Valley Authority, a name choice that McSwain always claimed. The Senate and House versions shared much common language because the House draftees also borrowed from earlier bills. The House Military Affairs Committee made significant changes in the House bill, and these changes further weakened it in Norris's judgment.

By agreement with Roosevelt, both Norris and McSwain helped secure limits on debate and by this assured early passage. Each bill was bound to pass, as opponents realized from the beginning. After six hours of intense debate the House bill passed by a vote of 306 to 92. In the Senate Norris moved to replace the language of his amended and perfected bill with that of H.R. 5081, and thus to vote on what amounted to a Senate version of H.R. 5081 (this strategy made Hill and not Norris the listed sponsor of the TVA Act). The Senate approved the substitution by 65 to 20. Since both houses held firm on their wording, the bill had to go to conference. The Senate passed the final bill on May 16 without a roll call. The slightly more resistant House passed it by 258 to 112 on May 17, and a jubilant Roosevelt signed it on May 18.[31]

The similarities in the Senate and House bills far outweighed differences. The common preamble listed, as purposes, not only the prime constitutional basis of the act—improved navigation, flood control, and defense—but reforestation, the proper use of marginal land, and agricultural and industrial development. Everyone now agreed on an independent government corporation with its own, nonpolitical employment policies, and with much-debated payments to Tennessee and Alabama in lieu of taxes. Both House and Senate agreed on three presidentially appointed directors, but only the House version contained older provisions for a general manager and two assistant managers (dropped in conference). Small differences in the wording of the long sections stipulating the legal status and administrative rules of the new corporation, and the responsibility of the directors, were easily resolved in conference. Both versions gave wide leeway to the board in the complex fertilizer section, in the ingredients manufactured and in types of experimentation and demonstration, but the House version had a stronger commitment to actual fertilizer production and sale. The conference changed the House's "shall produce" to an authorization to produce, and thus further widened the options available to the board.

The most divisive differences all involved power. The House version had a more sweeping authorization for future dams along the whole watershed, without limits as to who would construct them (the Senate version mentioned the Corps of Engineers). But to the horror of Norris, the House added a qualifying clause that postponed any new power-producing dams beyond Wheeler and Cove Creeks until such time as a reasonable demand existed for the power ("reasonable" meant rates sufficient to amortize the dams in sixty years). This, in effect, meant that the TVA would be unable to proceed with dams until it had power contracts in hand. Both bills gave the Authority full power to market its surplus electricity, but the House bill transferred to the Federal Power Commission the final rate determination for power sold to private utilities. Here the stronger Senate version won, leaving TVA with full rate-setting authority. Also, the final bill included a Senate clause authorizing the board to make studies or experiments to promote a wider and better use of electricity. The House, in what its conferees referred to as a more "businesslike" approach, qualified the Authority's right to build transmission lines. It could do so only with presidential approval and if it could not reach a satisfactory contract with persons, firms, or corporations to lease or purchase existing facilities. Sensible as this seems, it left TVA open to endless injunctions before it could build its own lines, and seemed to Norris and his supporters a last dire threat to the TVA by the private power interest. The most bitter debates in the House and Senate revolved around this transmission issue, and led a frightened Norris and other congressmen to appeal directly to the president. Roosevelt, who preferred the House wording on several minor issues, insisted upon the strongest language on both dam construction and transmission lines. Norris thus won, and the resulting bill granted a broader mandate to the board than had either of the two bills alone.[32]

The House and Senate never really debated Sections 22 and 23, except for one lone senator's complaint that Section 22 was so broad and indeterminate as to give the president carte blanche power. Section 22 on planning (Section 27 in the original House bill) did not apply directly to TVA. It authorized the president, by means he deemed appropriate and subject to congressional appropriations, to "make surveys and general plans" useful to the states or federal government in fostering an orderly and proper physical, economic, and social development of the Tennessee River drainage basin. These surveys were to aid in the proper use, conservation, and development of the natural resources of the basin and adjoining territory. The day after he signed the act, Roosevelt by executive order assigned responsibility for such surveys and plans to the directors of the TVA. Section 23 (Section 28 of the House bill) was linked to Section 22 and again did not specifically enable TVA to do anything. It directed the president, as the plans in Section 22 proceeded, to recommend to Congress appropriate legislation to maximize navigation, flood control, and the production of power consistent with the first two goals. Such new legislation was also to promote the proper use of marginal land, the reforestation on all suitable lands, and, most broadly, "the economic and social well-being of the people living in the said river basin." The first TVA chairman, Arthur Morgan, would appeal to this section, or to the purposes reflected in presidential speeches, to justify some of his famous vagaries—the planning of Norris village, extensive employee training programs, handicrafts and local self-help cooperatives, and malaria and other health control efforts.[33]

Several last-minute amendments to the act reflected the influence of Arthur Morgan, then president of Antioch College. In March, 1933, Roosevelt selected Morgan as his choice as first board chairman of the forthcoming TVA. He invited Morgan to the White House on April 13, and apparently the two hit it off perfectly. Morgan, a self-made engineer and innovative college administrator, loved to talk in the same vague language as Roosevelt about planning, the correct use of human and natural resources, community building and cooperation, forestry and the proper use of marginal lands. A latter-day Victorian, Morgan was rigorously honest, moralistic, and supremely self-confident. Experienced in drainage and flood control projects, he seemed technically well qualified to direct the engineering projects in the Tennessee Valley. An early version of Buckminster Fuller—full of enthusiasm, innovative, almost utopian in his dreams, yet always a bit superficial—Morgan wanted to shape the larger philosophy of TVA and to bring a kind of uplift or even redemption to the people of the Valley. Morgan asked and received permission to begin gathering a staff of qualified officials even before the TVA Act passed. He also consulted with Norris as well as Roosevelt , and in the process suggested changes in the founding act.

The Morgan impact on the TVA Act can be easily exaggerated. Later he did just this. At Morgan's request, Norris added some clarifying language that did not basically alter TVA policies, including one minor alteration affecting the job description of the forthcoming chairman. Morgan, who later claimed credit for Sections 22 and 23, actually contributed only a final clause to Section 22, a provision for TVA planners to cooperate not only with state governments but with local governments, cooperatives, or other organizations, and for it to carry out studies or experiments on behalf of its planning goals. But of critical importance, as it turned out, was a last-minute change in the provisions for Cove Creek and, by implication, for all future dams. The House bill never clarified specifically who would do the construction. The early Norris bill, following his Muscle Shoals bills, directed the corps to build Cove Creek. The corps had made the engineering surveys and had the needed expertise. Morgan did not want to work under, or with, the corps. He wanted to build his own dams. Thus the final version included two changes. The original Norris mandate to the secretary of war (i.e. the corps) was expanded to include the secretary of the Interior. This, said Norris, was to accommodate any possible shifts of government functions, but it also fit what happened to a limited extent, since the Bureau of Reclamation, not the corps, drafted the plans for both Wheeler and Norris dams. More crucial, an added section gave Roosevelt the option of designating to the corps which engineers would design and construct TVA facilities, or even of placing planning and construction in the hands of a chief engineer of his choice drawn from private life. Obviously, Morgan was his engineer of choice, and by executive order Roosevelt appointed him chief engineer the day after he signed the TVA Act. Although he drew no separate salary, Morgan had a dual appointment in the Valley.[34]

Morgan never better served the TVA than in this one legislative contribution. The fact that he was chief engineer, and free to begin accumulating his own construction crews, made TVA a quite different agency from what it would have been under Norris's original bill. Morgan was now able to hire and direct thousands of construction workers, experiment with dramatic new personnel and administrative policies, and gain all the local loyalty and support due any agency that offered so much work in the midst of a great depression.

The TVA, even if a quite distinctive agency, derived from a quite typically complicated legislative process. At least a dozen strands combined in a complex, even confusing bill. Typical of so much Depression legislation, the act was a bit of a blank check. Subject to legal challenges, the early directors could have added different programs or altered the priorities they gave to the ones they implemented. Yet historical tradition reinforced the more explicit enablements of the act—power, agricultural development, navigation, and flood control. These were to dominate the early, as well as the later, TVA programs. Perhaps appropriately, the one issue that had most complicated the decade-long fight over Muscle Shoals—the government's role in producing and distributing electricity—would also remain the one most controverted and divisive issue in TVA's first decade. In its first four years TVA would spend 89.1 percent of its approximately $150 million appropriation on its large construction projects, that is, on the linked issues of power, navigation, and flood control; 6.7 percent on fertilizer and agriculture; and only .08 percent on regional studies, experiments, and demonstrations. Despite all the verbal flourishes of Roosevelt, or the wistful hopes of Arthur Morgan, TVA remained very close to the agency envisioned in the earliest version of Norris's old Muscle Shoals bill.[35]

NOTES

1. Wilmon H. Droze, *High Dams and Slack Waters: TVA Rebuilds a River* (Baton Rouge: Louisiana State University Press, 1965), pp. 10–17.

2. This map, plus other survey data, is in Official File 44 (Muscle Shoals), Franklin D. Roosevelt Library, Hyde Park, N.Y.

3. "The Tennessee River: Wilson Dam," a consolidated data report of Jan. 1, 1933, in Official File 42 (TVA), Roosevelt Library.

4. *Ibid.*; Droze, *High Dams*, pp. 26–34.

5. Judson King, "Legislative History of Muscle Shoals" (MS, TVA Technical Library, Knoxville, Tenn.) pp. 2–12.

6. Judson King, *The Conservation Fight: From Theodore Roosevelt to the Tennessee Valley Authority* (Washington, D.C.: Public Affairs Press, 1959), pp. 1–13.

7. *Ibid.*, pp. 13–19.

8. *Ibid.*, pp. 42–58.

9. King, "Legislative History," pp. 16–26.

10. *Ibid.*, pp. 57–62, 74; King, *Conservation Fight*, pp. 59–70; Preston J. Hubbard, *Origins of the TVA: The Muscle Shoals Controversy, 1920–1932* (Nashville , Tenn.: Vanderbilt University Press, 1961), pp. 1–2.

11. Hubbard, *Origins of the TVA*, pp. 2–3.

12. *Ibid.*, pp. 5–27.

13. *Ibid.*, pp. 28–32; *Congressional Record*, 67th Cong., 1st sess., 67:4285–86; Senate Report 831, 67th Cong., 2d sess., pp. 12–16.

14. Hubbard, *Origins of the TVA*, pp. 28–138.

15. Senate Report 831, pp. 32–33, 34.

16. Senate Report 678, 68th Cong., 1st sess., pp. 1–5, 12.

17. Hubbard, *Origins of the TVA*, pp. 147–93.

18. *Ibid.*, pp. 196–220; *Congressional Record*, 70th Cong., 1st sess., 69:8209–10, 9949–51, 10056.

19. *Congressional Record*, 71st Cong., 2d sess., 72:6399–6412.

20. Senate Document 321 in *ibid.*, p. 4286.

21. *Ibid.*, p. 311; Thomas K. McCraw, *TVA and the Power Fight, 1933–1939* (Philadelphia: J. B. Lippincott, 1971), pp. 26–32.

22. *The Public Papers and Addresses of Franklin D. Roosevelt*, vol. 1, *The Genesis of the New Deal*, ed. Samuel I. Rosenman (New York: Random House, 1938), pp. 733–42; McCraw, *TVA and the Power Fight*, pp. 33–34.

23. *Public Papers and Addresses of Franklin D. Roosevelt*, 1:887–89.

24. *New York Times*, Feb. 3 and 4, 1933.

25. See Roy Lubove, *Community Planning in the 1920's: The Contribution of the Regional Planning Association of America* (Pittsburgh: University of Pittsburgh Press, 1963).

26. *Public Papers and Addresses of Franklin D. Roosevelt*, 1:496–97; Franklin D. Roosevelt, "A New Rural Planning," *Proceedings of the 14th National Country Life Conference* (Chicago: University of Chicago Press, 1932), pp. 10–17.

27. Nancy Grant, "Blacks, Regional Planning, and the TVA" (Ph.D. dissertation, University of Chicago, 1978), pp. 103–33.

28. Copies of S.J.R. 4 and H.R. 1672 are in Official File 42 (TVA), Roosevelt Library.

29. *The Secret Diary of Harold L. Ickes*, vol. 1, *The First Thousand Days, 1933–1936* (New York: Simon and Schuster, 1953), p. 15; Frank Freidel, *Franklin D. Roosevelt*, vol. 4,

Launching the New Deal (Boston: Little, Brown, 1973), p. 351; memo, FDR to Norris, Mar. 13, 1933; Edward B. Almon to FDR, Apr. 8, 1933, both in Official File 42 (TVA), Roosevelt Library.

30. *Congressional Record*, 73d Cong., 1st sess., 77:1423.

31. Informational memo for FDR, Apr. 10, 1933, Official File 44 (Muscle Shoals), Roosevelt Library; *Congressional Record*, 73d Cong., 1st sess., 76:3554–3600.

32. *Ickes Diary*, 1:32; memo, FDR to Conference Committee, Apr. 18, Official File 44 (Muscle Shoals), Roosevelt Library; a detailed comparison of the Senate and House bills is in *Congressional Record*, 73d Cong., 1st sess., 77:3562–90.

33. Arthur Morgan, *The Making of the TVA* (Buffalo: Prometheus Books, 1974), pp. 56–60.

34. *Ibid.*, p. 18; *Congressional Record*, 73d Cong., 1st sess., 77:2634–87.

35. Report of a three-member panel to FDR, 1937, Official File 42 (TVA), Roosevelt Library.

2

Richard Lowitt

The TVA, 1933–45

IN April, 1922, George W. Norris introduced his first Muscle Shoals bill. On the sixth effort he succeeded with a measure that became law on May 18, 1933. The Nebraska senator's vision of "taking the Tennessee River as a whole and developing it systematically, as one great enterprise, to bring about the maximum control of navigation, of flood control, and of the development of electricity" could now be realized. The eighth longest river in the nation, about 650 miles in length, with a basin roughly the size of Scotland and England inhabited by about 2 million people, would be developed "as a whole, not by piecemeal." Approved in the first hundred days of the New Deal, the act creating the Tennesee Valley Authority was the only significant measure during the first session of the Seventy-third Congress not directly related to the Great Depression.

Though primarily a regional agency with headquarters in Knoxville, TVA received congressional appropriations and national as well as international scrutiny. While serving states, counties, municipalities, and individuals within its seven-state region, the agency had to devote much time and attention to broader concerns as well. The enabling act, amended significantly three times prior to 1945 with George W. Norris playing the leading role in shepherding the amendments through Congress, was a unique piece of legislation. Heretofore most government corporations were established for a specific purpose and were not autonomous, separated from other departments or branches of government. Moreover, TVA, besides having a specific mission to develop a river, also had a more general one, as noted in Sections 22 and 23 of the enabling act, to make surveys and prepare reports that might be useful to both Congress and to interested states "for the general purpose of fostering an orderly and proper physical, economic, and social development" throughout the region, as well as providing for "the economic and social well being of the people living in said river basin." No other agency previously established received as broad a mandate from Congress.

Several points follow from the mandate granted to the Tennessee Valley Authority. Most obvious is that the constitutionality of the agency would be challenged by powerful utility companies, by what Norris and others called the "power trust" and their minions, who never accepted the concept of multipurpose development and who insisted that TVA was nothing more than a specially favored and protected power company. The industry was hard pressed, and both congressional and Federal Trade Commission investigations already had revealed shady dealings and actual malpractice by powerful figures associated with leading utilities. There was increasing sentiment in the press and in Congress to severely regulate the industry, which was on the defensive as the New Deal got underway. Wendell Willkie, installed in 1933 as president of the Commonwealth and Southern, a holding company controlling the leading utilities in the TVA area, proved himself a capable, eloquent, and attractive leader who tried to turn the situation around by defending his industry and attacking TVA. This theme of challenging TVA is central to the early history of the agency and to this essay.

Another obvious point is that the agency would have to engage in some sort of planning. It was granted the power to put its own programs into execution, and this represented a marked advance in the United States for creative government and instrumental planning. As it turned out, however, there was little overall, long-range planning; most of it was focused on resolving specific problems among the multitude for which the agency assumed responsibility. In developing the river through the construction of a series of dams, TVA practiced multipurpose development, a concept whose time had finally come. Though earlier championed by Theodore Roosevelt, Gifford Pinchot, and others, multipurpose river valley development had not been widely accepted. Arthur E. Morgan, for example, had constructed a series of dams on the Miami River in Ohio designed specifically to prevent the recurrence of the disastrous flooding that devastated Dayton in 1913. By the 1930s, though, multipurpose dams designed to assist in navigation, flood control, the generation of hydroelectric power, land use, and recreation became established procedure. Every major dam constructed by

TVA, and virtually every dam designed by the Bureau of Reclamation, was a multipurpose dam. TVA harmonized different functions, such as flood control, power development, transportation, soil conservation, and forestry, to a degree not previously practiced elsewhere on the American scene.

At first glance TVA appeared to be a planner's paradise. Thorstein Veblen would have been delighted with the opportunities presented in planning for the region. Here was an agency divorced from the pecuniary considerations of business manager, one in which attention could be devoted to the social goal of improving the welfare of the people in the Valley. Moreover, efficiency and productivity would not be restrained by the pecuniary culture of business. And other benefits accrued to planners at the outset.

For one thing, the area to be served by TVA was located in what was possibly the poorest part of the poorest region in the nation at that time. East Tennessee, southwest Virginia, western North Carolina, northwest Georgia, north Alabama, and northeast Mississippi were the most deprived sections of their respective states and generally were not favored by the political factions dominating their states. Moreover, the services provided by state, county, and local government throughout the Tennessee Valley were very limited in 1933. In seeking to develop the region, TVA would not be competing with agencies of these entities. In many instances TVA assisted in the development of state, county, and local agencies and turned over to them some of the programs it developed. In addition, TVA did its best to keep some federal agencies out of the Valley and therefore unable to compete with or challenge its programs. In short, TVA had unprecedented opportunities for planning and developing one of the most neglected regions in the eastern part of the United States, a region in which unemployment was endemic, in which the cash income per family in many instances averaged less than $100 per year, in which the mountains had been slashed and forests burned, in which a barter economy, even in a city like Knoxville, was becoming widespread, in which spring flooding was taken for granted. In the Tennessee Valley, if I again can follow Veblen, a technical intelligentsia allied with workers and farmers could create from a devastated region a garden of beauty and well-being, a region in which the capitalist and financier would be relegated to a marginal role and in which intelligence and good will could prevail.

How successful planning would be and what kind of programs could be developed throughout the Tennessee Valley depended in good part upon the caliber and training of the men who comprised the initial board of directors. This leads to the final point I wish to make, with the benefit of perspective, about evident developments in the early history of TVA; namely, besides legal battles and opportunities for multipurpose planning, it was most likely that serious conflict would develop among the board members.

Much has been written about the controversy involving Arthur E. Morgan on the one hand and David E. Lilienthal and Harcourt Morgan on the other, and I need not extensively probe the details of the conflict. Arthur Morgan served as chairman for almost a month before the other directors were selected. During that period he made decisions and in effect was general manager of the agency. At the first board meeting on June 16, 1933, in the Willard Hotel the new directors were asked to ratify or comment upon actions already initiated. Unwilling to comply with this approach as poor administration, the two directors soon forced the chairman to agree to allocating areas of responsibility. At the outset, then, it became evident that planning and programs would follow each director's area of responsibility.

Moreover, at this first board meeting Arthur Morgan sought cooperation with private utilities throughout the Valley by laying before them "our views and plans as they develop, and in other ways deal[ing] with them in an open and frank manner, with the understanding that they would deal with us in the same spirit." Harcourt Morgan and Lilienthal disagreed, and a Knoxville editor, believing Arthur Morgan "either opposed to competing with the power companies or afraid of them," wrote at the end of July that "the members of the authority are at the breaking point. Fortunately, H. A. Morgan . . . has very definitely swung to Lilienthal and it appears the two of them will probably outvote Chairman A. E. Morgan on fundamental questions."[1]

In addition, Arthur Morgan, a man of great ability and renown, was a person of tremendous moral rectitude and self-righteousness. By great determination he had overcome almost monumental handicaps in his youth to become an outstanding construction engineer and innovative educator. Largely self-educated, capable of complete concentration and with a wide range of interests, but contemptuous of "small talk," Arthur Morgan found it difficult to tolerate opposition equitably. At Antioch, when he experienced "a certain amount of dissention and rebellion" against his leadership among "the faculty and administration," he fled to Europe for a year and was saved from further controversy and possible resignation under pressure by being selected to chair the Tennessee Valley Authority.[2]

Among the initial directors Arthur Morgan was the most interested in broad-gauged planning, despite the fact that in previously construct-ing dams he had shown no concern for multipurpose development. TVA, to Arthur Morgan, was to be far more than an agency concerned with fertilizers, navigation, electricity, flood control, and the like. He envisioned it as an experiment in regional reconstruction that could provide an example of the reawakening of the American spirit along lines that would de-emphasize self-interest by encouraging people to work together. Under his aegis, among other things, TVA encouraged the creation of cooperatives, constructed what Morgan envisioned as a model community with an innovative school, pioneered in establishing a meaningful labor union for TVA employees, and stimulated small business. Building character was more important to Morgan than build-ing dams.

While Arthur Morgan was focusing on planning possibilities, Har-court Morgan and David Lilienthal were more concerned with the spe-cific provisions of the enabling act. Lilienthal at thirty-four was the youngest of the directors. Harcourt Morgan was sixty-six in 1933, and Arthur Morgan was fifty-four when the president called him to Wash-ington to discuss the new agency. Lilienthal, however, was the only di-rector to have served on a regulatory commission, which meant that he had worked closely with others in seeking to resolve complex issues that affected the economic well-being of large numbers of people. Ap-pointed by Governor Philip LaFollette to the Wisconsin Public Utilities Commission and previously a lawyer in practice with Donald Richberg in Chicago, Lilienthal had been noticed as a promising student by Felix Frankfurter at the Harvard Law School. He was a progressive in his poli-tics, and his association with the LaFollettes impressed upon him the necessity of relating directly to the people of the Tennessee Valley and of involving them as much as possible in the programs of the agency. Like Arthur Morgan, a man of intense energy and will, Lilienthal was dubious about the possibilities of long-range, broad-gauged planning because he realized that conditions changed and that people could easily become involved with specific matters of immediate and press-ing concern.

Harcourt Morgan, with a long background in agricultural education, also understood the necessity of relating to people and their concerns. Though a Canadian by birth, virtually his entire career had been spent in the South, and as president of the University of Tennessee he knew both the people and the problems of the area to be served by TVA. His chief concern had been, and remained, agriculture. The agricultural programs all bore his stamp, and he cooperated closely with the agencies he knew best: the agricultural colleges located at the state universities, the experiment stations, the Extension Service of the U.S. Department of Agriculture whose agents penetrated almost every county in the Valley, and the Farm Bureau Federation. All served the more prosperous and better-educated farmers. In the 1930s this meant farmers who still owned their land.

Given the different approaches and outlooks of the directors, the tensions that arose at the outset were eased by allocating areas of responsibility and by providing in 1937 for a general manager. Planning focused on specific programs and was not considered, except by Arthur Morgan, as broad-gauged policy. To be sure, Harcourt Morgan talked about "a common mooring," but he never defined exactly what he meant. At best, it remained a vague, ambiguous approach calling for general melioration that combined individual initiative and publicly controlled resources in an effort to further the education and outlook of people throughout the Valley.

The differences in the TVA leadership came to national attention only when Arthur Morgan saw moral issues that made civility and continued relations impossible. His position was most difficult because, despite his role as chairman, he was continually outvoted. When Lilienthal's term expired in 1936, Arthur Morgan asked the president not to renew it. Roosevelt in an election year managed to placate the chairman but later reappointed Lilienthal. However, within a year the differences burst forth upon the national scene. Harcourt Morgan and Lilienthal claimed that the chairman no longer fully believed "in the feasibility and wisdom" of the act:[3] in several articles, statements, and speeches they say he had presented a utility-company bias at a time when TVA was fighting for its very existence.

Arthur Morgan, on the other hand, publicly suggested that his fellow directors were guilty of possible criminal behavior as well as moral neglect in supporting what he considered fraudulent claims for lands purchased by TVA in the vicinity of Norris Dam. By December, 1937, the president could no longer avoid these conflicts and sought to resolve differences among the directors.

The further dimensions of this controversy will be commented upon briefly later in this essay. However, the controversy is an integral part of the main theme of the early history of TVA, namely, that until 1940 TVA was engaged in a series of struggles any one of which could have terminated or drastically changed its status as an independent agency. Most have been extensively written about and need not be fully developed here, but briefly mentioning them in sequence should establish the validity of this premise.

The attacks on TVA came from three sources. Two already have been mentioned: the legal challenge and the conflict within the agency. The other source came from within the government itself: efforts within the legislative and executive branches to diminish, if not to destroy, the agency as initially constituted. Even a cursory study of TVA's constitutional litigation quickly reveals the seriousness of the struggle it faced.[4] Litigation, as was expected, involved primarily the power program of the agency.

Within a year of TVA's creation construction was underway on the Norris and Wheeler dams. TVA purchased transmission lines from Commonwealth and Southern subsidiaries at Muscle Shoals and began expanding its holdings and service in that area while at the same time encouraging municipalities to purchase power company distribution systems. An agreement was achieved in 1934 among TVA, the city of Knoxville, and the subsidiary of Electric Bond and Share serving that area. Contracts also were signed with Mississippi utilities. But only the latter were successfully carried out. During the summer of 1934 and continuing for the rest of the decade, TVA, several communities, and other public bodies desiring to purchase TVA power were involved in litigation that stalled the power program, considerably increased the costs, and threatened the existence of the agency as conceived in its enabling act.

TVA and its friends hoped to avoid these court suits. At the outset, while selling electricity to private power corporations, TVA was also negotiating to purchase some of their facilities. The first contract for the sale of TVA power was made with the city of Tupelo, Mississippi. It went into effect on February 1, 1934, while other groups were applying for Public Works Administration loans to construct facilities enabling communities and farmers to more quickly secure TVA power. By the end of 1934 TVA had spent at least $24 million in purchasing facilities; rate reductions were estimated at $16 million, and a more rapid decrease was expected. David Lilienthal testified that more than 300 communities had applied for TVA power. Senator Kenneth McKellar believed that TVA would "reduce the price of electric current by probably one half." Litigation either halted or suspended these activities: municipalities were unable to pursue their distributing plans; most consumers found that electric rates were not being reduced; and at the same time investigations by the Federal Trade Commission revealed "more than $1,000,000,000 in watered stock in power company set-ups throughout the country."[5]

The debates of the *Ashwander* case concerning the validity of TVA's generation and sale of power from Wilson Dam need only be mentioned here. In February, 1935, Judge William I. Grubb for the U.S. District Court in Birmingham granted an injunction restraining both TVA from selling electricity to municipalities in northern Alabama and those communities from seeking PWA funds for the purchase or construction of distributing systems to utilize TVA power. Until the case was settled, until the constitutionality of TVA's right to generate hydroelectric power was fully recognized, the power program of the agency would be stalled.

The decision in the *Ashwander* case, following the Supreme Court's toppling of the New Deal's agricultural program, heartened New Dealers and the friends of TVA; eight of the nine justices upheld the Circuit Court of Appeals reversal of Judge Grubb's injunction. But the constitutional question remained undecided in 1936 and litigation continued. Utilities delayed or refused to convey their properties to TVA, nor did they negotiate seriously with municipalities for the sale of their distributing systems. At the same time the power companies utilized the courts to throw expensive roadblocks in the way of those municipalities that attempted to find funds for the construction of duplicating facilities. Injunctions were secured in both state and federal courts against municipalities and public groups, such as farmers in a particular area seeking public power, and also against TVA and PWA, preventing this agency from lending money for power purposes. The joint congressional committee that later investigated TVA noted that these legal proceedings, besides involving losses and expenses amounting to millions of dollars, impaired the efficiency of TVA by smothering the agency "with duplicating cases and multiplied attacks."[6]

Nineteen utility companies took up where the preferred stockholders of the Alabama Power Company left off. They sought to prevent TVA from conducting its power program except as it related to Wilson Dam, now sanctioned by the Supreme Court in the *Ashwander* decision. This time it was Federal District Court Judge John J. Gore who prepared a sweeping injunction restraining TVA. The agency was prohibited from extending or enlarging its transmission facilities. While it could complete substations and transmission lines already under construction, no new construction could be negotiated and no new service provided. In short, the power program was restricted to functions already being provided.

TVA successfully appealed the injunction, but the trial on its merits did not get underway until late in 1937. In August of that year Congress approved legislation providing for the issuance of injunctions affecting the constitutionality of acts of Congress only after a hearing was held before no fewer than three judges, including at least one circuit court judge. The case was heard before such a court in Chattanooga, with Circuit Judge Florence E. Allen presiding. Judge Gore was also a member of this court.[7] The trial lasted almost two months, and the court was deluged with exhaustive testimony and over a thousand exhibits. The court decided, with Judge Gore dissenting or qualifying many of "the other judges' conclusions," for TVA on almost all counts. It upheld TVA's constitutionality and endorsed its power program as a meaningful extension of its mandate to provide navigation and flood control. TVA now could sell power in competition with that being marketed by private utilities.

This 1938 decision is the only determination ever rendered on the constitutionality of TVA's power program. The case was unsuccessfully appealed to the Supreme Court. Its conclusion did not mean that TVA's legal difficulties with its power program were at an end, but they were on their way toward being resolved. Earlier, the Supreme Court held that private utilities also were without standing to contest grants and loans by the PWA for the construction of electric distribution systems by municipalities.[8]

While not deciding constitutional issues, these Supreme Court holdings, nevertheless, broke the legal log-jam that had brought the TVA power program to a standstill. Most private utility companies, now faced with the possibility of duplicate facilities, sold their properties, chiefly from late in 1938 through 1940, to TVA or to municipalities and rural cooperatives. Commonwealth and Southern, the parent company for several of the more prominent private utility companies, and its president, Wendell Willkie, played a prominent role in some of those negotiations, particularly the sale of Tennessee Electric Power Company facilities to the city of Chattanooga and to TVA.

The constitutional issues raised by the litigants in challenging TVA's power program were resolved in two cases decided by the Supreme Court in 1940 and 1941 in which utilization of hydroelectric power resources on a navigable stream, even at the headwaters above its navigable portion, was deemed part of commerce control and therefore subject to federal jurisdiction.[9] By the summer of 1941, eight years after its creation, at a tremendous cost in money as well as in time and effort on the part of key personnel, and with its power program stalled and challenged for most of these years, TVA could now proceed unimpaired with the full development of its program. The delay meant that its costs were increased in some areas and that the rates it charged in part reflected these increases. The damage done the defendants throughout this extensive litigation far outweighed the damage that would have occurred to the plaintiffs had the work continued. More serious was TVA's inability to help provide the blessings of cheap electricity to many deprived people during these Depression years.

The challenge in the courts was not the only major threat that TVA faced during its early years. It was rivaled both in importance and in the public attention it received by the spectacular controversy among the original directors, which prompted a presidential removal of the chairman and a full-scale congressional investigation of the agency itself. Already noted were basic differences among the board members evident at the outset, and others soon appeared. Arthur Morgan, through his lack of tact and abrupt remarks, managed to offend prominent people. Senator Norris, for example, during his 1935 tour of the Valley had to assure several of them as to Morgan's many admirable qualities: his high ideals and great abilities as well as his honesty and sympathy for oppressed people.[10]

By the summer of 1936 it was evident to Senator Norris that Arthur Morgan "was not willing to subordinate any of his own ideas to the Board itself, insofar as his policies were concerned," that some of the construction engineers he recruited had "no sympathy whatsoever with the ultimate purposes of TVA," and that he was "rather insistent that his ideas must always prevail." Others also complained about Arthur Morgan's difficulty in getting along with equals, his suspicious and jealous nature, his "Messiah complex," and his occasionally fuzzy thinking. More important, because it was this perception that led to his downfall, Arthur Morgan appeared increasingly willing to cooperate with private power companies. In turn, his fellow directors and others viewed him as endeavoring to cripple TVA and its power program. Arthur Morgan, meanwhile, was criticizing Lilienthal in caustic terms for getting TVA involved in politics and for spending excessive sums to promote the use of TVA power, giving him what one of his listeners described as "unshirted hell." This widening breach continued throughout 1937, and by the end of the year all the directors, according to Herman Finer, "seemed to have a sense of impending catastrophe." The crisis came to a head early in the new year in such a way that the president had to act, just when the special three-judge court in Chattanooga was upholding the validity of TVA's power program.[11]

On January 18, 1938, Harcourt Morgan and Lilienthal submitted to the president an official memorandum carefully enumerating "how the Authority's work had been accomplished in spite of the reported failure of Arthur E. Morgan to accept and cooperate in carrying out provisions of law and Board decisions." In public statements on March 3 and March 5, 1938, Arthur Morgan charged his fellow directors with dishonesty, malfeasance, and lack of integrity. Roosevelt then made public the official memorandum and summoned the board to appear before him on March 11. When asked by the president to provide particulars or to note any instance where Harcourt Morgan and Lilienthal had failed in their public duty, Arthur Morgan refused to answer, claiming that the hearing would not result in any good and that Congress was the appropriate place for him to testify. What information the president received was presented by the other members of the board.

Their testimony also indicated that besides impugning the integrity of his fellow directors, Arthur Morgan in the recent injunction suit charged the engineers and the attorneys in the case with inefficiency, unprofessional conduct, and dishonesty. He reportedly said that the engineers had told him that TVA's lawyers were trying to get them to testify contrary to facts. When asked by the president to specify a single instance of unprofessional or dishonorable conduct on the part of either TVA engineer or lawyer, Arthur Morgan again refused to respond, leaving the president no choice but to dismiss him for "insubordination and contumacy."[12]

Arthur Morgan, though removed from office, had his way. After some dickering a joint committee—approved on April 4, 1938, consisting of nine members, and chaired by Senator A. Victor Donahey of Ohio—launched an exhaustive investigation of TVA. By January, 1939, the committee sought further funding and promised its report not later than April 1, 1939. Already it had heard 101 witnesses and acquired 15,470 pages of testimony and 588 exhibits. Its findings, presented as promised, indicated that the controversies embroiling TVA were coming to an end. All the directors testified at length, as did fourteen of twenty-one TVA department heads. Representatives of private utility companies testified for nine days. Hearings were held in Washington, Knoxville, and Chattanooga. All aspects of TVA's programs and policies were reviewed and the controversies engulfing it deeply probed. As expected, there was a majority and a minority report, the latter submitted by three of the Republican members. But before the hearings were concluded, Arthur Morgan was no longer a dominant figure attracting national attention. The majority report conclusively stated that his "charges of dishonesty . . . are without foundation, not supported by evidence, and made without due consideration of the available facts." The minority report could condemn TVA only for not cooperating with other agencies and for what it considered a deficient accounting system.[13]

In January, 1939, President Roosevelt appointed former Idaho Senator James P. Pope, who possessed a first-hand acquaintance with the problems of erosion control and of phosphate development in the West, to the TVA board. Disagreement among the directors evaporated with Pope's appointment, and the agency now entered a period of relative harmony. His appointment was followed by congressional approval of the April report of the joint committee. And by July, 1939, with the transfer of the electric system of the Tennessee Electric Power Company to TVA and thirty-three municipalities and cooperative associations, the power fight that had involved the agency in controversy from the outset came to an end. TVA would survive with its mandate intact, but it paid a heavy price in expensive litigation, in the delay and confusion about its program, and in the excessive attention given to hydroelectric power at the expense of the other notable things TVA was accomplishing. It also took a heavy toll on the directors. Harcourt Morgan was absent from board meetings for months on end. Arthur Morgan's erratic behavior in his last years on the board certainly reflects the pressures affecting him. Morgan confessed in 1934 that he had "never worked under such pressure before," and one student noted that he "suffered several nervous breakdowns" during his tenure with TVA.[14] David Lilienthal, while ill with undulant fever, also suffered from what Senator Norris called "an extremely nervous condition" and spent almost a year recuperating, serving as a board member on a limited basis.

Another set of battles needs to be briefly considered. Defeat in any one could have seriously crippled TVA. These battles, while never receiving the attention of those already discussed, nevertheless commanded the full attention of TVA administrators, who understood what was at stake. Enumeration of these controversies should suffice to establish their significance. They emanated from both the executive and legislative branches of government and continued throughout the early history of TVA.

As TVA was acknowledging its second birthday with a parade and barbecue attended by more than 6,000 people in Knoxville on May 17, 1935, Comptroller General John R. McCarl presented his official audit of TVA operations for the 1934 fiscal year. He challenged the agency's administrative freedom by insisting that it follow federal regulations and statutes in its procurement policies and in the general conduct of its fiscal affairs. Following Judge Grubb's March 4 injunction, McCarl's audit prompted critics to denounce TVA as inefficient in its operations, wasteful of public funds, and fraudulent in some of its practices.

Senator Norris criticized McCarl's audit as unjust, unfair, and "untrue," citing many instances of the comptroller general's unfamiliarity with the provisions of the enabling act as well as with previous contractual arrangements made by the government with the Alabama Power Company. He concluded that "it almost looks as if you must be moved by some desire to injure, if not destroy, the entire usefulness of the Tennessee Valley Authority." Along with Congressman John E. Rankin, Norris introduced an amendment to the enabling act. It perfected arrangements for financing loans to municipalities, enabling them to purchase or construct distribution systems for TVA power, and thereby partially resolved some of the questions raised by McCarl's audit.

The appointment of a new comptroller general, replacing McCarl, whose term came to an end in 1935, eliminated future attacks from this quarter and established recognition of the fact that TVA, as a government corporation, was not subject to the same auditing procedures as other departments or bureaus. But the point to be noted here is that Congress at this time was considering legislation affecting the operation of holding companies. Controversy over TVA was intermeshed with the broader battle; if McCarl's critique prevailed, TVA could have been crippled in some of its operations. However, when he testified before the House Military Affairs Committee, McCarl backed off from his previous comments by stating he had found no evidence of fraud on the part of TVA officials.[15]

Another impediment to TVA was Congressman Andrew J. May; because he chaired the Military Affairs Committee, where all TVA legislation was considered in the House, he could pigeonhole measures and thereby impair the effectiveness of the agency. May, an unremitting critic of TVA, almost engineered its first defeat on Capitol Hill when in 1939 he precipitated a conference on the measure introduced by Norris in the Senate providing for the issuance of bonds by TVA for the purchase of Tennessee Electric Power Company properties. On the third try a compromise was reached and May proved unable to restrict the territory in which TVA could operate. But he and other critics in Congress would continue their efforts and eventually succeed.[16]

Norris and the friends of TVA in Congress learned their lesson well. When Norris in the Senate and John Sparkman in the House considered a question injected into the debate of the TVA bond measure—namely, the amount of money to be paid by TVA in lieu of taxes—they also had to consider ways of avoiding Andrew May and the Military Affairs Committee. The measure, amending the TVA enabling act, provided for payment in lieu of taxes and easily passed the Senate. But the Military Affairs Committee refused to report the bill to the House floor. The amendment was approved, however, because it was tacked on to a bill appropriating work-relief funds and in this version was enacted in June, 1940.[17]

Far more serious as a congressional impediment to TVA during the last years of the period 1933–45 was the senior senator from Tennessee, Kenneth D. McKellar, who tried to turn TVA into a vast patronage operation. His transition from friend to foe occurred in 1941 when he successfully, because of his great power as acting chairman of the Appropriations Committee and as chairman of the Post Offices and Post Roads Committee, tabled a proposal calling for the construction of a storage dam across the French Broad River. He did this, despite a personal plea from the president, for reasons that have not yet been precisely clarified. It was this controversy, however, that marked McKellar's open hostility to TVA in general and Lilienthal in particular.[18]

In March, 1942, Lilienthal introduced a measure requiring TVA to turn its proceeds from the sale of electricity and the disposition of other property into the treasury and to request all expenses necessary for the operation of its business from congressional appropriations. If successful, McKellar, as acting and subsequent chairman of the Senate Appropriations Committee, would have become the dominant figure in TVA. He failed in 1942. But he tried again in 1943 and 1944 to hobble TVA by curbing its control over finances and appointments. And at every opportunity he attacked board chairman David E. Lilienthal.

Equally threatening were the behind-the-scenes efforts against TVA by Secretary of the Interior Harold L. Ickes. His reasoning, unlike McKellar's, was clear. He wanted to absorb TVA into his department, which he hoped the president would agree to reorganize into a Department of Conservation. In his capacity as Public Works Administrator, providing funds for major construction projects throughout the country, Ickes, who easily commanded the attention of the president, was a foe to be reckoned with. Senator Norris expressed his opposition to Ickes's reorganization proposal to the president, who by late 1939 was increasingly involved with foreign affairs, and Ickes soon found other challenges to occupy his attention. But he posed a potent threat to TVA.

By reviewing these controversies, tensions, and antagonisms, we can see that during its earliest years TVA was almost continually engaged in battles that diverted the energies of key personnel from more constructive endeavors. In addition, some of these controversies stalled crucial TVA programs and added to their expense. Defeat in one or several of these battles, while not necessarily bringing about the demise of the agency, certainly would have kept TVA from fulfilling its multipurpose mandate. That most of these controversies in one way or another revolved around public power and were related to the power fight waged on numerous fronts throughout the New Deal was, as already suggested, almost inevitable. The New Deal merely continued and brought to a relatively successful conclusion a conflict that raged throughout the 1920s. By the eve of World War II this fight was finished, and TVA entered the war years prepared and able to make a significant contribution in that endeavor. However, the prewar years, the years of the power fight and other controversies, still produced meaningful endeavors on the part of TVA.

To discuss fully these endeavors is beyond the scope of this essay. However, it is worth mentioning some and briefly commenting on others to suggest the impact and diversity of TVA's activities in its earliest years. Lorena Hickok, reporting to Harry Hopkins on June 6, 1934, about her visit to the Valley, conjured up the image that most Americans and many foreign visitors held about TVA: "A Promised Land, bathed in golden sunlight, is rising out of the grey shadows of want and squalor and wretchedness down here in the Tennessee Valley these days."[19]

Though few were as excited about TVA as Hickok—and she had the impression that many people in the Valley "don't really know what it is all about"—she nevertheless concluded that "the people as a whole" were "beginning to 'feel' the presence of TVA." She guessed correctly that within "another decade you wouldn't know this country," that TVA could help create a better life by offering, besides a chance for decent wages and better housing, opportunities that people had never before considered. It was this vision, stated succinctly and eloquently at the outset of her report, that helped make TVA, despite the turmoil surrounding it, one of the showpieces of the New Deal.

One of the notable changes TVA brought about was the eradication of malaria, endemic throughout a large portion of the Valley. By slightly raising and lowering the water level at the various dams controlling the impounded lakes, TVA medical officers were able to create an environment in which larvae of the anopheline mosquito were unable to thrive. The editor of the *Florence Times*, reminiscing in 1970, considered eradication of malaria the greatest achievement of TVA. It is an accomplishment largely taken for granted because since 1949 not a single case of malaria has been recorded within the vicinity of TVA reservoirs.[20]

TVA also helped to change northern Alabama from one of the more backward and poorer parts of the state into one of the most progressive and prosperous. TVA dams—Pickwick Landing, Wilson, Wheeler, and Guntersville—helped make the river navigable and, along with cheaper power, created numerous commercial and industrial opportunities for businessmen in north Alabama communities. Research at the TVA National Fertilizer Development Center at Muscle Shoals developed and encouraged the use of inexpensive phosphate fertilizers so that north Alabama farmers were getting far better yields per acre than before the dams were constructed. By becoming involved with TVA test demonstration programs, presented to farmers through their county agents, north Alabama farmers were able, besides increasing their yields per acre, to overcome erosion on their lands. TVA also assisted them in forming cooperatives to bring electricity to their farms and thereby encouraged better farm management so they could both better conserve their lands and improve their earnings. From an agriculture based on cotton and corn, the area was converted into a balanced agricultural economy. What was meaningful for north Alabama farmers was meaningful for all farmers throughout the Valley who cooperated with TVA and the Extension Service in seeking better yields while restoring and improving their acreage.

The devastating flooding that occurred throughout the Ohio and Mississippi River valleys in 1937, which left about a million homeless, brought to national attention the fact that flood control on the Tennessee River was already quite effective. At that time only three dams and reservoirs were in operation. This situation inclined Congress to provide further funding for Gilbertsville (now Kentucky) Dam, the largest on-river dam. Its construction would ensure a nine-foot channel on the river, making it navigable all the way from Knoxville to Paducah. Completion of this dam along with the others also under construction in 1937 (Hiwassee, Guntersville, and Chickamauga) meant that destructive flooding would virtually be eliminated from the Valley. Congressional concern about flood control and navigation forced TVA to emphasize on-river construction rather than, as originally intended, to alternate construction on river with dams on tributaries.

If Congress exerted influence in determining some of TVA's priorities, so too did TVA influence the growth of institutions hitherto not widely accepted throughout the Valley. Its role in the development of cooperative enterprises, already mentioned, was notable not only in the Tennessee Valley, where they served as a fulcrum for social and economic improvement, but also as a model for similar endeavors elsewhere in the United States. In January, 1934, the Tennessee Valley Associated Cooperatives, Inc., was chartered, with the TVA directors serving as its directors, "to promote, organize, establish, manage, finance, coordinate and assist in any way in the development of cooperative enterprises in the Tennessee Valley." Arthur Morgan played the leading role in this endeavor and in securing a Federal Emergency Relief Administration grant to effectively get it underway.[21]

TVA also encouraged the establishment of union and collective bargaining with its employees. A 1935 statement of policy asserted, as did the Wagner Act approved in 1935, that employees "had the right to organize and designate representatives of their own choosing." Earlier Senator Norris had inserted a provision in the enabling act, which effectively removed TVA from the sphere of patronage-hungry politicians, stating that "no political test or qualification shall be permitted or given consideration, but all such appointments and promotions shall be given and made on the basis of efficiency." Though the enabling act also stated that the provisions of Civil Service laws were not applicable to TVA, the agency quickly adopted a merit system of its own and paid its employees at prevailing rates agreed upon through collective bargaining.

At the outset each of the directors possibly violated TVA's mandate by recruiting key personnel in the area that concerned him. Nevertheless, in the early years employee morale, with one notable exception to be discussed later, was high, and TVA helped encourage the trade union movement in the South through its program of labor relations. Employee morale was high not only because of wage rates but because of an effective grievance procedure and ample opportunities for advancement through the acquisition of new skills obtained in TVA training programs. TVA tried whenever possible to fill technical and executive positions from within the ranks of its own employees.[22]

TVA also pioneered in the development of rural regional libraries, including bookmobiles. Originally set up to provide reading material for TVA families at distant or isolated construction sites, these libraries were soon turned over to developing state and county systems. This example illustrates another major theme of TVA's development during these early years. TVA helped create organizations, systems, and procedures that it then turned over to counties and states, or it assisted them in their establishment and growth. Plans, ordinances, and codes developed in the villages constructed by TVA at the various dam sites were usually adopted by the councils of these communities as they were absorbed into the structure of county government. Their school systems, notably in the case of Norris, were innovative and well staffed and quickly became some of the better systems in their respective counties. Some of their innovative methods and programs were copied, while others were adapted for use in neighboring communities and counties.[23]

The same could be said for parks. Tennessee started a state park system only after TVA turned over to the state some of its lakeshore lands. Neither Tennessee nor Alabama had state conservation departments until TVA assisted in their creation. It assisted, too, in the development of state planning and other agencies. It also insisted on uniform accounting practices on the part of municipalities and power districts to which it sold power. In later decades various state, county, and local agencies would complain that TVA had usurped their authority and responsibility. But in the 1930s it was the other way around. TVA encouraged the development and expansion of agencies and programs related in one way or another to work it initially started.

At the outset TVA had to face a most difficult task in its relations with people in east Tennessee. Construction of Norris Dam at the confluence of the Clinch and Powell rivers necessitated the removal of thousands of people. TVA assisted in their relocation and tried to move their churches and cemeteries. It worked out grievance procedures to ensure displaced people adequate compensation. Roads, bridges, and other structures, whenever possible, were either rebuilt or replaced. But not everyone could be satisfied; tenant families, for example, received no compensation and were placed in dire straits once they left the land. While TVA came in for serious criticism, no follow-up is possible to ascertain how many displaced individuals, for example, secured jobs at the Norris Dam site.[24]

Population removal remained a serious problem with the construction of later dams and installations. About two-thirds of a million acres were flooded by reservoirs prior to World War II. But TVA, working with county agricultural agents in dealing with displaced persons, accelerated its procedures and sought to be even more generous in its payments to involved individuals. Despite whatever policy it pursued, however, many people were annoyed, aggrieved, and some became openly hostile. In the case of Douglas Dam, where lands leased to leading farmers and cannery operators were involved, TVA earned the open animosity of Senator Kenneth McKellar. But it was the dispossessed mountain people of east Tennessee, already exposed to a life of deprivation and harshness, who chiefly bore the cost of disruption involved in TVA's massive construction projects.

Involved in administering this program, and all the others as well, was an able group of young, largely professionally trained, men and some women from all walks of middle-class American life and from all sections of the nation. Together they helped create possibly the ablest and most dedicated staff of any agency during the New Deal. Many rose within the ranks to top positions in TVA, including that of general manager and board chairman. Others moved on to top-level positions in other government departments, bureaus, or agencies on both the national and state levels. Some returned to or entered the business world where they assumed similar positions. Two held cabinet seats: one as secretary of the interior, the other as secretary of the treasury. Most recalled their service with TVA during its early years as exciting and meaningful and with satisfaction.

Americans concerned about architecture and other cultural manifestations during the 1930s also looked upon TVA as exciting and meaningful and with satisfaction. In May, 1941, the Museum of Modern Art opened an exhibition of TVA architecture that attracted widespread attention. As *Time* stated, "TVA's designers had coordinated its myriad parts into a unified symphony of structure." Lewis Mumford, recently returned from a tour of the Valley, claimed that TVA structures—dams, powerhouses, bridges, highways, dormitories, generator and control rooms, even drinking fountains, as well as facilities provided in its parks and recreation areas—"are as close to perfection as our age has come." He gave credit to Roland Wank, TVA's chief architect, and his staff for achieving with free labor what other civilizations had accomplished with slave labor, namely, functional structures with few, if any, superfluous touches, blending harmoniously with the landscape, imaginatively utilizing glass, tile, brick, stone, earth, and concrete in the most economical treatment possible. TVA had successfully coordinated the science of engineering with the art of architecture.[25]

On the eve of World War II, most Americans were favorably impressed with the physical manifestations of TVA. They saw that through cooperation and large-scale planning great national works, as Talbot F. Hamlin concluded, "exist for the advantage of simple human persons, for the common good." In a world rapidly being engulfed by the rampant forces of totalitarianism, in which many democratic societies were being overrun, the effusive remarks of critics and commentators can be best understood. But by almost any standard TVA in late 1941 was an outstanding American success story—not in the traditional sense based on individual effort but as a planned enterprise indicating what a free people, dedicated and concerned, could accomplish.

An additional point, before briefly examining TVA during the war years, needs to be made, and that is the rural thrust of the agency and its programs. In a nation already heavily urbanized, TVA was helping fulfill Arthur Morgan's vision of vibrant, cooperating smaller communities, realizing Harcourt Morgan's goal of assisting farmers and restoring the land, and providing Lilienthal the means to bring cheap electricity to people and business firms throughout the seven-state area. TVA was constructed largely in a rural setting, and it helped to invigorate rural life throughout the region it served.

With the outbreak of war in Europe in 1939, and the increasing concern for national defense, the thrust of TVA, as of all federal agencies and programs, dramatically reflected this shift of emphasis. National defense was the reason for developing the Muscle Shoals site back in 1916, and national defense was cited as the first interest of the Tennessee Valley Authority in the opening section of its enabling act. With American participation in World War II, Congress and the administration emphasized the need for greater amounts of electric power necessary to manufacture the aluminum utilized in the nation's rapidly expanding production of airplanes. Late in the war period equally large amounts were needed for the secret work being done under military auspices at Oak Ridge in utilizing uranium-235 to produce atomic weapons. Plants utilizing the gaseous diffusion method and the electromagnetic process were to be constructed at Oak Ridge, as was another authorized late in 1944 using a thermal diffusion method. All called for prodigious quantities of electricity to be provided by TVA. Oak Ridge, which did not exist at the end of 1942, employed 82,000 workers by May, 1945, and already had some of the trappings of a cosmopolitan city. By the end of 1943 production of uranium-235 was well advanced and that of plutonium was getting underway. TVA provided the necessary power for the plants and the rapidly growing community, which it assisted in such other ways as providing designs for prefabricated housing. In November, 1943, for example, the first uranium chain reactor in the world with a production potential went into operation.[26]

The energy for Oak Ridge, the plants at Alcoa, and other war plants and industries came largely from the two storage dams started early in 1942: Fontana and Douglas. Fontana, the highest dam east of the Rocky Mountains, was constructed in a highly picturesque and inaccessible area on the Little Tennessee River beginning in January, 1942. It took three years to complete, and its construction village became the basis of a resort community in the Great Smoky Mountains. In addition, five smaller tributary dams and a steam generating plant, plus eleven hydroelectric units in vacant stalls, were completed during the war years.

Douglas Dam, whose construction was delayed for a year in good part through the efforts of Senator McKellar, got underway a month after Fontana. It was operative, impounding water and generating electricity on the French Broad River, only thirteen and one-half months after its groundbreaking. By moving workers and equipment from the newly completed nearby Cherokee Dam on the Holston River, as well as by adapting many of its designs and details, TVA was able to complete Douglas Dam in record time. Though TVA functioned during the war years with a diminishing labor force, with a shortage of materials, and with a sense of urgency, by utilizing its now efficient and skilled design and construction crews it was able to meet all of its wartime demands on or ahead of schedule. In 1942 Robert P. Patterson, under secretary of war, indicated the new thrust of the agency in a letter to Lilienthal: "The War Department has leaned heavily on the TVA to provide a tremendous amount of the power required for the military program." And, he added, "Its confidence in the TVA to produce results is well justified."[27]

The fertilizer operations at Muscle Shoals were restored to their original purpose, that of producing hundreds of tons of ammonium nitrate daily. The chemical was then shipped in either crystal or liquid form to ordnance plants where it was a base ingredient in the production of bombs and other munitions. Women now entered TVA's labor force in greater numbers, operating compressors, watching gauges, and checking the proportions of components utilized in making ammonia. TVA chemists, meanwhile, cooperated with the War Department in preparing red phosphorus for use in ammunition and calcium carbide for use in the manufacture of synthetic rubber. In addition, TVA cartographers assisted the Army in preparing maps that provided information necessary for military operations from aerial photographs. And TVA provided engineering designs for hydroelectric dams under construction in Russia beyond the Ural Mountains, replacing facilities destroyed during the German invasion. TVA did this work at the request of the Treasury Department and under the auspices of the Lend-Lease Administration.[28]

The war years saw the capacity of TVA's power system increase more than fivefold, from a little less than a half-million kilowatts in 1940 to more than 2.5 million in 1946. By war's end the nine-foot navigation channel from Paducah to Knoxville was substantially completed, adding a major new inland waterway to those already operative in the United States. By 1945 the Tennessee River was the most completely controlled river system in the nation, and TVA's contributions to the

Valley, to the United States, and to the war effort were widely recognized and applauded. The power fight had ended and most critics had either retreated into silence or had started to praise TVA and its contributions to the war effort. TVA finished its first dozen years as a widely accepted and well-established institution on the American scene, and one that was highly regarded abroad as well.

Late in December, 1942, before Senator Norris, recently defeated in his bid for re-election, departed from the national capital, Lilienthal sent a message informing him that TVA had already returned to the federal treasury "net in cash" the complete cost of the dam named in his honor. Norris Dam had only been in operation six and a half years. In addition, Lilienthal noted, one-fourth of the cost of Wheeler Dam had been returned. In all, up to June 30, 1942, TVA had returned to the federal treasury in cash "for reappropriation and reinvestment in its projects, nearly $35,000,000"; by the end of the year he estimated the figure would be more than $42 million. While emphasizing power aspects, the war years, as Lilienthal indicated, enabled TVA to start paying off its obligations, thereby more firmly establishing itself as a permanent part of the nation's institutional apparatus. It already had a varied and exciting history as well as loyalties and traditions well rooted both in agency and throughout the Valley.[29]

Though TVA emerged from the war years on a sounder base than before, controversy had not disappeared completely. Rather, the storms that engulfed TVA, and that constitute the heart of this paper, had abated, and the existence of the agency could now be taken for granted. Nevertheless, criticism continued. Some of it was penetrating and should be considered at this time.

TVA brought some criticism upon itself because it used vague and ambiguous terms that allowed critics to prove their erudition by attacking it. "Yardstick" and "grass-roots democracy" are two such examples. The term "yardstick," initially used by TVA officials when discussing their power rates as a guide for those to be charged by private companies, allowed private power spokesmen to show that TVA enjoyed all sorts of advantages not available to private companies. TVA officials soon either limited their use of the term or broadened its scope to allow TVA to serve as a model for the development of other river valleys. By the end of the 1930s the term was no longer widely used.

Such was not the case with "grass-roots democracy," a term favored by David E. Lilienthal in countless speeches, articles, and his 1944 study of TVA subtitled *Democracy on the March*. It was relatively easy to show that TVA, and not the people in the Valley, provided the impetus for its widely accepted projects. Few, if any, were directly initiated by the people themselves before the appearance of TVA and few, if any, would have occurred without the intrusion of federal authority into the region during the New Deal. Moreover, many TVA programs, most notably those in agriculture under the aegis of Harcourt Morgan, were conducted through established agencies, such as the Extension Service and the agricultural colleges, while other New Deal agencies, such as the Soil Conservation Service, were virtually excluded from the Valley.

One scholar used the term "cooptation" to indicate how older, established institutions and relatively affluent farmers benefited most from TVA. While the thesis can be debated, what it implied about grass-roots democracy was valid. The term "grass-roots democracy" was subject to devastating criticism. Nevertheless, I think at least two things can be said in seeking to understand Lilienthal's use of the term. First, it was excellent public relations not only for TVA but for the New Deal. In a world in which democratic nations were fighting for survival, this approach suggested that a free people working together with their government could accomplish meaningful things in overcoming economic adversity and in promoting the general welfare. Second, and undoubtedly of equal or greater significance to Lilienthal at the time, was that the successful use of the term virtually assured TVA's existence as a separate independent agency permanently based in the Valley. And his concern was justified—Harold Ickes, opposed to the idea of decentralized regional agencies, was in late 1944 and 1945 again seeking to discredit TVA as part of his effort to prevent the creation of a contemplated Missouri Valley Authority.[30]

The Southern Agrarians, espousing a traditional view of southern life and society in the 1920s and 1930s, should have been hostile to TVA. And, indeed, some were—but not all. Donald Davidson, most notably, was critical of TVA. Others (Lyle H. Lanier, John Donald Wade, John Crowe Ransom, Andrew Nelson Lytle) never expressed themselves in print, but John Gould Fletcher, Frank L. Owsley, Herman C. Nixon, Allen Tate, and Henry Blue Kline expressed varying degrees of support for TVA because they viewed it as a decentralized regional agency concerned with rural values and life. Kline worked for TVA for several years while he prepared a study examining the effect of discriminatory railroad rates on southern industrial development. Robert Penn Warren told a graduate student interviewing him in 1965 that he supported TVA. What becomes clear in examining their views of TVA is how widely they differed despite their belief in economic decentralization and the values associated with an agarian way of life.[31]

If the Southern Agrarians seemingly should have been hostile to TVA, then certainly blacks should have been favorably inclined, since TVA promised to hire them in proportion to their percentage of the population and offer them the opportunities available to all TVA employees. This meant that more blacks should be hired, for example, for the construction of Wheeler and Pickwick dams than for Norris and Cherokee dams because they comprised a larger portion of the population in north Alabama and southwest Tennessee than in east Tennessee. But such was not the case. Early on TVA came under criticism as a New Deal agency that offered blacks few of the benefits it was making available throughout the Valley, that it was lily-white in most of its practices and services, and that where it employed blacks, it generally discriminated against them, for example, by using Jim Crow training programs and employing blacks, despite these programs, chiefly as unskilled and semiskilled labor. In short, black leaders noted, there was no rehabilitation for the Negro in the programs and policies espoused by TVA. This view, expressed as early as 1934 in *The Crisis*, was continued throughout the decade in that journal and in statements by leaders of its parent organization, the National Association for the Advancement of Colored People.[32]

Earlier, in December, 1933, a black lawyer in Knoxville had written Harcourt Morgan requesting opportunities for blacks, noting that men of both races had worked together for years in east Tennessee "without any conflict" and suggesting that blacks should be represented in an advisory capacity to speak for their interests. TVA responded by recruiting a black educator, J. Max Bond, and placing him in charge of personnel work among blacks. Bond, a brother of Horace Mann Bond and a son-in-law of Rufus Clement, both prominent black educators, explained to his father-in-law in 1935 that Chairman Arthur Morgan and the "powers that be" had promised permanent villages for black employees at Pickwick and Wheeler Dam sites, but he protested the inferior quality of homes being built, so poor that one of the white foremen refused to continue with the work. He also complained that white labor was being used exclusively on this construction work, with blacks digging the ditches.

Throughout his tenure with TVA Bond found that his protests were of no avail. While people in Knoxville might be willing to listen, "the white southerners in charge [in the field] go on unheeding." Bond thought the solution was to get the facts to a "militant Negro organization," the NAACP, which could investigate and expose them. To that end, throughout his career at TVA, he provided such investigators,

Charles H. Houston and Thurgood Marshall among them, with information about discriminatory practices and unkept promises on the part of TVA officials and employees.[33]

Throughout the New Deal the NAACP, with information provided by their own investigators, J. Max Bond, and a handful of black lawyers in the Tennessee Valley, maintained a constant barrage of criticism against the racial policies of TVA and the treatment of black employees. Thanks in part to Francis Biddle, who was general counsel for the Joint Committee on the Investigation of the Tennessee Valley Authority and a member of the National Legal Committee of the NAACP, the situation regarding blacks was fully explored. The committee report stated, "On paper the Authority policy toward Negroes is one of no discrimination and a proportionate share of jobs. In practice the Authority has not felt able to enforce this policy as fully as could be desired." Gordon Clapp, director of personnel and in charge of labor relations, candidly stated TVA's position by testifying, "The Authority in general does not feel that it has any special responsibility for attempting to revise or reconstruct the attitude of this area or any other area with respect to the racial question." In the face of such a policy, black complaints received minimal attention throughout the early history of TVA. There were very few skilled black workers in the employ of TVA, and the labor unions refused to admit black employees to apprenticeship training.[34]

While witnesses recognized that TVA could not solve the race problem in the Valley, NAACP spokesman Charles H. Houston stated, and the committee report agreed, that TVA "can and should do more for the Negroes than it is doing." Specifically it recommended that field supervisors who had ill-treated black workers be disciplined. There was no evidence that one had ever been disciplined. Further recommendations were that recreational facilities be provided for blacks in areas already provided for whites and that blacks be employed on projects even in areas where they represented a small proportion of the population. None, for example, were employed on construction work at the Hiwassee Dam site. When TVA constructed separate recreational facilities for blacks and turned them over to fledgling state park systems in Alabama and Tennessee, black leaders protested that they should have been integrated and kept under TVA auspices because federal agencies officially did not authorize segregation. Finally, the committee recommended that a director of Negro work be employed by TVA. By 1939 J. Max Bond, principal supervisor of Negro training, was no longer listed on the roster of TVA employees.[35]

The chief complaint of black leaders—that TVA was too inclined to yield without protest to what it conceived to be local attitudes—applies equally well to TVA's initial lack of interest in tributary development, in seeing that people in the more inaccessible mountain region were brought into the areas served by TVA. In short, during the early years of TVA the people who benefited most were farmers and residents of communities located along or relatively close to the Tennessee River. Only after 1935 did the agency launch a program of tributary development and indicate an interest in people located "up in the hollows."

Larger, landowning farmers benefited far more from TVA's programs than did those less secure, including tenants, sharecroppers, and black farmers. This pattern, of course, was valid for southern agriculture in general during the New Deal, the possible exception being the work of the Farm Security Administration. TVA did not actively cooperate with this agency, as it did not actively cooperate with most New Deal agencies concerning agriculture, preferring instead to supervise its own programs and work with the older groups serving established farmers throughout the Valley. This was done, as already noted, largely at the wish of Harcourt Morgan.

By the end of World War II the first phase of TVA's history came to an end. The president who had brought TVA into being and the senator who had been its legislative godfather were already deceased. Within a year Lilienthal left the Tennessee Valley for Washington and the Atomic Energy Commission. Two years thereafter, in 1948, Harcourt Morgan, the last of the original directors, resigned. On October 8, 1945, President Harry Truman dedicated Kentucky Dam, the last of the on-river dams to be completed and the sixteenth dam built by the TVA. Truman said that TVA was no longer an experiment but "a great American accomplishment," one that "firmly established the basic principle of development of resources on an autonomous regional basis."

He also quoted his predecessor, when Roosevelt recommended the creation of TVA in 1933: "The usefulness of the entire Tennessee River . . . transcends mere power development; it enters the wide fields of flood control, soil erosion, afforestation, elimination from agricultural use of marginal lands and distribution and diversification of industry." Truman then made the obvious conclusion: "His prophecy has been fulfilled, for in the TVA the Congress has provided for a tying together of all things that go to make up a well-rounded economic development."[36]

People throughout the Tennessee Valley, with the exceptions already suggested, agreed with President Truman's evaluation. Herman Finer, who spent most of 1938 in Knoxville studying TVA, observed that when TVA entered the Valley, "it was met, as it were, by a large question mark." But as its programs became clear and its benefits more manifest, "a very large proportion of the population now talk of 'our dams' and 'our TVA' with pride."[37] What is ironic in Finer's observation is that TVA, representing the most massive intrusion of federal authority into the South since Reconstruction, alienated the one group of people who benefited most from the presence of federal authority in the years following the Civil War. The people most hostile to the federal presence during Reconstruction were now among TVA's most ardent champions, proclaiming, both individually and through their numerous civic organizations, that their welfare would continue to improve through the manifold contributions of TVA.

This, assuredly, was the view of the governors of the seven Tennessee Valley states. All agreed when interviewed at their state capitals by a reporter from the *St. Louis Post-Dispatch* in December, 1944, that TVA had brought numerous benefits to their states. All denied that TVA could be considered a "superstate" that violated states' rights and robbed them of tax revenues. In addition, the governors testified to the cooperative approach of the agency and its avoidance of high-handed methods. All further agreed that the interests and rights of their states in balance had been strengthened by TVA's operations. Seven separate statements appearing in the last issue of the newspaper for 1944 provided eloquent testimony to the favorable impact TVA had made. The governors were asked "for frank statements of what is good and what is bad about TVA," and they had nothing negative to say.

On the national scene most of the conflict had abated. Many old enemies had become silent; some had modified their views. According to his friend and biographer, Wendell Willkie "found much to regret in his own record" during the power fight.[38] By 1945 TVA could be measured in terms involving more than a good investment of federal funds. It proved to be a sound investment in developing a region and providing a symbol of a stronger America.

TVA practiced regional planning on a larger scale than any other agency during the New Deal. While its approach prompted criticism and led to real grievances on the part of some dispossessed people, and while at times it exacerbated racial tensions, its integrated use of land, water, and power made for a dynamic trinity in harmony with technological imperatives. In the realm of social planning large segments of the population benefited from TVA programs throughout the Tennessee Valley. It is clear, however, that TVA fulfilled the more specific functions of its mandate more easily than the general planning suggestions contained in Sections 22 and 23 of the enabling act.

Throughout its early history TVA programs and policies were guided by the perspectives of its remarkably able and diverse first board of directors. Its energies, however, were largely devoted to a tumultuous series of battles that, if lost, could have markedly changed the structure, outlook, programs, and policies of the agency. In one way or another most of these controversies concerned the power program of TVA, and this aspect received excessive public attention to the detriment of the broad range of constructive programs the agency pursued. The war years, however, necessitated an emphasis on hydroelectric power, and TVA's focus definitely tilted in that direction. It entered the postwar period as a tested and valued American institution with a firm regional base. It achieved its maturity during a decade of depression and global conflict. It had met its responsibilities and the challenges and opportunities they incurred under the aegis of an administration and Congress that with some exceptions were favorably inclined. It had occupied a position at once symbolic and experimental. It provided an exciting example while incurring risks and a liability to error inherent in all developmental states. Inevitably, all of these conditions would change. But during these early years were forged many of the practices, procedures, policies, and programs, as well as loyalties and traditions, that guide TVA a half-century later in a region and a nation markedly different from that which existed at its creation.

NOTES

1. David E. Lilienthal to Arthur E. Morgan, July 21, 1933; Benton J. Stong to George B. Parker, July 31, 1933, both in Herman Finer Papers, Record Group 200, National Archives Gift Collection.

2. Walter Kahoe, *Arthur Morgan: A Biography and Memoir* (Moylan, Pa., 1977), p. 66.

3. Section 2H of the TVA Act was included at the insistence of Senator Norris.

4. Joseph C. Swidler and Robert Marquis, "TVA in Court: A Study of TVA's Constitutional Litigation," *Iowa Law Review*, 32 (1947): 296–326, is the best introduction. In 1947 Swidler was general counsel and Marquis was assistant general counsel of TVA. See, too, the excellent TVA Oral History Interviews with Henry H. Fowler in 1971, in the Mississippi Valley Collection, Memphis State University.

5. Richard Lowitt, *George W. Norris: The Triumph of a Progressive, 1933–1944* (Urbana: University of Illinois Press, 1978), pp. 111–12, including footnotes. Campaigning for re-election in 1934, McKellar endorsed TVA, called on the voters to support the TVA referendums, and noted that "the major federal projects now total $318,000,000, more than the total invested by all previous administrations since Tennessee statehood in 1796." Speech delivered Nov. 5, 1934, and summarized in John Howard Riggs, *A Calen-*

dar of Political and Occasional Speeches by Senator Kenneth D. McKellar, 1928–1940, with Summaries and Subject Index (Aug., 1962), Memphis Public Library.

6. Swidler and Marquis, "TVA in Court," p. 312 n.44.

7. Tennessee Electric Power Company et al. v. Tennessee Valley Authority, 306 U.S. 118 (1939).

8. Alabama Power Company v. Ickes, 302 U.S. 464.

9. United States v. Appalachian Electric Power Company, 311 U.S. 377, and Oklahoma v. Atkinson Company, 313 U.S. 508.

10. Lowitt, Norris, p. 120.

11. Ibid., pp. 204–5; memo by George Fort Milton, May 11–14, 1936, re reappointment of Lilienthal, Box 89, George Fort Milton Papers, Library of Congress. For Arthur Morgan's activities, see the syndicated "New York Whirligig" column in the Birmingham News, Aug. 28, 1936. The comment by Finer is in the memo of his Sept. 14, 1937, interview with David E. Lilienthal, Herman Finer Papers.

12. The White House hearings are conveniently available in Senate Document 155, 75th Cong., 3d sess., entitled Removal of a Member of the Tennessee Valley Authority. For an indication of Arthur Morgan's concern about TVA lawyers and engineers, see the lengthy memo by James Lawrence Fly, general counsel of TVA, Nov. 18, 1937, copy in Box 79, Arthur Morgan on folder, David E. Lilienthal Papers, Princeton University. Fly comments upon Morgan's desire to set the record straight at the Chattanooga trial.

Morgan later brought suit against TVA charging that the president had no authority to dismiss him. The case never reached the Supreme Court, but both the East Tennessee District Court on Aug. 11, 1939, and the Sixth Circuit Court of Appeals on Dec. 6, 1940, affirmed that the power of the president to remove members of the board is not limited to specific causes enumerated in the enabling act. (Section 6 gave the president authority to remove any board member found utilizing political considerations in appointments and promotions. Section 2b defined the terms of office of board members appointed by the president.)

13. The two-volume report of the joint committee was printed as Senate Document 56, 76th Cong., 1st sess., Investigation of the Tennessee Valley Authority. See also Francis Biddle, In Brief Authority (Garden City, N.Y.: Doubleday, 1962), pp. 52–78. Biddle was general counsel for the joint committee.

14. This assertion is made in a 1973 term paper by Jeffrey Moeller entitled "Making a New Heaven in an Old Earth: Arthur Morgan and the TVA Idea," copy in TVA Technical Library, Knoxville, Tenn.

15. Lowitt, Norris, pp. 115–16, including n. 16. See, too, C. Herman Pritchett, The Tennessee Valley Authority (Chapel Hill: University of North Carolina Press, 1943), pp. 251–53.

16. Lowitt, Norris, pp. 279–81.

17. Ibid., pp. 282, 286.

18. James R. Stokely, whose family canneries suffered from the flooding of leased farmlands by the construction of Douglas Dam, in a senior essay submitted to the Department of American Studies at Yale in 1972, viewed the Douglas Dam controversy as a crisis in leadership between McKellar and Lilienthal, who along with other Authority officials was animated by "an almost obsessive desire to see the dam built" (p. 4). A copy of Stokely's essay is on deposit in the TVA Technical Library.

19. Richard Lowitt and Maurine Beasely, eds., One Third of a Nation: Lorena Hickok Reports on the Great Depression (Urbana: University of Illinois Press, 1981), pp. 269–72.

20. TVA Oral History Interview with Louis Eckl, June 16, 1970, Mississippi Valley Collection, Memphis State University. See, too, the discussion by O. M. Derryberry in Roscoe C. Martin, ed., *TVA: The First Twenty Years: A Staff Report* (University: University of Alabama Press; Knoxville: University of Tennessee Press, 1956), pp. 195–99.

21. For a discussion of TVA cooperatives which, besides those sponsored by TVAC, were related to the growth of the agency's electricity and fertilizer programs, see Joseph G. Knapp, *The Advance of American Cooperative Enterprise: 1920–1945* (Danville, Ill.: Interstate Printers & Publishers, 1973), pp. 325–41.

22. Section 3 of the TVA Act calls for wages at not less than "the prevailing rate" for work of a similar nature "prevailing in the vicinity." From 1933 through 1945 no dispute arose over these ambiguous terms.

23. TVA built eight villages in four states at Norris, Wheeler, Pickwick, Guntersville, Kentucky, Watts Bar, Hiwassee, and Fontana dams.

24. Michael McDonald and John Muldowny, *T.V.A. and the Dispossessed* (Knoxville: University of Tennessee Press, 1982). Through the sophisticated use of various methodological approaches this study examines population removal for the construction of Norris Dam.

25. Data on TVA architecture and some of the responses it elicited came from *Time* (May 12, 1941), p. 46; *The New Yorker* (June 7, 1941), p. 58, containing comments on the Museum of Modern Art exhibition by Lewis Mumford. See, too, F. A. Gutheim, "Tennessee Valley Authority: A New Phase in Architecture" *Magazine of Art*, 33 (September, 1940): 516–27; Talbot F. Hamlin, "Architecture of the TVA," *Pencil Points*, 20 (Nov., 1939): 721–31; and the pictorial essay on TVA in *Architectural Forum*, 71 (Aug., 1939): 74–114.

26. See George O. Robinson, *The Oak Ridge Story* (Kingsport, Tenn.: Southern Publishers 1950), and Charles W. Johnson and Charles O. Jackson, *City behind a Fence* (Knoxville: University of Tennessee Press, 1981).

27. Robert P. Patterson to David E. Lilienthal, Sept. 5, 1942, Box 32, Curtis-Morgan-Morgan File, TVA Archives, Knoxville, Tenn. See, too, Don McBride, "TVA and National Defense" (MS, 1975), TVA Technical Library.

28. For information about assistance provided to Russia, see Gordon R. Clapp to Kenneth D. McKellar, June 7, 1944, Box 32, Curtis-Morgan-Morgan File, TVA Archives.

29. For Lilienthal's message, see Lilienthal to George W. Norris, Dec. 28, 1942, George W. Norris Papers, Library of Congress. From 1933 to 1944 TVA received about $700 million from the federal government. By the summer of 1944 power revenues were more than $100 million and increasing. These figures were cited in an article by Stuart Chase, "What the TVA Means," abridged in *Reader's Digest*, 45 (Oct., 1944): 37.

30. For Ickes's views, see Ickes to FDR, Dec. 18, 1944, and Jan. 13, 1945; Ickes to Alan Barth, Jan. 18, 1945; Ickes to Kenneth D. McKellar, Jan. 24, 1945, all in Box 364, Harold L. Ickes Papers, Library of Congress. Ickes was seeking material critical of TVA as he prepared his strategy in opposition to a proposed Missouri Valley Authority. Lilienthal, incidentally, favored such an authority.

31. Edward Shapiro, "The Southern Agrarians and the Tennessee Valley Authority," *American Quarterly*, 22 (1970): 791–806.

32. Charles H. Houston and John P. Davis, "TVA: Lily-White Reconstruction," *The Crisis*, 41 (Oct., 1934): 290–91, 311; John P. Davis, "The Plight of the Negro in the Tennessee Valley," *ibid.*, 42 (Oct., 1935): 294–95, 314–15; Rollins L. Winslow, "An Alley in the Valley," *ibid.*, 44 (Jan., 1937): 12–13, 29. The second half of a 1978 University of Chi-

cago Ph.D. dissertation by Nancy Grant, "Blacks, Regional Planning, and the TVA," presents a comprehensive and devastating examination.

33. C. A. Cowan to Harcourt Morgan, Dec. 26, 1933; J. Max Bond to Rufus Clement, Feb. 25, 1935; Bond to Walter White, Aug. 5, 1935, all in NAACP C407, Library of Congress. In Sept., 1934, the NAACP Press Service released a story concluding that TVA projects were of little benefit to blacks, who suffered in jobs, wages, and housing.

34. Boxes C407 and C408 of the NAACP Papers contain the files, including press releases and correspondence, pertaining to their investigation of race relations in TVA. See, for example, Walter White to A. Victor Donahey, July 11, 1938, C408. Senator Donahey chaired the Joint Committee on the Investigation of the Tennessee Valley Authority. The NAACP sent Charles H. Houston and Thurgood Marshall to Tennessee to examine race relations in TVA. Houston testified before the committee. Their reports are available in C408. See, too, Senate Document 56, 76th Cong., 1st sess., *Report of the Joint Committee on the Investigation of the Tennessee Valley Authority*, pt. 1, pp. 56–58.

35. Senate Document 56, pt. 1, pp. 56–58. In 1941 TVA tried to adopt "a more definite program on Negro employment" and to expand "placement opportunities for Negroes." See memo prepared by George F. Gant, Aug. 25, 1941, Box 42, Curtis-Morgan-Morgan File, TVA Archives.

36. Harry S. Truman, *Public Messages, Speeches, and Statements of the President, 1945* (Washington, D.C.: U.S. Government Printing Office, 1961), pp. 389–92.

37. Herman Finer, *The TVA: Lessons for International Application* (Montreal: International Labor Office, 1944), p. 215.

38. Joseph Barnes to Mrs. Alice W. Milton, Aug. 13, 1954, Box 3, Joseph Barnes Papers, Library of Congress.

3

Wilmon H. Droze

The TVA, 1945–80:
The Power Company

LONG before Congress created the Tennessee Valley Authority in May, 1933, public and private power interests battled for control of the power sites on the Tennessee River.[1] In the presidential campaign of 1932 power issues clearly divided the two candidates. Franklin Roosevelt's victory in 1932 assured comprehensive, multipurpose development of the Tennessee River by public rather than private interests. During the next decade the struggle between public and private interests shifted to the courts, where the utilities battled TVA.

On August 25, 1933, the TVA board announced its power policy. In item eight of that pronouncement the board gave notice that TVA ultimately intended to provide electricity for the whole drainage area of the Tennessee River and possibly also for such cities as Birmingham, Memphis, Atlanta, and/or Louisville. Moreover, it left open the possibility of service to areas well beyond the Valley region if the public interest required.

Nineteen of the thirty sections of the original TVA Act prescribed, in some fashion, how the Authority was to produce and distribute electricity. Later amendments mostly concerned power activities.[2] The agency thus summarized its statutory power assignment in its 1936 *Annual Report*:

. . . sections 9a, 10, 11, 12, 12a, 13, 14, 15, 15a of the act . . . direct the Authority (1) to generate and sell electric energy, in quantities consistent with streamflow regulations primarily for the purpose of promoting navigation and controlling floods, in order to avoid the waste of water power, and (2) to give preference in sale of this surplus power to states, counties, and municipalities, and cooperative organizations of citizens and farmers not organized or doing business for profit, and (3) to construct or acquire transmission facilities to provide outlets for the sale of power, and (4) to promote the wider and better use of electric power for agricultural and domestic use, and for the development of the resources of the region.[3]

To carry out this mandate, the TVA board chose to create its own utility service area.[4] The sale of its power at dams or steam plants to private utilities probably would have subverted its mission. First, it would have been unable to market its power over a wide area at the lowest possible rates. Second it could not have sold its power to preferred groups as directed by Congress. Finally, the mass production and distribution of electricity at low rates set by the Authority were regarded by TVA officials as the key for promoting the region's economic and social development.

It was primarily the TVA board's early decision to displace the existing private utility companies in the Valley that provoked the nearly fatal court battles of the 1930s. It also underlay the Lilienthal-Morgan feud. Morgan favored the creation of a small service area and full cooperation with private utilities. Lilienthal believed that only the elimination of private power companies in nearly all of the Valley would allow TVA to satisfy its statutory mandate. By 1939, with TVA's victory in the Tennessee Electric Power Company (TEP) case, the Lilienthal power program and Harcourt Morgan's agricultural improvement program dwarfed the other functions of the agency.[5]

The power program also overshadowed TVA's other programs in visibility, assets, and budgets. When TVA took control of the Muscle Shoals properties in 1933, the Authority had an installed hydro-electric capacity of 184,000 kilowatts at the Wilson Dam and a 60,000-kilowatt steam plant under lease to the Alabama Power Company.[6] By June 30, 1941, the Authority had an installed generating capacity of 1,063,905 kilowatts and had another 969,200 kilowatts of capacity under construction.[7] It had an estimated $111,993,946 in power assets compared to an estimated $110,098,728 in navigation and flood control facilities. Power revenues totaled $21,137,371 in 1942. It had power operating expenses of about $14,000,000, or more than double its expenses for navigation, flood control, fertilizer, and resource development.[8] By 1941 TVA was the largest distributor of electric power in the South and the sixth largest utility company in the nation in point of energy output.[9] In the summer of 1940 it began expanding its power capacity to meet national defense goals, especially the higher power needs of aluminum and munitions plants.

World War II accelerated TVA's power development. It shifted its fertilizer program to the production of nitrates and phosphates for munitions. It abandoned or reduced other programs or gave them a defense orientation.[10] Since the Aluminum Company of America near Maryville, Tennessee, vastly increased its production of aluminum for aircraft, the president and Congress asked TVA to expedite its construction of power dams. TVA speeded the completion of the Kentucky, Watts Bar, and Fort Loudoun dams, began Cherokee Dam on the Holston, and built its first new steam-electrical generating plant near Watts Bar Dam. It installed extra generating units at Pickwick and Wilson dams and planned additional ones for the incomplete Fort Loudoun and Kentucky dams. On July 1, 1941, TVA had an installed generating capacity of 1,063,905 kilowatts. By war's end it owned a combined system of hydro, steam, and internal combustion plants with a capacity of 2,513,102 kilowatts—a 127 percent increase in five years. In the process it completed the main-river dams that provided a navigation channel from the Ohio River to Knoxville and created 14 million acre-feet of flood storage. TVA boasted in 1945 that it produced more electricity than any other single integrated system in the nation in that year.[11]

TVA's increased electrical potential made the Valley a prime site for the Manhattan Engineer District's Clinton Engineering Works (CEW) at Oak Ridge. Its mission was to produce U-235, through two power-hungry separation methods, a gaseous diffusion and an electromagnetic process.[12] The needs of Oak Ridge ensured that TVA's power production would become more than a byproduct of river control and development.[13] The coming of the nuclear age gave the Authority a vital place in the nation's defense and domestic energy picture.

The first new steam plant at Watts Bar Dam set an important precedent. It provided power for the Alcoa plants near Maryville, Tennessee. Ironically, when President Roosevelt authorized its construction in July, 1940, the TVA board was reluctant to build it. Agency officials argued that while "steam generated power is desirable to provide supplementary power during periods of extreme drought and to allow flexibility in system management, any considerable addition to steam capacity during the present emergency appears inadvisable."[14] There are several explanations for TVA's position. Officials felt it would require more time to build a steam rather than new hydro plants, since steam turbines were not immediately available from suppliers because of orders from the Navy, the merchant marine, and contractors in regions of the country where hydro sites were not available. Also, TVA had an eye to the future: at that date, hydro power cost .642¢ per kilowatt-hour to produce compared to 2.8¢ for steam-generated power.[15] Moreover, power production expenses at its small number of steam and internal combustion plants were more than one-half of total expenditures of the combined hydro-steam system, which at the time included fourteen multiple-use and twelve single-use dams.[16] Expenses for coal, a major cost factor, totaled $3,694,831 for 879,500 tons in fiscal 1945. Clearly, any increase in steam generation tied to increases in the price of coal would, in time, create difficulties for the agency. In spite of TVA's concern, national defense needs were primary and the Authority built the Watts Bar steam unit in record time.

Before the war ended, TVA successfully carried out three emergency construction programs. Rapid growth and "bigness" were not without concern for TVA officials because by law they were required to operate their system on a self-liquidating basis. An unused surplus of power capacity could send rates soaring, which was hardly consistent with the agency's philosophy of low-cost power and mass consumption. Supporting these fears was the general belief that a postwar depression might follow the closing of defense industries. One can readily understand TVA's concern over the War Department's insatiable demand for more and more energy.[17] While the agency expanded its capacity at a much faster rate than projected in its 1936 plan, TVA Chairman David E. Lilienthal believed that over a period of time the excess power would be absorbed.[18]

TVA won acclaim for its wartime achievement. Few except TVA officials gave much thought to its postwar role. Chairman Lilienthal moved to Washington to head the newly organized Atomic Energy Commission (AEC), and Gordon R. Clapp, former general manager, became chairman after a thorough review of his qualifications by the Senate Public Works Committee. Clapp and his associates began to take stock of their war-built power system and, in conjunction with the TVA distributor system of municipal and rural cooperatives, began vigorously to seek new markets for TVA's power.[19] After World War II the Authority's power system experienced only about a ten-month decline in power consumption. By using hydro power only, TVA kept production costs down. By the end of its first postwar year its power revenues were down only about 10 percent and its return on its expanded power system was only .6 percent less than in fiscal 1945. Conversion from war to peace accompanied a substantial increase in the use of electricity by farmers and small commercial establishments, while eight new distributors joined the TVA system. Behind this successful reconversion lay an aggressive promotional campaign by TVA and its distributors. They gave particular attention to rural electrification. Surveys revealed that 150,000 farms, or more than double the number served in 1945, were potential users of TVA electricity. TVA and its distributor organizations agreed that TVA would provide technical advice and assistance in various electrical services, and the distributors would determine which phase of the program they would emphasize in their particular service areas.[20] The Authority's consumers, who numbered 1,258 on February 7, 1934, consisted of 668,752 households in seven states by 1946.[21]

The rapid reconversion made several considerations obvious. If the power market continued to grow, TVA would have to have new generating capacity, since it had all but exhausted its hydro capacity. This meant that it would have to turn to steam generation or purchase more expensive power from neighboring utilities.[22] From 1945 to 1947 the annual residential use of electrical energy on its system increased by 60 percent, rising from 900 million to nearly 1.5 billion kilowatt-hours; average consumption per family increased 1,790 to 2,320 kilowatt-hours per year. The agency expected this use to double by 1952.[23] An equally compelling factor was the evolving Cold War, followed later by the Korean War, both of which put new emphasis on the need for atomic weapons; this, of course, accelerated electrical needs at Oak Ridge. TVA officials emphasized that its generating capacity had not kept up with consumption. From 1945 to 1948 generating capacity had increased by only 2 percent whereas average annual use increased by 43.7 percent.[24] TVA, which tried to plan ten years ahead, began seeking the means to augment its power capacity in 1946,[25] when it concluded that its region would be subject to unparalleled economic growth. By that date steam power was increasingly needed to "firm up" hydro power during periods of low stream flow and at time of peak load. In addition, the increased use was greater in the western portion of its service area, where additional hydro capacity was unavailable. Its east-to-west power transmission lines were already carrying capacity loads. After considerable study TVA asked Congress in April, 1948, for funds to construct a steam plant at New Johnsonville, Tennessee. It planned a plant of 375,000 kilowatts, with the first of three generating units to become operational in the fall of 1951.

For the first time in nine years private power interests challenged TVA plans. The utility companies saw an opportunity to limit the growth of TVA's power program and to curb any possible future expansion of its service area. The Eightieth Congress now had to weigh the consequences of slowing power development in the Valley or of recognizing the agency's legal right to be the Valley's sole power company.[26] The Republican majority in the House, in spite of President Harry Truman's intervention on behalf of TVA, refused to vote the funds. The Senate passed the bill, but strong opposition by House members in conference defeated it.

The refusal of Congress to supply $4 million to initiate construction at New Johnsonville marked the beginning of several years of intermittent warfare in Congress between TVA and a resurging coalition of private power advocates organized in the National Association of Electrical Companies. At issue was the fear of the privately owned utility companies that if TVA could legitimately build one steam plant, it could embark upon a program of unlimited future expansion, which might extend its market area well beyond the Valley.[27] The utilities argued that TVA was authorized to produce power only if incidental to navigation, flood control, or national defense. Since the new plant would not deliver large amounts of power to military installations or to the atomic facilities at Oak Ridge, private utility spokesmen contended that TVA had no statutory authority to erect it.

The surprising election victory of President Harry Truman and the resurgence of Democratic party control of Congress in the 1948 election gave TVA renewed hope. Moreover, President Truman campaigned for public power development in his election campaign, so his support of an appropriation was assured.[28] The Authority's chairman, Gordon R. Clapp, told Truman and Senate and House Democrats that TVA could no longer meet its defense commitment or its obligation to provide power to its service area unless it developed additional steam capacity. In the spring of 1949 the Senate followed House action and approved $2,950,000 for New Johnsonville.[29] The vote followed party lines, with Democrats supporting TVA.

George Rawson has concluded that the vote for the appropriation legitimated TVA's expansion into a new technological area.[30] Of even greater significance was Congress's recognition that TVA, as Director Arnold Jones wrote, had "public-utility responsibility."[31] The action by Congress also meant that it would not place a ceiling on the Valley's power supply, provided TVA could secure adequate funds for expansion of its power system.

Funds to construct new generating capacity quickly became TVA's most acute problem. In 1947, just prior to the rapid increase in demand for electricity, TVA and Congress had worked out a new financial relationship. There seemed no likelihood that TVA's growth would level off or that power revenues would be sufficient to pay operating costs, to underwrite capital plant expansion, to make payments in lieu of taxes to the states, and still return a surplus to the treasury. These assumptions led Congress in 1947 to include provisions in the Government Corporation Appropriations Act of 1948 requiring TVA to pay $2.5 million annually on its outstanding bonded indebtedness, incurred in 1939 when TVA sold bonds to purchase properties of the private utilities in the Valley. It also was told to pay, over a forty-year period, a sum equal to all appropriations Congress had made for power facilities.[32]

The steady-state philosophy and the plan to make TVA's power program "self-supporting" and "self-liquidating" fell victim to the Korean War and the subsequent national emergency. The Authority was called upon again to supply vast amounts of energy to federal installations at Oak Ridge and Tullahoma, to its Muscle Shoals fertilizer works, and, later, to the AEC plant at Paducah, Kentucky. National defense needs led to an unprecedented expansion of TVA's steam generating capacity. Congress, in the latter years of the Truman administration, provided generous appropriations to build two dams in northeast Tennessee, six steam plants scattered throughout the Valley at optimum load distribution points, and many more transmission lines.[33] The demands upon the TVA power system continued to increase dramatically. Between 1945 and 1956, when defense power expansion was nearing completion, annual system power consumption grew from 12.5 billion to nearly 60 billion kilowatt-hours.[34] While a majority of this power was destined for defense facilities, it should be noted that Valley municipalities and cooperatives correspondingly increased their demand; their annual power usage grew from 3.3 billion kilowatt-hours in 1945 to 15.5 billion kilowatt-hours in 1956.[35]

In spite of a greatly enlarged steam construction program, growth in power demand appeared endless. Appropriations by Congress from 1950 to 1954 totaled $1,077,610,000, most of which was allocated to steam plant construction. Power expansion soon created a growing reluctance in Congress to continue appropriating such large sums year in and year out to keep pace with the normal peacetime development of the region.[36] Congressional unwillingness to expand the federal debit, a widespread belief that TVA's peacetime expansion should be financed by its power sales, and the sweeping Republican victory of 1952 brought to an end appropriations for new TVA power plants. By 1954 earlier authorized steam plants were nearly complete. From 1954 until July, 1961, when TVA began to receive funds from bond sales, the Authority had to rely upon power revenues to finance any construction. Congress, of course, continued to supply small amounts of money for TVA's non-power functions. That the Authority was able to continue to finance the load growth from its revenues for nearly six years was a rather remarkable accomplishment. Director Jones explained: "Several unusual factors contributed to TVA's ability to do so. Two business recessions slowed the growth of very large industrial loads; the city of Memphis withdrew as a customer of TVA and built its own steam plant; being ahead of schedule in its Treasury payments under the 1948 Appropriations Act . . . TVA held payments after 1956 to a nominal sum; [and] system earnings were relatively large in comparison with capital requirements once the federal loads leveled off." [37]

While TVA struggled to meet its system needs, it again incurred the wrath of private power interests and faced a hostile presidential administration. TVA's need to enlarge its generating capacity in the Memphis, Tennessee, area brought matters to a head. The outgoing Truman administration, in its budget for fiscal 1953, approved a TVA budget request of $4 million to construct a large steam plant at Fulton, Tennessee, near Memphis. [38] After a delay of five months the new Eisenhower administration eliminated from TVA's budget any funds for the facility. Its opposition to TVA became clear when Eisenhower implied on June 17, 1953, that TVA was an example of "creeping socialism." [39] For the next several weeks a debate raged over TVA's request. When Congress adjourned in August, 1953, it had provided no funds for the Fulton plant, since the administration was anxious to reduce government spending, was committed to a balanced budget, and wanted private interests to develop future power supplies. This impasse forced TVA to use its own revenues to expand its capacity, while President Eisenhower and private power supporters tried to curb any further growth of TVA's power-generating capacity. More extreme devotees of private power advocated either selling TVA or dividing it up into small units. The plan that won presidential favor led to the Dixon-Yates controversy.

Energy demands by federal agencies proved insatiable. The AEC's plant at Oak Ridge, the Arnold Engineering Development Center at Tullahoma, and other federal facilities purchased nearly one-half of TVA's electrical production by 1954. The agency concluded in 1954 that "at the end of 1956, the margin for meeting unforeseeable developments, affecting either TVA's generating capacity or now unpredictable demands for new blocks of power, will be dangerously small—in fact, only about half the average margin deemed advisable and [currently] being provided by the nation's private utilities."[40] The problem led TVA in 1955 to ask the AEC to reduce TVA's commitment to the AEC plant at Paducah, Kentucky, by 500,000 kilowatts by the fall of 1957. TVA planned a new steam plant at Fulton, Tennessee, if it received appropriated funds from Congress. The Bureau of the Budget, headed by Joseph Dodge, developed a plan for meeting TVA's power needs without appropriations for the Fulton plant. He asked AEC to contract with private utility companies to build a plant in the Memphis area to replace part of the power TVA supplied to the Paducah facility. The Middle South Utilities Corporation, headed by Edgar H. Dixon, and the Southern Company, headed by Eugene A. Yates, worked with the bureau and the AEC to organize the Mississippi Valley Generating Company to build a steam plant near Memphis. From the spring of 1953 until July, 1955, this Dixon-Yates scheme was subjected to a national airing that daily lessened its chances of being accepted by Congress or the administration. President Eisenhower ordered the Dixon-Yates contract canceled in July, 1955, after the city of Memphis decided to build its own generating plant and conflict-of-interest charges were leveled at the Dixon-Yates organizers.

The failure of the Dixon-Yates organizers did not result in new TVA appropriations. As Aaron Wildavsky has pointed out, the TVA could not now look to southern Democrats and representatives from the Pacific Northwest to support its appropriations.[41] Since TVA did not receive funds to develop any new generating capacity, it began to seek other means for continuing to supply low-cost power to its consumers. In 1955 the TVA faced some hard realities. It was the sole supplier of power for its 80,000-square-mile service area. Its power system load was growing at a rate of 12 percent annually, which required $150 to $200 million a year in new capital funds. Larger annual outlays loomed ahead. Like other utility firms, TVA could not meet those capital requirements from its own revenues. After several months of discussion with the Bureau of the Budget, TVA distributors, and Valley power organizations, the Authority proposed on April 1, 1955, that Congress amend the TVA statute so that it could use revenue bonds to finance capital expansion. The proposal rekindled the fight between public and private power interests and initiated a debate that, when concluded four years later, produced a "new national consensus on the terms under which it [TVA] could continue to operate."[42]

Both private power supporters and the Bureau of the Budget opposed TVA self-financing. The bureau, reflecting the views of the Eisenhower administration, believed that the president and Congress should more carefully scrutinize TVA's activities. Those who supported TVA believed it should remain "a corporation clothed with the power of government but possessed of the flexibility and initiative of private enterprise." These differences created a number of issues that had to be compromised before a self-financing bill could secure congressional approval. Among the questions to be answered were: Should the nation recover its cost in TVA power facilities? Should the bondholders or the tax-payers have first call on TVA's revenues? Should TVA be limited on the amount of bonds it could sell? Should Congress have prior approval of all bond sales? Should the TVA service area be limited to its existing boundaries?[43]

After prolonged debate, and concessions between contending groups, the TVA Revenue Bond Act became law on August 6, 1959. The law did not cripple TVA or eliminate the agency's flexibility. Full responsibility for management of its power system remained with the TVA board. The act enabled TVA to finance new power facilities from both power revenues and proceeds from the sales of bonds. Although prohibited from having more than $750 million in bonds outstanding at any one time, TVA could, with Congress's approval, raise its debt ceiling. The law required that TVA use bond money only for its power program.

The act also established a new schedule for the repayment of congressional appropriations made for the power program. The Government Corporations Act of 1948 had required that TVA pay $2.5 million annually from net power proceeds to liquidate its bonded indebtedness incurred in 1939 and 1940 when it purchased the Tennessee Electric Power Company and other smaller firms. Also, it required TVA to repay $348,239,240 in appropriations to the treasury by 1990. The self-financing law replaced the 1948 pay-back schedule and required that the Authority make payments to the Treasury Department as a return on the unrepaid balance of appropriated funds invested in TVA power facilities. The return was to be repaid at an annual rate equal to the computed average interest rate payable by the treasury on its total matchable public obligation as of the beginning of the fiscal year. TVA might defer such payments for up to two years. This provision required the agency to pay much higher interest rates than those that prevailed at the time of the original appropriations. The TVA was to pay back only $1 billion over a forty-year period, although by 1959 Congress had appropriated about $1.25 billion for the power system. Neither President

Eisenhower nor his associates wanted TVA to pay back all of the appropriated investment, lest such provide a basis for ratepayers to claim a
role in the governance of TVA.[44]

TVA was authorized by the act to sell its bonds in the open market
without approval of the treasury, although the treasury had to be notified in advance and could delay the sale of an issue for as much as eight
months. In the meantime TVA could issue short-term notes. The payments of interest and principal to bondholders gained first claim on
TVA's power earnings.[45] To pacify private utility interests, coal companies, and others who feared that TVA would now expand its service
area well beyond its present 80,000 square miles, the law included a
territorial limitation freezing the area served as of July 7, 1957, with a
few exceptions along the watershed's periphery. The advocates of fixed
limits won a hollow victory, since TVA had no real interest in expanding its service area.[46]

Finally, the statute permitted Congress, by concurrent resolution, to
alter or change TVA's programs without presidential agreement. This
was a concession to TVA's congressional opponents, who contended
that by giving up its control over appropriations, Congress was losing control over TVA's power program. President Eisenhower took exception to the provision because he believed that Congress had no
authority to limit the president's veto power. He threatened to veto the
bill unless Congress repealed that provision. Congress quickly rushed
through a repeal amendment. Changes in the bill left TVA with greater
flexibility and less congressional supervision. The nonpower programs
remained subject to annual congressional review. TVA also had to make
annual reports to the president and Congress of all its activities, especially financial ones. The comptroller general and the General Accounting Office could conduct periodic audits of TVA's operations.

The Revenue Bond Act gave TVA more flexibility in planning and
building needed generating capacity. It could now plan well in advance
of its new demand. In 1959, under normal circumstances, a coal-fired
plant required approximately three years to build. The construction of
nuclear plants in the mid-1960s required five to seven years, and today
nearly twenty years are needed. It would have been extremely difficult
to persuade Congress to appropriate funds that far ahead. Passage of the
Revenue Bond Act marked the end of an aggressive drive by private
power interests to discredit the agency.[47] This is not to say that all criticism of TVA ceased, for spokesmen representing such organizations as
the U.S. Chamber of Commerce and the Edison Electric Institute frequently scored TVA because it was not private owned and because it

did not pay income taxes. Other cities found TVA's programs unjustified by the results achieved. But, as Marguerite Owen observed, TVA's reliance on bond funds removed "the obligations of utility lobbyists to organize annual campaigns against the appropriation of money for capacity increases."[48] She also observed that bond sales may have given TVA greater respectability among financiers who also handled the capital fund needs of private utilities.[49]

By 1960 TVA had to add about 1 million kilowatts of generating capacity each year to keep pace with demands. This required an investment of $175 million by June 30, 1961, and $225 million annually thereafter. TVA planned to raise about two-thirds of these amounts from bond sales and the remainder from power revenues. Power officials believed that it would be five or six years before it had to ask for a higher ceiling on its bond-issuing authority. The increased generating capacity had to come from coal-fired steam plants, since TVA had only a few new hydro sites and the needed nuclear technology was still several years in the future.

In November, 1959, TVA began construction of its Paradise steam plant in Kentucky. The first two units there would produce 650,000 kilowatts each and the plant had an ultimate installed minimum capacity of 2,600,000 kilowatts. It ordered an even larger 900,000-kilowatt unit for the Bull Run steam plant in east Tennessee. These huge plants consumed prodigious amounts of coal. The Bull Run facility was expected to use 23.4 million tons of coal during its first fifteen years of operation. Coal then sold for $3.00 a ton, f.o.b., at the mine. One can readily understand the consequences of future increases in coal prices, or how restricted coal supplies could threaten the TVA's system. Aware of these dangers, the TVA, in its 1959 Annual Report, announced that "when nuclear plants became economically competitive with coal burning plants, TVA will doubtless design and build some nuclear plants."[50] For the time being, however, the Authority concentrated on the rapid expansion of its coal-fired steam plant system, which in 1959 was producing some 75 percent of the agency's electrical power. Between 1960 and 1966 TVA expanded its installed generating capacity from 11,373,460 to 17,149,500 kilowatts. At that time it had a total of 4,648,040 kilowatts under construction, which by 1971 would bring system capacity to 21,697,840 kilowatts.

The building of massive coal-fired steam generating stations, the immense sums required for their construction, and the effort to satisfy the insatiable demands for more and more electricity dwarfed all of TVA's other activities. This contributed to a widespread image of TVA as just another power company. New, economically justified power interchange agreements with old competitors, Alabama Power Company, Mississippi Power and Light Company, American Electric Power Company, Arkansas Power and Light, must have raised eyebrows among the older proponents of public power. Seasonal power exchanges reached 2.4 million kilowatts by 1974.[51] The TVA system interconnected at numerous places with other electric utility systems. In 1972 TVA joined with Commonwealth Edison Company of Chicago to begin building the nation's first breeder reactor demonstration plant near Oak Ridge. Because of the project's initial expense, nearly $700 million, all segments of the electric utility industry pledged financial support.[52] It is instructive to find that in the TVA oversight hearings held in 1975 by the Senate Public Works Committee, not a single private utility spokesman came forth to criticize TVA's programs.[53] Thus, prior to embarking upon the nation's largest nuclear-fired steam power program, TVA comfortably coexisted with other utility systems. When its nuclear power age dawned in the 1960s, the Authority had become the pacesetter[54] for the utility industry, and public power exponents expected it to take the lead in developing low-cost nuclear power.[55]

In 1966 TVA opted to build its first nuclear-fired steam generating station, the Brown's Ferry plant in northern Alabama. In October, 1965, Gabriel O. Wessenauer, TVA's brilliant, long-time manager of power, reported to TVA General Manager Louis J. Van Mol that studies had confirmed the feasibility of installing a large light-water nuclear power plant in the TVA system:[56] "This detailed study confirms our tentative conclusions of a year ago [1964] that a large light water reactor plant is closely competitive with a large conventional coal-burning plant. Therefore, we [Division of Power] are proposing that TVA consider a light water reactor plant for the next addition to the power system."[57]

Economic and engineering considerations had determined the choice to develop nuclear power. A few weeks earlier the TVA board had authorized the preparation of specifications and bid invitations for both a coal-fired plant and a nuclear plant. Bids were opened in March, 1966, and on June 17, 1966, the board finally approved the award of contracts for equipment and fuel for the Authority's first light-water nuclear plant at an estimated cost of $313,373,000.[58] The plant was expected to provide its first power in the fall of 1970, in time to meet the peak loads projected for the winter of 1970–71. Wessenauer and his associates were convinced that a nuclear plant could produce a kilowatt-hour of electricity for 2.39 mills as against 2.90 mills for a coal-fired plant. Fuel costs over a twelve-year period and operating and maintenance expenses would all be less for a nuclear plant. They believed that during the nuclear facility's first twelve years, TVA would save $100 million.

Thus, TVA joined five private utility companies that already possessed commercially operating nuclear plants. An important difference was that the first unit of TVA's planned three-unit plant would produce 1,152,000 kilowatts, whereas the largest of the plants owned by private concerns had a capacity of only 265,000 kilowatts. Three years prior to TVA's decision "to go nuclear," the New Jersey Central Power and Light Company had announced plans to build, without a federal subsidy, a 650,000-kilowatt plant, the first truly large-scale nuclear plant.[59] TVA was "going nuclear" but on a grand scale. The three-unit Brown's Ferry plant, located near Huntsville, Alabama, would, when eventually completed in 1975, have an installed capacity of 3,456,000 kilowatts. System capacity in 1976 amounted to 27,071,480 kilowatts.[60] Power Manager Wessenaur, who had led TVA power engineers in the building of some of the world's largest coal-fired steam power plants and who had pioneered in effecting economies of scale by such large power plants, confidently predicted that "TVA's engineers already are anticipating the day when the region's power requirements will reach 50 million kilowatts, and the facilities TVA is building are designed with a 50-million-kilowatt-system in mind."[61] Aubrey J. Wagner, chairman of the TVA board, informed the Madison County Chamber of Commerce of Huntsville in August, 1966: "Regardless of the source—from hydro generation to nuclear fission—it has been TVA's responsibility for 33 years to provide abundant, low cost electricity to this region. Our decision to enter the nuclear field represents no [italics his] departure from this original responsibility."[62] Wagner was correct. TVA was simply expanding its program technology. Did it really matter whether steam was created by the burning of coal or by nuclear fission? Time will tell.

At the time of the change in technology, few expressed any concerns. Coal industry spokesmen, who feared that TVA, the nation's largest consumer of coal, would reduce coal use and thereby limit their market, pushed Congress to decline TVA's request for increased ceilings on its bond-issuing authority because of the dangers of nuclear generation and the uncertainty of future supplies of uranium.[63] Private utility leaders did not react at all to TVA's decision, and members of Congress, although informed by TVA of its plans to begin a nuclear plant, appeared disinterested in how TVA created its steam and seemed so satisfied with its financial soundness and fiscal management that it permitted the Authority to increase its debt ceiling from $750 million to $1.75 billion.[64]

TVA's entry into nuclear construction began a new era in its history. In less than a decade the Authority initiated work on five additional very large nuclear plants and began planning two more, for an eventual installed nuclear capacity of 18,116,960 kilowatts. This potential capacity was greater than the capability of all of TVA's coal-fired steam plants in 1980.[65] The TVA expected that nuclear plants would ultimately replace coal-fired stations as producers of its base loads.[66]

Confidence alone does not explain why TVA entered the nuclear power generation in such a grand manner. The Authority's first nuclear facility was larger than any in the world. It planned and began constructing between 1966 and 1969 the largest number of nuclear units of any utility in the nation.[67] TVA General Manager Lynn Seeber may have best explained this commitment when he told Senator Howard H. Baker's oversight committee that TVA's statute was explicit: "Thou shalt supply power at the lowest possible cost consistent with financial soundness."[68] TVA officials were convinced that low-cost power could be obtained only from nuclear stations.[69] Coal was not only costly but dirty as well. Its use had greatly increased TVA's operating expenses and had forced the agency to shop in uncertain markets. Nuclear plants, on the other hand, offered TVA an opportunity to strike a balance between the costly environmental problems associated with coal-fired plants and consumer demands for electrical rates they could afford. Safety was a concern, but in 1966 it was not viewed as a deterrent at all by TVA staff, for no serious nuclear accidents had been recorded at that time.

In July, 1973, TVA expanded its nuclear role when it committed its technology and nearly $21.7 million to a joint venture with the AEC and Commonwealth Edison Company in Chicago to design, construct, and operate the nation's first liquid-metal fast breeder reactor, a 300–500-megawatt demonstration plant.[70] TVA, Commonwealth Edison, and 753 privately owned public utilities jointly undertook to finance the Clinch River Breeder Reactor, which in 1973 was estimated to cost $700 million. Three years later projected costs rose to $3.2 billion. Cost overruns and concern over the safety of the experimental reactors resulted in the reorganization of the Clinch River project, and control of it reverted to the Energy Research and Development Administration in 1976.[71] President Jimmy Carter refused to provide further funds for the project. In spite of the president's action, Congress continued to appropriate $172 million annually for it. The Reagan administration encouraged the continuation of the project by budgeting $254 million for fiscal year 1981.[72]

TVA's initiation of nuclear power development followed nearly two decades of close cooperation with the AEC. TVA assigned its employees in the 1950s to work at AEC-sponsored installations. TVA also cooperated with the AEC in developing a gas-cooled reactor, a venture that was abandoned after a few years. Agency staff members went to England to view nuclear projects, since England, France, and the Soviet Union were well ahead of the United States in breeder reactor development. These involvements made TVA officials feel ready, in 1966, to undertake its large nuclear program.

The history of TVA's power program since the 1970s consists of the Authority's efforts to carry out its program in a period of challenges. Its efforts to produce low-cost power in a clean and safe environment have been challenged by individuals and groups who question TVA's standards for environmental quality. Equally as controversial, and probably of even greater importance to TVA's future, has been the agency's inability to sell its power in volume amounts at traditionally low prices. High-priced coal, escalating interest rates, and rampant inflation forced TVA to raise its wholesale electrical rates in 1967 for the first time in thirty-four years. Rates increased from slightly over .5¢ per kilowatt-hour in 1967 to nearly 3¢ in 1980. The product of these frustrations over environmental quality and seemingly unending rate increases has been a growing source of criticism of TVA by Valley residents. Their frustrations have been enhanced by what they feel to be a major problem— their inability to communicate their dissatisfactions to TVA's board. When TVA would not or could not respond adequately to its public, the dissidents turned to Congress, the courts, and federal regulatory agencies for redress. As might be anticipated, the continuing controversy eroded TVA's credibility, brought closer congressional scrutiny, led to an increase in TVA's court battles, and produced numerous confrontations with state and federal regulatory agencies.

In the half-century after 1933, TVA built a power-generating system larger than any other in the nation. Its concern with its mission to provide low-cost electricity to its service area led the Authority first to construct coal-fired steam plants in the 1950s and 1960s and later to build its first nuclear plant in 1966. In an effort to supply its major consumer, the AEC, with its seemingly insatiable demand for power, TVA planned seven nuclear plants and seventeen reactors. Relying too much on the Department of Energy's (formerly AEC) projections for a huge demand for power in the Tennessee Valley, and failing to be adequately critical of its own estimates of load growth, created for TVA and its ratepayers a financial nightmare. The Authority overbuilt its nuclear generating capacity when the Federal Power Commission and many private electrical utilities were reducing their estimates for future electrical consumption.

TVA began to reap the results of its overly optimistic projections in the form of rate increases over protests by ratepayers and demands by antinuclear proponents that the nuclear construction program be scrapped or severely reduced. The Authority sought to sell its excess power to neighboring private utilities, but it has had only minimal success.[73] Its inability to secure markets for the nuclear plant system has forced TVA to cancel a major part of its nuclear construction program. The Tennessee Valley Industrial Council in a news release on January 31, 1982, summarized public sentiment in the Valley when it said that "deferral of nuclear reactors is absolutely mandatory, if TVA is to live up to its statutory obligations"[74] to produce electricity at the lowest possible cost. Thus, TVA, like other public and private utilities, has had to adjust to structural changes in the nation's economy brought about by the 1973 Arab states' oil embargo, the escalation of energy prices in 1979, and the tremendous increases in interest rates. In TVA's fiftieth year it is trying to learn how to live in a market in which people conserve energy. The power program must now await another period of defense preparation and a more effective and safe nuclear technology before it will again become the growth catalyst for the Tennessee Valley.

NOTES

1. Preston J. Hubbard, *Origins of the TVA: The Muscle Shoals Controversy, 1920–1932* (Nashville, Tenn.: Vanderbilt University Press, 1961).

2. Elliott Roberts, *One River—Seven States: TVA-State Relations in the Development of the Tennessee River* (Knoxville: University of Tennessee, Bureau of Public Administration, 1955), p. 59.

3. TVA, *Annual Report* (1936), p. 25.

4. An alternative to outright ownership of the region's privately owned power production and distribution systems was the establishment of a regional power pool. This possibility was discussed by President Roosevelt, TVA's directors, Wendell Willkie, and other private power leaders in Sept., 1936. Demands by Commonwealth and Southern's operating companies in the Southeast for territorial limits to TVA's service area, Lilienthal's strong opposition to the idea because he felt that TVA would not be able to carry out the intent of Congress or the provisions of the TVA Act, and the advent of the Tennessee Electric Power Company's case brought all discussion to an end. See "Power Pool," Folder 951.04, Administrative Files, TVA Archives, Knoxville, Tenn.

5. George E. Rawson, "The Process of Program Development: The Case of TVA's Power Program" (Ph.D. dissertation, University of Tennessee, Knoxville, 1978), p. 52.

6. TVA, *Annual Report* (1934), p. 24.

7. *Ibid.* (1941), pp. 86–87.

8. Most of TVA's hydro-steam system in 1941 consisted of main-river dams whose cost of $212,092,671 was allocated 65.8 percent to power, 21.8 percent to navigation, and 12.4 percent to flood control. Additional plant for power purposes had a depreciated value of $83,983,231. *Ibid.*, pp. 38, 66–68.

9. *Ibid.*, p. 3.

10. Don McBride, "TVA and the National Defense" (MS, 1975), TVA Technical Library, Knoxville, Tenn., pp. 22–23.

11. TVA, *Annual Report* (1945), pp. 36, 57.

12. Charles W. Johnson and Charles O. Jackson, *City behind a Fence: Oak Ridge, Tennessee, 1942–1946* (Knoxville: University of Tennessee Press, 1981), p. xx.

13. McBride, "TVA and the National Defense," p. 3.

14. TVA, *Annual Report* (1941), p. 12.

15. *Ibid.* (1945), p. 106.

16. *Ibid.* See Schedule C: "Details of Power Expenses for Year Ended June 30, 1945," pp. 105–7.

17. This concern over wartime capital plant expansion produced nearly fifteen years' discussion and debate between TVA and the War Department over the rate the department would pay for power sold to its defense plants. The department thought it should be provided virtually free, but TVA by law had to dispose of its power at a "reasonable rate." Long after the war ended, TVA won its arguments that the department should pay the lowest commercial rate. This controversy is discussed in McBride, "TVA and the National Defense," pp. 29–30.

18. *Ibid.*, p. 38.

19. W. E. Herring to David E. Lilienthal, Sept. 18, 1945; Gordon R. Clapp to W. E. Herring, Oct. 11, 1945, both in Folder 047.2-30, Administrative Files, Office of the General Manager, TVA Archives.

20. TVA, *Annual Report* (1946), p. 76.

21. *Ibid.*, p. 79.

22. Power purchased in 1948 cost the TVA 4.3 mills per kilowatt-hour whereas its Watts Bar steam plant produced power at a cost of 3.5 mills per kilowatt-hour. TVA, *Annual Report* (1948), "Schedule C," p. A21.

23. "The Case for the New Johnsonville Steam Plant" (undated but ca. 1949), Box 20, Folder 312, Chairman's Files, TVA Archives; TVA, *Annual Report* (1948), p. 80.

24. During fiscal 1948 TVA was adding or had on order twelve new generating units for its dams and had agreed to purchase the electrical energy being produced by the Corps of Engineers' three-dam system nearing completion on the Cumberland River north of the Tennessee River. TVA, *Annual Report* (1948), pp. 84, 94.

25. "Recommended Program for Additional Generating Capacity" (Mar., 1948), Box 20, Folder 312, Chairman's Files, TVA Archives.

26. Rawson, "Process of Program Development," p. 61; Aaron Wildavsky, *Dixon-Yates: A Study in Power Politics* (New Haven, Conn.: Yale University Press, 1962), pp. 10–13.

27. Wildavsky, *Dixon-Yates*, pp. 10–13.

28. Craufurd D. Goodwin, "Truman Administration Policies toward Particular Energy Sources," in Craufurd D. Goodwin, ed., *Energy Policy in Perspective: Today's Problems, Yesterday's Solutions* (Washington, D.C.: Brookings Institution, 1981), p. 180.

29. *Congressional Record*, 81st Cong., 1st sess. (1949), pp. 1260, 4482.

30. Rawson, "Process of Program Development," p. 63.

31. Arnold R. Jones, "The Financing of TVA," *Law and Contemporary Problems*, 26 (Autumn, 1961): 732.

32. TVA, *Annual Report* (1946), p. 90.

33. In 1947, when the act was passed, appropriated investment and bonded indebtedness totaled $348,239,240. TVA, *Annual Report* (1948), p.A10.

34. Appropriations to TVA for fiscal years 1950–52 totaled $592,782,650. From 1946 through 1948, when Congress was controlled by the Republican party, TVA received only $68,250,000. TVA, *Annual Reports* (1946–48, 1951–53): see "Notes Pertaining to Financial Statements," sec. 6.

35. O. S. Wessel, "The Power Program," in Roscoe C. Martin, ed., *TVA: The First Twenty Years: A Staff Report* (University: University of Alabama Press; Knoxville: University of Tennessee Press, 1956), pp. 124–25; TVA, *Annual Report* (1956), pp. 26–27.

36. Wessel, "Power Program," p. 125; TVA, *Annual Report* (1956), p. 3.

37. Jones, "Financing of TVA," p. 737.

38. *Ibid.*

39. TVA first requested funds for the Fulton steam plant in 1951, but President Truman and his Budget Bureau had rejected the appeal for inclusion in the budget for the 1952 fiscal year. In his final year in office (1952) Truman agreed to an appropriation of $30 million to start construction of the facility.

40. Marguerite Owen, *The Tennessee Valley Authority* (New York: Praeger, 1973), p. 97.

41. TVA, *Annual Report* (1954), p. 38: Jones, "Financing of TVA," p. 738.

42. Aaron Wildavsky, "TVA and Power Politics," *American Political Science Review*, 50 (Sept., 1961): 577–79.

43. Wildavsky, *Dixon-Yates*, p. 323.

44. Jones, "Financing of TVA," p. 738.

45. TVA, *Annual Report* (1959), pp. A10–A11; Herbert D. Vogel, "TVA Financing Legislation" (Dec. 23, 1958), memo for Chairman's Files, Folder 133, Chairman's Files, TVA Archives.

46. Jones, "Financing of TVA," p. 739.

47. Arnold R. Jones to C. C. Kilker, Mar. 6, 1958, Folder 133, General Manager's File, TVA Archives.

48. According to Marguerite Owen, TVA's Washington representative, the Electric Companies Advertising Program spent $17 million for anti-TVA advertising. Owen, *Tennessee Valley Authority*, p. 120.

49. *Ibid.*, pp. 120–21.

50. TVA, *Annual Report* (1959), p. 84.

51. Rawson, "Process of Program Development," p. 71.

52. TVA, *Power Annual Report* (1974), p. 2.

53. Senate Public Works Committee, *Tennessee Valley Authority Oversight Hearings, 1975*, 94th Cong., 1st sess. (1975), pt. 1, pp. 15–16, 705, 717, 728, 730, 806.

54. Arnold Jones to C. C. Kilker, Mar. 6, 1958; Senate Public Works Committee, *TVA Oversight Hearings, 1975*, pp. 213–14, 693; TVA, *Annual Report* (1967), p. 92.

55. J. Frank Ward to Gordon R. Clapp, Dec. 23, 1952; Clapp to Ward, Jan. 20, 1953, both in Folder 901.002, Administrative Files, TVA Archives.

56. Gabriel O. Wessenauer, "Light Water Nuclear Plant Feasibility Study" (Oct. 29, 1965), to L[ouis] J. Van Mol, Folder 319, General Manager's Files, TVA Archives.

57. *Ibid.*

58. TVA, board of directors meeting, Aug. 25, 1966, Minute Entry 946-16.

59. James L. Cochrane, "Energy Policy in the Johnson Administration," in Goodwin, ed., *Energy Policy in Perspective*, p. 366.

60. *TVA, Annual Report* (1980), 1:61.

61. Wessenauer, "Evaluating the Cost of Nuclear versus Fossil Fuel Power Plants," paper presented at Nuclear Power Briefing for the Coal Industry, U.S. Atomic Energy Commission, Oak Ridge, Tenn., Sept. 30, 1966, Folder 319, General Manager's Files, TVA Archives.

62. Aubrey J. Wagner, an address before the Huntsville–Madison County Chamber of Commerce, Huntsville, Ala., Aug. 10, 1966, copy in Chairman's Office Files, TVA Archives.

63. Rawson, "Process of Program Development," pp. 89–91. This same line of argument was pursued by the spokesman of the United Mine Workers, Tom Bethell, at the 1975 oversight hearings. Senate Public Works Committee, *TVA Oversight Hearings, 1975*, pp. 691–92.

64. Rawson, "Process of Program Development," pp. 100–101.

65. TVA, *Annual Report* (1980), 1:62. By 1974 some fifty-three nuclear plants were in operation, two were licensed to operate, sixty-three were under construction, and nineteen others had limited work permits allowing initial construction activities. Some ninety-three plants were in various stages of planning. U.S. Energy Research and Development Administration, "News Release" (Jan. 28, 1975), Folder 319, General Manager's Files, TVA Archives.

66. Senate Public Works Committee, *TVA Oversight Hearings, 1975*, p. 49.

67. Rawson, "Process of Program Development," p. 103.

68. Senate Public Works Committee, *TVA Oversight Hearings, 1975*, pt. 1, p. 712.

69. *Ibid.*, p. 61.

70. A breeder reactor of the type that was planned for the Oak Ridge demonstration plant was an advanced power reactor utilizing fissionable plutonium as its fuel. Plutonium is produced in nuclear reactors from the ordinary kind of uranium. Light-water reactors in use in today's nuclear plants produce some plutonium but only enough to supply a small portion of their own fuel needs. They rely principally on naturally occurring fissionable uranium (U-235) for their fuel. This kind of uranium is quite scarce, comprising only 0.7 percent of the uranium found in nature. The breeder reactor produces more plutonium than it uses; therefore, after several productive years it would provide additional plutonium to fuel other reactors. W. B. Behnke to James Watson, Mar. 24, 1971, with attached copy of "Fact Sheet on the First Large Scale Liquid Metal Fast Breeder Reactor," Folder 319, General Manager's Files; "Document Summary: Briefing on TVA's Commitments to Clinch River Breeder Reactor" (July, 1981), Folder 319, Chairman's Office Files, TVA Archives.

71. "Briefing on TVA's Commitments to Clinch River Breeder Reactor" (July 24, 1981).

72. *Ibid.*

73. *Knoxville News–Sentinel*, Aug. 25, 1981, p. B-10.

74. *Albany* (Ga.) *Herald*, Feb. 1, 1982, p. 3-B.

PART TWO

Leadership and Government

4
Erwin C. Hargrove

The Task of Leadership:
The Board Chairmen

THE crucial task of leadership for a TVA chairman is to combine technology and politics in the definition and creation of support for TVA missions. The task arises from two necessities. Changing historical conditions have required the development of new technology, e.g. the shift in emphasis from hydro to steam power and, subsequently, to nuclear-powered plants. Political support for such shifts has never been automatic. The principal task of leadership has been to construct a creative synthesis of technology and political support that will sustain the work of the organization until a new adaptation and redefinition are required.

It is ironic that the TVA has portrayed itself as a nonpolitical organization in which policy decisions are made on technological grounds. This is a "noble lie" in the sense that the "myth" of a non-political organization has itself been a political resource for those who knew how to use it.

Creative leadership has been necessary when TVA missions have been in doubt. The first board was required to decide between competing visions of TVA purposes. Arthur Morgan wished TVA to be a demonstration agency for the nation that would experiment with different modes of regional development. David Lilienthal opposed this vision and sought to strengthen specific statutory responsibilities such as the production and role of electric power, the management of the river, and the production of fertilizer for agricultural use. Lilienthal defeated Morgan because his vision created technological achievements, such as cheap power, that won political support and because, unlike Morgan, he understood the need for such support. The second variation is that of fashioning new technological means to achieve accepted ends. Such adaptations also require political support. Gordon Clapp carried TVA into steam power by winning support from the political coalition that had been constructed by Lilienthal. Herbert Vogel and his associates succeeded in reconciling a Republican administration to the continued development of the technology and the mission. Aubrey Wagner sought an adaptation of means similar to that achieved by Clapp, in the decisions to develop nuclear capacity. But political support for nuclear power, and for other policies of the Wagner TVA, gradually eroded, so that the organization increasingly found itself in tension with its environment. A technological imperative, as conceived by TVA, could not by itself create political support. The chairmanship of S. David Freeman was characterized by the search for a new creative synthesis in which both ends and means would be redefined.

This paper employs a biographical method to delineate an organizational role. The task of combining technology and politics faces every chairman, and they are compared in regard to how well they did it. The risk of using biography as a method to explain the actions of organizations is that a focus on individuals may exaggerate their importance and fail to identify the contributions of others. This is especially true of TVA, which has a three-member board, strong department heads, and a collegial mode of operation. But it is true that the chairman is the only person at TVA who must, by virtue of his position, deal with both technology and politics.

Arthur E. Morgan, Chairman, 1933–38 *

Arthur Morgan emerged from a crisis of identity in young adulthood with a philosophy of life and a practical mode of action that were joined to a deep commitment to the perfection of his own moral character. He had rejected Protestant dogma but embraced a vague social ethic

* The portraits of Morgan and the others draw on twenty-one interviews with past TVA employees, including three former chairmen, and twenty interviews with present TVA employees. In addition to formal interviews, the author was a participant in TVA's 1979 Summer Study of TVA missions for regional development and was thus a party to many informal discussions among TVA officials. The names of those interviewed are cited in the notes by their permission. Not all those interviewed agreed to the use of their names.

and joined the goal of creating a cooperative society to a belief in technology as the means. His personal success in achieving self-control and in establishing a professional career as an engineer convinced him that all things were possible. He believed that his striving for righteousness had brought him professional success and drew the conclusion that all men could improve themselves if they would only emulate his example. He believed that institutional changes were meaningless unless personal character was also transformed.[1]

Ordinary workaday politics was too practical and too subject to compromise to satisfy his prophetic urge. His criterion was whether a policy or action contributed to the long-run perfection of man and society, and he relied on personal intuition to tell him which actions were "ethical" in this sense. He was determined to see the whole context of every decision and had an abiding concern with the long run.[2]

Morgan viewed politicians critically as those who lived entirely in the short run. He believed that leaders, by which he meant professional experts, should create codes for the mass of persons to follow. He abhorred conflict and did not believe that social progress could be achieved through antagonism. His faith in the natural goodness of human beings was manifested in his belief that progress might come through persuasion and that it must be gradual. It is important to understand this combination of the gradualist and the utopian because Arthur Morgan both was more visionary in his goals for TVA than Harcourt Morgan or Lilienthal and, yet, was also more willing to compromise with the private power companies. The TVA was to set a good example by which society would seek to transform itself, and private power companies would embrace this transformation. Conflict was therefore unnecessary and undesirable.[3]

Morgan's prophetic urge and his gradualism led to tensions. Those who worked with him saw these different aspects of his character and alternately described him as authoritarian and experimental. To him this was no contradiction for he was intent on achieving a consensus, but continuing disagreements upset him. He had not had the discipline of a formal education and had not subjected his beliefs to criticism by others. His associates in his engineering work had been disciples.[4] One person who observed him closely from the beginning remembered: "A.E. had a simplicity about him that was almost pathetic. He was a strict disciplinarian of himself and others. He wanted to tell other people what to do."[5] This statement refers to the code of ethics Morgan prepared for TVA employees. Yet a former assistant reports that when asked why he had recommended the appointment of Lilienthal to the board, to his later regret, Morgan replied: "I thought that three intelligent men could work things out cooperatively."[6] Talbert explains that Morgan believed in the Quaker manner of conducting business through consensus rather than formal votes. Therefore, it was easy for him to interpret divisive votes and policy disagreements as unwarranted conflict.[7]

Morgan brought to the TVA chairmanship lessons to be applied from his two great successes, the Miami Conservancy and Antioch College. The dams his firm constructed on the Little Miami River were extraordinarily innovative in their design. Morgan also saw the Miami project as a social experiment that provided comfortable housing, schools, and adult education for the families of workers. The workers were encouraged to develop self-government in their living arrangements. He negotiated a general labor policy for the conservancy with the multiplicity of unions that helped build the dams. He thus believed he had achieved both practical success and social progress.[8]

Morgan also believed that Antioch College exemplified ideals that Americans could emulate. The central theme of the Antioch experience was the integration of education and work, but the very vagueness of the ideal as a vehicle for social transformation was an impediment to its realization, even in the life of the college.[9] The prophetic urge was inclined to overreach the available instruments in Morgan's mind.

Franklin Roosevelt, on first meeting Morgan in 1933, claimed to have read *Antioch Notes*. From this alumni publication FDR gathered that they shared a common commitment to the integrated development of human and natural resources, which was what TVA was to be all about.[10] In fact, it is unlikely that FDR knew much about Morgan. They understood each other only on the verbal level. One of Morgan's assistants at TVA remembers that A.E. had long talks with Roosevelt about TVA and thought that he was carrying out the president's ideas. However, this person adds: "Mrs. Roosevelt told A.E., in my presence, that FDR responded to the last person he talked with." Still, "Morgan had tremendous admiration for and belief in FDR, almost to the end."[11]

Morgan saw the TVA as a laboratory for social experimentation that would serve as a beacon to the nation.[12] Despite the claims that he was an authoritarian who wished to impose his values on people, he was opposed to the form the TVA agricultural program took under Harcourt Morgan because there was too little self-help. He thought that TVA should have its own agricultural staff. Three close associates concur in this.[13] One of them remembers the reason: "He had a vision of small scale developments. He wanted people to develop their own land for their own use—to produce their own chickens, eggs, and cattle. . . . A.E. did not approve of H.A. delegating the agricultural program to the colleges. It should be in the hands of the individual people. If it went through the agricultural colleges, it benefited very few farmers."[14]

Morgan's commitment to the TVA as a demonstration organization is perhaps not fully understood. Edward Falck, a former aid to Lilienthal, remembers:

A.E. thought I was the only honest person in the Lilienthal camp that he could talk to. He asked me to explain the Lilienthal position (on public power) to him. He never understood. I told him the private companies were trying to kill us, e.g., the Ashwander case. He ignored these cases. His conception was artistic and intellectual. TVA would act like a limited scope model that would be so perfect and idealized that the utilities would copy it. No need for large scope. One demonstration farm and one demonstration cooperative and one TVA municipal power company would be enough. The yardstick would exemplify the right way of doing things.[15]

Morgan was accustomed to throwing out ideas in speeches without sufficient forethought simply to stimulate discussion. Suggestions about local communities using scrip instead of money, of the need to reduce the number of counties in Tennessee, of the state confiscating the land of farmers who failed to prevent soil erosion, of hopes for reform of the real estate business, and numerous suggestions for the stimulation of local artisanship and handicrafts were greeted with derision by Harcourt Morgan, Lilienthal, and many others. It is an error to interpret this as an authoritarian desire to "improve" life in the Valley in spite of its inhabitants. Morgan habitually advanced such ideas for discussion purposes. One of his long-time associates remembered: "He always had crazy ideas (in the Memphis engineering firm), but would give in on them. His last book, 'Wholemanism,' was not published. It was a theory that every decision ought to be thoroughly explored."[16] The TVA Act provided little leeway for such experimentation. Section 22, which provides for planning studies, was insufficient. More important, Morgan was oblivious to the effect of his words on his credibility as chairman. Tugwell and others warned him that it was politically unwise for him to talk publicly in this manner before TVA was well established, but he ignored the advice.[17]

Morgan's chief contributions to TVA were derived from his achievements with the Miami Conservancy. He was, in large part, responsible for the engineering and architectural ingenuity of the dams. It was his proposal to build the town of Norris over the objection of Lilienthal and Harcourt Morgan, again following the Miami pattern.[18] An efficient personnel system, free from political patronage, was surely his creation, and his stubborn resistance to politicians in this regard became a TVA tradition.

But Morgan's enduring achievements were all technocratic. He was unable to construct a creative synthesis of the technological and the political because he did not accept or understand politics. He began a TVA tradition of the chairman making effective presentations on technological questions to congressional committees.[19] But as conflicts about policy directions developed with Lilienthal, he had no understanding of how to make his case or protect himself politically. Lilienthal and Harcourt Morgan believed A.E.'s utopian ideas to be harmful to the survival of the precarious TVA. Personality clashes soon developed an independent momentum. Former staff members who attended board meetings present a clear picture of an aggressive Lilienthal, a silent Harcourt Morgan, and a confused and depressed Arthur Morgan, who did not know how to respond to Lilienthal's attacks.[20] One assistant remembered how reluctant A.E. was to use negative information about Lilienthal with FDR and others because he "wanted the whole to be beautiful."[21]

Morgan's inability to deal with conflict with the board was a manifestation of the tragic flaw that led to his ultimate defeat on the larger stage. He lost the fight with Lilienthal over the character of the TVA power program because he did not understand, as Lilienthal did, that the TVA struggle to best the private power companies was a chapter in the effort of the Roosevelt administration to identify enemies and cement a political coalition. Morgan wished to compromise with the power companies by demarcating separate competitive areas. The TVA "yardstick" would reveal its superiority. As a close associate remembered: "A.E. got along well with the utility people. He didn't want to take their jobs away, but to teach them how to do better."[22] McCraw has told the story of how A.E. gradually forfeited the confidence of FDR and Senator Norris at the very time when Lilienthal was so assiduously cultivating them and creating broad support for a fight with private companies. He has also recounted Morgan's strategic blunders in a continuous advocacy of cooperation with the power companies despite the intensification of their legal attacks on TVA.[23]

Arthur Morgan was no match for Lilienthal in a personal or political fight. He did not know how to persuade others that he was right. One of Lilienthal's aides remembers: "If given political advice on strategy, for example, call on the editor of The Chattanooga Times. A.E. saw that as stooping too low. His personality was not suited to that."[24] Morgan

trusted Willkie, Norris, and Roosevelt to the end. He did not understand that his credibility with them depended upon his ability to construct a technological and political synthesis that would justify and win
support for the TVA.

Harcourt Morgan, Director, 1933–38, 1941–48, Chairman, 1938–41

Harcourt Morgan became chairman in 1938 only because FDR removed Arthur Morgan and Harcourt was a respected figure who could
replace him. In fact, H.A. did not enjoy the job and deferred both public
and organizational leaderhip to Lilienthal. H.A.'s contribution to the
TVA was his vision for the resource management programs, particularly agriculture. He had cut his teeth in Louisiana persuading individualistic farmers to create land strips to stop the boll weevil.[25] Through
his experiences as an administrator of land grant colleges he had developed the basic insight that one persuaded people to persuade themselves to change. One of H.A.'s closest associates described his style:

He was a natural leader. People followed him because they respected his vision
for the valley, ability and honesty. He was the most popular man in the region. It
was due to H.A. that people accepted TVA. People don't like outsiders telling
them what to do. So H.A. formulated the idea of letting the people decide. For
example, he got a Nashvillian, the president of Rotary International, Bill Man-
ier, to organize and lead the Tennessee Valley Association to promote TVA programs. They served their purpose and went out of existence in four or five
years. That was typical of H.A.'s leadership. He persuaded Bill that he should
lead the effort.[26]

In oral history interviews conducted by his daughter in the late
1940s, H.A. recalled a 1933 meeting of the administrators of the seven
land grant colleges. They were worried that TVA would compete with
their research and service programs and invited Morgan to attend and
tell them what TVA was going to do. His answer was: "We were not
going to do anything except to promote their programs, help them carry
out what they had in mind." H.A. did not see this as cooptation. He remembered that these educators had "mediocre ideas" so that "the program had to evolve step by step through experience."[27]

Morgan believed TVA should use the colleges as its agent for two
reasons. First, TVA could best develop the Valley through the better
farmers, who would find ways to help themselves. Second, the modernization of southern agriculture, meaning for Morgan a change from

cotton and corn to livestock and pasture, required the expertise of the colleges and the Extension Service and the cooperation of the progressive farmers. He retrospectively justified his cooperation with the colleges: "If it weren't today for the power of agriculture, the leadership of these land grant institutions, the Department of Agriculture and the forces of the farm organizations, you would have a peasantry."[28] Morgan believed that agricultural improvement had to come through slow education and that only the large-scale farmers could afford it.[29] The kind of agricultural self-help favored by A.E. appeared to H.A. to be perpetrating a "peasantry."

The search for political support for TVA did not seem to have been the basis of H.A.'s reliance on the colleges.[30] A former director of TVA agricultural programs argues:

TVA could not have gotten anywhere without the cooperation of the extension service. They had too much power. If we had tied up with the Soil Conservation Service in the early thirties, we might have survived. But, we would have lost the opportunity to tie the research and extension people together. The universities valued working with TVA. It catalyzed their research departments. H.A.'s insight here was not political. It was an ideal. . . . The land would never have changed unless you had all the universities tied into it. For example, the university home economists had a hold on the women, unlike the Soil Conservation Service.[31]

Morgan's concern with effectiveness may have been politically sound, but his dominant note was technological rather than political.

H.A. assumed early control of the other resource development programs and set a pattern similar to that of agriculture. The Forestry Division did not develop a large staff but worked through the state departments of forestry. He subordinated regional planning within TVA to agriculture. H.A. wished to carry out planning and studies, under Section 22 of the act, with Valley groups and state and local governments. He argued strongly that independent TVA planning would be resented and disregarded by those governments.[32]

It is not difficult to understand how this practical man would find Lilienthal a more congenial colleague than the other Morgan. H.A. remembered A.E. as a "self-educated man" who had "some very immature conceptions." He felt that if A.E. had been a product of the land grant system rather than a private college, he would have been a more accommodating man.[33] H.A.'s associates remembered that he sponsored Lilienthal in the Valley and taught him a "grass-roots" philosophy. One close associate of Lilienthal remembers that by "grass-roots," H.A.

"meant the power structure, not ten farmers."[34] H.A.'s reliance on successful farmers was similar to Lilienthal's belief that members of the boards of municipal electric companies should be prominent local businessmen.[35]

H.A. saw the grass-roots principle as an extension of his "common mooring" idea, which was simply an ecological conception of the unity of man and nature, human and natural resources. He was critical of the sociologist Howard Odum and other social scientists for believing that human resources could be developed independently of natural resources.[36]

The following statements by Harcourt Morgan, made at the end of his life, suggested that his vision of TVA as an integrated entity for the development of resources was, in some ways, close to that of Arthur Morgan and was utopian in its own way. He says that in Lilienthal's book, *TVA: Democracy on the March,*

much of this concept (common mooring) is lost. [It] simply looked at the administrative. He didn't get what I was after at all.

Q— Do you think Gordon (Clapp) has this?
A— No, Gordon doesn't have this. He has been forced by the demands of the Congress and the political pressures . . . to recognize that the only route . . . to have it accomplished is to take the political method.
Q— Who in TVA really has this understanding now?
A— Nobody. . . . The point is that you've got to have a devotion to nature's contribution. . . . They don't think anything at all about it. They just grab nature to make their own personal promotions. . . . Dave was as bad in that as anybody, grand as he is.[37]

Morgan's vagueness, which was so frustrating to his associates, is apparent in these words, as in the following: "I gave up a long time ago that the valley was going to be set up as an integrated agency by the staff. . . . They couldn't get it by Congress if they were in favor of it."[38] He added: "I thought that we did wrong when we didn't utilize some of the income from the power to build the land to save the water to increase the power . . . if you would say here, we are going to determine what is the value of this cover of grass, cover of winter legume, etc. . . . what returns do we get out of that in power? Well, of course, engineers with all their multiplying precision, they just said . . . you can't get any data. You can't do anything with that."[39]

Grass-roots democracy was linked in Morgan's mind with resource development, but the connection was obscure. One can infer the implication that progress must come from an understanding of man's dependence on nature in human settings but that, unfortunately, ". . . the tendency was for the human activity or achievement to be the whole thing." He added that this was all discussed a lot at TVA, "but they would pass it off," and "I don't feel that you can carry on the processes of democracy without a full understanding of nature's contribution."[40]

As chairman from 1938 to 1941, Morgan gave his attention to agriculture and the other programs that interested him and let Lilienthal lead the organization, both internally and externally. It was always his habit to work through others. In addition, as one close associate remembered: "He hated to come to Washington. He was hard-of-hearing and hated congressional hearings when he couldn't hear. He liked to work in the background. He hated being chairman, hated speeches. His false teeth didn't fit."[41]

Harcourt Morgan's principal contribution to TVA was the policy that resource management programs would be carried out by TVA in cooperation with state and local governments. As these governments strengthened their professional capacities, there was less for TVA to do in regard to regional development. These changes coincided with the increasing role of the TVA power program in the organization, about which H.A. was uneasy. But he had no conception of how to integrate the resource development and power programs.

David Lilienthal, Director, 1933–41, Chairman, 1941–46

Lilienthal was a political man. His principal skills were rhetorical and inventive, and the two were closely joined. He spent hours writing speeches and books, which he hoped would capture the imagination of wide audiences. He was always looking for a new invention that would solve an immediate problem which he could then elevate into a general principle. Thus the first power contracts, which he negotiated between the TVA and municipalities, eventually became the basis for his articulation of grass-roots democracy. Lawyers and engineers developed the legal and technical details, and he borrowed the grass-roots idea from Harcourt Morgan, but Lilienthal furnished the drive and the inspirational language.

Lilienthal's former associates remember him as a man of consuming personal ambition. Some, who knew him well in the post-TVA years, felt that he used his diaries to construct a public persona for history. One of his closest associates remembered: "He was designing a life of David Lilienthal—the only one most people would know."[42] Lilienthal did not keep the diary regularly until the late thirties when he was fully in charge of TVA, and his friends suggest that it did not become the primary focus of his life until after he left government service in 1950. The important point was that he invested his actions with significance beyond the immediate situation. He harnessed a tremendous egoism to the imperative to invent new institutions.

Lilienthal's initial achievement as a board member was to dramatize to plain people in the Valley what electric power could do for their lives. One of the men who worked on the first TVA contracts with municipalities remembered that local commercial property owners were opposed to TVA because high electric rates were providing taxes for cities which businessmen would have to pay if TVA introduced low rates. So "we took our case above the city fathers to the public. . . . We felt that everybody was hostile to us but the people. . . . Lilienthal was pictured as Prometheus bringing light to the dark valley."[43]

Lilienthal's achievement was to be able to persuade both the high and the low. An aide remembers:

He had enormous gifts of leadership—a carpetbagger who was adopted warmly by the people of the valley.

He had a good feeling for what they were interested in and knew how to combine economic aspirations with expressions of idealism so that following their economic interests would seem comfortable to them.

His obvious qualities of mind impressed the people with whom he dealt. . . . Look at his career as combining idealism and opportunism. He impressed people of great discrimination, Brandeis, Frankfurter, FDR, Acheson. He could take a difficult task and carry it out.[44]

He drew strength from his talks on the courthouse steps of small towns, as his 1935 diary description of an Alabama speech attests: "The most gratifying thing about the whole trip is to see how meeting directly with people out in the field revitalizes you and makes you feel that the program is worth carrying on. . . ." But he also thoroughly understood the political value of his personal role in dramatizing the introduction of public power. In a 1939 retrospective letter to a friend he assessed the ingredients of his success: "Electricity is something people understand and respond to, the fact that a fight is involved doesn't hurt a damn bit either, for it dramatizes the point."[45]

Later that year he asked, in his diary, why TVA water and agricultural programs had failed to capture the public imagination as had the power program, and answered:

Isn't the answer that all the eloquence about land and water omits two factors almost essential to wide public interest of a lively kind, to wit, emphasis upon human beings and a fight? In my activities "crusading" on the power issue, when we were surrounded by a "ring of steel" and the getting of a market presented a problem, indeed, I sensed the crucial importance of stressing the human factors, the concrete picture of men and women benefitting from low electric rates, etc. It was something that came into everyone's life and affected it. The farm electricity matter was especially good in that connection. And, of course, the utility companies furnished the "fight" element.[46]

Lilienthal rejected Arthur Morgan's conceptions of social planning and downgraded the TVA regional planning staff after Morgan left.[47] Lilienthal did not believe in planning for people. TVA was to provide new resources and energy through which people were to shape their own lives.

Lilienthal was de facto chairman from 1937 to 1941 and actual chairman from 1941 to 1946. In February, 1941, he wrote in his journal, "The Board has come to mean me." He did not regard the chairman's role as administrative. His role was to lead by stimulating new ideas to prevent bureaucratic complacency. In July, 1939, he wrote in his journal: "There is a slowing down of new ideas for the very reason that we are catching our breath. . . . It is important that I somehow find time to do the thing I am best at—to stimulate and prod and drive ahead. And that takes time—time to talk things over, time to visit the job and people in the valley."[48] In October of that year he wrote a memo to the board and general manager complaining that the board was too preoccupied with current business and that too few new ideas were coming up through the organization. He called for a board-management conference to develop ways that ideas developed within the organization might better rise up.[49] His journal in these years is filled with references to the actions taken to rouse the organization: a fighting speech against private power companies; assessing the effect of his speech on grass-roots democracy on the understanding of TVA professionals of the "regional idea"; an attack on féderal departments for poaching on TVA responsibilities; an attempt to explain to power staffs that TVA was not just another utility and should not sell power to the Army at a "profit."[50]

Lilienthal, as chairman, devoted himself primarily to TVA's contribution to national defense, in particular, for the manufacture of aluminum and for the mysterious Oak Ridge facility. FDR's shift from Dr. New Deal to Dr. Win the War was followed on a smaller scale by TVA. TVA officials, thinking about future missions, were subtly transformed by this process. They began to discuss the need to build steam plants to accommodate postwar industrial development.[51] Lilienthal accepted this need and appealed to Congress in 1940 for appropriations for the Cherokee Dam and a steam plant that was later built at Watts Bar, thus preparing the way for Clapp's postwar initiative for a large-scale steam plant program.[52]

By all accounts, he did not enjoy working with members of Congress, although a close observer testifies that he was good at it.[53] He was persuasive in appropriation committee hearings because of his verbal skills. He would also visit individual members at the request of the TVA Washington office—a practice followed by all subsequent chairmen. He did believe that his role with Congress was important. For example, he interpreted the victory over Senator McKellar about the site of the Douglas Dam as a vindication of the principle that TVA would not knuckle under to political demands. And he added to himself, ". . . our fights have made TVA."[54] Lilienthal understood that political insecurity could be a source of policy creativity.

By 1941 Lilienthal was again fearful of a TVA relaxation and asked himself how it could adapt to a changing world. He was beginning to think of TVA financing its power program through bonds, a scheme that came to fruition much later. He feared that TVA's role as a model of regional organization for the nation would fade unless it explored such new ideas as making alumina from clay or developed new modes of timber cutting. He concluded that Washington was so full of timid men that fresh policies could only come from a region. He gave considerable thought to how he might publicize the TVA idea nationally. "Now what? What next? How can the progress made be further developed? How can new avenues be opened to this idea?"[55]

David Lilienthal was the most creative of all the TVA chairmen in his ability to unite technology and politics. He made the power program the central theme of TVA and created a continuing tension between the multipurpose idea and actual reality. Finally, he articulated the central TVA "myths": grass-roots democracy, freedom from politics, and the decentralization and integration of functions as a model for regional development.

Gordon Clapp, Chairman, 1946–54

Clapp went to work for TVA in 1933 at age twenty-seven as deputy director of personnel. He was the director of personnel for four years, the general manager for nine, and chairman for eight years. The Personnel Department was the nerve center of the early TVA because it selected staff members and issued organizational bulletins. The director of personnel was thus familiar with the staffs and work of all divisions. In this job, and subsequently as general manager, Clapp developed a complementary relationship with Lilienthal in which the latter supplied creative ideas and Clapp managed the communication of those ideas between the board and the working units. Lilienthal regarded Clapp as a source of stability for himself.[56] Former associates remembered that Clapp helped Lilienthal sift his ideas critically, and that he was Lilienthal's executive arm in the organization.[57]

If Lilienthal ensured TVA's political survival and defined its missions, it was Clapp, more than any other man, who created the management system to carry out those missions. The general picture of Clapp that emerges from conversations with former colleagues, from contemporary descriptions, and from Clapp's own writing is of a man who had a clear philosophy about what TVA should do, how it should do it, and of his role in nurturing the organizational vitality to ensure that it was done well.

Clapp carried TVA into the era of steam plants after World War II, but such a move was inevitable once favorable court decisions had ensured TVA of a monopoly within its service area. From that point on, TVA was responsible for developing a power program that would keep pace with demand.[58] Clapp's Walgreen lectures at the University of Chicago in 1954 articulated this point of view and argued the comparative advantage of TVA over private companies in developing the capital necessary to anticipate and meet an expanding need for power. Supply must precede demand, he contended, in order to stimulate economic development.[59] An additional argument used by Clapp illustrates the continuing effect of war and Cold War on the organization. He reported that almost three-quarters of the industrial and commercial load of TVA was for users who served national defense; atomic energy, aluminum, aircraft, and guided missile production.[60]

In a 1948 article in the *Public Administration Review* he idealized TVA as developing an institution that recognized the unity of a region's resources and so organized itself that programs reflected an awareness of such interdependence.[61] Aubrey Wagner remembered of Clapp, "His conception of TVA was to touch the region lightly, with subtle leadership. The Tributary Area Development program was his idea. He would never tell you what to do, e.g., they took TAD away from McAmis (head of agricultural division) and gave it to me. I finally figured out that Gordon wanted the Governors to work with us, get people involved in development."[62]

This remark contains a key to Clapp's style. He saw himself as a manager of institutional processes through which fresh ideas might emerge. His admirers in TVA praise him in these terms. The following descriptions by those who worked with him are consistent:

Clapp made no mistakes. Nobody ever lived who had more antennae out than he. He had a cold and calculating intellect.

Clapp accomplished what he was after quietly, with few mistakes. He made no overwhelming impression on the TVA group.

Clapp was a philosopher. He wouldn't tell me what to do but gave the philosophical base for decisions, e.g., in local planning assistance work one step below the political level.

Clapp would describe a situation and then leave others to work out ways to solve the problem.[63]

He was respected as a thorough professional. Harcourt Morgan assessed Clapp late in his life: ". . . he's the man that will utilize the ability that he has, and the information that he gets and the obligation that he owes about as well as anybody I ever knew."[64]

Clapp, as head of personnel, had been instrumental in formulating the central administrative philosophy of TVA—the delegation of responsibility for policy development throughout the organization.[65] He was general manager under Lilienthal in the crucial years when that administrative philosophy was developed. This conception of authority required the board to make policy decisions, the general manager to structure questions for board discussion and to take responsibility for the integration of perspectives across divisions, and for the divisions continually to take the initiative on new problems. The entire system depended upon facilitative leadership at the top. The emphasis was primarily apolitical. Decisions were to be made on the basis of expert knowledge as it was applied within the organization. It also required a high degree of unity and morale throughout the organization if there was to be a genuine integration of functions.[66] In a 1943 talk to the Power Division managers, Clapp stressed the principles of decentralization, continuous review of policies, the authority of knowledge, and the importance of communication within TVA.[67] John Oliver, general manager at the time, told the story of the director of the Power Division coming to his office after a meeting in which the power group had prevailed over other divisions on a matter to point out that the opposition could have made a strong case. He added: "There were a lot of self-correcting devices in TVA which have been lost. . . . The self-correction came from people who cared about the organization. Clapp instilled this."[68]

Without such leadership a bureaucracy may become sluggish and compartmentalized. However, the self-correcting devices encompassed technical rather than political knowledge. There is a risk that an organization with the competence and esprit de corps of TVA may come to regard its standards for decision as the only standards. In his 1954 lectures on TVA Clapp told the story of the opposition, in Congress and the Valley, to the site chosen by TVA for the building of the Douglas Dam in 1941. Much valuable farmland would be covered, but TVA engineers had chosen the site that would produce the most power. Contending that this was the best site for the war effort, TVA resisted the efforts of Senator McKellar and others to change the site. Pearl Harbor resolved the issue in TVA's favor. Clapp drew the moral; he recognized that Congress had the responsibility for deciding whether the Douglas Dam was to be built. But if TVA had yielded on the site, it would have lost its authority as an engineering organization: "Administrators pay a high price for yielding to pressures that break into the circle of their responsibility. They are, in effect, making political decisions under the guise of administrative, engineering or other professional responsibilities."[69] It seems not to have occurred to Clapp that what appears to be an engineering decision may depend on certain goals, like war production, rather than others, such as land and food production. In this sense all technological decisions are political.

By all accounts, he made superb presentations before congressional appropriations committees because he was so thoroughly prepared. Paul Evans, the director of information, remembered how able Clapp was in asking Congress for new steam plants: "There is a difference between arguing resource development and power supply. In the latter, cold and calculated figures will persuade. This was his logic and personality, e.g., the need for supplying the AEC was a big factor. And he had the major valley politicians with him."[70]

But most observers thought that he did not handle fluid political situations well. His virtues became a fault. He was so anxious to keep politics out of TVA that he stayed aloof from Congress and from groups in the Valley that supported TVA. Several people were critical of Clapp's decision to move TVA headquarters to Muscle Shoals, Alabama, because that was friendly Lister Hill, Democratic country, and Knoxville was unfriendly Republican country. But it was quixotic because the Tennessee senators would never permit it, and Clapp unnecessarily took on a peripheral, losing fight. In a sharp letter to Congressman Howard Baker, Sr., he complained that he was not being allowed to administer TVA. This letter prompted Evans to conclude: "He did not think intuitively and strategically as Lilienthal did. He had no gut feeling for public relations but went by the book."[71] A division head remembered that Clapp had little contact with interest groups or Valley publics. Consistent with his administrative theory, he depended on office heads to develop such ties. John Oliver recalled Clapp telling him that the engineers must decide in which state a new steam plant was to go in order that politics not influence the decision. He, Clapp, preferred not to know until after they made the decision.[72]

Clapp had political foresight in his function as a planner. He understood that Congress would not continue to appropriate funds for the development of the TVA power program and ordered a staff study to consider alternative modes of financing. According to Aubrey Wagner, the staff could not develop a convincing idea. Clapp thus had to deal with a skeptical Eisenhower administration on the old basis because "he liked a factual basis for action and had none."[73]

The system of management that Clapp constructed was well designed for technological achievement. Its success depended upon considerable autonomy and freedom from external politics and, even more, upon political support in Congress for such autonomy. The "myth" of TVA as an apolitical organization was itself a strong political resource that Clapp knew how to invoke.

Herbert Vogel, Chairman, 1954–62

When Vogel arrived in Knoxville in 1954 as the appointee of a Republican president who had referred to TVA as "creeping socialism," many people in the organization believed that he came to dismantle it. Vogel denied that he received any such directive from Sherman Adams, but clearly the administration wished the new chairman to carry out the Dixon-Yates plan. By this plan a private company would provide power for Memphis so that TVA could meet its commitments to the AEC.[74] This episode was the most dramatic manifestation of a more fundamental problem. Neither the administration nor the Democratic Congress was willing to continue an unending stream of appropriations for TVA steam plants.[75]

The Eisenhower administration had developed the Dixon-Yates plan in response to TVA requests for appropriations to build additional steam plants. Dixon-Yates, so called after the names of the two officers of the private utility company that would build and operate the new facility, was a stopgap remedy that would not have solved the long-term TVA need for increased capacity in order to meet the region's need for power. The Dixon-Yates proposal became a partisan issue that congressional Democrats used to paint the Eisenhower administration as reactionary and anti-TVA, thus reviving the public versus private power crusade. The president, in turn, fought to resist the "creeping socialism" of the TVA. The matter was resolved when a private consultant to the Bureau of the Budget, which had formulated the plan, was revealed also to have been an adviser to the Dixon-Yates firm. Burying the issue opened the way to a long-term compromise in 1959 by which the TVA was authorized to market its own bonds to finance expansion.

The Dixon-Yates issue dissolved soon after Vogel's arrival. Before that time his relations with the other two board members, Harry Curtis and Raymond Paty, were strained because they refused to open discussions with the AEC about a contract. The head of the Power Division and the chief counsel were required by Paty and Curtis to represent their position to congressional committees in opposition to the chairman.[76]

With Dixon-Yates behind him, Vogel gradually educated himself and was educated by TVA officials so that in time he became popular in the organization and was an effective external advocate for TVA programs. These changes were eased by the appointment of new board members in 1958, but stability was achieved before that time. By all reports, General Manager Aubrey Wagner worked closely and well with Vogel and introduced him to people and established procedures. Vogel was impressed that Wagner and others were open with him.[77]

Vogel admits that he knew little about TVA when he arrived but that gradually he learned and developed good internal relations by "going around and talking with people and leaving my door open."[78] Paul Evans, who worked daily with Vogel, remembers:

The thing that saved TVA was Vogel's respect for competent engineering and Wagner's absolute integrity. Wagner always told it exactly like it was. Vogel didn't always like that but he learned that Red didn't lie to him, . . . and he also saw TVA engineering competence.

I have no question that Adams told Vogel to go down and take care of "that nest of socialists." Vogel once called me in to show me a letter he had written to Adams saying that TVA employees were not socialists but were fine people. I advised against sending the letter and I don't think he did.[79]

A former chief counsel recalled ". . . the day of his (Vogel's) conversion. I was with him before the House Appropriations Committee. . . . He thought he had (Republican) friends on the Committee. They ate him up. . . . It later dawned on me that this may have been the best day TVA ever had for Vogel suddenly realized that he was not one of the hounds but one of the rabbits. He saw that he was trying to run the agency and the hard line Republicans were no help."[80]

Vogel's background as a district and regional engineer in the Army Corps of Engineers provided valuable experience and skills that could be adapted to the leadership of TVA. He was thoroughly familiar with water projects of all kinds. But, perhaps more important, his experience had given him an understanding of the need for a technical organization to keep on good terms with public opinion and relevant interest groups in its area of activity. Paul Evans, former TVA information director, recalled:

Vogel had the best sense of public relations of any director I knew, next to Lilienthal. He had a gut feeling for it. . . .

(He) used his adroitness to carry groups in the valley with him. He spoke to groups, for example the distributors, with the aim of winning them over. . . .

He is a good speaker, took speech lessons when he was in the Corps. To run a Corps region and district you have to be more than a competent engineer but must have public relations skills.[81]

The general himself agreed that his corps experience had given him "political antennae; you always have to be listening to people."[82] Finally, testimony suggests that he was an effective administrator. Evans describes his style as chairman: "Vogel was a good internal operator. He worked with the staff and worked with the General Manager. It was a chain of command similar to the Corps. He maintained a good relation with staff. He could knock an idea down from behind in Board meetings—would sneak up on it, never a frontal attack. People would hardly know they had been contradicted, the product of long experience in the army."[83]

The achievement of which Vogel was most proud was the passage of the TVA Revenue Bond Act in 1959 to permit the power program to be financed through TVA commercial bonds rather than appropriations. The act also delimited the power service area, which meant that TVA finally achieved peace with the private power companies. These developments, and the absence of any outstanding controversies about TVA programs, created an atmosphere of good feeling that was Vogel's legacy to the future. Clapp had initiated discussion of the self-financing problem, and TVA legal and power experts worked on the question throughout the Vogel years. Vogel remembered that it took five years for

Marguerite Owen, TVA's Washington representative, to put together a congressional majority for self-financing against the opposition of the Bureau of the Budget, which felt that it would lose control of TVA.[84]

Vogel's contribution was to persuade President Eisenhower to sign the act. White House legal advisers urged a veto because Congress reserved to itself a right to veto TVA bond financing that was denied the president. Vogel was told by Gerald Morgan, the counsel to the president, not to bother trying to see Eisenhower, that the veto was set. He and his staff worked out alternative language for the bill to eliminate the offensive passages. Vogel sent a telegram to the president and asked to see him before he acted, and Eisenhower agreed. The president was adamant that he would not surrender presidential prerogatives to Congress. At that point Vogel carried out his plan:

I reached into my pocket, took out my pencil and said with the appropriate gesture, "What do you say we strike out both paragraphs.". . . He said, "That's a good idea! Let's do that." Jerry Morgan, sitting over by the wall, appeared propelled from his chair. "You can't do that" he said. . . . By this time the President, anxious to get to his next appointment, stood up, came around his desk and said "O.K., that's fine. . . . You boys go and work this out now. . . . We'll just strike out those paragraphs."[85]

Vogel and the president had amended the bill by excising the offending passages. Morgan and the Bureau of the Budget could do nothing because Marguerite Owen persuaded Senator Kerr to introduce the appropriate amendment, and the self-financing issue was settled.[86] TVA officials who were involved in this event agreed that no one at TVA except Vogel could have carried it off. He had the brass to insist on seeing the president, and he had the confidence of the president.

Vogel's leadership ushered in an era of good feeling in which TVA made peace with the private power companies, continued its expansion to meet the demands from economic growth, and appeared to be on good terms with president, Congress, and the people of the Valley.

Aubrey J. Wagner, Director, 1961–62, Chairman, 1962–77

Gordon Clapp and Aubrey Wagner are the two career professionals who have risen through the organization to become chairman. Wagner was head of navigation, assistant general manager, general manager, and a board member before he became chairman in 1962. Clapp was his ideal of what a chairman should be, in both style and purpose. Wagner admired Clapp's self-disciplined steering of organizational discussions so that the best ideas emerged. He shared Clapp's distrust of political pressures and prized the nonpolitical TVA ideal. And, while he devoted his primary attention to the power program, he saw it as part of a multipurpose mission.[87]

Wagner had originally been a water man, and he never lost his fondness for water projects. His chief contribution in this regard was the Tributary Area Development program. Under this program TVA built small dams in tributary streams and provided technical assistance for social and economic development to watershed communities. Wagner gives Clapp credit for TAD, and there is also evidence that Marguerite Owen stimulated the original idea. TVA would do developmental demonstrations with selected counties as an analogue to the test demonstration farm.[88] A former division head remembered: "The board was trying to keep power from overriding all other programs and talked about it in 1952–53. Wagner saw TAD as a counterbalance. He was a waterway man."[89] He saw TAD as an extension of the goal of multipurpose development: "We have painted with the big brush, now have to do it with the fine print. The TAD program could make local government more meaningful. Counties could give way to larger units."[90] Arthur Morgan had hoped that TVA planning might encourage the enlargement of Tennessee counties. This is only one illustration of the persistence of submerged ideas in TVA history.

Wagner saw TVA as something more than a power company. He regarded controversial water projects like the Tellico, Columbia, and Normandy dams as worthwhile.[91] He also had mixed feelings about the power program, calling it a "curse and a blessing": a curse because it caused so many problems and a blessing because TVA could not have survived politically without it.[92] However, Wagner accepted the logic of Clapp's thinking about the obligation of TVA to meet the needs of the Valley for electric power. TVA agricultural officials report that, as a midwesterner, Wagner felt that southern agriculture was not nationally competitive, and he therefore gave little attention to the agricultural program except to encourage innovations in the manufacture of fertilizer.[93] Cheap power was the strongest path to economic development for Wagner.

The board of TVA has the obligation to provide power for the Valley. The difficult questions have to do with how much and at what financial and environmental costs. Wagner was the first chairman required to face these hard questions. But he had no choice. Rawson captures the reality: "As the demand for electricity has increased in the valley, TVA officials have repeatedly decided to expand the means to meet the ends rather than modify ends to meet the means available."[94] Wagner remembers the context of the TVA decision to develop a nuclear program: "If we had not done this, we would have failed in our mission. We would have had to buy power from the outside. The people of the valley would have been distressed. Clapp faced the same situation after the war in regard to steam plants."[95]

He believed that the TVA Act gave the board the authority and the responsibility to achieve a changing balance among the several objectives of TVA.[96] In his mind TVA was not to be compared to a government department, which is immediately responsive to presidential policy: "The statute (TVA Act) fixes responsibility on the Board. The Board has autonomy within that Act. That is the basis for accountability. As long as I stayed within the Act I was OK."[97]

At first look, it appears that the 1959 self-financing decision freed TVA from congressional scrutiny and political accountability for its power program. It is surely true that Congress could never have been persuaded to appropriate funds for the succession of nuclear plants that TVA developed after 1965. But the 1959 decision made TVA accountable to the ratepayers for the first time in its history, since they had to bear the cost of power and of the construction of new plants. Yet the only forum in which the ratepayers could express their views was Congress.

The initial decisions to build nuclear plants were not controversial. The congressional public works committees had the right to ask about them but did not do so. The relative cost of coal and nuclear power were compared for each plant by TVA. Wagner and the board were increasingly under pressure from Congress, from segments of public opinion, and, in the 1970s, from the Environmental Protection Agency to act against air pollution from coal, and he saw nuclear energy as an alternative: "I saw nuclear as a means of getting continuing power, at lower cost, with less harm to the environment."[98] Wagner also resisted the dictates of EPA that TVA install expensive scrubbers on smokestacks because he thought the scrubber technology was ineffective, the pollution problem exaggerated, and the costs unjustified in view of the limited life of the many existing steam plants.[99] However, congressional hearings became more heated and intense during the 1970s as critics raised questions about strip mining, air pollution, nuclear construction, and rate increases.[100]

Wagner's management style was based on his understanding of Clapp's philosophy. He used the office heads as his principal advisers and assumed that fresh ideas would emerge from the organization, as in past years. However, critics of Wagner within the organization felt that he relied too much on his personal knowledge and on his old friends and that there was too little systematic analysis of policy options.[101] General Manager Lynn Seeber became concerned about this question and in the early 1970s created a small central planning staff in his office. The economist who directed the staff saw Wagner as having no interest in their work: "He believed the offices (divisions) were making their best recommendations. He had great self-confidence and felt personally close to each of these office managers. He had grown up with them."[102] Wagner confirmed this report, saying that it was a mistake to have central planners tell people what to do because they were not responsible for results.[103] However, a former board member felt that the board was seriously limited in its knowledge by the TVA mode of operation during Wagner's period. He saw the opposition to a central planning staff as a defensive move by the program offices to prevent the development of information that might prove unfavorable to them.[104]

Wagner self-consciously acted according to his understanding of TVA norms. His methods of dealing with Congress and the public were thus clear and deliberate in his own mind. The general strategy developed by TVA chairmen over the years in dealing with Congress had been to emphasize their own expert testimony and work with a few close congressional friends of TVA to secure favorable votes. Wagner and Marguerite Owen worked very closely together in this regard. She would identify particular problems and people with whom Wagner should talk, and he would see them. He paid particular attention to Congressmen Bob Jones from northern Alabama; Jamie Whitten, a Mississippian who was chairman of the House Appropriations Committee; Senator Lister Hill of Alabama; and, after Hill's retirement, Senator Howard Baker of Tennessee.[105] One close colleague remembered that Wagner "hated" such work.[106] After Miss Owen retired in 1970 and as Senator Hill began to lose power and then retired, Wagner had few ties in Congress and did not receive the help he needed from a weakened TVA Washington office.[107]

Wagner did not look to public opinion for guidance in making TVA decisions. For him this would have meant abdicating the responsibility of the board. But according to Frank Smith, a former board member, Wagner never thought that he was acting in a way contrary to the majority of public opinion. He was trying to give people what they wanted, electric power at the most reasonable cost.[108] Wagner's response to public criticism was, as Paul Evans put it, ". . . to explain things. He saw people as rational and intelligent."[109] Another colleague added: "Wagner was never able to awake the assistance of the customers about costs. . . . Are we engineers poor at selling things to people. . . . Red's speeches fell flat."[110] The difficulty was the intractability of the issue of rising costs and the absence of a forum in which the question could be resolved with public participation. TVA had developed an elaborate publicity machine that had proclaimed the virtues of cheap power, and Valley publics could not adjust to the brute reality. Wagner was apolitical and therefore seemed autocratic. In fact, he was acting in a technocratic way to base TVA decisions on his projections of the future power needs of the Valley.

Wagner's critics charged him with carrying TVA into an expensive program of nuclear construction without engaging in sufficient analysis of its ultimate costs. As one power manager recalled in 1979: "Self-financing relaxed constraints on planning (in the power division). We turned in pro forma budgets to the Board and OMB. Our program planning went to pot. Wessenauer (long-time head of the power division) retired in 1970. He had used the budget as a control device for 25 years. After he left budget preparation was a paper exercise."[111] A contrary view, defending Wagner, was taken by a former power official:

In authorizing new capacity in the late '60s and early '70s, the choice was not to select a project that could produce power at a lower cost than previously had been attained. Rather, since power from all alternatives would be more costly, the choice was which would best meet the objectives of the Act. The nuclear alternative showed up best at the time and that conclusion was not unique to the Tennessee Valley region.

It seemed to me that Wagner should be recognized for his accomplishment in leading the organization in developing a power supply which was faithful to the Act's directive. Had world economic conditions been normal. I believe the modest rate increases which would have been required would have been accepted with little furor.[112]

This paper cannot resolve the question of whether the Wagner TVA carefully felt its way into the future or whether organizational imperatives overwhelmed careful analysis. That task must be left to future research on the decisions taken to develop the nuclear program. What is clear is that Wagner based his leadership of TVA, in part, on the model set by Clapp. This style sustained him and the missions he supported for most of his tenure. But popular restlessness was so troublesome in his last years that his successor resolved on an altogether new approach.

S. David Freeman, Director, 1977–78, 1981–, Chairman, 1978–81

S. David Freeman was a lawyer-engineer who made a career of being in the forefront of developments in national energy policy. He was the first energy adviser on the White House staff in the Johnson and Nixon administrations, and directed a study for the Ford Foundation that anticipated shortages of energy. Freeman was primarily a generator of ideas. Contradictions did not bother him; he believed in a free-for-all. His approach to organizations was therefore unsettling to those who were comfortable with routine. His style of public leadership had the same catalytic quality, which was better suited to introducing fresh ideas than to building coalitions.

Freeman and his fellow board member Richard Freeman returned to the TVA, after a twenty-year absence in both cases, with the belief that the organization was moribund and divorced from the public it served. They perceived TVA as an unenlightened power company that no longer listened to its constituencies. Their remedy for this problem was to inspire the organization to develop new missions that would recover the original TVA spirit. They hoped that the adaptation of mission would reflect public perceptions of need and win widespread support.[113]

Freeman's chairmanship illustrated the difficulty of leading TVA when major constituencies disagree about appropriate missions. This problem had not presented itself since the first decade. In the intervening years TVA had succeeded in constructing a battleground between friends and enemies on which the friends always won. The later Wagner years revealed the disappearance of the traditional enemies and the development of conflict and criticism among friends. Freeman sought to transcend existing issues and divisions by inventing new missions that would unite factions on altogether new principles. He sought a synthesis of policy and technology, but the weakness of the political element in the vision undermined it.

Freeman, in his initial articulation of reformulated missions, presented the TVA as an "energy laboratory" for the nation and called for a rejuvenation of the resource management programs on behalf of economic development. The guiding theme was "quality growth." The policies that followed from this principle were respect for environmental quality, conservation of energy, and economic development compatible with both. Freeman consciously sought to revive TVA idealism and appealed to the spirits of both Arthur Morgan and Lilienthal. In

1979 the board commissioned a group of academic advisers to do studies of how TVA might contribute to regional development through the resource management programs. Freeman's charge to these "Summer Study" professors revealed his idealism: "The sole purpose of TVA is to demonstrate the capacities of regional government, to attempt grand experiments which will help the people of the nation. This is the (A. E.) Morgan rhetoric and the Lilienthal tools. Should TVA take the Morgan rhetoric seriously?"[114]

It was clear that Freeman took it seriously. In his talk he praised TVA's role as an energy lab, citing the development of a coal gasification plant and work on the electric car. He also asked what TVA might do to combat rural poverty, promote regional planning, and contribute to the alleviation of economic problems such as unemployment.

One of Freeman's first actions was to end the long conflict with the Environmental Protection Agency. He negotiated a settlement that conceded EPA demands that TVA install sulfur dioxide scrubbers in power plants. He interpreted this action in a newspaper interview as TVA performing its "yardstick role":

It sets the kind of example TVA needs to set for the utility industry. . . .

The gap between TVA and the rest of the utility type organizations is going to grow. . . . We are going to move swiftly into a leadership role in demonstrating new technologies in conservation measures and new sources of energy . . . and the difference between the TVA rates and utility rates generally is going to grow. . . .[115]

He accepted the nuclear program but in his early statements articulated values of conservation and quality growth. He clearly hoped to put controversies about nuclear power behind him by appealing to environmentalists. The settlement with EPA brought forth another challenge. Twenty-two electrical cooperatives filed suit to block the settlement. They argued that it was unnecessary and too generous.[116]

The innovations of the energy lab were modest because the Carter administration never backed hopes with appropriations. The administration itself cut funds for the coal gasification plant because they thought it an inappropriate project for TVA.[117] However, TVA adopted the conservation of energy as a source of power supply, and programs for home energy audits, home insulation, and solar hot water heaters were valued by many distributors as means to popularize the need to conserve. In addition, the distributors and manufacturers began to experiment with "cogeneration" of energy, through recycling, under prodding from TVA.

The search for new missions was necessarily linked, in Freeman's mind, with new styles of leadership and organization. He thought it important to reach out to the public:

TVA has made a career out of preaching grass roots democracy. We need a network to find out what people are thinking. Our mandate is so broad that we need to tap broad questions. . . .

We hear from the power distributors, a few concerned citizens; when I came I found an absence of links with blacks, the women's movement, the people of the valley. . . .

There are a lot of things that people are concerned with that they don't link with TVA, that TVA could do something about if we knew, for example recreation, or, to help small, weak communities get federal aid.[118]

Contrast this view with those of two TVA top managers, in power and agriculture respectively:

Dave asks how power will be responsive to public opinion. We don't have a mechanism to know what public opinion is.

Public opinion was never a factor in the agricultural program. Our constituents were the fertilizer industry, the land grant universities and the organized farmers.[119]

Freeman pursued responsiveness to public opinion by his many trips and speeches, the holding of open board meetings throughout the Valley, and the establishment of a free "hot line" for TVA consumers. But a more fundamental and less visible change was his challenge to the TVA mode of decision making. In his mind, new missions that were responsive to the public would have to be developed at board level, through planning. He lacked confidence that the divisions could generate fresh ideas.[120] Therefore, he and Richard Freeman, the two board members in the spring and summer of 1979, strengthened the central planning and budget staff in its capacity to develop policy ideas and analytically appraise division recommendations. For example, the Community Development Office would develop plans to nurture economic development of the poorest counties in cooperation with a newly appointed chief economist. The Freemans saw a great deal of previous intervention of this kind as blundering. Richard Freeman summed it up:

There is no analytical tradition in TVA. It is a "can do" ethos. Dave and I are trying to create one. . . .

Our budget decision process has been "projectitus." We need a framework, plus data, expertise and method. . . .[121]

The Summer Study professors suggested demonstrations in land use planning, assistance to small farmers, and help with community economic development, but none of the papers suggested how the power and regional development programs might be complementary nor did they fully assess the limits of TVA authority for regional development.[122]

The newly strengthened central planning staff distilled the Summer Study ideas into a 1980 planning document that identified the central TVA missions as the provision of sufficient electric power at the least possible cost and programs of technical assistance for rural and community economic development. The overall goal was the economic development of the Valley.[123] These issues were superseded in 1980 by a firestorm of controversy. The precipitating factor was growing public unhappiness about electric rate increases, on an average of 15 percent per year over the previous seven years. The TVA distributors were both defensive about the increases and critical of TVA management for not keeping costs down. The distributors were most critical of the new emphasis on resource management programs and of changes such as the consolidation of all TVA offices into regions under the direction of regional officers reporting to the general manager. Integrated regional development did not interest them.

In 1980 and 1981 David Freeman began to place increased stress on the power program as the basis for the economic development of the Valley. Freeman cited studies indicating that the anticipated economic development of the Valley would be dampened unless TVA could provide ample power at reasonable cost to new industry. The nuclear building program could give TVA a power surplus that would make it an oasis in a nation hungry for power.[124] It was difficult to distinguish his language from that of Clapp in 1947 or Wagner in the 1970s, and he compared TVA opportunities in 1980 to those of 1947 and derided the critics who charged, on both occasions, that TVA was expanding beyond any possible market.[125]

However, the search for a supportive constituency still eluded TVA. The complexity of Freeman's goals had alienated the distributors so that even though he eventually got on board the power and development bandwagon, he was not fully trusted. Representatives of the TVA distributors called for his removal in the March, 1981, Senate hearings.[126] His advocacy of the nuclear program and the justification he gave in behalf of future growth angered ratepayers, who were paying for power they would not use for years, and the congressional politicians who represented them. Both Freemans contend that their chief contribution to TVA has been the legitimation of power conservation as a leading TVA mission. But both also admit that a visible constituency for conservation has yet to emerge.[127] It is perhaps difficult to reconcile conservation with economic development. To many critics, the board seemed to be moving in contradictory directions.

Senator Howard Baker was a stabilizing force in the spring of 1981. A number of Valley congressmen seriously proposed that the TVA board be enlarged to seven members, presumably to make the organization more responsive to the publics of seven states. Baker was opposed to such action and supported the general directions of TVA policy. S. David Freeman lost his chairmanship as a necessary sacrifice on behalf of policy continuity. Possibly the two Freemans, and the new chairman, Charles Dean, acting in concert as a collegial board, will be successful in combining the goals of energy conservation, resource management, and economic development in a way acceptable to the Valley. If this occurs, TVA will have generated a new creative synthesis.

Conclusion

TVA history does not illustrate Marver Bernstein's theory of the life cycle of organizations in which innovativeness is succeeded by bureaucratization and rigidity.[128] I take my text from Marguerite Owen, who contends that the continual organizational creativity of TVA has been a direct consequence of political insecurity.[129]

The "myth" of the apolitical organization has been a political resource sustained by politics. The TVA was first supported politically as an extension of the New Deal. In the 1950s congressional Democrats used the protection of TVA as a weapon against a Republican administration. After 1959 the TVA ceased to be an agent of national policy, and political support depended on the view of the people of the Valley and their congressional representatives. In the 1970s the TVA technocratic impulse conflicted with the interests of TVA constituencies. The appeal to future benefits is not appealing when present costs are escalating. The TVA had legitimized itself with the people it served by providing electric power at low cost. It was a beneficent force. Only a malevolent force would ask for sacrifice now in hope of distant goods— or so it seemed.

Finally, this sketch of seven men may tell us something about creative leadership. Political scientists have characterized leadership in terms of the ability to develop and use influence in bargaining situations. Primary attention has been given to strategic and tactical skill in managing others. This is a necessary but incomplete picture of leadership. These seven profiles suggest that leadership also requires the ability to clarify and define ambiguous situations for others. Part of this clarification is the suggestion of new historical possibilities.[130] But before we idealize creative leadership, we should remember Shakespeare's skepticism, as expressed in the conversation between Hot Spur and Glendower in *Henry IV, Part I:*

Glendower: "I can call spirits from the vasty deep."
Hot Spur: "Why so can I or so can any man. But will they come when you do call for them?"

NOTES

1. Roy Talbert, Jr., "Beyond Pragmatism: The Story of Arthur E. Morgan" (Ph.D. dissertation, Vanderbilt University, 1971), pp. 10, 71, 70.

2. *Ibid.*, pp. 95, 137–39, 131.

3. *Ibid.*, pp. 135–36, 140–41, 218.

4. Edward Falck and Harry Wiersma, former TVA engineers, summer, 1981.

5. Neil Bass, former chief TVA conservation engineer, summer, 1981.

6. Ruth McGee Falck, assistant to Arthur Morgan, summer, 1981.

7. Talbert, "Beyond Pragmatism," p. 124.

8. *Ibid.*, pp. 65–68.

9. *Ibid.*, pp. 119–20, 106–7.

10. Roy Talbert, Jr., "The Human Engineer: Arthur E. Morgan and the Tennessee Valley Authority" (M.A. thesis, Vanderbilt University, 1967), p. 13.

11. Ruth McGee Falck, summer, 1981.

12. Thomas K. McCraw, *Morgan vs. Lilienthal: The Feud within the TVA* (Chicago: Loyola University Press, 1970), p. 36; Talbert, "Beyond Pragmatism," p. 105.

13. Neil Bass, Harry Wiersma, and Edward Falck, summer, 1981.

14. Edward Falck, summer, 1981.

15. *Ibid.*

16. Harry Wiersma, summer, 1981.

17. McCraw, *Morgan vs. Lilienthal*, pp. 33–35.

18. Talbert, "Beyond Pragmatism," p. 70.

19. Harry Wiersma, summer, 1981.

20. Harry Wiersma and Ruth McGee Falck, summer, 1981.

21. Ruth McGee Falck, summer, 1981.

22. *Ibid.*

23. McCraw, *Morgan vs. Lilienthal*, ch. 3 and pp. 81, 87–88.

24. Edward Falck, summer, 1981.

25. McCraw, *Morgan vs. Lilienthal*, p. 13.

26. Neil Bass, former assistant to Harcourt Morgan, summer, 1981.

27. Oral History transcripts, spool 5, Harcourt A. Morgan Papers, University of Tennessee Library, Knoxville, pp. 7, 8.

28. *Ibid.*, p. 10.

29. McCraw, *Morgan vs. Lilienthal*, pp. 15, 39.

30. *Ibid.*, p. 40.

31. Leland Allbaugh, former head of TVA Agricultural Office, summer, 1981.

32. Memo, Harcourt Morgan to board, Oct. 3, 1933.

33. Spool 5, Harcourt Morgan Papers, pp. 2, 4–5.

34. Joseph C. Swidler, summer, 1981.

35. David E. Lilienthal, *TVA: Democracy on the March* (Chicago: Quadrangle Books, 1966).

36. Spool 5, Harcourt Morgan Papers, p. 14.

37. *Ibid.*, spool 6, pp. 77–79.

38. *Ibid.*, spool 5, pp. 13–14.

39. *Ibid.*, spool 1, p. 7.

40. *Ibid.*, spool 3, p. 3.

41. Former TVA official, summer, 1981.

42. Joseph C. Swidler, former TVA counsel, summer, 1981.

43. Edward Falck, summer, 1981.

44. Joseph C. Swidler, summer, 1981.

45. David E. Lilienthal, *The Journals of David E. Lilienthal*, vol. 1, *The TVA Years, 1939–1945* (New York: Harper and Row, 1964), Oct. 5, 1935, pp. 53–54, 79–80.

46. *Ibid.*, Apr. 13, 1939, pp. 106–7.

47. A. J. Gray, former TVA regional planner, summer, 1981.

48. Lilienthal, *Journals*, Feb. 5, 1941, p. 280; July 3, 1939, p. 116.

49. Memo, Lilienthal to board of directors and general manager, Oct. 4, 1939, Curtis-Morgan-Morgan File, TVA Archives, Knoxville, Tenn.

50. Lilienthal, *Journals*, Nov. 12, 1939, p. 143; Dec. 24, 1939, p. 150; Oct. 16, 1941, p. 387; Oct. 22, 1941, pp. 394–95.

51. George Palo, former TVA chief engineer, summer, 1981; memo of conference of Julius Krug, G. O. Wessenauer, Joseph Swidler, and A. D. Spottswood about the TVA role in industrial development, Feb. 20, 1942, TVA Administrative Files, Knoxville.

52. Lilienthal, *Journals*, July 31, 1940, p. 198.

53. Former TVA official, summer, 1981.

54. Lilienthal, *Journals*, Nov. 22, 1941, pp. 403, 482; June 19, 1942, p. 498.

55. *Ibid.*, Mar. 26, 1941, pp. 289–91; Aug. 13, 1941, pp. 371–72; June 17, 1944, p. 643.

56. *Ibid.*, July 19, 1941, p. 360.

57. John Oliver, general manager under Clapp, and Aubrey J. Wagner, summer, 1981.

58. George E. Rawson, "The Process of Program Development: The Case of TVA's Power Program" (Ph.D. dissertation, University of Tennessee, 1979), pp. 54–57, 165.

59. Gordon R. Clapp, *The TVA: An Approach to the Development of a Region* (Chicago: University of Chicago Press, 1955), pp. 93–94.

60. *Ibid.*, p. 109.

61. Gordon R. Clapp, "Public Administration in an Advancing South," *Public Administration Review*, 8 (Summer, 1948): 171.

62. Aubrey J. Wagner, summer, 1981.

63. Comments by four former Clapp colleagues in TVA (Lee Greene, George Palo, A. J. Gray, John Oliver), summer, 1981.

64. Spool 5, Harcourt Morgan Papers, pp. 9–10.

65. John Oliver, former general manager, summer, 1981.

66. Harry L. Case, "Gordon R. Clapp: The Role of Faith, Purposes and People in Administration," *Public Administration Review*, 24 (June, 1964): 86–91.

67. Memo, Clapp to board of directors, July 3, 1943, Harcourt Morgan Files, TVA Technical Library, Knoxville, Tenn.

68. John Oliver, summer, 1981.

69. Clapp, *The TVA*, p. 41.

70. Paul Evans, former TVA director of information, summer, 1981.

71. *Ibid.*

72. John Oliver, summer, 1981.

73. Aubrey J. Wagner, summer, 1981.

74. General Herbert D. Vogel, June 5, 1981, Washington, D.C.

75. Interview with Herbert D. Vogel, conducted by Dr. Charles W. Crawford for the TVA Oral History Project, Memphis State University, Jan. 9, 1970.

76. Joseph C. Swidler, former chief counsel, summer, 1981.

77. Charles J. McCarthy, former TVA counsel, summer, 1981.

78. Herbert D. Vogel, June 5, 1981.

79. Paul Evans, summer, 1981.

80. Charles J. McCarthy, summer, 1981.

81. Paul Evans, summer, 1981.

82. Herbert D. Vogel, June 5, 1981.

83. Paul Evans, summer, 1981.

84. Herbert D. Vogel, June 5, 1981.

85. Vogel interview with Charles Crawford, Jan. 9, 1970.

86. *Ibid.*

87. Aubrey J. Wagner, May 13, 1981, Knoxville, Tenn.

88. *Ibid.*

89. Leland Allbaugh, summer, 1981.

90. Aubrey J. Wagner, May 13, 1981.

91. Aubrey J. Wagner, A. J. Gray, and a former TVA board member, summer, 1981.

92. Aubrey J. Wagner, May 13, 1981.

93. Lewis B. Nelson, former director of TVA Agricultural Office, summer, 1979.

94. Rawson, "Process of Program Development," p. 178.

95. Aubrey J. Wagner, May 13, 1981.

96. Senate. Public Works Committee, Oversight Hearings, *Tennessee Valley Authority*, parts 1–2 (Apr. 30–May 12, 1975), p. 36.

97. Aubrey J. Wagner, May 13, 1981.

98. *Ibid.*

99. Interviews with former board member and former TVA power official, summer, 1981, and with Aubrey J. Wagner, Nov., 1981.

100. Rawson, "Process of Program Development," p. 136.

101. Interviews with former budget director, power official, and two former board members, summer, 1981.

102. David Patterson, former head of TVA central planning staff, summer, 1979.

103. Aubrey J. Wagner, May 13, 1981.

104. Former TVA board member, summer, 1981.

105. Interview with Aubrey J. Wagner, Nov., 1981.

106. Former TVA official, summer, 1981.

107. Frank E. Smith, former TVA board member, summer, 1981.

108. *Ibid.*

109. Paul Evans, summer, 1981.

110. George Palo, summer, 1981.

111. Hugh Parris, director of TVA Power Office, July, 1979.

112. Former TVA power official, summer, 1981.

113. S. David Freeman, July 27, 1979, Knoxville, Tenn.

114. S. David Freeman, talk to Summer Study advisers, June, 1979, Knoxville, Tenn.

115. Interview with S. David Freeman by James Branscome for the *Mountain Eagle*, Jan., 1979.

116. "TVA Clean Air Settlement Block Attempt Seen," *Nashville Tennessean*, Mar. 18, 1979, p. 20A.

117. Christopher Madison, "Murphy Hill—Is It the Wrong Plant at the Wrong Time by the Wrong Agency?" *National Journal* (Feb. 28, 1981), pp. 346–49.

118. S. David Freeman, July 27, 1979.

119. Hugh Parris and Lewis B. Nelson, July, 1979, Knoxville, Tenn.

120. S. David Freeman, July 27, 1979.

121. Richard Freeman, July 26, 1979, Knoxville, Tenn.

122. TVA, *1979 Summer Policy Study: The Role of TVA Programs in Regional Development* (Knoxville, Tenn., Mar., 1981).

123. TVA, *Strategies for the 1980s: A TVA Statement of Corporate Purpose and Direction* (Knoxville, Tenn., Jan., 1981).

124. Testimony of S. David Freeman before the Energy and Water Development Subcommittee of the Senate Appropriations Committee, Dec. 11, 1980.

125. S. David Freeman, lecture at Vanderbilt University, Jan. 30, 1981.

126. "Baker Blames TVA Rate Hikes on Inflation," *Nashville Tennessean*, Mar. 18, 1981, p. 1.

127. S. David Freeman and Richard Freeman, Nov., 1981.

128. Marver Bernstein, *Regulating Business by Independent Commission* (Westport, Conn.: Greenwood Press, 1955).

129. Marguerite Owen, former director of TVA Washington office, summer, 1981.

130. Robert C. Tucker, *Politics as Leadership* (Columbia: University of Missouri Press, 1981), pp. 15–16. For a full discussion of the theory of institutional leadership implicit in this paper, see Philip Selznick, *Leadership in Administration* (New York: Harper and Row, 1957), pp. 12, 17, 21, 28. Selznick is particularly sensitive to the importance of leadership incorporating technical means into larger goals.

5

Avery Leiserson

Administrative Management and Political Accountability

I T is important that persons making political appraisals of
TVA's growth and experience adequately understand the
"bureaucratic variable," the administrative aspects of the
agency's record and performance. Too often, political analysts dismiss
problems of organization and administration as *mere* matters of conflicting personalities, exasperating procedures, unnecessary red tape,
or personal incompetence easily disposed of by selected firings and re-
placements with persons possessing the requisite capacity for policy
execution. Policy capacity, over and above an indeterminate level of
technical competence and public reputation, is conceived as the ability
to make and carry into effect decisions in controversial situations generally consistent with a person's world-view, value position, or attitude orientation. Persons who evaluate public officials and agencies by
such criteria find it easy to downgrade administrative problems as involving "no important questions of principle." As a consequence, vital
difficulties of structure and material contradictions of policy are assumed away by reference to general standards of belief, labels that leave
important theoretical issues inadequately stated, political discussion
empirically uninformed, and programmatic outcomes operationally
misconceived.

An illustration of this is the tendency to appraise TVA in terms of
the familiar dichotomy between liberalism and conservatism. In the

contemporary situation, protagonists of both viewpoints are uneasy, uncertain, and dissatisfied with particular directions the agency has taken. During the first twenty or thirty years of its life TVA tended to be defended by persons thinking of themselves as liberal or progressive, and attacked by self-styled conservatives. Since the early 1960s the volume and frequency at least of negative criticism have been largely reversed. It seems likely that these discontents are due not just to agency decisions and policies but to the lurking suspicion that criteria of liberalism and conservatism are insufficient to explain why TVA institutionally acts as it does. Saying that the agency "has gotten too big for its britches" doesn't help much to specify the structural and organizational factors that are part of the problem and have to be considered explicitly in the formulation of alternatives for change. Admittedly, administrative and technical considerations should not wholly determine how political conflicts of value, interest, and power are settled. Proposals for remedial action should, however, as far as possible be publicly discussed on the basis of tested knowledge and experience, not solely in terms of conformity with group demands, preconceived values, and deliberately unbalanced, one-sided phrases designed to evoke passionate reactions of support or hostility. The latter are notoriously unstable and dissatisfying in the long run.

In order to sharpen our awareness of how administrative considerations are central to understanding TVA's political survival, as well as its present difficulties, reflect on the following statements.

1. TVA's original statute of 1933 has often been interpreted as a political victory by liberal-progressive forces in America. It may be more realistically viewed as a successful alliance of liberal and other political groups mobilized by timely political leadership to transcend the cleavages that between 1918 and 1932 had completely stymied congressional resolution of the separate but closely related issues of the government's chemical plant disposal at Muscle Shoals, flood control, navigation and use of the Tennessee River watershed, production and distribution of electric power generated at dams and other facilities, and the broad, intransigent problem of poverty and economic underdevelopment in the Valley and adjacent region.

2. The 1933 law embodied a political decision by Congress and the president to approach these issues comprehensively by administrative resolution rather than legislative specification. The law listed several purposes and prescribed in considerable detail the Authority's powers and limits, but it did not establish priorities among its objectives or in-

dicate how the board was to settle conflicts arising between them as to timing or allocating its available resources. The law did not bypass all controversial issues of board authority, but by and large it left problems of emphasis, substance, and conflicting purposes to administrative discretion.

3. The inference is clear that the two political branches, Congress and the president, intended to delegate vital political controversies to the TVA board to decide on ostensibly "nonpolitical" grounds, that is, scientific, engineering, legal, and administrative expertness. This political stance of taking substantive policy questions out of politics of course did not mean that Congress and the president thought TVA policies and programs would not have political repercussions, that the board would not be held answerable for its acts or that the president and Congress would not exercise their reserved powers to oversee and modify the board's interpretations of its responsibilities by executive direction or statutory amendment.

4. Over the first six or seven years of its existence, the TVA board developed a fairly clear working order of priorities, although these were not always explicitly set forth in policy statements and particular decisions. In very broad terms TVA concentrated on dam construction, water control and integrated use of the river system, experimentation and application of fertilizer and related products to agricultural and industrial use, and construction of transmission lines and production facilities for the sale of electricity under policies prescribed by the act. By 1939, when the act and the board gained constitutional (judicial) approval, this "production-for-mass distribution" orientation had pretty clearly won out over the ideal of redistribution and reallocation of regional resources advocated by social planners within and outside TVA's staff. Between 1940 and 1960 the issue of financing TVA's capacity to meet the steadily growing demand for cheap electricity for war and domestic consumption took increasing precedence over other purposes. Throughout this period TVA gradually diminished, without wholly terminating, its early emphases upon culturally innovative projects, experimental programs in community building, modernization and alteration of local-regional patterns of landownership, race relations, forestry management, and the balanced development of commercial, recreational, and aesthetic resources associated with its civil, electrical, and industrial engineering facilities. Not until after 1960, however, when TVA secured authorization to finance its power operations by selling its own revenue bonds (the 1959 "self-financing" amendments),

did it become clear to many groups in its political constituency—environmental, antinuclear, coal mining, and different classes of electrical consumers: distributive, governmental, industrial, and residential—that their material interests could not be immediately or satisfactorily met by TVA's record of efficient performance or assertions of its public power philosophy and democratic administration. On the other side, TVA's practical accomplishments, measured by size, financial standing, and performance as a publicly owned and operated electric utility, muted, if they did not eliminate, the attacks of critics viewing the agency as unsound, unworkable, uneconomic, and un-American.

Enough perhaps has been said, by way of introduction, to justify the importance of explicitly incorporating the organizational and administrative dimension into the matrix of explanatory factors accounting for TVA's development, success, and problems. But what does this mean? Upon what operative organizational theory or model, and by what managerial principles governing its choice of means, has TVA pursued its assigned duties and won acceptance in the American political system?

II

TVA offers for political analysis the challenging case of a public corporation, wholly owned and operated by the U.S. government, endowed with specified statutory powers to be interpreted and carried into effect by a three-member board of directors reporting directly to the president and Congress. Although the government corporation was by no means a complete novelty at the time of TVA's creation in 1933, the scope of its mission was explicitly justified by the degree of its independence from the established department structure and political supervision by presidential and congressional staff agencies. This autonomy was hailed at the time and has been emphasized by TVA observers ever since.

In perspective of political capabilities as distinct from its legally defined status, however, TVA's corporate autonomy has been much more a contingent, fluctuating variable than a constant, stable assumption. TVA's public life can be mapped by periods of political struggle over the limits of its corporate powers. TVA's development looks like a series of stages, initiated and terminated by political, usually congressional, actions redefining the agency's formal authority, confirming or establishing a different order of priority among its multiple, partly conflicting,

TABLE 1

**Stages of Uncertainty in TVA's Political Environment:
The Balance between Autonomy and Accountability**

Period	Characteristics of Power Struggle
1933–39[a]	Internally: Goal clarification. Externally: Nullification of agency's mission and power program.
1939–49[b]	Efforts to redirect and limit TVA's legitimized status as a public utility.
1949–59[c]	Primarily external harassment aimed at inhibiting TVA's capital expansion program through appropriations.
1960–75[d]	Relative detachment and insulation from political pressures through the first half of the 1960s; escalating external pressures after 1966, deriving from decisions to "go nuclear," environmentalist forces, rising coal and equipment costs and rates.
1975–present	Continuation of trends in previous stage, intensified by uncertainties generated by conflicts over TVA's regional and national roles in the nation's energy program, accompanied by heightened demands for statutory revision of board's size, composition, and powers.

[a]Initiated by the organic act, 48 Stat. 58 (1933); terminated by Senate Document 56, *Report of the Joint Congressional Committee on the Investigation of the TVA*, 76th Cong., 1st sess. (1939), and *Tennessee Electric Power Co. v. TVA*, 306 U.S. 118 (1939). The 1936 ruling of the Supreme Court in the *Ashwander* case did not pass upon the constitutionality of TVA as a federal enterprise for the unified development of the river, region, and power distribution area.

[b]Terminated by the Government Corporation and Appropriations acts of 1948 and 1949, which stabilized the long-range financial relationships between TVA and the treasury, and enabled TVA to begin construction of steam (coal-fired) plants to supplement hydro-generated power.

[c]Highlighted by the actions of the Executive Office of the president and the Dixon-Yates contract (1953–55), and terminated by the revenue bond–financing amendments to the TVA Act in 1959, 73 Stat. 280.

[d]Terminated by the oversight hearings before the Senate Public Works Committee in May–June, 1975, after which TVA formally notified the Peabody Coal Company of its intent to cancel its 1974 offer to purchase the company's coal assets.

interrelated goals. Table 1 suggests five such periods of change, brought about by the efforts of interests, internal and external to the agency, to nullify, redirect, expand, or limit its goals and performance capacity.

This thumbnail summation suggests that TVA's survival and controversial political history cannot be satisfactorily explained solely by its formal statutory powers and relative political autonomy. Important as these factors are, controversiality has been endemic throughout the board's career. The board's success in maintaining and expanding its legal and operating authority has made it the envy of many privately owned, publicly regulated utility corporations. However, the record of presidential involvement through appointment and removal; congressional investigation, oversight, and annual appropriations hearings; about twenty separate statutory amendments; its relations with BOB-OMB, GAO, and GSA; its litigation caseload; and, not least, several studies critical of agency decision making—all reveal that the board and staff have constantly been obliged to act within political, legal, and administrative constraints. TVA has constantly recognized that it is required to answer publicly for its programs, acts, and performance; the board, as distinct from its subordinate officials and agents, has throughout taken anticipated consequences into account in arriving at policy and program decisions—both of the self-regarding (agency) and other-regarding (external) variety.[1] On at least one occasion—the proposed acquisition of the Peabody Company's coal properties—the board retrospectively found it advisable to revoke a major policy commitment.

From a system perspective, if not from that of particular individuals, scholars, or interest groups who define accountability in terms of personal accessibility and policy convergence with their articulated and negotiable demands, TVA's organizational history may be regarded as a shifting balance on a continuum between formal (legal) autonomy and informal (operating) accountability in an unstable environment of political forces and pressures. From time to time these tensions culminate temporarily in some symbolic, usually legislative act, indicating a modified line of agency development confirming or altering the agency's order of policy priorities. In a dialectic of TVA's development, relegitimation rather than transformation describes the outcome of each stage of struggle between the protagonists for priority among the agency's clienteles.

Analyzing TVA from the viewpoint of the highest level of the Authority's management system has negative as well as positive aspects. It exposes the observer to the charge of oversympathetic identification with the interests and survival of the agency. It incurs the danger that the analyst will subconsciously subordinate the immediate personal and group concerns of consumers, competitors, and suppliers, and local, state, and even national considerations, to the collective well-being of the TVA as an organization. The counterbalance to these possibilities lies in remembering that the organization's welfare is not an end-in-itself.

One other point should be mentioned in connection with TVA's pattern of organizational change. In the literature of governmental bureaucracy, this is commonly assumed to take the form of constant or increasing stability, rigidity, and resistance to change. Some years ago a fresh analysis of governmental regulatory commissions (which perhaps belong to a different class of organization from orthodox executive departments or public corporations) elaborated the conception of a universal bureaucratic life cycle consisting of four periods (gestation, rambunctious youth, devitalized maturity, and ossifying old age).[2] George E. Rawson's thorough study of TVA's power program casts serious doubt on whether the agency conforms to a pattern so analogous to an individual human being. Closely examined, TVA's power policies appear to have been characterized by changes of rapid pace and extensive magnitude.[3] Rawson's focus was on program, not organization, but his work supports the hypothesis that TVA's administrative organization has been change-susceptible and flexible, reflecting relatively frequent program modifications and considerable, but not excessive, turnover of policy staff personnel.

III

TVA's central decision-making machinery, consisting of a three-member board with a chairman designated by the president, a chief counsel, and a general manager, has characterized its existence almost since its creation.[4] Although the policy input of the general counsel to this day remains incalculable and deserves further study, it is the relations among the board, the general manager, and departmental staff that primarily concern us here. Nineteen members have served on the board since 1933; their average age when appointed was fifty-two, and their average length of service was eight years. There have been nine general managers since 1937, with an average age of just over forty when appointed and an average term of six years in office.[5]

A board system of executive responsibility operates under a heavy burden of proof in administrative theory. In the TVA case there is good reason to believe that the three-member board (not five, seven, or nine) is inextricably associated with the institutional character of agency. Emphasis upon unity of purpose, in the sense symbolized by a single-headed agency, has not been an outstanding feature of board behavior. From the early days of the Arthur Morgan period, much of the Vogel regime, the Wagner board, and the brief tenure of S. David Freeman, the board operated on a two-to-one majority basis, with the chairman for several periods being in the minority. However, not since 1937–38, when the Morgan-Lilienthal controversy required presidential intervention and a six-months' congressional investigation, has conflict within the board disrupted the staff and threatened the whole life of the organization. This result has only in part been due to the general manager. The clear-cut conception of a board restricting itself solely to policy, with the G.M. exclusively responsible for operations and execution, has never been applicable to TVA. Because of the variety of functions imposed by law, the host of problems never dreamed of when the act was drafted, the complexity of relations with other federal agencies and state-local governments, and the urgency of interdivisional relationships requiring board attention, the board has never confined itself to consideration of such matters as a general manager in charge of operations might choose to present to it. "Coordination" gets closer to describing his role, but the premise of board responsibility for policy and decision has kept the general manager from effectively channeling or controlling communications to and from the board. A more accurate term to describe the practice of effective TVA general managers would be that of executive or administrative assistant to the chairman for budgetary and organizational matters, plus acting as the board's official channel of communication to the staff and public when it acts as a collective entity. Board chairmen and members have exhibited a marked inclination to get involved in policy matters at an early stage, and to play an accommodating role in deciding technical, economic, and ideological differences within the staff. Active board-staff participation in policy has produced a pluralistic pattern of soliciting and thrashing out, if not bargaining, with frank expressions of policies being advocated. It was also consistent with the continuing conception of an agency with novel, ground-breaking grants of authority, endowed with full sublegislative and executive discretion as to means of accomplishing those ends.[6]

If unity-in-process fails to describe the TVA board in action, it does not follow that the board has been paralyzed, ineffective, unable to reach decisions. On the contrary, the board has followed the Harcourt Morgan example—one member acts as a key, "swing" figure to provide the board with a working majority and an articulate minority position. This also has reinforced the board's pluralistic tendency to listen, if not to respond directly, to diverse interests and views. Critics have charged the board with being overly responsive (1) to advocates of a "high use–low rate" public power philosophy;[7] (2) to the "Farm Bureau–Extension Service–state university agricultural research" alliance, as opposed to those desiring to raise incomes and life conditions of the poorest levels of rural society in the region,[8] (3) to coal producers, as opposed to union miners and opponents of cheaper strip-mining operations; (4) to residential and industrial consumers of electricity, rather than to recreational and environmental protectionists;[9] and (5) to the exigencies of expanding capacity to meet national energy policy requirements, rather than reducing demand estimates to short-run levels favored by its local-state close-to-home constituents.[10] What is noteworthy about these accusations is that the board has been accused not of inability to act but of alignment with wrong interests or pursuit of mistaken policy ends. The criticisms go to the board's exercise of responsibility, to the policy objects it has chosen to accept accountability for, and to the interest alignments benefited thereby—not to board refusal or inability to respond to conflicting demands. As to the three-member board's ability to reconcile conflicting goals and interests with a reasonable degree of continuity and acceptability, such a judgment will vary with time, circumstance, and perspective. It can only be conjectured whether the dynamic symbolism projected by TVA's growth and accomplishments would have been brought about by a single administrator or larger board–cum–executive director.

Besides corporate autonomy and a pluralistic decision-making structure, two other principles, the merit system of personnel administration and organizational flexibility, characterize TVA as an organization. These stem from Sections 3 and 6 of the act. The latter is most frequently referred to. It provides that in appointment, selection, and promotion of employees and officials, "no political test or qualification shall be permitted or given consideration, but all such appointments and promotions shall be given and made on the basis of merit and efficiency." It is not always realized that the mandatory freedom from partisan political considerations in employer-employee relations imposed by law represents a compromise between the alternatives of placing TVA under the federal Civil Service law and Commission regulations and giving it complete freedom to establish its own system of personnel administration. While subsequent congressional legislation has modified somewhat TVA's autonomy from government-wide policies in personnel matters, the original ban on partisan political influences in appointment and promotion has never been relaxed in agency policy or practice. This principle is closely associated with a doctrine of decentralizing responsibility for personnel to operating management under general oversight and assistance from the central personnel office. This is intended to unify personnel and general management at the top, and to avoid continuous conflict between personnel and operating management in the field.[11] That merit and efficiency have in fact characterized TVA operations has never been seriously challenged, even by critics who argue that TVA is too insensitive to political "realities."

Even before merit and efficiency in appointment and promotion, Section 3 of the act requires that the board "shall provide a system of organization to fix responsibility and promote efficiency . . . without regard to provision of civil service laws applicable to officers and employees of the United States." Under this mandate the board proceeded to build and maintain what may be called a unified system of delegated management ("decentralized" perhaps goes too far to describe the degree of operating managerial discretion). Comparison of TVA organization charts in 1937, 1951, 1970, and 1981 reveals a great deal of variation in divisional name and position, but the basic functional responsibilities and scheme of intercommunication appear remarkably similar. In 1937, besides the top layer of general management (including the legal, financial, and information offices), the operating divisions were: Water Control on the River, Water Control on the Land, Water Power Utilization, Management Services, and Regional Planning Council. By 1951 management services had been recognized as an auxiliary staff position under the general manager; water control was combined with design and construction under the chief engineer; a manager of power had been made responsible for power utilization and operations; forestry, chemical engineering, and agricultural relations had been placed under a chief conservation engineer; and a manager of reservoir and community relations was in charge of regional planning studies, health and safety, and reservoir properties. In 1970 the four main divisions were Power, Engineering Design and Construction, Agricultural and Chemical Development, and Health and Environmental Science, while four diminishing or embryonic functions were recognized as divisions of Water Control Planning, Navigational Development and Regional Studies, Tributary Area Development, and Forestry, Fisheries, and Wildlife Development. By 1980 the eight divisions of 1970 were again reduced to five: Power, Natural Resources, Economic and Community Development, Agricultural and Fertilizer Development, and General Service Activities.

This account of agency organization emphasizes organization by program and service function, and perhaps conceals TVA's system of "pooled administration," which brings together from each division engineers, chemists, agronomists, and experts in commercial, industrial, recreational, and community planning on any designated problem. Conscious attention to the requirement of concerting technical specializations toward the achievement of multiple purposes has been perhaps the organizational earmark of TVA, perhaps least visibly in power operations, but quite openly in reservoir and waterway management, recreational development, land use and wildlife conservation, health and disease control, industrial expansion, and community assistance.

Finally, two other features have characterized TVA's organizational continuity from the beginnings to the present day. The first is that for all activities other than power, with the exception of proceeds from non-power operations like fertilizer, recreation, and reimbursable services, the Authority seeks and relies upon annual congressional appropriations, with all the review and accountability checks implicit in that process.[12] The other corporate feature that distinguishes TVA is the variability of its decentralization of authority, by program. Power, fertilizer, and agricultural operations have been allowed substantial functional and geographic autonomy (power to Chattanooga, fertilizer and agricultural relations to Muscle Shoals). The board has kept closer track of resource conservation and development programs by locating them in Knoxville and Oak Ridge. Functionally, decentralization has occurred in production and applied research operations, while research and experimental projects involving human, economic, regional, and community innovation have received closer central supervision. Occupationally and professionally, the civil and electrical engineers, chemists, and agronomists have been allowed more autonomy than the foresters, recreationists, and community planners. The board has allowed most decentralization in construction, facility operation, energy, and fertilizer production. Where the board has pursued developmental, facilitative, and cooperative relationships with other governmental agencies and private associations, it has kept them under more restrictive control.

IV

Section 1 of the Tennessee Valley Authority Act provides:

that for the purpose of maintaining and operating the properties now owned by the United States in the vicinity of Muscle Shoals, Alabama, in the interest of the national defense and for agricultural and industrial development, and to improve navigation in the Tennessee River and to control the destructive flood waters in the Tennessee River and Mississippi River Basins, there is hereby created a body corporate by the name of the "Tennessee Valley Authority. . . ."

From this language it is readily seen that it was by no means after-the-fact rationalization for the board to articulate as its overriding policy goal "unified river and regional development." The same paragraph mentions navigation, flood control, and agricultural and industrial development, and Sections 4, 5, and 9 explicitly authorize land acquisition and sale, production and marketing of fertilizer, provision and operation of facilities for generation, transmission and sale of electric energy to assist in liquidating the cost or aid in the maintenance of the projects of the Authority. Reforestation and proper use of marginal lands followed navigation and flood control in the list of stated purposes. At least at the beginning, and down to 1940, the several objectives the board was directed to pursue were practically perceived as separate operating programs that, taken together, rationalized an overall policy mission of river development and resource management. The significance of the distinction between collective policy goal and separate operating program is that it provides an analytical standpoint from which to differentiate between the policy goals of TVA as a systemic whole (body corporate) and the goals of the several component programs and constituent groups interested in or affected by those programs.[13]

Between 1940, when TVA was mobilized to produce power for the war effort, and 1960, the year the self-financing amendments to the act came into effect, the question inescapably arises: did not the TVA power program change from that of a partial, instrumental goal complementing those of river control and navigation, land resource conservation, and industrial and community development, into that of the controlling, overall policy goal and criterion of TVA performance, with the functions of river control and resource management reduced to subordinate programs to power?

From the outside, such charges, and defenses against them, were stated in terms of "sell-out" or agency collusion and corruption by "the interests." In the case of the power program alone, this charge cannot hold water. To whom did the Authority sell out? The 160 municipal power systems? The electricity consumers of the TVA service area? The private electric power companies, the Budget Bureau, the Atomic Energy Commission? Or does it indicate a loss of influence and dollar allocation to the other programs within TVA compared to power? None upon analysis turns out to be a charge of de facto or legal culpability. Rather, it is an expression of disappointment and disagreement with the board, which took direct responsibility for river control and power production, compared with its delegation and cooperation with other agencies in the area of land use, forestry, and industrial and community development.

TVA spokesmen, while not denying the shift in magnitude of the power program, insist that it is still a part of the agency's overall policy of coordinated river and regional development. Of this, more later. In explaining the shift, however, they tend to use the language of technological necessity or fiscal-financial requirements to meet TVA's multiple goals. Both have considerable factual foundation.

Factors beyond the control of the TVA board have contributed in part to the long-range trends in energy production over fifty years, but board inititative and policy also explain some remarkable shifts: waterpower dropped from 100 to less than 20 percent of energy generated by TVA betwen 1933 and 1980; the share of coal-fired steam plants rose from 0 to 65 percent over the same period; and nuclear power increased spectacularly from 0 in 1966 to 15 percent in 1980, with a planned projection to 30 percent or more by 1990. Flood control, navigation, and nonpower programs declined from approximately half the Authority's annual expenditures in 1940 to 13 percent in 1960 and 4 percent in 1980. But shifts in program emphasis, measured by kilowatt-hours and dollars, are not the only guides and constraints that have influenced the board. Chairmen from Arthur Morgan to Aubrey Wagner and S. David Freeman have, in differing accents, all proclaimed the theme of coordinated control of river, natural, and human resource development. No board member has challenged or sought to redirect that overriding symbol, although some have pressed for a different program balance on specific issues. This policy continuity cannot be wholly downplayed as rationalization and propaganda for the power program. Nonetheless, the board's very success in securing financial autonomy and political sanction for the balance it has established among the several program objectives specified in the act, contributes to the economic consequences and controversies it finds itself in today. To understand them, it is necessary to consider the Authority's personnel and their place in the TVA's environment of political influences.

V

Vocational skill and professional competence are no less an earmark of TVA organization, as noted in section II, than corporate autonomy. Table 2, showing the agency's principal offices and distribution of employees by program, suggests the broad categories of expertness and training composing the staff. The power program, with 45,000 employees estimated for 1982, is by far the largest, accounting for 94 per-

TABLE 2

TVA Personnel by Major Program
(estimated for 1982)

Program	Number of Employees
Management and General Services	255
Board of directors	
General manager (budget and planning staffs, information, D.C. office, EEOC)	
General counsel	
Management services (union-management relations, property, finance, purchasing, personnel, medical, occupational health, safety, and environmental compliance)	
Agricultural and Chemical Development (agricultural and chemical R&D, fertilizer and chemical production)	1,014
Community Development (economic development, community services, regional studies)	255
Engineering Design and Construction (included with Power)	
Natural Resources (land, water, and forest resources, services, and Land between the Lakes)	1,878
Power and Energy Demonstrations (production, operations, transmission, construction, fuels, utilization, rates, conservation, research)	45,628 ⎯ 49,000

Sources: TVA, *Organization Bulletin* (July 27, 1979); *Budget Program* (1982), p. 215. From the beginning TVA, unlike the Corps of Engineers and Bureau of Reclamation, has employed its own construction workers on "force account" rather than spending on private construction.

cent of employment in the two Offices of Power and Engineering Design and Construction. Natural Resources (1,900) is second, followed by Agricultural and Chemical Development (1,000), and Economic and Community Development, Energy Demonstrations, and General Services, each with about 250.

Occupationally, TVA employees are distributed among hourly paid construction (19,870, or 41 percent), plant operations and maintenance (11,462, or 24 percent), scientific and engineering (9,728, or 20 percent), service and clerical (6,269, or 13 percent), and administrative (1,238, or 2 percent).[14] For 1982, personnel compensation is estimated at $1.5 billion, with $1.4 billion attributed to the power program and $100 million for all other purposes.

One of the ground-breaking decisions by the first TVA board was to recognize and bargain collectively with the Tennessee Valley Trades and Labor Council, representing its construction and maintenance workers through fifteen craft and other organized unions. Under these agreements TVA has established an outstanding record of stable, if not wholly harmonious, relations with its manual, hourly paid, blue-collar employees, evolving informally toward a form of open but pro-union shop.[15] Unions have argued that their members' terms of employment have not kept up with those in the private construction and electric utility industries, notwithstanding "the prevailing rate" provisions of the Davis-Bacon Act and other federal employment practice laws, but nevertheless have felt impelled to go along to "make this thing work." Less research attention has been paid to office and white-collar workers.

Reference has previously been made to the importance of scientific, engineering, and technical specialists in the TVA enterprise. Two board chairmen who have been most articulate in expounding the conditions under which it was made to work have laid the greatest emphasis upon the difficulties, as well as the success, involved in promoting pooled, interdisciplinary cooperation between such specialists in developing and administering programs.[16] Internal conflicts of training, perspective, and commitment are intensified among men whose vocational rather than pecuniary interests are involved. The insider accounts of cases of land acquisition, dam and plant site location, water use, disease control, fish and wildlife protection, and commercial development never fail to stress the factors of personnel selection, awareness of common purpose in promoting the well-being of the people of the region, and board protection of staff from outside political interference, in achieving whatever success TVA has had.

In addition to the differentiated interests of its staff and the supplier and customer groups affected by its operations, TVA's political environment includes the several components of its electric power system: 110 municipally owned distributing utilities,[17] 50 rural electric cooperatives, 50 direct industrial consumers, and several federal (DOE) installations. Its Office of Natural Resources is concerned with the management of 300,000 acres of land along 11,000 miles of reservoir shoreline. One or more divisions are involved in programs of land and forest reclamation, air and water pollution control, nuclear safety and storage, hazardous and solid waste disposal, 14 reservoir areas, and 250 access points to valley streams for recreational purposes. Industrial, commercial, community, and town development through planning and financial assistance is conducted on a project basis throughout the Valley from Virginia and western North Carolina, north Georgia, Alabama, and Mississippi, to west Tennessee and Kentucky. All over the region businessmen and farmers, workers and manufacturers, educators, doctors, and social workers, have come to see TVA as a resource for information, technical advice, and material aid in their self-help efforts. Their experiences, positive or negative, reflect back to the congressmen, senators, and governors of the tributary Valley states.

Other studies have elaborated the differences and oppositions, supports and alliances, among the interests composing TVA's political environment, which cut across and include elements both internal and external to the formal organization. Not least among the variables affecting this configuration are the payments-in-lieu-of-taxes to states and local governments (estimated at $158 million in 1982), repayments to the federal treasury of appropriations and the investment in power facilities (totaling an estimated $1.6 billion over the period 1961–82), and interest on revenue bonds (estimated at $1.3 billion in 1982 alone, almost one-third of the annual power system budget). TVA ratepayers have a distinctly wry reaction to the charge that the rest of the country is subsidizing TVA power rates; to them the reverse seems more accurate. (More than half of TVA's interest burden is directly related to the nuclear plant construction program.)[18] The average annual rate to TVA residential customers in 1980 ws 3.3¢ per kilowatt-hour as compared to an annual average national rate of 4.8¢, coupled with an annual average per-customer use of 15,130 kilowatt-hours compared with 8,944 nationally. These comparisons provide small comfort to ratepayers who have had to absorb increases in their electric bills of several hundred percent over the last five years.

Nationally, TVA's supporters have historically included public power sympathizers, particularly in the Pacific Northwest, advocates of rural electrification, liberal thinkers favorable to planned river and regional development, and unions particularly in the building and construction trades. The electric utility industry, the ideological opponents of government ownership and operation, and other federal departments like Agriculture and Interior, concerned over expansion of the autonomous regional agency principle to other sections of the country, comprise continuing elements of TVA's political opposition. Erosion has occurred among both national supporters and opponents, but the more serious from TVA's viewpoint has been the cleavage among liberal and labor sympathizers, brought about by environmental population shifts and nuclear issues, declining business and employment conditions in the industrial Northeast, partly attributable to cheaper power and anti-union attitudes. Perhaps more threatening have been rifts in the agency's congressional lobby, highlighted by coal industry problems in Kentucky and West Virginia, and resentment of the Alabama delegation over the seeming domination of TVA affairs by the Tennessee senators and congressmen. So far as the Tennessee delegation is concerned, from Kenneth McKellar to Howard Baker there has been an unbroken record of bipartisan support for TVA programs and appropriations, if not always on particular personnel recommendations and decisions on location of dams, purchase, reservoir management and water use, and environmental effects of power operations.

The major political sign of growing disruption in TVA's regional support base has been the increasing frequency of references in the press and congressional statements to the possibility of enlarging the size of the board. The option of opening up the statute to revise the board's powers, responsibilities, and consultative procedures has appeared less often and more vaguely. Although it is difficult to see how changes in board size, composition, and procedures could offset structural factors necessitating higher power rates, such "political" variables offer an obvious tactical means of allaying discontents, trading off autonomy-and-efficiency to accountability considerations.

VI

As an organizational model, the first question usually asked about TVA is, "Why have the managerial principles underlying its examples of coordinated development of a natural region's resources (autonomy, decentralization from the national capital to its area of operations, appointment by merit rather than partisan pressures and affiliations, a public agency committed to encourage and promote private and local enterprise) not been transferable to other regions of the country?" Indeed, they have been more admired and emulated by other countries than its own. As Derthick and Peirce have noted,[19] the very continuity of these organizational features helps to explain the decline of the agency's own missionary zeal and the rise of vigorous opposition from political, economic, geographic, and federal bureaucratic "interests" to export the unified public resource development agency from the Tennessee to the Missouri and Columbia valleys and elsewhere. In addition, the Southeast seemed to be almost a vacuum of hope in the depressed days of 1933; the TVA idea then was breathtakingly new and exciting; advocates of alternative development policies and agencies were unprepared to cope with the breadth and imagination of ideas mobilized by Senator Norris and President Roosevelt; awareness of the implications of what it was doing was probably limited both in Congress and the nation. The special circumstances surrounding TVA's creation are not likely to recur, and the more TVA establishes itself as a respectable public utility, primarily responsible for power and flood control, subject to market forces making for higher costs and rates, the less attractive the government monopoly alternative appears to the privately owned, publicly regulated form.

The next common question arising from TVA's organizational experience is, "What happened to its associations with regional and national planning?" Beside the fact that the planning concept nowhere receives explicit authorization and sanction in the act, as early as 1936[20] the dominant board majority had relinquished any definition of planning that denoted a blueprint of targeted objectives or mandatory criteria the board would implement and enforce, in favor of the doctrine of a coordinated approach to resource problems, physical and human, mobilizing all available technical and social skills to advance the interests and welfare of the Valley people. During the 1940s and 1950s Lilienthal and Clapp frequently identified TVA with democratic planning, arguing that the Valley people not only supported the objectives of the act but approved by their involvement and acquiescence TVA policies and procedures. Later chairmen, notably Vogel and Wagner, muted the democratic note by emphasizing the requirement of balanced administrative judgment imposed by Congress on the board and TVA staff to work out the several purposes of the act in concert, pointing to the necessity for the board's discretionary responsibility and accountability for results to president, Congress, courts, institutions, and people of the Valley. The board, of course, never relinquished its devotion to planning in the sense of applying scientific intelligence and skills to defined problems, carefully weighing the consequences of alternative policy proposals in decision making. But as a matter of staff training and public information, organization charts and administrative manuals, the planning ideas, bodies, and councils of early days have mostly been replaced by research units, regional studies, lines of staff communication and coordination. As Durisch and Lowry reported in 1953, one of TVA's early decisions was to discard staff preparation of a regional plan in favor of searching for a regional role where "planning is the democratic task of many institutions and countless individuals."[21]

Organization doctrine is one thing, evaluation of policy and program results another. Realistic research has not been lacking to probe beneath the rhetoric of "balanced attention" to all purposes and interests affected by TVA. Not surprisingly, it shows no consistent pattern

of approach among the several programs. TVA has never delegated
or shared responsibilities for the river control system and the public
power program. In these missions the pattern has been one of firm federal assumption of responsibility and control of operations, with little
delegation to lower administrative levels except for retail power distribution, where consumers scarcely control rates.[22] By way of contrast,
the Harcourt Morgan doctrine of working with and through state university experiment stations and agricultural extension services to promote farmer use of fertilizer and soil conservation practices has prevailed. In fact, the question arises whether, in the area of agricultural
relations, TVA has not delegated completely (let alone been co-opted,
in Selznick's terms) its responsibilities to state and county agencies
and farm organizations. Forestry started out with a commitment to a
7 million–acre program of purchase and management, but after 1941
this was abandoned in favor of joint collaboration with state and federal
conservation agencies, relying less on subsidization and more upon
public information and demonstration programs. TVA after 1940 withdrew from extensive land purchase and demonstration operations except as incidental to reservoir operations, extending a previous decision in 1935 that shifted from a policy of public ownership of marginal
lands toward educational processes to improve land use by state and
local agencies. About 1947, however, it began to terminate continuing
agreements, substituting a policy of negotiating preliminary arrangements for joint, interagency research and planning, temporary financial
support for limited periods, and then withdrawal from direct support
in favor of state or local appropriations.

Even this short summary shows how many different criteria—
administrative decentralization, popular participation and control,
"cost-benefit" analysis of each program, the attitudinal and working relationships between public-public and public-private agencies—have
been applied to TVA, each of which produces conflicting judgments. By
the standard of organizational continuity and survival, TVA has clearly
demonstrated the workability of a unified system of federal regional
management for river control and power supply, while exhibiting almost infinite flexibility in sharing and delegating responsibilities for related aspects of resource use and agricultural, industrial, and educational development. This organizational criterion does *not* say that TVA
has dealt equally and emphasized adequately each program of regional
resource administration. Taken separately, land use, forestry and wildlife, commercial and industrial development, might have fared better
under separate regional bodies or established federal agencies. Assum-

ing the necessity of coordination by a single regional agency, however, it is wholly speculative and unprovable to assert that such programs would have received more equal or adequate treatment than TVA has given them.

In the opening section of this paper it was asked whether TVA could be fitted into a four-stage theory of gestation, youth, maturity, and old age. Given the elastic duration of these stages, it would be difficult to argue that the largest electric utility in the nation ($13 billion in assets, operating 47 dams and 650 miles of waterways, with a power-generating capacity of 30 million kilowatts producing annual power revenues of $5 billion) has not reached maturity. Beyond that, among all recent controversy over nuclear construction, increasing rates, and charges of program imbalance, there is no mention of TVA devitalization or ossification. On the contrary, the criticisms of giantism, doing too many things, overcommitment to nuclear energy, failure to hold down electricity rates—these attest to the Authority's continuing vitality.

TVA's opposition to statutory revision of its basic charter reflects a clear, vigorous conception of its regional development responsibilities as a public corporation, not a mere, negative-passive acquiescence to vocal demands for responsiveness to change in the interests of bureaucratic survival.[23] The cross-cutting counterpressures from outside may indeed converge upon the need for clarifying TVA's priorities as between national and regional energy priorities. If that happens, and the act is opened up for revision, the opportunity will arise for stripping away or transferring to other agencies the river control system, fertilizer production and agricultural applications, forestry, fish and wildlife conservation, recreation, and commercial-industrial and community development. This would indeed remove the confusion between TVA's mission as a regional resource management agency versus that of publicly owned and operated electric utility. Whether the longer-range result would be devitalization and decline is problematic, but there is little doubt that TVA would evolve into a different kind of organization.

The outstanding factors that have contributed to TVA's longevity seem to be: its publicly perceived dedication to the material needs of the people and circumstances of its seven-state region; its sense of balance between its legal powers of discretionary initiative and the requirements of legal and political accountability; its unremitting attention to coordinating each of its program responsibilities in arriving at decisions; its flexibility in redefining an early doctrine of "planned experimentation in social reform" to a "grass-roots approach to regional development"; its sustained policy of sharing responsibilities with other federal agencies and state and local governments in land and resource management and community self-help, implemented both by payments-in-lieu-of-taxes and limited grants-in-aid; its concern with financial integrity by making electricity consumers repay all federal appropriations and the capital and maintenance costs of the power program. It is not singleness of purpose, but ability to demonstrate the compatibility of pursuing a plurality of public values over intermediate and long-range time periods, that has established TVA's legitimacy as a *productive* governmental enterprise.[24] Such diversity of purpose contains its own built-in costs and restraints, including the seeds of divisiveness and disintegration. Even if TVA's success in advancing the welfare of the people in the region and the nation has been only partial, and satisfied the needs of some groups more than others, it must be accounted a considerable democratic achievement to have expanded the marketplace of viable public choice between governmental and nongovernmental forms of collective enterprise, and greatly increased the opportunities for voluntary effort to improve conditions of human life throughout a once-depressed, highly deprived service area.

The final question is, "What about the corporate accountability of TVA compared with conventional government bureaus, departments, and independent agencies?" Our study of the TVA "case" has not included the Army Corps of Engineers, the Federal Power Commission (now the FERC), the departments of Energy, Agriculture, Interior, and Treasury, with all of whom TVA has important working relationships as well as interesting points of comparison with respect to political accountability. We have given only passing attention to TVA's relationships with presidential staff agencies and congressional committees seeking to bring TVA operations into line with the policies of their political superiors. A comprehensive assessment would take account of structural differences and variations in agency authority, program, and scope—the balance between geographic and interest-group foci of attention. We confine ourselves to generalizations from data gleaned during this limited study concerning TVA's accountability (answerability) to the following sources: (1) nongovernmental "interests," (2) presidential and congressional staff agencies and committee staffs, (3) the president, and (4) Congress.

1. *Interest-group accountability.* The most striking contrast that TVA presents to clientele and service departments of government like Agriculture, Commerce, Labor, Interior, HUD, Transportation, Health and Human Services, Education, and the Veterans Administration is

the widespread, if not wholly accurate, public impression that the latter have become the prisoners of the constituent groups they are supposed to serve and regulate. Much the same charge is levied against independent regulatory commissions, whose original establishment, independent of the president and his politically appointed department secretaries, was supposed to remove them from partisan political influences and expose them directly to the adversarial arguments of individuals and groups subject to their "quasi-judicial" jurisdiction. Today we are more skeptical about "accessibility to group demands" as an unqualifiedly acceptable criterion of administrative accountability, just as previous generations were of partisan intervention by political party agents. "Fair and competent execution of duties under their oath of office," at least openly and publicly, is the standard that most citizens and group representatives expect from public officials.

As an organization, TVA clearly passes such a test. To the writer's knowledge, no one seriously accuses TVA of "being in anybody's pocket," whether of politicians, bankers, businessmen, other public utilities, or least of all its own distributors and consumers. In fact, its corporate status and image today are attacked as too remote, detached, and insensitive. To the extent that this is true (it does not conform to the self-image of any board member the writer has observed or interviewed), it is probably due to the mounting evidence that the board in recent years has been more sensitive to the requirements of national energy policy, inflationary conditions, and the costs of borrowing money than to the angry outcries of public interest groups and residential and business ratepayers in the region who deeply resent paying the huge financial costs of constructing nuclear plants, at least until they start producing into the system. This dilemma is not likely to go away very soon. TVA is dealing with a balance-of-sensitivities problem here that is more complex than simply spending more time in public hearings and consultation with consumer, business, and financial groups, helpful as such procedures may be. The Authority will be fortunate if it does not escape the fate of many independent corporations and government agencies whose statutory authority has been so legislatively diluted, and their policy-making structure so infiltrated by persons representing partial group viewpoints, that they have lost most of their effective powers of initiative and discretion to take a comprehensive view of the public interest.

2. *Presidential and congressional staff.* Extremely conscious of their responsibility to act on behalf of their superiors, and necessary and useful as they are to them, central staff agencies like the Office of

Management and Budget, the General Accounting Office, congressional committee and subcommittee chairmen, their staff directors and professional employees, constitute a more immediately threatening instrument of official interference with everyday TVA policies and practices than the pressures of nongovernmental groups. The legitimate influence over budgetary and expenditure processes possessed by such agencies and committees, plus their more intimate access to the attention of their political employers, give them a continual and troublesome initiative to which TVA executives cannot avoid making reasonable responses.

Marguerite Owen, the director of TVA's Washington office for more than thirty-five years, has provided a fascinating account of the conflicting motivations and viewpoints of Washington staff and TVA as a federal field agency, together with a description of the negotiated outcomes of their interchanges on such matters as personnel, budget making and financial reporting, legal procedures, acquisition, use, and disposal of government property, plant and facility construction, transmission and marketing programs, rate schedules, and services.[25] The short-lived Dixon-Yates contract of the early Eisenhower years was a complex arrangement instigated through the Budget Bureau, involving a presidentially approved division of labor between TVA and two private utilities for meeting power needs of the Atomic Energy Commission and allocating shares of TVA's power marketing area among them. Owen's analysis, avowedly favorable to TVA, found that in general TVA has been able to protect its autonomy and integrity from arbitrary interference and direct policy control from Washington. She showed quite clearly, however, that the Authority has felt obliged on numerous occasions to bring its operating practices into line with what the Washington people would agree was substantial conformity to requirements of national policy. This finding most emphatically does not imply that all or most Washington staff people agree with the ways that TVA has interpreted its statutory responsibilities. The point is that TVA boards have for the most part succeeded in establishing their political accountability to the president personally and Congress as a whole, paying the price of bargaining with central staff agencies on administrative matters in order to avoid the necessity of automatically accepting as binding policy directives from the latter in particular cases.

3. *The president.* The Government Reorganization Act of 1939 and the Employment Act of 1946 are often said to symbolize the twentieth-century view of the American chief executive as "general manager" of the federal government. While some observers, pointing to the un-

deniable fact that American voters tend to hold incumbent presidents accountable for the state of the Union (including the economy), it should be kept in mind that Congress and the courts have not yet sanctioned such a sweeping conception, with the possible exception of wartime and extraordinary national emergencies. The foregoing acts of legislation implement only the president's responsibilities to manage the executive departments and agencies of government, by providing him with an expanded analytical and coordinating staff structure in the Executive Office to do that. In addition to the previously discussed supervision of operating policies and practices through such means, TVA offers a famous example of the president's authority to remove the chairman of an independent corporation for "contumacious" conduct, as well as the continuing authority to appoint or replace board members who resign or complete their nine-year terms of office. These managerial powers of the president, significant as they are, are neither symbolically nor effectively sufficient to authorize him to superimpose directly his policy preferences over the board's interpretation of its statutory responsibilities. Personally and practically, he is far too busy with other duties to intervene directly in TVA affairs beyond seeing that the board is in control, managing its affairs smoothly, and coordinating its activities with the duties of other federal agencies.

This, of course, does not completely describe the board's relationship with the president. If, for example, the terms of its members were made coterminous with the chief executive's tenure, it is undeniable that the White House incumbent could more directly influence the direction of board policy by an infusion of three, or even two, new members every four years. It is thought by many that presidents are able to attract high-grade managerial talent to government service only because overlapping, legally secure terms of office guarantee them against sanctions of political removal. At the same time, board members need the good will and support of the president, not only for their own morale but for the help that support can be in encouraging them to do their best job in the face of threatening opposition from all points of the political compass. His refusal to support damaging amendments to the law can be of enormous help. The aftermath of the Arthur Morgan removal in 1938, and the relationship of Herbert Vogel to President Eisenhower, first in disposing of the Dixon-Yates incident and later in securing presidential agreement not to oppose the self-financing amendments, illustrate the importance and kind of mutual dependence in political accountability of the board to the president. Not compulsory substitutability of policy preference, but informal, personal assurance that the conduct of government is better carried out by the available responsible persons, is the most relevant criterion of presidential evaluation in the TVA case. It is impossible to say with certainty that this principle is better implemented by government corporations generally than by regulatory commissions or bureaus within the executive departmental structure, but by the same token presidents likely have no better performance standard for most agencies at the operating level, at least in domestic, as opposed to military and national security fields. The limits of the interpreting, exempting, and equity powers of the executive ought, after all, to be as clear to political observers as they were to Abraham Lincoln.

4. *Congress.* It is Congress, then, upon which the effective, ultimate responsibility for ensuring political accountability of the public corporation rests. With the exception of the 1959 law, statutory amendments from 1933 to 1980 have been minor, of an effectuating nature, such as the authorizations to increase the amount of outstandings bonds from $750 million to $30 billion. Laws like the Government Corporations Act and the Administrative Procedures Acts have been adjusted to by negotiated settlements. Such thorny problems as allocation of costs among uses at joint facilities, and schedules for repayment of appropriated funds, have been disposed of by riders to appropriation bills. As we have seen, Congress now appropriates generally less than $150 million annually for TVA's nonpower functions, as compared with a total annual budget of $5 billion, but this provides ample leverage upon TVA for informational and suggestive purposes at the important appropriations committee and subcommittee level.

It is the standing authorization committees of the Senate and House, dealing with energy and public works, to which major attention for oversight of the Authority has been directed in recent years. Senator George Norris was a tower of strength to TVA in its formative years, and in a different way so was Senator McKellar until 1946. More recently, in 1975, within a month after four or five days of exhaustive hearings, TVA found it expedient to cancel its proposal to purchase the physical assets of one of the largest coal-mining companies in the country. In 1981, within six months after another set of oversight hearings before the Senate Public Works Committee, TVA publicly revised downward its estimates of future demand for electricity in its service area, and announced plans for reducing its long-range construction program of nuclear power plants and units from seventeen to fourteen, and perhaps further. The quiet role of Tennessee Senator Howard Baker in advising Chairman Aubrey Wagner no doubt contributed to the latter's longevity in office. His more prominent connection with President Reagan's replacement of S. David Freeman as TVA board chairman with Charles Dean, after Robert Clement's term ended in the spring of 1981, illustrates the opportunities arising from informal cultivation of personal relationships between strategically placed congressmen and TVA board members. An even more explicit political use of the oversight hearing was employed by Senator James Sasser in March, 1982, when he used the occasion of a report by the General Accounting Office, suggesting ways the board's statutory composition, powers, and procedures could be weakened or circumscribed, to announce a series of investigative hearings he proposed to conduct throughout the state into TVA affairs, inferentially as part of his campaign for re-election.[26]

Fortunately or unfortunately, the imminent possibility of TVA's organic statute being opened up for either "ripper" legislation or selective, weakening amendments describes the agency's contemporary problem of political accountability. What general propositions, as opposed to anecdotal precedents, would be helpful in appraising the dilemma facing its executives and managers? For the members of Congress interested and concerned with the welfare of the people of the Valley and the nation (their number is not restricted to those senators and congressmen from TVA's seven-state region), there is the usefulness of the board's reasoned defenses of its difficult decisions, even to those congressional politicians who might not agree with them from a personal or elective standpoint. From the TVA side, there is the record, over fifty years, of having struck a practical balance between statutorily justified intransigence to any sort of political interference, on the one hand, and such opportunistic deference to political pressures that the agency could not be trusted even by recipients of its accommodations, on the other. Different persons evaluate differently the balance required by both sets of considerations. The agency is not wholly without political resources of the kind recognized by politicians. It may be able to mobilize them to meet contemporary dangers to its historic structure and powers with the wit and ingenuity exhibited by board members and chairmen in the past.

NOTES

1. "Taken into account" is an ambiguous term. The *weight* given by the board to political demands such as Senator McKellar's personnel recommendations, the Douglas Dam case, the Alabama senators' concern over the location of the agency's principal office, the Kentucky politicians' resentment of TVA's handling of the strip-mining problem, and the environmental impact of coal policies was obviously unsatisfactory to them.

2. Marver Berstein, *Regulating Business by Independent Commission* (Princeton, N.J.: Princeton University Press, 1955), ch. 3.

3. George E. Rawson, "The Process of Program Development: The Case of TVA's Power Program" (Ph.D. dissertation, University of Tennessee, 1979), esp. chs. 4–6.

4. By law, in legal matters the general counsel has reported directly to the board since 1933. The general manager's position was not created until 1937. Three balanced accounts of that story, one from the inside and two from outside observers, are: Marguerite Owen, *The Tennessee Valley Authority* (New York: Praeger, 1973), ch. 3; C. Herman Pritchett, *The Tennessee Valley Authority* (Chapel Hill: University of North Carolina Press, 1943), chs. 6–7; Thomas K. McCraw, *Morgan vs. Lilienthal: The Feud within the TVA* (Chicago: Loyola University Press, 1970).

5. These figures supplement an analysis prepared by the East Tennessee Research Corporation, *TVA Decisionmakers* (Knoxville, Tenn., 1976).

6. The House and Senate committees' views on this point may be found in 73d Cong., 1st sess. (1933), House Document 15, House Report 130.

7. Rexford G. Tugwell and E. C. Banfield, "Grass Roots Democracy—Myth or Reality," *Public Administration Review*, 10 (Winter, 1950): 47–55.

8. Philip Selznick, *TVA and the Grass Roots* (Berkeley: University of California Press, 1949).

9. Senate Public Works Committee, *Oversight Hearings, Tennessee Valley Authority*, pts. 1–2 (Apr. 30–May 12, 1975); House, Public Works Subcommittee of Appropriations Committee, *Public Works for Water and Power Development . . . Appropriations Bill*, 93d Cong., 2d sess. (1973).

10. *Nashville Tennessean*, Mar. 15, 1981, p. 1B; June 27, 1981, p. 11.

11. R. S. Avery, *Experiment in Management* (Knoxville: University of Tennessee Press, 1954), pp. 10–14.

12. This is sometimes overlooked or forgotten by "ideological" opponents of TVA, whose major influence base has historically been BOB-OMB in the Executive Office of the president. Whether or not they were trying to restrict or invade TVA's service area, as in the notorious Dixon-Yates contracts of 1953–55, or to make TVA act more like a privately owned electric utility, their policy thrust was to cut off appropriations for nonpower purposes and oblige all TVA expenditures to be paid out of rates to power customers. The OMB under Carter and Reagan maintained this policy pressure no less than the old BOB under Truman and Eisenhower. See Aaron Wildavsky, *Dixon-Yates: A Study in Power Politics* (New Haven, Conn.: Yale University Press, 1962).

13. Daniel P. Moynihan, "Policy vs. Program in the 1970s," *Public Interest* (Summer, 1970): 90–100.

14. TVA, Office of Public Information, Aug. 7, 1981. The total as of June 30, 1981, is 48,567 employees.

15. Avery, *Experiment*, ch. 6.

16. David E. Lilienthal, *TVA: Democracy on the March*, 2d ed. (New York: Harper, 1953), ch. 8; Clapp, *TVA*, chs. 2–3.

17. Its latest chairman, Charles Dean, was appointed by President Reagan from the general managership of the Knoxville Utilities Board.

18. TVA, *Annual Report* (1980), p. 9.

19. Martha Derthick, *Between State and Nation: Regional Organizations of the United States* (Washington, D.C.: Brookings Institution, 1975), ch. 2; N. R. Peirce, *The Border South States* (New York: Norton, 1975), "TVA: Still Our Best Model?" pp. 362–87.

20. TVA, *Annual Report* (1936), p. 2.

21. Lawrence L. Durisch and Robert E. Lowry, "The Scope and Content of Administrative Decision—The TVA Illustration," *Public Administration Review*, 13 (1953): 219–26.

22. Elliott Roberts, *One River—Seven States* (Knoxville: University of Tennessee Press, 1955); Victor C. Hobday, *Sparks at the Grassroots* (Knoxville: University of Tennessee Press, 1969).

23. TVA's robust defense of its organizational mission stands out in interesting contrast to the intellectually soggy, self-defeating posture of much of the "business ethics" and "social responsibility" literature in the universities and private corporate sector. See T. Bradshaw and D. Vogel, eds., *Corporations and Their Critics* (New York: McGraw-Hill, 1980); *Public Interest* (Spring, 1981), no. 63.

24. This conception of "legitimacy" has been elaborated by Harold Lasswell and other outstanding social scientists. See K. W. Deutsch, "Constraints on Value Allocation in Society and Politics," in A. A. Rogow, ed., *Politics, Personality and Social Science in the 20th Century* (Chicago: University of Chicago Press, 1969), pp. 347–365; J. D. Thompson, *Organizations in Action* (New York: McGraw-Hill, 1967); E. C. Lindblom, *Politics and Markets* (New York: Basic Books, 1977); T. Sowell, *Knowledge and Decisions* (New York: Basic Books, 1980).

25. Owen, *TVA*.

26. *Nashville Tennessean*, Mar. 21, 1982, p. 1.

6

Vernon W. Ruttan

The TVA and Regional Development

I N this paper I attempt to assess how some of the economic forces dominating the development of the U.S. economy have enlarged or constrained the role of TVA in the development of the Valley region. This is in contrast to several other papers presented in this volume that concentrate on the impact of changes in the political environment on the scope and context of TVA decision making.

The TVA was established and grew to maturity during a period when the value and contribution to economic development of human and institutional capital was rising relative to the value and contribution of natural resources and physical capital. The contradiction between the program instruments available to TVA and the changes in the economic environment has represented a major constraint on TVA's contribution to regional development.

The Valley as a Developed Region

By any objective standard the economic performance of the TVA region over the last fifty years has been impressive. In the 1930s per capita income in the TVA region was less than half the national average. By 1980 it had risen to a level approaching the national average.[1] The industrial composition of the region's labor force is roughly similar to the rest of the United States. There are still serious problems of poverty in both urban and rural areas in the Valley. But the remaining inequities in income and level of living are primarily due to intra-Valley differences rather than differences between the Valley and the rest of the nation.

It might be argued that in the absence of TVA comparable support for regional development would have been provided by other federal and state agencies and by the private utilities. But in fact such support was initiated with federal support through the instrumentality of the TVA, at a time when similar support was not fully available in other regions. Few critics have been willing to argue that the regional development services provided by TVA would have been provided more efficiently or at lower cost under alternative arrangements.

There can be no question that TVA has had a vital impact on Valley development,[2] yet a definitive answer to the TVA impact on regional development will not be available until sufficiently realistic models of the economy of the Valley and the South become available to permit counterfactual simulations of Valley performance in the absence of the TVA. The models have not been constructed and the simulations have not been run. I can, therefore, do little more than share in the satisfaction with the region's economic progress over the last fifty years. I hope that the remaining inequities in the distribution of development among Valley communities will be further reduced over the next several decades.

National Economic Growth and Regional Development

A natural resource–based theory of economic development was implicit in both the TVA legislative history and in early TVA board policy. The framers of the TVA Act anticipated that the development of the region's land and water resources would provide the major leverage for regional economic growth. This view was consistent with much of economic thought in the 1930s about national economic development. A slowing of urban-industrial growth and a dampening or reversal of the rural-urban transition were feared by many economists and planners and welcomed (especially at Vanderbilt University) by rural fundamentalists.[3]

These expectations turned out to be inconsistent with the sources and direction of national economic growth. Throughout most of its history, the TVA board and program managers have been confronted with a national economic development thrust that has been primarily urban-based. TVA planners have been confined by a resource-based planning orientation. But interrelated urban-based regions rather than river basins have emerged as the most viable focus for regional planning and development. The TVA program has also been confronted with a pattern of national economic development that has drawn more heavily on the quality of human than of natural resources. Both the private and social rates of return to investment in human resource development have risen relative to the returns to investment in natural resource development.[4]

Two major implications for TVA regional development efforts flow from the transition from a natural resource–based to urban and human resource–based sources of development. One implication was that the structural transformation of the Valley region, from a primarily agricultural to a primarily urban and industrial economy, would dominate the rural development efforts of the TVA. Neither the magnitude nor the rate of this transformation was anticipated in the 1930s or 1940s or, indeed, until well into the mid-1950s. Because the dynamic sources of growth were misread and resisted TVA rural development programs (test demonstrations, tributary watersheds, rapid adjustment farms), leaders were continuously confronted with the need to adjust their activities to changes in the rural economy rather than anticipating or directing that change.

A second implication was that the focus of any comprehensive planning effort would be more consistent with long-run development opportunities if oriented primarily around urban-based rather than natural resource–based regions. TVA staff analysis has, at least since the early 1950s, suggested the importance of an urban-oriented planning strategy.[5] Until recently there has been little response by the TVA board or operating divisions to such suggestions. TVA urban initiatives have been selective and tentative rather than comprehensive and consistent.[6] The only consistent involvement with Memphis, the major urban center of the region, has been as a supplier of electricity to the municipal utility boards.

The TVA has been criticized for excessive reliance on the land grant colleges for the operational aspects of its rural development activities.[7] In retrospect it appears that the rural people of the Valley were better served by TVA cooperation with the agricultural extension services and experiment stations of the Valley universities than if the TVA agricultural and rural development activities had been organized under its own direction and/or its own field staff. By linking the fertilizer distribution programs to newly formed cooperatives and land use and farm management education to the university extension services, TVA established a partnership with an agency that was at least as much concerned with the development of the farm family—with farm and home development—as with the conservation and use of land and water resources.[8]

It was the colleges, drawing on experiment station research, that took the lead in urging the TVA toward change from a fertilizer research and development program, focused primarily on meeting the soil needs of the Valley (the phosphate gospel), to a more balanced program that would include the nitrogen fertilizers—toward a program that would more effectively enhance the productivity of the land and the people engaged in agricultural production. The programs of the state universities have been committed to the development of rural people and rural institutions as well as to the region's natural resources. They have been able to respond more effectively to the changing economic forces impinging on Valley development than the TVA, which has felt it necessary to link each new rural initiate (e.g. the tributary development program) to a perceived natural resource development mandate.

Planning for a tributary watershed development program began in the early 1950s in an effort to link regional and local planning efforts. Following the implementation of several pilot watershed planning and development programs, an Office of Tributary Area Development was established in 1961. By the late 1960s fifteen watershed area development associations had been formed. The program was continuously confronted by the awkwardness of the watershed definition as a basis for integrated area development efforts. As the federal government began to channel its local economic development assistance through multicounty planning districts, TVA gradually de-emphasized its watershed orientation. As this occurred, however, the TVA role as a source of support for local development declined relative to state and federal support.[9]

TVA's other major continuing institutional linkage to communities in its region has been through the municipal and cooperative electric power distribution system. These institutions played an important role in the emergence of the TVA as the nation's largest electric utility.[10] The separation of the power wholesaling from the retailing function enabled the distribution agencies to become an important institutional resource for the Valley regions. Although there is considerable disagreement over how much countervailing power the distributors are able to exercise, they do provide the communities they serve with an institutional mechanism for engaging in a dialogue with TVA over power development and pricing policy. Few other utility customers are as well represented in negotiations with their power suppliers.[11]

The economic forces generated by national economic growth, largely unanticipated by TVA in the 1930s and 1940s, have confirmed the wisdom of the early board decision "to reject the concept of a 'planned' region in favor of the idea of a 'planning' region." The planning region concept was emphasized in the 1979 Summer Policy Study report.[12] Efforts are again being made to revive TVA support for the planning region concept following a series of highly disruptive reorganizations in the structure of TVA's regional development activities in the late 1970s.

TVA Policy and Valley Region Development

The contribution of the TVA to Valley region economic development has been conditioned not only by the external economic and political forces impinging on Valley regional development but by a series of policies emerging out of board discussion and action. A number of these decisions have been detailed by Lawrence L. Durisch and Robert E. Lowry in their now classic article, "The Scope and Content of Administrative Decision—The TVA Illustration."[13] I would like to focus on two major areas—facilities construction and fertilizer research and development—because of their significance in determining TVA's capacity to contribute to regional economic development.

Force Account Construction

At the time TVA was established, it was faced with the major operational problem of initiating construction activity as soon as possible. Funds for building Norris and Wheeler dams were available. But the traditional system of contract construction would have meant months of delay as designs were completed, bids sought, and construction activity organized. The TVA board decided to initiate the construction of the Norris and Wheeler projects with its own staff and work force even while the design work was being completed. As the advantages of this action became apparent, a formal decision was made to engage directly in engineering design, purchase of land and materials, and employment and training of labor. The effectiveness of the force account construction policy was reinforced by the decision to acquire an integrated power service area that was large enough to realize the gains from scale economics in construction.

In retrospect it appears that the force account construction decision was a critical factor in providing TVA with the technical capacity to make an orderly transition from a construction program oriented primarily to flood control and navigation to a program oriented primarily to expansion of electric power generation—and to make a relatively smooth transition from construction of hydro to thermal and then to nuclear power facility construction. This investment in human resources, at both the technical and managerial levels, necessary to construct the electric generating facilities to supply a large, rapidly growing service area, enabled the TVA to successfully harness the power of technical change to overcome successive resource constraints on the sources of electric power supply.[14]

The evolution of the power program in a manner consistent with the emerging sources of national economic growth also carried with it a number of political advantages. The economic and political viability of an organization with over 20,000 employees during much of its history has not been without interest to the political leadership of Valley communities and states. The interest was reinforced by the early organization of TVA employees through the Tennessee Valley Trades and Labor Council.

The distribution of the benefits of the power program for the nation and the region has been a matter of continuing dispute.[15] But however the benefits are allocated, they did not come without cost. Power construction and operations activities dominated both the TVA budget and managerial attention. The creative effort available for other dimensions of regional development was severely constrained. But it can hardly be disputed that the early decision to engage in force account construction and to acquire a power service area large enough to realize economies of scale in construction and operations has been an important factor in TVA's economic and political viability.

TVA Fertilizer and Rural Development

Fertilizer has occupied a central role in TVA rural development programs. An important element in the political support for the series of legislative efforts that culminated in the TVA Act was the anticipation by southern agricultural leaders that the energy potential of the Tennessee River could be used to reduce the cost of fertilizer production. TVA inherited two obsolete synthetic nitrate plants that had been built during World War I.[16] An immediate question facing the TVA board in its early sessions was how the Muscle Shoals chemical facilities might be used to encourage regional development.

Early discussion within TVA and with representatives of the regional universities led to a decision to de-emphasize nitrogen production and to engage in a research and development effort that would make low-cost phosphate fertilizers available to Valley farmers. Both ideological and developmental considerations appear to have been involved in this decision. An emphasis on phosphate fertilizers was consistent with the view of the future of Valley agriculture that emerged out of the mature economy perspective that dominated a good deal of thinking about the future in the 1930s. The dominant view was that the Valley region would remain primarily rural. In this environment a viable Valley agricultural system would consist of small-scale farms practicing a soil-conserving system of grassland-livestock agriculture. Nitrogen fertilizers were associated with an exploitive row-crop agriculture. Phosphate fertilizers were needed to meet the soil needs of a conservation system of agriculture that both the agrarian fundamentalists and the planners saw as the future of Valley agriculture.

But there was also a second reason for emphasizing fertilizer. A major problem faced by any rural development program is how to generate the income growth needed to sustain the development of family and community amenities and services that contribute to the quality of life in rural areas.[17] TVA rural development activities were faced with the problem of how rural families could generate the new income streams necessary to support farm development, home improvement, and community development. Fertilizer was viewed as the strategic input that would permit the intensification of crop and livestock production that was necessary to generate new income streams in a small-scale agricultural system. Fertilizer was the strategic input that would enable Valley farmers and communities to "take off" into self-sustained growth.[18]

By the late 1940s it was recognized that the "phosphate philosophy" of regional development was obsolete. The demand for labor from rapidly expanding urban-industrial development in the national and regional economy was resulting in rapid migration of people from rural areas. Advances in mechanical technology were rapidly increasing the optimum size of the farm unit even in Valley agriculture. Advances in biological technology, such as hybrid corn, were resulting in increased demand for nitrogen as well as phosphate fertilizer. These developments combined to reduce the pressure on the more fragile soil resources of the Valley, not by permitting a shift to conservation systems of farming but by making these resources redundant for agricultural production.

As these changes began to impinge on national and Valley agriculture, the capacity for scientific research and technical development at the Muscle Shoals laboratories and pilot plants was expanded to include research and development on nitrogen as well as phosphate fertilizers. The TVA combined a unique capacity for basic research on the chemistry of fertilizer materials; the facilities to carry fertilizer technology development from the bench to the plant level; and the arrangements, in cooperation with the university experiment stations, to integrate fertilizer production research with research on the agronomic aspects of fertilizer use. This capacity was established during the period when the primary focus had been on the development of phosphate fertilizer. In the early 1950s it was refocused to enable TVA to make important contributions to the advancement of nitrogen fertilizer production technology. By the mid-1950s much of USDA fertilizer research was transferred to the TVA. Today the TVA National Fertilizer Development Center is the world's major fertilizer R&D organization. Its work is complemented by an internationally funded International Fertilizer Development Center, also located in Muscle Shoals, which has been given access to the national center's laboratory, pilot plant, and related facilities.[19]

An Inference

Let me now attempt to draw what I consider to be a major inference from both the power program and the fertilizer program. In both cases the TVA built up—within its own organization—the scientific, technical, and managerial capacity to respond to the changing forces of national development that have impinged on its program responsibilities in these two areas. Its human resource capabilities have enabled it to transcend the constraints of initial commitments to particular natural resource–based development strategies.

TVA as a Regional Development Agency

The perspective from the last section is that the TVA has emerged, over the past fifty years, as an efficient supplier of specific inputs into Valley region development. It has been particularly effective in supplying electric power, flood control and navigation services, and fertilizer research, development, and education. Other chapters in this volume, as well as the general literature on the TVA program, suggest that TVA has been less successful or at least less consistent in its role as supplier of a number of other services—industrial location assistance, community development assistance, health and education services, and others. This is not to suggest that many of these other services and activities have not been cost-effective. Certainly they have not cost very much! TVA has rarely allocated more than 2 percent of its budget to these other regional development activities.

But the TVA board and staff have typically been uneasy about their role as a supplier of a limited range of development inputs and services. After all, they stand charged by the expansive language of the TVA Act and judged by the inflated rhetoric of the members of the first TVA board with responsibility for total regional development. It was this concern that led the TVA board to commission in 1979 an external review committee to evaluate the regional development effort and recommend change in regional development program management and initiatives.[20]

In my judgment there have been both demand-side and supply-side constraints on TVA effectiveness in supplying a broad range of development services to the Valley region.

Demand-Side Constraints

A distinguishing feature of the services that TVA has attempted to provide the Valley, except for electric power and fertilizer, is that these services are typically provided outside of market channels. Even in the case of power and fertilizer TVA has at times attempted to pursue objectives that were not interpreted to TVA directly through market channels. This has meant that for most development services TVA has not been able to rely on market signals to interpret what the Valley (and the nation) has wanted from it. In some cases it has been possible for TVA to use market simulation methods such as benefit-cost calculations.

In the absence of direct market tests for the demand for TVA inputs and services, less objective methods have been used to establish development priorities and service levels. Traditionally three methods have been employed to establish the demand for development services.

Through local, state, and federal political processes. These processes have the great virtue of establishing a high degree of legitimacy. However, the political process is so diffuse that it has great difficulty in expressing specific demands for technical inputs of the type that TVA is able to provide.

Through the informal power structure. Selected individuals— because of their status in the economic system, the political system, and the media—have had direct access to the TVA staff and management. The problem in relying on this system is that individual notables and influentials have great difficulty, and often little interest, in distinguishing their personal economic and political interests from the interests of the broader community of which they are a part.

Through organized interest groups. These range from very specific special-purpose interest groups concerned with, for example, the development or preservation of a particular historical or environmental feature, to more broadly based intergovernmental and privately organized regional development agencies. It is not always possible, in the case of the relationship between an agency and a special-interest group, to distinguish the patron from the client.

The TVA cannot afford to ignore any of the traditional methods through which the demands for nonmarket services are traditionally expressed. Yet these mechanisms have not been effective for either resolving conflicts among special-interest constituencies or interpreting local and regional needs for specific technical services. Grass-roots democracy, as a source of TVA program inspiration, has remained ineffective because no broadly representative constituency for TVA nonmarket services has been institutionalized at the local level. In effect, the TVA has had no legislative body capable of expressing a clear-cut economic or political demand for a broad range of TVA development services.

Supply-Side Constraints

The TVA has been most successful in maintaining program continuity and impact in those areas where it has had exclusive or at least primary responsibility for program development and execution. In these areas it has developed a unique TVA scientific, technical, or managerial expertise that has been brought to bear on the delivery of inputs and services into regional and national development. The TVA has been least effective in those areas involving heavy reliance on cooperative program development or operation. In these areas TVA has gradually lost the expertise needed to cooperate effectively with the relevant federal, state, or local programs.

I have argued above that Valley agricultural and rural development was better served by cooperating with the regional universities than if it had attempted its own agricultural development program. But one consequence of this collaborative mode has been to erode TVA agricultural and rural development program delivery and planning capacity except to those areas directly related to fertilizer technology and use. A similar point can be made in the case of TVA support for state and watershed planning activities. In these cases it can also be argued that the Valley was better served through TVA support of state and local planning agencies than if TVA had attempted to centralize regional planning within the organization.

Conclusion

The TVA has been most effective where it has functioned as a technocratic rather than a grass-roots operation. Appeal to a grass-roots ideology has not enabled the TVA to escape either the strengths or the limitations of its role as an agency of the federal government. But its image as an apolitical technocratic organization has been a major source of political strength in dealing with critics and supporters in both the Valley and Washington.

This perspective has significant implications for TVA's future pattern of evolution. The role of TVA as a regional development agency can be expected to continue to recede in response to the evolution of federal and state economic development activities. But in an era in which the sources of energy supply and the structure of the electric power industry are expected to undergo considerable change, it is somewhat easier to imagine the TVA developing a national electrical energy R&D capacity, along the lines of the National Fertilizer Development Center, than a national laboratory for the development of urban-based regions.

NOTES

I have benefited from comments on an earlier draft of this paper by Richard M. Freeman, Erwin C. Hargrove, John V. Krutilla, Stefan H. Robock, Wesley G. Smith, and George W. Wilson.

1. For a useful description of the regional dimensions of economic development in the Tennessee Valley, see Wesley G. Smith, "Demographic and Economic Trends in the Tennessee Valley Region," in TVA, *Final Report, Core Policy Analysis Group* (Knoxville, Tenn., June 20 , 1980, mimeo). Even by the mid-1950s it was apparent that the remaining differences in family incomes between the South (and the TVA) and the rest of the United States were due primarily to differences in racial composition, differences in city size, and differences in the ratio of farm to nonfarm population. In 1950 family incomes of white urban families in the South were approximately the same in cities of comparable. size as in the rest of the country. See D. Gale Johnson, "Some Effects of Region, Community Size, Color and Occupation on Family and Individual Income," in *Studies in Income and Wealth*, 15 (New York: National Bureau of Economic Research, 1952): 50–74; Edwin Mansfield, "City Size and Income, 1949," *Studies in Income and Wealth*, 21 (New York: National Bureau of Economic Research, 1957): 271–307. The effect of city size and urbanization has been neglected in a number of recent studies that point to a narrowing but continuing disparity in family income or earnings between the South and the rest of the

United States. See, for example, Charles Hirschman and Kim Blankenship, "The North-South Earnings Gap: Changes during the 1960s and 1970s," *American Journal of Sociology*, 87 (Sept., 1981): 388–403.

2. The results of several TVA staff studies conducted in the 1950s have been summarized in Stefan H. Robock, "Integrated River-Basin Development and Industrialization: The Tennessee Valley Experience," in *Science, Technology and Development*, U.S. Papers Prepared for the UN Conference on the Application of Science and Technology for the Benefit of the Less Developed Areas, vol. 4, *Industrial Development* (Washington, D.C.: U.S. Government Printing Office, 1963); Stefan H. Robock, "An Unfinished Task: A Socio-Economic Evaluation of the TVA Experiment," in John H. Moore, ed., *The Economic Impact of TVA* (Knoxville: University of Tennessee Press, 1967), pp. 105–20. See also the very useful discussion in Hans Knop, ed., *The Tennessee Valley Authority Experience*, 2 vols., CP-76-2 (Laxenburg, Austria: International Institute for Applied Systems Analysis, 1976).

3. For a useful expression of the 1930s version of the mature-economy thesis, see the presidential address to the American Economic Association by Alvin Hansen, "Economic Progress and Declining Population Growth," *American Economic Review*, 29 (Mar., 1939): 1–15. Several of the papers in this volume, particularly those by Paul Conkin and Craufurd Goodwin, trace the implications of the mature-economy perspective for the TVA Act and early TVA program development.

4. Theodore W. Schultz, *Investing in People* (Berkeley: University of California Press, 1981).

5. See John R. P. Friedman, "The Spatial Structure of Economic Development in the Tennessee Valley: A Study in Regional Planning" (Chicago: University of Chicago Program of Education and Research in Planning, Mar., 1955); Vernon W. Ruttan, "The Impact of Urban-Industrial Development on Farm and Nonfarm Income," *Journal of Farm Economics*, 37 (Feb., 1955): 38–56. For a more recent discussion see Ralph R. Widner, "Regional Development in the Tennessee Valley Region," in TVA, *The Role of TVA Programs in Regional Development: The 1979 Summer Policy Study* (Knoxville, Tenn., Mar., 1981), sec. 2.

6. A number of TVA urban initiatives have been reviewed by Ally Mack, "TVA and Urban Development," in TVA, *Role of TVA Programs in Regional Development*. See also the report on energy conservation activities by the Division of Energy Conservation and Rates, *Program Summary, 1981* (Chattanooga: TVA Office of Power, Apr., 1981).

7. Philip Selznick, *TVA and the Grass Roots: A Study in the Sociology of Formal Organization* (New York: Harper and Row, 1966, reprinted); Norman F. Wengert, *Valley of Tommorrow: The TVA and Agriculture* (Knoxville: University of Tennessee, Bureau of Public Administration, 1952).

8. A more serious charge against the TVA agricultural and rural development program is that, until recently, TVA had not worked directly with the traditionally black agricultural colleges (referred to as the 1890 colleges, in contrast to the land grant colleges established under the 1862 legislation) to strengthen services to disadvantaged farmers. See Handy Williamson, Jr., "TVA and Rural Development," in TVA, *Role of TVA Programs in Regional Development*.

9. For background on TVA tributary area development activities, see Donald T. Wells, *The TVA Tributary Area Development Program* (University: University of Alabama, Bureau of Public Administration, 1964); George J. Gordon, "Intergovernmental Relations in the Tennessee Valley" (Ph.D. dissertation, Syracuse University, 1971).

10. See Chapter 9 of this volume.

11. The TVA may represent an important institutional prototype for the delinking of energy production and wholesaling functions from energy retailing. I would hypothesize that the countervailing power inherent in such a market structure would result in better market performance than under existing regulatory regimes. The delinking of wholesaling and retailing was suggested in a 1968 staff study by Resources for the Future, *U.S. Energy Policies: An Agenda for Research* (Washington, D.C., 1968). The RFF report raises the question of whether "prospective changes in technology argue for a limited number of regional generation and transmission organizations which serve as wholesale power supply organizations to retail distribution systems" (p. 98). The RFF argument is based primarily on technical considerations. There is a rapidly growing literature on the issue of deregulation of electric generation. However, this literature has not confronted the issue of the structural reforms in the organization of the electric power industry that would be necessary to induce competitive behavior and efficient performance.

12. Richard W. Poston, "TVA and the Region's Communities," in TVA, *Role of TVA Programs in Regional Development.*

13. Lawrence L. Durisch and Robert E. Lowry, "The Scope and Content of Administrative Decision—The TVA Illustration," *Public Administration Review*, 13 (Autumn, 1953): 219–26. The Durisch-Lowry paper has been reviewed and updated by Charles M. Stephenson, "Administrative Decision Revisited: TVA Experience since 1953" (Oct. 15, 1975), copy in TVA Technical Library, Knoxville, Tenn.

14. For a brief overview of the development of the TVA nuclear power program, see George E. Rawson, "The Process of Program Development: The Case of TVA's Power Program" (Ph.D. dissertation, University of Tennessee, 1978), pp. 74–104. Rawson indicates that the TVA was much less successful in dealing with the environmental consequences of its coal and nuclear power programs (pp. 104–56). See also Hans Knop, ed., *The Tennessee Valley Authority: A Field Study* (Laxenburg, Austria: International Institute for Applied Systems Analysis, June, 1979).

15. Considerable attention has been focused on the development implications of low-cost power relative to the implications of an adequate power supply. See, for example, Bruce C. Netschert, "Electric Power and Economic Development," in Moore, ed., *Economic Impact of TVA*, pp. 1–24. There can be little argument about the contribution to the quality of life of the extension of electric power to farms and communities where it had previously been unavailable. Nor can there be much doubt about the importance of the availability of electricity as a factor in the decentralization of economic activity. It would be of interest, however, to ask what would be the employment and income effects on the Tennessee Valley if electric power had been available at a price equal to the national or regional average rather than at the prices that have actively prevailed. Given the large share of TVA power that is used by a relatively few energy-intensive industrial firms and federal facilities, my guess is that the reduction in total nonfarm employment in the Valley (2,578,500 in 1977) would be surprisingly small. Such a finding should not be taken to imply that the investment in the power capacity to respond to energy-intensive private and public sector demand has not had a reasonable rate of return when evaluated at the national level.

16. Plant no. 1 was an experimental plant designed to produce synthetic ammonia (Haber process). Plant no. 2 was a commercial-scale plant designed to produce cyanamide. For a more complete discussion see Chapter 1 of this volume.

17. Vernon W. Ruttan, "Integrated Rural Development Programs: A Skeptical Perspective," *International Development Review*, 17 (Dec., 1975): 9–16.

18. Gordon R. Clapp, *The TVA: An Approach to the Development of a Region* (Chi-

cago: University of Chicago Press, 1965), p. 144; Wilmon H. Droze, "TVA and the Ordinary Farmer," *Agricultural History*, 53 (Oct., 1979): 188–202. See also Wengert, *Valley of Tomorrow*.

19. For a useful review, see Office of the General Manager, *The Federal Government's Role in Fertilizer Research and Development* (Knoxville: TVA, June, 1978, mimeo).

20. TVA, *Role of TVA Programs in Regional Development*.

PART THREE

Contemporary Problems

7

William Bruce Wheeler
Michael J. McDonald

The "New Mission" and
the Tellico Project, 1945–70

B Y the end of World War II, TVA could look back on its
record since its birth in 1933 with a certain amount of
justifiable pride. Its high-dam program on the Tennessee
River had been nearly completed; in terms of power production, navigation, and flood control, its goals had been achieved; through Alcoa
and AEC it had made itself vital to the war effort. Indeed, by almost
every criterion TVA had been one of the great success stories of modern
history. In 1945 TVA was triumphant.

Yet the end of World War II marked the beginning of a period of uncertainty, indecision, and drift. With the achievement of its earlier
goals, TVA recognized the need to rearticulate its mission. Many within
the agency had come to realize that abundant, cheap power alone would
not rejuvenate a region thrust from a premodern to an industrial climate
in less than two decades. Clearly a "new mission" was necessary for
TVA to save the Valley and itself. The search for such a mission, from
1945 to 1970, caused considerable internal conflict. In the 1950s, owing
to a complex interaction of national mood, budgetary considerations,
and backgrounds of policy-making administrators and intra-agency politics, the notion of tributary area development had emerged triumphant,
symbolized in 1961 by the creation of the Office of Tributary Area Development (OTAD) and the elevation to the directorship of Aubrey J. Wagner, the principal supporter of that concept.

The building of the Tellico Dam on the Little Tennessee River forced TVA to publicly articulate its new mission. Although technically not a tributary but a main-river project and hence not within the purview of OTAD, Tellico was the place where TVA believed it had to take a public stand in defense of its new mission as the agency that could change nearly every aspect of life in the tributary areas. The Tellico debate, however, revealed that TVA's postwar new mission was in fact a reduced version of its old mission, in which each tributary area was seen as a microcosm of the entire Valley. The Tellico controversy also revealed that TVA still viewed the region much as it had in the Roosevelt years. Ambivalent about public involvement in Authority plans or projects, sensitive to criticism, and seeing themselves as "humanistic engineers" who could escort the region into the modern age, many TVA officials were confused, hurt, and angered by attacks against the Authority. By this time many of the Authority's first generation had retired, leaving a new generation to search again for mission and for vision.

Although not specifically mentioned in its charter, industrial development had never been far from the collective mind of TVA's first generation. However, the Great Depression and internal conflicts within the agency forced those advocates to bide their time. The Depression had seriously weakened industries throughout the country and (as economist John V. Krutilla recalled) "in the face of a depressed national economy . . . the prospects for expanding regional employment in manufacturing did not look at all promising."[1]

But if the notion of TVA's mission as that of industrializing the Valley was temporarily defeated, it was never obliterated. TVA's first generation was transplanted midwesterners, men who almost naturally had compared agriculture in the Midwest to that of the Appalachian South, and had found the latter wanting. If the Valley was to be brought into the modern age, they reasoned, it could never be as an agricultural region, given its average farm size, soil types, inability to mechanize, and agricultural practices. To these men, many of them engineers, the key to the Valley's future was its ability to use abundant and cheap power and the region's natural resources to attract industries. Their faith in science and technology to change the environment and those who lived in it showed them as both concerned, decent men and as *naifs*. That they presumed to know what was best for the region made them at once altruistic and skeptical of the people's own ideas.[2]

These men did not have to wait long to find willing audiences both inside and outside TVA. As World War II neared its end, many within

TVA openly began to ask, "What does TVA do now?" In 1942 General Manager Gordon Clapp directed the Department of Regional Studies to make postwar plans for the agency. By May 1944 Steps I and II of the working papers had been completed (Step III would be finished in late 1945). "Further industrial development of the Tennessee Valley region is necessary to accomplish the best use of its human and physical resources," the authors of the Step II working papers firmly asserted. Steps II and III went so far as to list several potential industries that might be attracted to the region.[3] By 1945 it was clear that an engineering mentality had come to dominate TVA, grounded on the assumption that most (if not all) problems could be solved by technology if the scientists and engineers had sufficient capital and were protected from both political and popular pressure and scrutiny.

The "power people" (concentrated in but not exclusively dominating the Office of Power) by the late 1940s had become more interested in industrial development. Their reasoning was simple: having been created, now power had to be consumed, used for the benefit of the Valley. "The 'power people' were very active," remembers one former TVA employee, "since they were always looking to sell power." Moreover, in order to justify further power development and projects (a number of which were planned for the postwar years), power consumption would have to increase dramatically. Industrial development was the most obvious answer. Hence G. O. Wessenauer (who eventually became director of the Office of Power and one of the most influential men in the agency) began actively to support this "larger mission" for TVA.[4]

Other groups joined the power people in moving the agency toward encouragement of industrial development. Economists and planners within the Office of Regional Planning (earlier the Department of Regional Studies) for some time had called for industrial development as one component of regionwide planning. So too had navigation and natural resources people. In a somewhat difficult vein, the once-important Project Planning Division of the Office of Water Control recognized that unless it embraced the new mission, its tasks and influence would be seriously diminished.

At the same time the agriculture people, who with the power people had virtually dominated TVA during its formative years in the 1930s, saw their power deteriorating and their ideas increasingly ignored. In the Step III working papers of late 1945 agriculture clearly played less of a role in TVA's postwar planning. Indeed, as agriculture's share of the Valley's combined income declined from 23 percent in 1929 to 18 percent in 1946 (and would reach 11 percent by 1953) and the percentage of

Valley residents employed in agriculture declined from 56.4 percent in 1929 to 29.1 percent in 1953, the influence of agriculture people within TVA seemed to decline too.[5]

Hence a host of internal and external factors by the late 1940s had led TVA to perceive its new mission as being a complete economic regeneration of the Valley, largely through industrial development. Industrialization was to provide the agency with the linchpin of a comprehensive plan for development that would enlist the cooperation of state agencies and local development groups.

It was almost natural that these planning and development projects would be on the tributaries rather than on the main river. Thus the agency could concentrate the full force of its expertise on one limited area and then move on to another until the whole Valley had been regenerated. In 1938 one TVA study had identified 100 watershed areas in the Valley that had serious problems. Within the agency many who championed industrial development were connected with construction projects (Power, Project Planning, Navigation, Resources, etc.). Since the main-river projects essentially had been completed by 1945, these groups supported tributary area development as the key to future construction. Others, economists and regional planners, for instance, recognized that tributary projects would allow the agency to acquire significant amounts of shoreline property that could be used for economic development. As Chairman Aubrey Wagner was to say later, "Should land [suited to industry] be preempted by homes or cabins or stores, the cost to industry for purchase and redevelopment would become prohibitive. A community which allows this to happen is depriving its future citizens of jobs and payrolls. . . ."[6] With approximately 10,000 miles of shoreline in the Valley (equal to that of the Great Lakes), the possibilities for planning and development appeared endless.[7]

This new mission received tremendous impetus from Aubrey J. ("Red") Wagner, one of the first generation who rose within the agency and brought his vision along with him. A native of Wisconsin and graduate of the University of Wisconsin School of Engineering, Wagner joined TVA in 1934 as an engineering aide. He became director of the Navigation and Transportation Branch of that division in 1948, assistant to the general manager in 1951, general manager in 1954, board member in 1961, and finally chairman of the board in 1962.

From his early years in TVA, Wagner became convinced that widespread industrial development of the tributary areas was preferable to concentration of industries in the region's few large cities. "Wagner was

rural oriented," remembers one former TVA employee. "The idea of factories in the fields was great for him." Wagner's notion was that each
tributary area was a microcosm of the entire Valley and that "we needed
miniature TVAs in the tributaries." Moreover, Wagner believed that the
cooperation of state agencies and local citizens in the tributaries was
vital to achieve lasting success. "It was part of our original grass roots
philosophy," he recalled, although there was little doubt in his—or
anyone's—mind that the agency's technological expertise ought to make
it the senior partner in any cooperative venture.[8]

Wagner's influence was an important factor in the organization of a
Tributary Area Committee in the early 1950s. Apparently he was concerned that the agriculture people would capture control of the tributary area movement, something he was loathe to let happen. As a result,
the Tributary Area Committee's membership (which reported to Wagner) was skewed away from agriculture and toward Wagner's preference
for industrial development. Included on the committee were Reed Elliot
(director, Division of Water Control Planning), J. Porter Taylor (director,
division of Navigation and Flood Control), Louis J. Van Mol (chief budget officer), and Leland Allbaugh (director, Division of Agricultural Relations). Eventual chairman of the committee, reporting to Wagner, was
Richard Kilbourne, director of the Division of Forestry, whose major
concern had been persuading industries to use the Valley's forestry
products.[9]

The first test case of this new mission came in the Chestuee watershed, a project so modest that former TVA people (except Kilbourne) do
not look back on it as such. The Chestuee watershed (near Athens, Tennessee) had been identified by the agency in 1938 as one of the 100
"problem areas." In 1939 local residents requested TVA's aid in arrest-
ing the periodic flooding of valuable farmland. Until 1951 the agency's
role was limited to conducting studies, many of which went far beyond
the local residents' requests for flood control assistance. Ultimately,
however, TVA did little except to direct local residents in the removal
of debris from the creeks and make some plans for the further development of the area.[10]

But although the Chestuee project was a modest one, TVA learned
lessons it would later apply to other projects. The Tributary Area Committee (and hence Wagner) learned, as Robert E. Lowry later stated,
"While the citizen group was primarily concerned with flood problems,
it was possible to channel local interests into other problems." Those
on the Tributary Area Committee also learned that influential groups
within TVA would not support a project which did not involve con-

struction of some kind and a broader planning vision than that assigned to TVA in its original charter.[11]

For this reason the Beech River Watershed Project was crucial to advocates of a new mission for TVA. Southwest of Nashville (in Henderson and Decatur counties), the Beech River area suffered from flooding and erosion, the lack of drinkable water for the city of Lexington, and the massive outmigration of its population because of lack of employment.[12]

"Beech River is where we really took off," recalls Kilbourne. Ironically, the project originated in complaints from local citizens that TVA had been responsible for flooding their land. The agency responded with a comprehensive effort that included flood control, reforestation, and (not surprisingly) planning for industrialization. "Beech River became a *total* project," Wagner remembered. "Anything needed for the development of the area, we could do." Indeed, Lowry's model report on Beech River (*Working with Areas of Special Need, with Examples from the Beech River Watershed*, 1952) projected that TVA's involvement in the area would produce improved land use, greater nonfarm employment and income, and better community services and facilities. TVA encouraged the creation of the Beech River Watershed Development Association (BRWDA), undertook construction and planning projects in the area (several dams were built), and in general focused its attention on a watershed area badly in need of it. The results were both remarkable and predictable.[13]

Kilbourne remembers the excitement the Beech River project elicited among those in TVA committed to the agency's new mission. "There was the idea floating around that TVA could come in and completely remake the community," he recalls with a sense of both wistfulness and exhilaration. Kilbourne also notes that the always influential power people were not initially impressed by the Beech River efforts: "The 'power people' didn't have much of a role in this. They sort of stood on the sideline and poo-pooed the whole thing. They thought they were above all this nonsense." Yet, as Wagner recognized, if Power couldn't be brought into line, then his "new vision" would be broken apart on the rocks of intra-agency discord and division.[14]

Yet if the Beech River Watershed Project was the true test case of the agency's new mission, TVA was slow to follow up this "model experiment" with expanded tributary projects. A number of factors account for this rather curious lethargy. To begin with, the power people had displayed mixed feelings toward both Chestuee and Beech River. Defense-related power consumption (largely at Oak Ridge) had helped to account for an elevenfold increase in power consumption between 1950 and 1955. Hence problems of consumption were less pressing than the power people had believed in 1945. More important, the Eisenhower administration created a good deal of uncertainty within the agency. Fearing that many of TVA's prior gains might be eradicated by a Republican administration apparently dominated by big business interests, the agency purposely kept a low profile. Too, budgetary limitations obliged TVA to pull back from its expansive—but also costly—new mission. The Dixon-Yates controversy and the return of the town of Norris to private ownership were but two incidents which convinced the Agency that it would be unwise to forge ahead. Indeed, although the first generation of TVA consistently maintained that it was independent of politics, the agency's response to the shifting political sands of the 1950s proved quite the opposite.[15]

Ironically, the Beech River Watershed Project caused a flurry of interest in the Tennessee Valley, even as TVA was drawing back in response to the political climate of the 1950s. A number of local communities (largely through chambers of commerce or development associations) came to the agency seeking planning, technological assistance, money, and jobs. "Other groups heard about Beech River," recalls Kilbourne, "and they wanted in." TVA's response was to encourage the formation of area development associations that (with the states) might be able to share the costs of future projects. In the 1950s the agency was unwilling—and unable—to take on the full financing of tributary area development projects. When the Elk River Association appealed to TVA for a dam, planning, and area development, Chairman Herbert Vogel replied coldly that the benefit-cost ratio would make it unfeasible unless state and local interests could assume part of the cost or (to be important later) unless new factors could be added into the benefit-cost ratio so as to make the project economically defensible. The same message was communicated to the recently created Duck River Development Association. Both groups lobbied in Congress for appropriations, but TVA sagaciously kept its low profile in these matters.[16]

By the late 1950s, however, pressure both inside and outside TVA was increasing for the agency to become more active in tributary area development. Beginning in 1959, Congress required TVA's power projects to be self-financing. This budgetary shift threatened the influential power people. Since congressional appropriations to TVA at that time were not earmarked for specific purposes, the power people (led by Wessenauer) conceived the idea of draining off funds from other offices within the agency. Recognizing that tributary area development not only would require additional power projects but also would be a convenient shield, Wessenauer and the power people began to push enthusiastically for tributary projects. Moreover, the victory of John F. Kennedy presaged a dramatic shift of attitudes in the White House, one that would be receptive to bold ideas for the uplift of "depressed areas."[17]

Wagner lost no time in setting the wheels in motion. In March, 1961, he created the Office of Tributary Area Development (OTAD) and named Kilbourne its first director. OTAD was charged with identifying high-priority projects, working with local groups, and planning for tributary development. In response to local appeals for projects, OTAD sent people into the areas ("men on the ground," as they were called) who formed local committees dealing with every facet of the area.[18]

Problems arose immediately. Inside TVA the creation of OTAD caused opposition, the majority of it coming from Regional Planning. By 1961 Regional Planning had become convinced that the future of the Valley lay in comprehensive planning that would encourage industrial development in small cities (Morristown, Kingsport, Newport, for instance), uplifting the service sector in the larger but declining industrial cities (Knoxville, for example), and cooperating with state agencies. In the eyes of Regional Planning, OTAD was going about the process all wrong: it maintained the notion of "factories amidst the fields," held to an exceedingly limited view of regional development, and worked through local rather than state agencies and organizations. "They wanted to start up little TVAs all over the Valley," one former TVA employer explained, "and that was taking the easy way out by trying to repeat TVA's successes, only on a much smaller scale." Apparently Wagner stifled this internal feud, though it left a residue of bitterness for years afterward.

Outside TVA there were problems too. Though it probably can never be proven, many got the impression that OTAD actually *created* the local interest groups which subsequently applied to TVA for projects. "They dangled the bait of dams, power, jobs and money," commented one former TVA employee (who requested that his name be withheld). More serious, however, was the problem of getting local groups and OTAD-created committees to bow to the agency's superior expertise. Kilbourne recalls that he "didn't like these local groups telling us what we ought to do. . . . We had to be diplomatic about the whole business." But TVA maintained the upper hand, giving much advice and accepting little input.[19]

In 1962 the United States Senate issued a report of the President's Water Resources Council, which called for multiple uses for rivers, lakes, and shorelines. Of course, TVA had been moving in that direction since 1945 at the latest. Later, TVA employees used Senate Document 97 as a justification for what the agency had decided to do years earlier.[20]

OTAD's accomplishments, noted in its yearly newsletter, were indeed impressive. At roughly a dozen tributary areas OTAD set up local committees, identified needs, and then moved to meet those needs. This approach to each tributary area meant that the projects OTAD carried out were as diverse as the Tennessee Valley. Educational programs were set up, as was school drop-out counseling; "townlift" projects, encouragement of tourism and recreation, collection of abandoned automobiles from roadsides, preparation of historical brochures—all were undertaken. Industrial site surveys were done, solid waste disposal problems were solved, reforestation and forest industry planning were done, dams were planned and constructed. Indeed, as Richard Kilbourne later stated, there was nothing OTAD would not do.[21]

On the other side of the ledger, OTAD's foray into local cooperation and popular participation must be judged as less than successful. On the Upper French Broad (Mills River) project, a group of retired people badly outmaneuvered the agency, turned the citizenry against TVA, and almost literally chased OTAD and TVA out. Too, once the gates of TVA had been opened to popular participation—however limited—they could never be closed completely again.

The history of the Tellico Dam parallels the postwar search by TVA for a new mission. Indeed, by the late 1950s the two movements had become tightly intertwined: the Tellico project became the conjuncture of the agency's revised land purchase policy, the intra-agency decline of the agriculturalists, the emphasis on industrial development, the devising of more imaginative methods of computing benefit-cost analyses, the use of citizen cooperation and support, and the affirmation of the new mission of creating "little TVAs" in the tributary areas throughout the Valley. In truth although the Tellico project always was seen by the agency as a main-river project (connected as it was to the earlier Fort Loudoun Dam project), it nevertheless became—especially after the failure at Mills River—the test case for the new mission, a mission which in many ways was not very new at all.

The controversial Tellico Dam project on the Little Tennessee River (known locally as the "Little T") owes its existence to the fact that TVA's main-river dam below Knoxville, the Fort Loudoun (earlier Coulter Shoals) Dam was built above the entrance of the Little T into the Tennessee River. From the beginning there was raised the possibility of a dam across the Little T (in 1936 called the Davis Ferry project and later Tellico) that would divert its waters into Fort Loudoun Reservoir via a diversion canal, to improve navigation on the Tennessee below Fort Loudoun and to increase power-generating and flood control capacities. Though planned in tandem with the Fort Loudoun Dam, the Tellico project was vetoed in the summer of 1942 by the War Production Board because of a scarcity of steel. But to TVA planners and engineers Tellico remained a main-river project through its connection with Fort Loudoun Dam, and even though TVA deftly turned aside congressional and local inquiries about the status of the Tellico project, the question was not whether it would be built but when.[22]

In 1959–60 there was a flurry of activity surrounding Tellico. In July, 1959, Chief Water Control Planning Engineer Reed Elliot informed Don Mattern (chief of the Project Planning Branch) and R. E. Frierson that "we had planned, in setting up the 1960 Budget, to concentrate on Fort Loudoun Extension."[23] Never one to misread between the lines, Mattern ordered a number of on-site inspections of "the area which would be flooded": mineral inspection, relocation, land costs, and navigation studies.[24] By the end of March, 1960, Elliot had digested these preliminary investigations and offered his own synopsis of them. The total cost, he estimated, would be $55,800,000 and the benefit-cost ratio of the project would be roughly 1:1. Although Elliot didn't know it then, the benefits-cost ratio would be a crucial issue.[25] Yet even though there were strong indications that TVA was determined to go ahead with the Tellico project, the agency continued to maintain a low public profile. Three months after Elliot's memorandum to Mattern, Vogel replied to an inquiry from a person interested in buying a farm in the area "to go ahead with his plans as if nothing would ever happen."[26]

Clearly TVA had raised the Tellico project to top priority by 1959. Why it did so is more complex. As noted above, several groups within TVA were pushing the agency toward embracing a new mission involving industrialization and tributary area development. At the same time, local citizens' groups, having seen what TVA was doing at Beech River, were appealing to the agency for dams and simultaneously lobbying in Congress for line item appropriations for their respective projects. Two of the most effective of these citizens' groups were those at Elk River and Duck River, both in middle Tennessee. Although General Vogel (an Eisenhower appointee) had echoed a version of the president's notion of federal partnership with the people when he urged the formation of a Valley-wide "citizens association" that would plan for the future development of the Tennessee Valley, what sprang up instead were local groups with limited vision and perspective.[27] Moreover, TVA seems to have feared that these local groups would throw enough political weight that the Authority would become a mere "pork-barrel" agency that would be ordered to build dams at the beck and call of local groups. TVA clearly *did* want to build more dams and (as Wagner said) "fill in the gaps with a fine brush," but not at the price of becoming a technological tool of others.

Replying to these local requests, Vogel explained that the poor benefit-cost ratios for those projects made them unfeasible. Clearly what Vogel wanted was for the state agencies or the local groups themselves to shoulder a portion of the costs. But the local groups remained firm, urging TVA to recalculate benefit-cost ratios by taking into account economic benefits in addition to navigation, flood control, and power. They suggested that the agency also figure in land enhancement, recreation, and water supply, something that TVA had heretofore been unwilling to do.[28]

But the scheme, once planted in the collective mind of TVA, would not go away. If the agency could recalculate benefit-cost ratios for local projects on the Elk or Duck rivers, why not for Tellico? Project Planning, regional planners, and the tributary people all were pushing for new projects. Moreover, because of its links to the Fort Loudoun Dam, Tellico (once Fort Loudoun Extension) was the uncompleted part of that ambitious project. In the mind of an engineer an uncompleted project was unacceptable. For all these reasons Tellico rose rapidly on the agency's priority list.

In late summer of 1960 General Manager Aubrey Wagner informed Chief Engineer George P. Palo that Tellico would not be included in the fiscal 1962 budget because of a poor benefit-cost ratio, but "the Tellico Project is a most promising one in which to try out new methods of economic justification." "It is essential," continued Wagner, "that we move ahead as rapidly as possible to apply to the Tellico project any new and different methods we can devise for justification and financing, looking toward construction of the project and starting to capture its benefits at as early a date as is feasible." Further, Wagner ordered Palo to have on his desk "by the beginning of 1961" a coordinated report on Tellico, "coming up with as many new ideas and methods of justification and financing as can be developed by that time to complement conventional methods of economic justification."[29]

In response to Wagner's order, Palo circulated a memo asking for suggestions on economic justification.[30] J. Porter Taylor suggested calculating benefits by each function.[31] From Richard Kilbourne, coordinator of the Tributary Watersheds Program, came more constructive advice. Kilbourne suggested that the key to benefit calculation came, or would come, from shoreline industrial development, especially in the "extensive areas of prime industrial development" up and downstream from the point where the L&N Railroad and highway 411 crossed the Little Tennessee at Niles Ferry. Kilbourne spoke of the need to acquire "adequate land" along reservoir margins.[32] TVA's Manager of Power G. O. Wessenauer only reiterated to Palo what Wagner had earlier stressed: "It is my present opinion that construction of the project depends entirely on finding means of justification which go beyond navigation, flood control and power programs." Wessenauer argued that preliminary figures put the power benefits too high and the cost too low.[33] Despite Wagner's urgings, however, by November not much had been done in calculating new benefit-cost ratios.

The benefit-cost ratio was the major obstacle. Kilbourne had the key, but internal conflicts within TVA (even among those favoring Tellico) prevented him from using it. Kilbourne saw the agency's future linked to industrial development on the tributaries. Once it became clear that TVA was going to shift its attention temporarily from tributary area development (Elk River and Duck River projects) to Tellico, Kilbourne shifted too. Obviously he saw Tellico as a slight variation of tributary area development and determined to get his tributary people involved. "'Red' [Wagner] asked us to get involved early," Kilbourne later recalled. To Kilbourne, the "tributary area approach" was just what Tellico needed.[34]

But Regional Planning had other ideas. As noted above, they insisted that the agency develop a Valley-wide plan for industrial development, scoffed at the "factory in the fields" notion, thought the tributary people were mistaken in cultivating local rather than state cooperation. Not opposed to industrial development per se, Regional Planning called for a "bigger picture" that would see Tellico through the prism of the needs of the entire Valley.[35]

"I'm not sure Wagner ever fully perceived the philosophical differences between what was to become OTAD and Regional Planning," explains one former TVA employee. "But Mike Foster [Millard 'Mike' Foster, economist and eventual head of Navigation and Regional Studies] fought the tributary people tooth and nail." Foster had access to Wagner and apparently was able to convince him that, since Tellico was a main-river project, the tributary people should not get involved. As it turned out, the loosening of congressional purse strings in the mid-1960s gave the tributary people (by then OTAD) plenty to do.[36]

Hence, in computing Tellico's benefit-cost ratio, Kilbourne's saga-cious suggestion was in essence ignored. Instead, by the end of 1960 the agency was concentrating on land value enhancement as a benefit to be added into the earlier calculations. As Robert Coker (chief, Land Branch, Division of Property and Supply) reported to Robert Howes (Division of Reservoir Properties), land purchased by TVA but not inundated would cost $3.6 million and its estimated land value enhancement (at the end of 100 years) would be $10,850,000.[37] This tactic represents the dramatic (though quiet) final victory of those advocating major land purchases above the projected waterline. Although supporters of this policy always had emphasized TVA's planning role as well as industrial and recre-ational development, by late 1960 the major-purchase policy, a reversal of TVA policy since the building of Fort Loudoun Dam, was being used initially to get the Tellico project off the ground.

The beginning of 1961 saw a flurry of news releases on the Tellico project, since it was listed as "under consideration" in the 1960 annual year-end report. The *Knoxville News Sentinel* reported Vogel as saying that costs and benefits were roughly equal and appealing to state and local governments and local individuals to foot the bill.[38] Local news media clearly identified TVA as looking to "justify" the Tellico dam, and seeing it as a stimulus to a locally flagging economy.[39]

By early 1961, then, the fact that TVA was bogged down over the benefit-cost ratio problem was general knowledge. In February, 1961, Palo informed Wagner that a further cost reduction for Tellico had been obtained. The first cost reduction (in November, 1960) had been from $55.8 million to $53 million. In terms of benefits, however, Palo added that increased power production alone was not enough to produce a de-sired ratio: ". . . inclusion of other benefits are needed to make Tellico an unquestionably justified project.[40] Such a justification, confessed Palo to Van Mol, was "difficult." Palo continued to maintain that the Tellico project should be built, but that it would have to be justified by unorthodox means.[41]

Kenneth Seigsworth, TVA's director of Forestry Development, pin-pointed the problem. "Sometime, somehow," Seigsworth wrote to Palo, "the sticky question must be faced of how the public can capture a sub-stantial portion of land enhancement which a publicly financed reser-voir project creates."[42] Put another way, Seigsworth asked precisely what "land enhancement" meant. Did it mean that TVA itself would develop recreational and industrial facilities on the Little Tennessee River? Or did it mean that TVA would purchase significant amounts of land above the projected waterline which in turn would be sold to those private interests who would develop the area in the proper way? Even if it was provided for in TVA's charter (and that point was unclear), the former would be too expensive. Hence the agency was led back to a position that embraced industrial and recreational development by private interests, and of adding those economic benefits to Tellico's benefit-cost ratio.[43]

By mid-1963 industrial and recreational development was being stressed heavily. Apparently the board agreed, for it approved the Tellico project and resolved that construction should begin in 1965. To protect itself, the board also ordered further justification studies, one of which spoke glowingly of the new jobs that Tellico would create in the area. Palo was enthusiastic: "We know of no better project than Tellico on which to test these new justification methods and believe that delay in Tellico may delay equally consideration of start of other water resource projects."[44]

If Palo can be taken literally (and there is nothing to suggest otherwise), then many within TVA saw Tellico as a test case; if it were successful, then several similar projects emphasizing industrial development on the tributaries could be initiated. Wagner clearly was committed, as were Palo, Kilbourne, Mattern, Wessenauer, Elliot, Taylor, Howes, and Foster. For them and for others, this was to be TVA's new mission and Tellico would be the opening salvo.

As seen above, this new mission required large land purchases above the projected waterline. But heavy purchase, whether done as in the thirties for watershed control and reservoir protection or as in the sixties for industrial siting and land enhancement, always does one thing—it raises severe agricultural opposition in local communities and offers opponents an excellent focus for resistance to TVA. In 1964 Bill Brock, a "comer" in Republican politics in Tennessee, made inquiries of TVA about "charges" he had heard "that in order to make the dam economically feasible, TVA proposes to buy the land surrounding the lake and sell it back at a high profit."[45] Replying to Brock, Wagner wrote that land had to be acquired "for maximum possible contribution to the economy of the region," and specifically used industrial and recreational developments as examples. Further, Wagner admitted that there would be great profits on the resale of land (which would be returned to the federal treasury) and that such enhancement was taken into account in computing the benefit-cost ratio. But Wagner denied that creating a good benefit-cost ratio had been the reason TVA adopted the heavy land purchase policy at Tellico.[46]

Despite TVA's obvious commitment to build the Tellico Dam and the advanced stages of its planning, as late as mid-1963 the agency continued to present mixed messages. A. J. Gray of TVA's government relations and economics staff told the State Planning Commission of the "uncertainty of the project." One TVA official told a landowner that the project had not been authorized as yet but hinted that TVA would be acquiring property, and Reed Elliot informed David Dale Dickey, president of the Tennessee Outdoor Writers Association: "Our studies are not at the stage where we can provide detailed information on its [Tellico's] feasibility and justification as requested in your letter." Technically Elliot was correct, yet the implications of his remarks are misleading.

In spite of the agency's relatively low-keyed approach to the project, opposition to the Tellico Dam began to mount in 1963–64. That opposition, however, was fairly localized, does not appear to have been exceedingly strong, and was itself divided. Even with the organization in October, 1964, of the Association for the Preservation of the Little Tennessee River, the opposition grew neither stronger nor more united.[47]

The principal sources of opposition are interesting, though hardly surprising. Fishermen and outdoorsmen, aided in part by the Tennessee Outdoor Writers Association and some members of the State Game and Fish Commission, complained that the area was the only section of the Little Tennessee River still undammed. The *Tennessee Outdoor Record*, a publication devoted to outdoor recreational activities, accused TVA of having a "to hell with everybody; we're running the show" attitude, and also insinuated that many within TVA were dubious about the project but were being ignored by "the engineers."[48]

Other early opponents of the Tellico project included some farmers, conservatives, and those concerned about the preservation of old Fort Loudoun, a fortification built by the British in the 1750s. Farm bureaus, livestock associations, farmers' cooperatives, and feeder pig associations opposed the project on the grounds that valuable farmland would be inundated. These groups (not all of which would be affected directly by the project) probably feared what they perceived as TVA's turning away from agriculture. Conservatives attacked the agency's large-purchase policy, seeing it as bringing the federal government into direct competition with private interests. In their view, to acquire property with the idea of selling it later at a profit was clearly a violation of the agency's charter. Finally, the Fort Loudoun advocates, many of them members of the Fort Loudoun Association (a local historical association some of whose members had political influence) objected that nothing

TVA could do would preserve the integrity of the site or the nearby Cherokee Indian village sites and burial grounds. Though active opponents later, the Cherokees themselves apparently were willing for others (especially the Fort Loudoun Association) to do their fighting for them in the early years.[49]

By early 1965 some twenty groups, most of them fishermen, outdoorsmen, and farmers, had gone on record as opposing the Tellico Dam. All available evidence, however, suggests that they represented only a minority of citizens of the three affected counties. Local businessmen's associations (Rotary, Civitan, chambers of commerce, Jaycees, and development associations) rushed to support the project. Indeed, a poll (based on reader responses to a questionnaire) taken by the *Monroe Citizen* in late 1964 showed that over 60 percent of the respondents favored building the dam.[50]

TVA had no intention of allowing public opinion to turn against the Tellico project. From Wagner on down, agency employees took to the hustings, defending the project at countless luncheons, association meetings, and public gatherings. Still believing that if the public were informed it would understand the benefits of the Tellico project, TVA people even accepted invitations to meetings where the groups were known to be hostile, as on September 22, 1964, when Wagner spoke to a large gathering at Greenback High School. One reporter covering the meeting estimated that 90 percent of the 400 who attended were opposed to the project, and only Wagner spoke in its favor. The TVA chairman was roughly handled verbally by the assemblage but managed to keep his composure, stating that the TVA didn't want to undertake any project where a majority of people were opposed. In response, Judge Sue K. Hicks called for a referendum on the dam, but Wagner avoided that by declaring that the project affected more people than just area residents. Disgusted, the *Madisonville Democrat* grumbled that "most persons believe that TVA will eventually 'decide what the people's choice is.'" Although the agency appears to have been determined to go ahead with the Tellico project, that charge was probably unfair.[51]

To assist Wagner and others engaged in public discussion and debate, the agency took great pains to make sure they were well prepared. Bernard Zellner and Kilbourne (both of OTAD) prepared lists of questions agency people were likely to encounter, together with well-researched answers. Simultaneously the Office of Information was bustling with activity, providing material for TVA people as well as for private groups supporting the project, as well as making sure that no local letters to editors remained unanswered. In November, 1964, the office

issued a white paper on "The Tellico Project" that was widely dissemi-
nated, run serially in some local newspapers, and provided in bulk to
private groups and citizens on record as favoring the project. Supporters might not always be well received, but they would never be ill
prepared.[52]

TVA took other approaches to neutralize criticism. What was needed,
many reasoned, was one local group to coordinate support and defend
the project. Hence the Tri-Counties Development Association was
formed in November, 1964. Though evidence is contradictory (and TVA
stoutly denies it), the Tri-Counties Development Association probably
owed its existence to TVA, which needed such a group to carry the Tellico banner. It is certain that TVA employees attended the meeting at
which the association was formed and lent considerable assistance. Exactly one week after the meeting the association met privately with the
TVA board to plan strategy, and the agency continued to provide information and materials to the association as long as it lived.[53]

The principal argument used by TVA to counter this early opposition was that the dam and large-purchase policy together would encourage industrial development in the area, bringing with it new jobs
and a halt to the debilitating outmigration of young people. Mike Foster
prepared analyses of regional outmigration and projections of how
many new jobs would be created, ammunition that Wagner used liberally both in his correspondence with influential political figures and in
public debates. Since Wagner believed that Tellico's flood control,
power, and navigation benefits would be "relatively insignificant" (a
statement TVA's Office of Information rushed to "correct"), he was playing what he considered to be his most powerful card.[54]

The delicate problem of Fort Loudoun still remained. Not only did
TVA not want to be cast as being insensitive to historic preservation (it
wasn't), but many TVA employees were emotionally attached to the fort
as a beautiful and historic landmark. Many had visited the fort with
their families, and Wagner used to take his Boy Scout troop camping in
this unique spot where men and nature met. In short, the agency was
determined to save Fort Loudoun if it could be done. The nearby Indian
sites, of course, could not be saved if the dam was built.[55]

However, every plan TVA devised failed to satisfy the Fort Loudoun
Association. At first TVA engineers proposed a series of earthen dikes,
but the association passed a resolution in December, 1964, that opposed
"any change in the topography of the region which would destroy
archaeological and historical evidence." In the end, the agency dismantled the fort, raised the level of the land seventeen feet, and recon-

structed the fort (with an attractive new visitors' center and museum) on that spot—all over the objections of many within the association.[56] As of 1982, all the work required by the original agreement with the Fort Loudoun Association has been completed at the site although additional constructs and improvements are still being made by the Department of Conservation of the state of Tennessee.

Hence, if TVA had not silenced the local critics of the Tellico project by 1965, at least it had contained them and stopped local opposition from spreading. President Johnson's 1966 budget (to be approved by Congress in 1965) carried a request for a sizable appropriation to begin the project. The agency was ready to begin construction in the spring of 1966. But speed was imperative, for new sources of opposition were beginning to crop up. If only it could be started, TVA probably reasoned, this new opposition would simply collapse.

But calamity then struck the Tellico project. In one of the most sagacious pieces of congressional wizardry in modern memory, Congressman Joe Evins of Tennessee's Fourth Congressional District was able to get the House Public Works Subcommittee to shift the Tellico appropriation to the Tims Ford project, which was in Evins's district. The House Appropriations Committee supported its subcommittee, and the whole House went along.[57]

TVA was stunned. Although Tims Ford was also an agency project, TVA believed it was vital to get Tellico underway before costs rose (thus destroying the delicate benefit-cost ratio) and opposition became stronger. In an effort to reverse the House's decision in the Senate, TVA encouraged private citizens and groups to endorse the Tellico project and put pressure on their congressmen. Forty-two local businessmen (including Knoxville Mayor Leonard Rogers) flew to Washington to plead Tellico's case, while the agency (according to some sources) began pressuring local groups for endorsement. Some members of the Knoxville Chamber of Commerce reported to one of the local newspapers that unseemly pressure had been applied, and Wagner made a personal appeal to the Knoxville City Council for its endorsement.[58]

At the center of the storm in the Senate was Democratic Senator Allen Ellender of Louisiana, hardly a friend of TVA. Always eager to embarrass the agency, Ellender concentrated on Tellico's most vulnerable spot: its suspicious benefit-cost ratio. The Louisiana senator ordered the Corps of Engineers, not exactly allies of TVA, to recompute the benefit-cost ratio. Few were surprised when the corps's report to Ellender stated that, in its opinion, TVA's ratio was much too high. In the end, however, the Senate subcommittee (over Ellender's objections) endorsed the Tellico project, switching the funds back from Tims Ford. Ultimately the full Senate went along.[59] But in the House-Senate conference committee, Evins again held sway. Once again the funds were switched from Tellico to Tims Ford. Tired of the battle, both houses deferred to Evins's wishes. In what he must have considered a magnanimous gesture, Evins told a group of disappointed Tellico proponents that he would support a Tellico appropriation in 1966.[60]

As the Tellico appropriations fight was being waged in Congress, Supreme Court Justice William O. Douglas visited the Tellico region, ostensibly to do some trout fishing. Once in Tennessee, the controversial jurist began making anti-Tellico statements. He met with representatives of the Eastern Band of the Cherokees at Chota, the site of an ancient Cherokee village that would be inundated by the Tellico project. Douglas promised the Cherokees that he would oppose the project, take their petition to Interior Secretary Stewart Udall, and write an article on the controversy for *National Geographic* magazine. While fishing, Douglas publicly lamented that this great trout stream would be lost (rumors circulated that the State Game and Fish Commission had stocked the river so Douglas's efforts would be rewarded).[61]

While Douglas probably was too damaged by past controversies to be of much help, his trip to Tennessee had several important consequences. For one thing, the Cherokees, who up to that time had kept a fairly low profile, now actively opposed the project. The inundation of their ancient burial sites had the potential of being an emotional issue that would put TVA in the worst possible light. Too, Douglas's visit for the first time focused national attention on the project, something TVA had tried desperately to avoid. The unpredictable and controversial justice was "good copy," and newspapers throughout the country rushed to take up the cause of Douglas and the Cherokees. Writing to Douglas, Wagner exercised enormous restraint, but he must have been terribly disappointed and inwardly seething.[62]

Were the Douglas incident not enough, the U.S. Chamber of Commerce waded into the fray. President Robert P. Gerholz attacked the Tellico project, calling it "a flagrant assault on free enterprise" because TVA was getting into the real estate and development business. In November, 1965, *Nation's Business*, the chamber's national publication, repeated those charges. Together with Douglas's utterances, the chamber's assault resulted in an avalanche of anti-TVA letters directed both to the newspapers and to the agency itself.[63]

Darker days were to come, but for TVA these were dark enough. One can see a marked drawing inward of the agency, hoping that the storm of controversy would blow itself out. Fewer and fewer reports exist of TVA officials taking to the podiums to explain or defend the project. Maintaining its determination to build the dam, the agency appears to have wanted to do so with as little fanfare as possible.

TVA was right. National attention simply could not be maintained once Douglas's statements had been forgotten (he returned briefly to the area in 1969) and the Chamber of Commerce became concerned with other things. America was at war in Vietnam, and that war intruded itself upon a progressively larger share of American life and thought. The president was an embattled chief executive, and Richard Nixon (once thought to be politically dead) was becoming increasingly visible. Civil rights for blacks continued to be a pressing national dilemma. No issue like a small dam on a small river could compete for the attention of the American people.

Hence there was comparatively little fanfare when President Johnson's 1967 budget (submitted to Congress in early 1966) contained a $3.2 million appropriation to begin the Tellico project. Evins announced he would go along this time ($8 million had been appropriated for Tims Ford) and the appropriation passed both houses with only modest debate, the only exception being an angry exchange between TVA Board Member Frank Smith and Democratic Congressman John Dingell of Michigan, who chaired the House Fisheries and Wildlife Subcommittee. President Johnson signed the 1967 budget on October 17, 1966. TVA planned to begin construction in the early spring of 1967, with an estimated completion date of 1970 or 1971.[64]

But even as construction began in March, 1967, forces were at work that threatened the project. By August, 1967, Palo was complaining to Van Mol that money was exceedingly tight and that the project was slowing down. In late 1968 the agency was forced to admit that construction would either slow or stop owing to lack of funds. Part of the problem was that the Vietnam War was eroding financing of domestic projects. Moreover, after President Nixon occupied the White House, funding was greatly reduced because of the administration's skepticism about TVA in general and Tellico in particular. But the principal reason was that, in order to maintain publicly a favorable benefit-cost ratio, the agency had minimized inflation of land and material prices.[65] Land prices had climbed rapidly, reaching $19.3 million in September, 1967, and $21.8 million by May, 1969. As costs rose, TVA continued to restudy and recalculate the benefit-cost ratio. In October, 1967, the agency increased land enhancement benefits by 18.5 percent. Even so, by the fall of 1968 new jobs and increased wages made up the largest benefit category.[66]

Obviously something was needed to get the project going again. Construction had stopped, TVA morale was low, the Nixon administration was unfriendly, costs were rising, local support groups were moribund, the benefit-cost ratio looked more porous than ever. In 1969 William O. Douglas returned to the Valley, wrote a scathing criticism of the project for *True Magazine*, and caused another avalanche of hostile mail.[67] In response to this most recent crisis, Wagner revived a pet idea that he had been nurturing for some time. In cooperation with private industry, TVA could build an all-electric model city, near the Tellico Dam, a showcase of what the agency could do for the Valley. Although Frank Smith had mentioned the concept to Van Mol as early as 1966, the weight of evidence suggests that (as one former TVA employee put it), "The whole thing was 'Red' Wagner's baby. It was his idea right from the start."[68]

In March, 1968, Wagner publicly broached the idea, and by May "Tellico New Community: A Proposal" had been drafted. Indeed, things moved with such uncharacteristic swiftness that by December, 1968, Van Mol was telling Mike Foster that TVA "is committed to the development of a new town in the Tellico Reservoir area" and that specific planning was being given to the Division of Navigational Development and Regional Studies. By September, 1969, "Timberlake" had become the new town's official name and by December of that year a detailed plan had emerged.[69]

The detailed report saw Timberlake as a demonstration of "public-private approach to new community development." It was to be a totally planned community, "a high-quality urban environment" whose population by the year 2000 would be approximately 50,000 people. By that year 25,000 new jobs would have been created, which would be a boon to the entire area. Indeed, it sounded like a utopia; cheap land, low taxes (estimated at 99¢ per $1,000 in the year 2000), gorgeous recreation facilities, model homes, prosperity. Timberlake had everything, especially the potential of being the imaginative concept that would turn the Tellico project around.[70] But Timberlake was not to be. In spite of the fact that the Boeing Corporation was interested enough in the cooperative venture with TVA to send planners to Tennessee, the stopping of the dam by the Environmental Protection Agency in the early 1970s caused Boeing to withdraw.[71]

The final threat against Tellico was the most timely: timely, because to watch it unfold is to glimpse a by now familiar process of bureaucratic self-destruction, and because the issue was the environment. The Environmental Protection Agency, founded in 1969, mandated that environmental impact statements be submitted for all federal projects. Although TVA was composing one, the agency insisted that it was doing so on its own and not because it was required to do so by EPA. An injunction followed that enjoined TVA from completion until an environmental impact statement was complete (twenty-one months). When TVA's statement was ruled acceptable in 1973, it coincided with the passage of the Endangered Species Act and the discovery by University of Tennessee ichthyologist David Etnier of a small, heretofore unobserved species of minnow, the snail darter, in the Little Tennessee River. With the project 75 percent complete in March, 1975, the U.S. Fish and Wildlife Service petitioned for the darter to be placed on the endangered list, and in October of that year it was. TVA claimed that retroactive application of a 1973 act should not be allowed to threaten the project, and argued that continued federal funding of the Tellico project proved tacit congressional (and, by implication, government) approval. It argued it was under no obligation to seek any alternative to closure of the dam and creation of the reservoir, despite the fact that closure was then thought to be the one act which would threaten the darter.

An attempt was made to stop TVA in federal district court (*Hill v. TVA*), but the suit was dismissed in May, 1976. An appeal brought an injunction against TVA that allowed some ongoing work on the Tellico project to continue but no closure of the dam itself. The Department of the Interior, in the fall of 1976, argued for the darter and against Tellico's completion. With the project 90 percent completed, the Sixth Circuit Court of Appeals reversed the district court, but in 1978 the U.S. Supreme Court stopped closure of the dam by a vote of six to three before TVA could act to create the reservoir. Eventually the Tellico Reservoir was created when the dam was closed by the back door: an amendment was attached to an Energy and Water Approprations Act (H.R. 43888) in June, 1978, that allowed TVA to close the dam regardless of the Endangered Species Act or other like laws. Carter failed to veto and the project was completed, the floodgates closed.

The change in resistance to TVA projects from a private to a public stance was voiced to the authors by a woman whose family was one of the 3,500-plus families removed from the Norris basin in 1934 by TVA to create the Norris Dam and Reservoir. At the time the Supreme Court decision stopped Tellico, she reminisced, "They stopped Tellico over a damned fish but they moved thousands of us—but we was only people."[72]

Ultimately, then, the Tellico Dam was built. But the residue of ill feeling had badly damaged TVA's reputation, perhaps irreparably. What had began as a showcase project to dramatize the agency's new mission (that of industrial development on the tributaries in "little TVAs") had ended in controversy, political in-fighting, and bitterness that many years will not altogether erase. Never malicious or vicious, TVA wanted only to bring the Tennessee Valley into the modern age in which a healthy, prosperous, well-educated people could enjoy all the fruits of technology. Though paternalistic, it was never knowingly wicked. But in its determination to carry out its new mission, the agency was often stubborn, occasionally duplicitous, and sometimes simply mistaken. To some, it appeared that the end truly justified the means. In the increasingly complex modern age the Tellico project and TVA's new mission stand as an important case study of the dilemma of a society that seeks both technology and democracy. Indeed, the issues raised by the Tellico project and TVA's new mission face all of us in modern America.

NOTES

1. John V. Krutilla, "Economic Development: An Appraisal," in Roscoe C. Martin, ed., *TVA: The First Twenty Years: A Staff Report* (University: University of Alabama Press; Knoxville: University of Tennessee Press, 1956), p. 220.

2. On midwesterners, see interview with Richard Kilbourne, Feb. 12, 1982; interview with Aubrey J. Wagner, Mar. 9, 1982.

3. Interview with A. J. Gray, Mar. 9, 1982; G. O. Wessenauer, "A Short History of TVA," remarks to Power Distributors' Electrical Development Personnel Training Institute, June 18, 1962, copy in TVA Technical Library, Knoxville, Tenn. On postwar planning, see Howard K. Menhinick, director, Department of Regional Studies, to Files, Aug. 7, 1944, attached to "Forecast of Physical Resources of the Tennessee Valley—1945," Step I Working Papers (Knoxville, May, 1944). For plans, see "Opportunities for Postwar Development of Tennessee Valley Resources," Step II Working Papers (Knoxville, May, 1944), E1-18, and "Development of Tennessee Valley Resources—Program Suggestions," Step III Working Papers (Knoxville, Nov., 1945), E1-8.

4. Kilbourne interview.

5. Krutilla, "Economic Development," pp. 225, 229; Step III Working Papers, A1–25.

6. For 100 studies, see Donald T. Wells, "TVA Tributary Area Development Program" (Ph.D. dissertation, University of Oklahoma, 1963), p. 66. See also Aubrey J. Wagner, "The Future of TVA," in John R. Moore, ed., *The Economic Impact of TVA* (Knoxville: University of Tennessee Press, 1967), pp. 153–54.

7. Wagner, "Future of TVA," p. 151.

8. Wagner interview; Gray interview.

9. Wagner interview. For Tributary Area Committee and composition, see Kilbourne interview.

10. Ralph F. Garn, "Tributary Area Development in Tennessee: TVA's Changing Perspective" (Ph.D. dissertation, University of Tennessee, Knoxville, 1974), pp. 68–72; Kilbourne interview; Wagner interview.

11. Robert E. Lowry, "Beech River Experiment" (unpublished TVA report, in OTAD files), p. 4.

12. TVA, *Working with Areas of Special Need, with Examples from the Beech River Watershed* (Knoxville, Tenn., 1953), pp. 6–12; Kilbourne interview.

13. *Ibid.* See also Wagner interview; Garn, "Tributary Area Development in Tennessee," pp. 72–79.

14. Kilbourne interview.

15. On power consumption, see Wessenauer, "Short History of TVA." On power people, see Kilbourne interview. On nonpolitical stance, see Wagner interview.

16. Vogel to Joe Sir, president, Elk River Development Association, July 9, 1959, OTAD Administrative Files; Garn, "Tributary Area Development in Tennessee," pp. 98–102.

17. Kilbourne interview; Gray interview.

18. Kilbourne interview; Wagner interview.

19. Interview with former TVA employee who requested that his name be withheld. See also Kilbourne interview.

20. U.S. Senate, Document 97, 87th Cong., 2d sess., The President's Water Resources Council. *Policies, Standards, and Procedures in the Formulation, Evaluation, and Review of Plans for Use and Development of Water and Related Land Resources* (May 29, 1962); interview with J. Fergurson, Feb. 3, 1982; Kilbourne interview.

21. OTAD, *Annual Reports* (1963–71); Kilbourne interview.

22. For background of the Tellico project, see Boxes 44-c-92 and 49-c-70, TVA Administrative Files; Boxes 26 H 31 and 26 H 29, TVA Commerce Department Files; Microfilm reel 614, TVA Central Files. Though linked inexorably to Fort Loudoun Dam, Tellico marked a return to land "overpurchase" while Fort Loudoun was the first TVA main-river dam for which purchase was minimized through flowage easements instead of large fee-simple purchase; see letters in Boxes 26 H 29 and 26 H 31, TVA Commerce Department Files; Box 44-c-92, TVA Administrative Files; Microfilm reel 667, TVA Central Files. For the War Production Board's decision and TVA reaction, see Box 44-c-92, TVA Administrative Files. For inquiries and responses in the 1940s and 1950s concerning whether or not the land for the Tellico project would be purchased and when, see Box 44-c-92, TVA Administrative Files; Microfilm reel 666, TVA Central Files: Folder 1, TVA Project Planning Branch Files (hereafter referred to as TVA, PPB).

23. Reed Elliot to Don H. Mattern and R. E. Frierson, July 15, 1959, TVA, PPB. During 1959 soil sampling was done for the Tellico project.

24. Memo, Jan. 15, 1960; Berlen C. Moneymaker to Robert J. Coker, Jan. 18, 1960; W. F. Emmons to Reed A. Elliot, Feb. 10, 1960; T. C. McCarley to Robert J. Coker, Feb. 11, 1960; J. Porter Taylor to D. H. Mattern, Mar. 31, 1960, all in TVA, PPB.

25. Reed Elliot to D. H. Mattern, March 31, 1960, TVA, PPB. In 1941 TVA had estimated the cost of the Fort Loudoun Extension at $31,300,000, which was revised upward (pending WPB approval at $46,400,000 [Serial Nos. 200.2 and 200.6 (1942) approval requests, Box 26 H 20, TVA Administrative Files]).

26. Vogel to Phillip Appleby, Aug. 28, 1959, TVA, PPB. Vogel told Appleby that the

situation was unchanged from 1952. For his Nov., 1954, advice to a landowner, see D. H. Mattern memo, Nov. 30, 1959, TVA, PPB.

27. See Garn, "Tributary Area Development in Tennessee," esp. pp. 89–102, for these developments. Pressure from Elk River residents was to result in a group similar to that called for by General Vogel, formed in 1960, the Tennessee River and Tributary Association, a Valley-wide organization.

28. Garn, "Tributary Area Development in Tennessee," pp. 119–23; Nashville Tennessean, Jan. 15, 1961, cited in ibid., p. 123. The Elk River Development Association urged TVA to include in calculation of benefit-cost ratios water supply, land enhancement, and recreation. Ibid., pp. 123–24.

29. Aubrey Wagner to George P. Palo and Robert M. Howes, Aug. 9, 1960, TVA, PPB. Howes had already been in touch with Reed H. Elliot about the recreational potential of the Tellico project (May 12, 1960).

30. Palo memo, Aug. 18, 1960, TVA, PPB.

31. J. Porter Taylor to George P. Palo, Sept. 15, 1960, TVA, PPB.

32. Richard Kilbourne to George P. Palo, Sept. 15, 1960, TVA, PPB.

33. Wessenauer to Palo, Sept. 28, 1960, TVA, PPB.

34. Kilbourne interview.

35. Gray interview.

36. Ibid. See Foster's obituary in the Knoxville News-Sentinel, Oct. 9, 1979.

37. Robert Coker to Robert Howes, Dec. 29, 1960, TVA, PPB.

38. "TVA Asks Help in Tellico Dam," Knoxville News-Sentinel, Jan. 1, 1961.

39. Knoxville Journal, Feb. 15, 1961; Knoxville News-Sentinel, Jan. 1, 1961.

40. Palo to Wagner, Feb. 10, 1961, TVA, PPB.

41. Palo to Van Mol, Mar. 19, 1962, TVA, PPB. Still benefit-cost ratios ranged from 1:1 to 2:1.

42. Kenneth Seigsworth to George Palo, Jan. 25, 1963, TVA, PPB.

43. Porter Taylor to Palo, Jan. 29, 1963; Palo to Van Mol, Feb. 7, 1963, TVA, PPB.

44. Reed Elliot to Porter Taylor, May 28, 1963; Elliot to Howes, May 28, 1963, both in TVA, PPB. C. J. Parrot of Land Acquisition, however, warned that TVA had calculated the benefits from selling purchased land around the reservoir too high, because they had now allowed a 12 percent reduction for the cost of selling the land, mailing surveys, etc. C. J. Parrot to Robert Coker, June 7, 1963; Palo to Van Mol, July 30, 1963; A. J. Gray to Files, May 28, 1963; Loose to Files, Aug. 12, 1963; Kilbourne to Palo, July 23, 1963, all in TVA, PPB. Robert Howes, however, thought it unlikely that these "new jobs" would be filled by "people presently employed in agriculture"; more likely, one would displace the other. Robert Howes to E. S. Brosell, Oct. 7, 1963; Porter Taylor to Reed Elliot, Oct. 28, 1963, TVA, PPB. Memos of Robert Howes urged development of the shoreline "to achieve maximum contribution to the economy of the region." Oct. 30, 1963, TVA, PPB.

45. Bill Brock to Bert Hoskins, May 26, 1964, TVA, PPB.

46. Aubrey Wagner to Bill Brock, June 9, 1964, TVA, PPB.

47. On founding of the association, see Maryville-Alcoa Times, Oct. 14, 1964.

48. Tennessee Outdoor Record, Sept. 13, 1963. On fishermen and outdoorsmen, see Knoxville News-Sentinel, Sept. 22, Oct. 13, Nov. 17, 1963, Jan. 9, Oct. 3, 1964; Knoxville Journal, Feb. 1, 1965; Nashville Tennessean, Oct. 15, 1963; Maryville-Alcoa Times, May 1, Sept. 24, 1964; Chattanooga Free Press, Aug. 6, 1964.

49. On opposition of farm groups, see Knoxville Journal, Feb. 1, 1965. On conservative attack, a typical example is found in Monroe Citizen, Sept. 16, 1964. On Fort Loudon,

see folders on Land Use, Old Fort Loudoun–Tellico, TVA Water Control Planning File, Knoxville. See also Project Planning Branch Correspondence File, Dec. 15, 1964, for Fort Loudoun Association resolution.

50. On the twenty groups, see Knoxville Journal, Feb. 1, 1965. For samples of support, see ibid., May 21, July 15, 1964; Sweetwater Valley News, Aug. 27, 1964; Monroe Citizen, Oct. 7, 1964; Knoxville News-Sentinel, Oct. 12, 1964. On poll, see Monroe Citizen, Oct. 14, 1964. For Wagner's statement, see Knoxville News-Sentinel, Sept. 11, 13, 1964; Chattanooga News–Free Press, Sept. 23, 1964.

51. On the Greenback meeting, see Chattanooga News–Free Press, Sept. 23, 1964; Knoxville News-Sentinel, Sept. 23, 1964. See also Madisonville Democrat, Sept. 24, 1964. For a similar opinion, see Knoxville Journal, Dec. 10, 1964.

52. Zellner to Kilbourne, Oct. 1, 1964. On white paper, see TVA Newspaper File, Nov. 25, 1964, TVA Technical Library. On serialization, see Loudoun County Herald, Dec. 3, 1964; Knoxville News-Sentinel, Dec. 6, 1964; Lenoir City News-Banner, Dec. 10 and 17, 1964; Monroe County Citizen-Democrat, Dec. 9, 1964. On answering critics, see Taylor to Van Mol, Nov. 13, 1964, and Van Mol to Files, Nov. 30, 1964, TVA, PPB.

53. An organization meeting had been held on Oct. 20. See Mavis Cunningham's report in Fort Loudoun Correspondence, Water Control Planning Files; Mavis Cunningham to OTAD files, Nov. 19, 1964, TVA, PPB. On combined meeting of Nov. 18, 1964, see same to same, Nov. 24, 1964, TVA, PPB. See also Gray interview.

54. On new jobs, see Wagner to Senator Ross Bass, Jan. 8, 1965, TVA, PPB. For Wagner on benefits, see Maryville-Alcoa Times, Nov. 10, 1964. For a different view, see Gilbert "Pete" Stuart's letter to the editor, Knoxville News-Sentinel, Oct. 7, 1964. For more on jobs and halting outmigration, see Madisonville Democrat, Nov. 11, 1964; Maryville-Alcoa Times, Nov. 5, 1964.

55. Wagner interview.

56. See Fort Loudoun Correspondence, 1961–65, Water Control Planning Archives. The decision to abandon the dikes scheme and raise the fort was made in Feb., 1965. Ibid.

57. Knoxville News-Sentinel, Apr. 27, June 8, 9, and 17, 1965.

58. On flying to Washington, see Knoxville News-Sentinel, July 12, 1965. On appeals and pressure, see ibid., May 20, 1965; Knoxville Journal, May 21, 1965. The Chamber of Commerce did not formally endorse the project, though the City Council did, on July 13, by a vote of four to three. See Knoxville Journal, July 14, 1965.

59. Ellender to Wagner, July 20, 1965; Gen. W. P. Leber to Col. Jesse L. Fishback, July 26, 1965, both in TVA, PPB; Congressional Record-Senate, 89th Congress, 1st sess., Aug. 23, 1965, pp. 20567–68; Knoxville News-Sentinel, July 16, Aug. 24, 1965; Nashville Tennessean, July 12, 1965.

60. Knoxville News-Sentinel, Oct. 14, 1965; Chattanooga News–Free Press, Oct. 14, 1965; Chattanooga Times, Oct. 16 and 17, 1965.

61. Madisonville Citizen-Democrat, Apr. 7, 1965; Knoxville News-Sentinel, Apr. 10, 1965; Knoxville Journal, May 11, 1965.

62. For open Cherokee oppositon, see Nashville Tennessean, Apr. 5, 1965; For a small sample of the national press coverage, see St. Louis Post-Dispatch, Apr. 5, 1965; Louisville Courier-Journal, Apr. 5, 1965; Christian Science Monitor, Apr. 7, 1965; Washington Post, Apr. 11, 1965. For Wagner's letter, see Wagner to Douglas, May 13, 1965, TVA, PPB.

63. On Gerholz, see Nashville Tennessean, Aug. 25, 1965. See also Nation's Business, Nov., 1965. For TVA responses to the chamber attacks, see Knoxville News-Sentinel, Nov. 26, 1965; Tullahoma News and Guardian, Dec. 8, 1965. In Dec., 1965, the National Parks Magazine also criticized the Tellico project.

64. *Knoxville News-Sentinel*, Jan. 24, May 3, Sept. 27 and 28, Oct. 12, 1966; *Knoxville Journal*, Sept. 20, Oct. 13 and 18, 1966.

65. Palo to Van Mol, Aug. 1, 1967, TVA, PPB; *News-Sentinel*, June 21, 1967; *Chattanooga Times*, Nov. 16, 1968; *Johnson City Press-Chronicle*, Jan. 21, 1969. On subsequent appropriations, see *Loudon County Herald*, Jan. 26, 1967; *Chattanooga Times*, Nov. 16, 1968; *Johnson City Press-Chronicle*, Jan. 21, 1969.

66. Reeder to Perry, Sept. 26, 1967; Elliot to Mattern, Apr. 26, 1968; Fergurson to Files, Sept. 6, 1968; Mattern to Elliot, Sept. 11, 1968; Clark to Perry, May 2, 1969; Perry to Rountree, May 5, 1969, all in TVA, PPB.

67. On deterioration of local support groups, see Cunningham to Zellner, Jan. 24, 1969; J. Richard Willson to Barron, Mar. 4, 1969, both in OTAD Files. On Douglas, see *Nashville Tennessean*, Apr. 14, 1969. For letters, see Project Planning Branch Correspondence, summer-fall, 1969.

68. Smith to Van Mol, Sept. 7, 1966, TVA, PPB; Gray interview.

69. For Wagner's public announcement, see *Knoxville News-Sentinel*, Mar. 7, 1968. See also TVA Task Force, "Tellico New Community: A Proposal" (May, 1968); Van Mol to Foster, Dec. 4, 1968, both in Division of Water Control, Tellico New Town Correspondence, 1968–79. On naming town, see Foster to Van Mol, July 27, 1969, and Van Mol to Heads of Offices and Divisions, Sept. 17, 1969, *ibid.*; TVA News Release, Sept. 22, 1969, OTAD Files.

70. Division of Water Control Planning, "Timberlake: A Preliminary Planning Report—Draft" (Dec., 1969), Water Control Planning Archives.

71. On Boeing, see Foster to Elliot, Oct. 26, 1971, Timberlake Commission.

72. TVA, *Alternatives for Completing the Tellico Project* (Knoxville, Tenn., 1978). For a strongly biased view, see Peter Matthiessen, "How to Kill a Valley," *New York Review of Books*, 27 (Feb. 7, 1980): 31–36.

8 Dean Hill Rivkin

TVA, the Courts, and the Public Interest

SINCE its inception the Tennessee Valley Authority has grappled continuously with complex questions of autonomy and responsiveness. Under its organic statute TVA was accorded unprecedented flexibility and insulation from national political interference. Over the years the agency has fought to retain its discretion in policy making. A prime arena in this struggle has been the courts, which TVA has used as both a shield and a sword.[1]

The creation of a decentralized national agency armed with a broad mandate to promote the development of a region defied the conventional wisdom of the New Deal. National agencies working on national problems, New Deal theorists believed, were most effective in solving the myriad economic and social problems plaguing the country in the 1930s. In a sense, the creation of the TVA permitted the Roosevelt administration to respond to decentralist critics by pointing to its decentralized and private features. Despite its unique features, however, TVA shared three characteristics with other national administrative agencies created by the Roosevelt administration: its apolitical character, its insulation from judicial review, and its reliance on experts in policy making.[2]

TVA was to be distinctly apolitical, a feature rooted in the expansive TVA charter. As long as the agency pursued the multitude of developmental goals broadly subsumed within its charter—navigation, flood control, and, ultimately, power generation—TVA was to enjoy significant insulation. The agency had authority to tackle problems without suffering the ordinary intrusions characteristic of the political process. In its hiring TVA was required to bypass the prevalent patronage channels and hire solely on merit. TVA created its own civil service system to ensure fairness in its employment practices. A requirement of competitive bidding also removed TVA's procurement policies from the political realm.[3]

A corollary to safeguards from political control is insulation from judicial review. In the view of New Deal architects, courts should not substitute their rigid legalistic judgments for the expert policy conclusions reached by administrative agencies. For many decades this principle left TVA officials free to try to escape even minimal judicial oversight.

From the beginning TVA directors emphasized the role of experts in formulating and implementing policy. In its early days the success of TVA's mission hinged on the technical expertise of architects and engineers. The agency prided itself on hiring the most competent and progressive professionals in its ambitious plan of water resources development. The agency left little doubt that the answers to the intractable problems of the region could be solved scientifically and technically.[4]

In these major respects—its apolitical design, insulation from the courts, and uncritical reliance on technical expertise—TVA mirrored its New Deal administrative counterparts. In addition, two other aspects of TVA's early years help explain its institutional role. First, despite its protective covering, TVA could not avoid disputes over policy with other federal agencies whose missions coincided with TVA. The bitter infighting between Secretary of the Interior Harold Ickes and the first TVA board foreshadowed the interagency struggles of the 1970s with EPA and others. TVA largely prevailed in these early encounters by stressing to the White House its broad mission and high purposes, a strategy that served it well in later years too.[5]

Second, TVA had to relate to the states in the Valley. TVA represented a considered judgment by the federal government that the states were unable to achieve the economic and social rehabilitation of the Valley. Given its ability to wield national authority and resources, TVA anticipated that it would encounter serious resistance from the states. "It expected to be charged with arbitrariness, with 'carpet-bagging,' and with pushing people around," stated close agency observers. That major confrontations did not occur in these early years is a tribute to the political skill of the agency's early leaders, who aligned TVA with powerful interests in the Valley, notably the Farm Bureau, in a successful effort to stave off state or local interference.[6]

In formulating policy, TVA officials always tried to promote its conception of the public interest. From its inception they construed this concept in distinctly utilitarian terms. What was good for the overall welfare of the Valley, what maximized resources for the people of the Valley, was considered by the agency to be in the public interest. To bolster its policies, TVA adeptly convinced the world that what it thought was in the public interest was also what the people of the Valley wanted. In TVA's view its major function was to aggregate grass-roots preferences and marshal resources toward the satisfaction of these agreed-upon goals.[7] In the early years this strategy was enormously successful. Few disputed that the Valley could benefit from rapid economic development. The means to this end, it was generally agreed, lay predominantly in power production. TVA seized this concern and embarked on an ambitious program of dam building.

TVA's model of decision making in formulating this early policy deserves mention. In making policy, government agencies have followed two general models: "incrementalism" and "comprehensive rationality." Under the former, policy is made in small chunks by numerous actors inside an agency responding with limited alternatives to short-range problems. Incrementalism was the dominant model of decision making by most New Deal agencies.[8] Comprehensive rationality requires the decision maker to select policy goals, identify alternative methods for achieving these goals, assess the costs and benefits of each alternative, and finally choose the alternative that best promotes the desired end.:

Comprehensive rationality emphasizes static choice. It seeks the best of all options available at a given moment. The prospect of change does not inhibit analysis but rather becomes a factor in the analysis. Comprehensive rationality does not, of course, deny that policies will need to be modified over time. But it is a system of comparative statics, not continuous motion: a series of vivid tableaux, each as complete as circumstances will permit. The synoptic thinker conceives of the world as a closed system in which the causal interrelationships of all elements can, in principle, be specified. Once goals are adopted, the system dictates the solution.[9]

Unlike its New Deal counterparts, TVA did not make policy incrementally. It embraced a model of comprehensive rationality with a vengeance. The agency's goals—spelled out in its charter and in the prevailing regional concerns about economic development—were reasonably fixed. The development of methods of reaching those goals was entrusted to the expert technicians at TVA. What emerged in these early years was a public works program of unrivaled magnitude. Little room was left for marginal adjustments in policy when that policy involved enormous construction projects scattered over a large geographical area. Throughout this process there was virtually no attempt by the agency meaningfully to involve the "public" in the process of choosing the best path toward achieving the developmental objectives handed the agency in its congressional charter. Thus comprehensive rationality worked extremely well for the agency in its early years. TVA was lauded as a model of fairness and efficiency. Yet these early successes fixed the agency on a course that would prove problematical in future years.[10]

Given its comprehensive mission, its special institutional character, and its synoptic model of administrative decision making, not unsurprisingly TVA enjoyed considerable autonomy in its early years. Significantly, it was the courts that, in the final analysis, protected the agency from the buffeting political tides. Two major judicial decisions stand out.

In *Ashwander v. TVA* TVA's institutional autonomy was at stake in a suit by dissident shareholders of the Alabama Power Company. They challenged (primarily on Tenth Amendment grounds) TVA's authority to engage in power generation and distribution. The *Ashwander* decision was a milestone in the bitter battle between TVA and national private power interests. The legal challenge, mirroring the acrimony of an accompanying political campaign, was framed by TVA's opponents in unusually strong terms: "This proceeding presents for review the constitutional validity of an effort through a corporate agency of the Federal Government permanently to the manufacture and distribution of electricity throughout an initial region comprising approximately one-fifth of the population of the United States."[11]

In *Ashwander* TVA's threshold legal strategy was to challenge the standing of the shareholders to raise the constitutional issues. In essence, TVA argued that the shareholders' stake in a power contract entered into between Alabama Power and TVA was insufficient to justify invoking the power of the courts to rule on the ultimate constitutionality of the TVA Act. Despite Justice Brandeis's classic analysis of the standing-to-sue issue, in which he concluded that the stockholders did not have a right to challenge the allegedly illegal actions by TVA officials, a majority of the court concluded that "it is enough for (the stockholders) to show the breach of trust or duty involved in the injurious or illegal action. . . . The illegality may be found in the lack of lawful authority on the part of those with whom the corporation is attempting to deal."[12]

On the merits, the Court concluded that TVA, a government instrumentality, possessed the constitutional authority to market power from the Wilson Dam in Alabama. Although the opinion concluded by limiting its ruling to the Wilson Dam, the language of the opinion, focusing on the promotion of the "public interest" by TVA, unmistakably foreshadowed vindication of TVA's broader power development efforts.

In the wake of *Ashwander* a collection of private power companies sought a final determination on the constitutionality of TVA's power program in *Tennessee Power Company v. TVA*. After an extensive trial the district court found that TVA's power program constituted a bona fide exercise of the federal government's commerce and war powers; consequently, power from TVA dams could be sold in competition with the sale of power by private utilities. Interestingly, the Supreme Court, in an apparent reversal of its closely divided position in *Ashwander*, found that the plaintiffs lacked standing to sue because, among other reasons, competition from TVA did not embody the type of economic injury needed to support a challenge to TVA's constitutional authority. The substantive constitutional issue was finally settled by the Supreme Court favorably to the federal governnent in 1940 and 1941 cases involving other national water resources agencies.[13]

The importance of the courts in TVA's early efforts to protect its institutional integrity is also exemplified in *Morgan v. TVA*. The Court sustained President Roosevelt's removal of Arthur Morgan. Morgan was removed by the president for his "contumacious" refusal to carry out executive policy. He claimed his removal was unlawful, pointing to two provisions of the TVA Act that authorized removal of a board member by the president for abuse of the merit promotion system, 16 U.S.C. Section 831e, and by Congress at will, 16 U.S.C. Section 831c(f). Roosevelt's intervention, Morgan claimed, contravened these two exclusive methods in the TVA Act. The Court held that the president's inherent right to remove appointees could be abrogated only by express statutory language to that effect.[14]

At first blush, *Morgan* might appear to conflict with the proposition that early judicial decisions permitted TVA to pursue its broad mandate relatively free from political control. Morgan himself, however, was perceived by his colleagues on the TVA board as a threat to TVA's nonpartisan functioning, an image crucial to the consensus that TVA relied on in shaping its institutional persona. Had the *Morgan* case reached a contrary result, the president's only recourse would have been to convince both the House and the Senate to remove the TVA chairman. Such an attempt would have provided a convenient forum for the private utility interests opposing TVA at the time. At bottom, the result can be considered as preserving rather than eroding TVA's independence.

These cases illustrate the predisposition of the judiciary to nurture this institutional experiment. The cases also established the indispensability of an able TVA legal staff whose primary mission was to engage TVA's adversaries in what was perceived at the time as mortal combat. The strategies employed—for example, the creative use of the standing doctrine—served the agency well in these early days and laid a pattern for the 1970s, when the agency was again embattled in the courts.

Fortified by its early victories, TVA embarked on a far-reaching program of power development. For purposes of this essay, the chief characteristics of TVA policy making in the 1940s, 1950s, and 1960s remained the same. The agency continued to adhere to a model of comprehensive rationality in its major policy decisions. The shifts to coal-fired steam plants in the late 1940s and early 1950s (twelve in all) and finally to nuclear power in the late 1960s had an inexorable logic of their own. Unlike its dam-building days, when TVA's institutional goal was the simple provision of abundant electric power to the masses, TVA's goal in this period became the provision of low-cost power.[15]

As in the past, the agency pursued this goal single-mindedly, justifying its decisions on largely utilitarian grounds. The details of TVA's decision making during these years are outside the scope of this paper. Suffice it to say, the little available evidence indicates that the agency went through the motions of assessing alternatives and optimizing policy. Questions have been raised, however, about the seriousness of the agency's efforts to analyze and incorporate into its decisions the full consequences of its major policy shifts. For example, although some data on health effects of air pollution from coal-fired plants were available during the years TVA was constructing its coal-fired system, the agency's unaggressive attitude toward the risks posed by these data hardly represented a model of thorough, sound, decision making. At bottom, once policy was made, it was fixed, and the ample resources of the agency were mobilized behind it.[16]

During these years the courts continued to defer to TVA policy making; no serious judicial challenge to TVA activities was even mounted. The agency continued to use litigation instrumentally to achieve its policy goals. TVA's condemnation cases pitted TVA lawyers against Valley citizens fighting for their land and way of life. These cases could not have been pleasant tasks for TVA's legal staff. But duty to the overarching public interest came first, and the legal staff systematically carried out their assignments.

The coal and nuclear decision cycles committed the agency to courses from which there was little room to stray. By any measure the agency, judged against its own goals, was a huge success. But as the consensus underlying these goals weakened in the 1960s, the agency's proven methods of the past faced serious challenge.

By the late 1960s the consensus that TVA had skillfully managed to promote its autonomy over the years was beginning to erode. Consumers, environmentalists, and public interest advocates—symbols of the emerging public law era—began to intrude on TVA's autonomy and reservoir of good will. This is not to suggest that TVA escaped criticism in its earlier efforts. As knowledgeable commentators have shown, TVA consciously avoided fundamental institutional and political reform in its formative years. The agency did little, for example, to empower small farmers or to confront racial discrimination in the Tennessee Valley. TVA's decisions to avoid these controversial issues no doubt contributed to the agency's image as a ponderous corporate machine removed from the hurly-burly of state and local politics.[17]

The reform issues of the late 1960s, however, collided with TVA's attempt to use strategies that were so successful for the agency in its earlier years. Prominent among these strategies were (1) the agency's continuing effort to transform political and social issues into technical ones, and (2) the agency's heavy reliance on the courts to ensure its autonomy. The strategies of the past then failed in major ways, leading to the crisis of accountability the agency faced in the early 1980s. The search for new mechanisms and strategies by TVA continues. The agency's success in adapting to a new political and legal climate, one based more on enduring values of process and substantive fairness, may determine the future course, if not the very existence, of TVA.[18]

Like its New Deal counterparts, TVA was not immune to shifting conceptions of administrative policy making that emerged in the late 1960s. In place of an earlier consensus, courts became the prime arena where competing social interests attempted to further their notions of sound policy. The discretion enjoyed by TVA under its broad legislative mandate began to narrow as interest groups challenged its expertise, drawing on competing technical and scientific information.[19]

As the accounts below show, TVA continued to insist that its policies advanced the collective good of the Valley. What the agency discounted in making this assertion was its own role in shaping preferences for environmental quality or low electrical rates. The formidable expertise TVA was able to bring to bear through the media, in the respective state legislatures and administrative agencies, and, to a lesser degree, in Washington played a powerful role in molding public opinion on controversial issues. This role was shaken in the public law era, as Valley interests drew on the resources of national organizations—the U.S. Environmental Protection Agency (EPA) and environmental and consumer organizations—and exposed fallacies in TVA's technocratic responses to public policy issues. TVA's brand of "comprehensive rationality" was challenged as a veneer for self-interested decisions. The role of the courts in this delegitimizing process, though not determinative, was significant. The accounts below chronicle that role.[20]

Most New Deal courts assumed that agencies like TVA could adequately protect the public interest. They believed that standing, liberally granted, would dissipate agency resources and permit hostile courts to thwart an agency's mission, as in such cases as *Tennessee Electric Power v. TVA*. With the emerging recognition that agencies might not incorporate the views of divergent classes of interests came a broadening of the standing doctrine.

The major watershed in the willingness of courts to pierce TVA's long-standing claim of autonomy was *Hardin v. Kentucky Utilities Co.* (1968). In it the Supreme Court repudiated TVA's claim that its interpretation of the TVA Act was judicially unreviewable and permitted a competing utility to obtain judicial interpretation of Section 15d(a) of the TVA Act delineating its mandated "service area." The decision established the ability of parties adversely affected by TVA's actions to seek judicial construction of the scope of TVA authority, a dramatic departure from the laissez-faire attitude of the Court in *Tennessee Electric Power*.[21]

The expansion of standing rights to adversely affected parties constituted a major chink in TVA's protective armor. Since *Hardin*, it has not been unusual for courts to conduct searching examinations of the purpose and meaning of various provisions of the TVA Act. For example, in *Young v. Tennessee Valley Authority* (1979) the U.S. Court of Appeals for the Sixth Circuit ruled on a claim by property owners seeking an interpretation of TVA's authority under Section 831c(i) & (j) of the TVA Act to construct the Hartsville nuclear plant on a site outside the watershed of the Tennessee River. In a divided opinion concluding that TVA possessed such authority, the court carefully examined the competing policy claims advanced by TVA and the plant's opponents. Similarly, in *State of Alabama v. Tennessee Valley Authority* (1981), in a suit brought by the attorney general of Alabama, *parens patriae*, the U.S. Court of Appeals for the Fifth Circuit carefully construed Section 8(a) of the TVA Act in light of Alabama's claim that TVA had improperly located its headquarters in Knoxville, rather than in Muscle Shoals, Alabama, as directed on the face of the act. The court approved TVA's decision to locate in Knoxville in light of long-standing congressional approval of this location.[22]

Despite the failure of TVA's adversaries to gain judicial approval of interpretations of the TVA Act inimical to the agency, *Hardin* signaled a new era of heightened judicial involvement in TVA activities. Most of the significant challenges were commenced by organizations purporting to represent interests whose viewpoints were significantly underrepresented in TVA decision making. A closer examination of some of these controversies will reveal the vulnerability of TVA's claim to unfettered autonomy in an era when courts and the public have viewed with increasing skepticism claims by government that its actions serve an elusive public interest.

The consequences of TVA's massive shift to coal-fired generation in the 1950s created great controversy in the 1960s. Rigidly adhering to its objective of low-cost power, the agency, as the largest coal purchaser in the country, had a significant impact on the eastern coal market and stimulated the development of strip mining as a marginally cheaper alternative to deep mining. As the external social and environmental costs of strip mining became better known, TVA paid lip-service to the necessity for strict environmental safeguards. For example, at the same time TVA publicly expressed concern for the damages resulting from strip mining, the agency was resisting through lobbying the enactment of strong strip-mining legislation, primarily in Kentucky.[23]

TVA did not account for the full social costs of its coal purchasing program. This resulted in certain classes of TVA consumers and others outside the TVA service area—those living in the coalfields of Kentucky and Tennessee—in effect paying more than the vast majority of TVA ratepayers for electricity. It was difficult to justify the inequity inherent in this policy even on the starkest utilitarian grounds. But the burden borne by these remote consumers did not register in TVA's rate calculus. The payments exacted from these persons were in the form not of higher utility bills each month but of road damage, intermittent flooding, and an overall lower quality of life.

One of the earliest efforts to hold TVA accountable for the external costs of its coal strategy was initiated by Save Our Cumberland

Mountains (SOCM), a citizens' organization dedicated to improving the quality of life in the east Tennessee coalfields. Through SOCM's organizational and educational efforts, some citizens perceived the disproportionate burden they were bearing as a consequence of TVA's failure to price coal at its full social cost. Having overcome the high transaction costs of engaging in collective action to redress this problem, SOCM turned to the courts to hold TVA accountable.[24]

The first effort revolved around TVA's steam plant in Kingston, Tennessee. In 1972 this plant was receiving nearly 2 million tons of coal, about 25 percent of the total output in east Tennessee. Most of the coal was transported over county and state highways in trucks consistently exceeding the 73,280-pound maximum permissible gross weight prescribed by Tennessee law. Immediately upon arrival at the plant, each truck was weighed to determine the quantity of coal delivered. The trucks that traveled to Kingston left substantial damage in their wake in large potholes, sharp indentations, craggy rises, and sizable chunks of fallen coal. In turn, the residents of the area suffered in a variety of ways. Their automobiles were subjected to extraordinary wear and tear, their driving safety was jeopardized by oversized trucks, and their counties were forced to allocate a much greater portion of tax revenues to road repair. In effect, these residents were subsidizing the price of electricity for other TVA consumers.

TVA's response to SOCM's complaints about this problem revealed the agency's fixation on low-cost power. Rather than exploring alternative solutions—for example, the renegotiation of higher contracts to encourage compliance—TVA insisted that it was contractually bound to accept the coal. The agency also disclaimed any law enforcement role, noting that it was the state's responsibility to enforce the truck weight limits.[25]

SOCM decided that TVA was in the best position to solve the problem and filed suit in the U.S. District Court for the Eastern District of Tennessee. The suit's main contention was that, as a matter of federal common law, federal courts should not condone policies and practices by federal agencies that frustrate state law. In making this argument, SOCM relied on the reasoning in *Tank Truck Rentals v. Commissioner of Internal Revenue*, in which the Supreme Court upheld the disallowance of deductions claimed by taxpayers, owners of a fleet of motor carriers, for fines and penalties imposed upon them for violation of Pennsylvania statutes governing the maximum weight limit for trucks operated on Pennsylvania highways. The rationale of the Supreme Court was directly analogous to TVA's conduct at Kingston: "Judicial deference to state action requires, wherever possible, that a state not be thwarted in its policy. We will not presume that the Congress . . . intended to encourage a business enterprise to violate the declared policy of the state. To allow the deductions sought here would but encourage continued violations of state law by increasing the odds in favor of noncompliance. This would only tend to destroy the effectiveness of the state's maximum weight laws."[26]

TVA's response to this argument in court echoes its prelitigation position. In addition, TVA asserted that neither SOCM had standing to sue nor the court jurisdiction to hear the case. In essence, TVA maintained that its policies were unreviewable and that it had no obligation to act.[27] The district court rejected SOCM's arguments, stating: "The Governor of Tennessee is charged with the responsibility for enforcing state laws, not the TVA." The court's reasons for ruling in favor of TVA were grounded in concepts of federal-state comity. Ironically, the Tennessee enforcement authorities expressed support for the SOCM suit and would have welcomed an order directing TVA to reject overweight deliveries to Kingston.[28] Despite its loss in court, SOCM persisted in seeking to halt the systematic violations of state law by overweight trucks delivering to Kingston. Finally, in 1979, TVA announced a change in policy: it would no longer accept overweight deliveries and would renegotiate its contracts with coal haulers to ensure that the trucks weighed within the legal limit. Why did the agency take so long in reaching a fair and effective policy result? A number of reasons suggest themselves.[29]

First, TVA was not accustomed to collective efforts by citizens seeking specific modifications of agency policies. Before the 1970s, TVA had not encountered the type of interest-group advocacy that SOCM presented. The agency fell back on its accustomed response to "outside" intervention in its policy making: it did not bargain, it did not provide formal mechanisms for hearing competing arguments, and it employed legal tactics designed to blunt the merits of SOCM's arguments.

Second, TVA appeared willing to sacrifice an insular portion of its consumer constituency for the benefit of coal interests with close relations to the agency. To grapple with the overweight truck problem on its merits would have meant antagonizing these interests by forcing them to change long-standing business practices. One futile attempt by TVA to reject overweight deliveries in 1972 precipitated a strike by small coal haulers that closed Kingston for days until TVA relented. TVA undoubtedly wanted to avoid accusations that it was adding to the distress of an economically marginal but politically influential segment of the coal industry.

Finally, it took TVA years to recognize the elementary principle that its electric generating activities should pay their full social costs. The agency seemed to believe that even small savings resulting in costs outside the system were justified in pursuit of its low-cost goal. TVA failed to respond on the truck issue at the very time it should have been seizing the initiative presented to it by organizations like SOCM to incorporate into agency policy legitimate perspectives that diverged from its preoccupation with low-cost power.[30]

The Tellico Dam controversy represents another illustration of TVA's consistent efforts to insulate its decision making from judicial scrutiny. The controversy also marks the beginning of meaningful judicial efforts to influence TVA decision making. The roots of Tellico extend back to TVA's early dam-building days. A history of the project is treated in Chapter 7 of this book. Suffice it to say that, until 1970, the opposition to the dam—conservationists, local farmers, the Cherokee Indians, and the state of Tennessee under the Dunn administration—was unable to convince TVA through the informal channels of persuasion that TVA made available, such as public hearings and responses to letters, that the project was an economically and environmentally unwise investment.[31]

One striking aspect of the history of the project—continuing a strategy common to other controversial TVA initiatives—was TVA's virtual monopoly on the technical data underlying its decision to construct Tellico. Without access to the data, project opponents predictably faced a barrage of superficially irrefutable technical arguments in favor of the project. TVA would not concede that the issue involved more fundamental values—issues of heritage and ecological diversity—than economics or economic development.[32]

In 1970 project opponents turned to a national environmental public interest law firm, the Environmental Defense Fund (EDF), which possessed a highly competent technical staff in water resources issues. In 1971 EDF, Trout Unlimited, and local citizens sued TVA under the National Environmental Policy Act of 1969 (NEPA), claiming that TVA's failure to prepare an environmental impact statement violated NEPA. In response, TVA contended that, as a threshhold matter, the plaintiffs did not have standing to sue. On the merits, the agency claimed it was not required to comply with NEPA, since the Tellico project was approved and the first appropriations of funds were made by Congress in 1966, four years before the effective date of NEPA. As part of its legal strategy, TVA, contemporaneous with the litigation, was preparing its own environmental impact statement on the project.

The U.S. District Court for the Eastern District of Tennessee rejected TVA's position and enjoined construction of the project until TVA complied with NEPA. This decision was later affirmed by the U.S. Court of Appeals for the Sixth Circuit. In their decisions the courts rejected TVA's limited approach to NEPA. The Sixth Circuit found initially that the plaintiffs alleged the requisite "injury in fact" and that these injuries fell within the zone of interests protected by NEPA. Accordingly, the plaintiffs (with the exception of EDF, which did not allege particularized injury to its members) were permitted to assert the interests of the general public in support of their claim for an injunction.[33]

On the NEPA argument, the court of appeals found that TVA's contentions "ignore the language and policy of NEPA, violate regulations promulgated both by the Council on Environmental Quality and the TVA itself, and are against the clear weight and trend of the case law that has developed under the Act." Responding to TVA's argument that an injunction was inappropriate because of the plaintiffs' delay in bringing suit, the court of appeals interpreted the requirement that the issuance of an injunction be in the "public interest" differently from TVA's narrower view of what the public interest demanded. The court found that the strong policy of NEPA mandating agency consideration of environmental values and the public interest in requiring public officials to obey federal law militated against TVA's contention that the suit should be barred.[34]

Complying with the courts' decisions, TVA prepared an environmental impact statement on Tellico that withstood the opponents' subsequent challenge that the 600-page document inadequately described a number of the significant impacts of Tellico. At trial, TVA presented expert testimony substantiating the completeness of its data in the impact statement in such areas as archaeology, water quality, and ecology. Ultimately, the continuing objections of the opponents were labeled "overly technical and hypercritical" by the Sixth Circuit.[35]

These were TVA's first major judicial defeats in years. The agency saw its time-tested arguments on standing and the unreviewability of its decision making fall before a national law that mandated more open government. Full disclosure of the assumptions and data supporting the Tellico project armed the project's opponents with new ammunition. The delay occasioned by the litigation also permitted further scientific investigation of the impacts of the project.

One of the resulting discoveries—the snail darter—gave project opponents a legal handle to return to court. The litigation, premised on the Endangered Species Act, was a conscious attempt to prolong the Tellico project in the courts in order to provide opponents an opportunity to present their arguments on the economic infeasibility of the project to the only forum with the authority to stop the project: Congress. The strategy almost succeeded. TVA, resting its legal case on a narrow interpretation of the Endangered Species Act and stressing the unique features of TVA's broad mandate, took the case to the U.S. Supreme Court and lost. The Court's opinion in *Hill v. TVA* rejected TVA's conception of the public interest and instead relied on the clear prohibitions contained in the Endangered Species Act. In essence, the Court chose Congress's long-run view over TVA's short-run notion of public good. Following the Court's decision, Congress created a panel of cabinet-level administration officials to review the merits of the dam.[36]

After reviewing current project data, the Endangered Species Committee concluded that the economics of the project were not justified, despite the large expenditure of money already spent. Project proponents persisted, and the power of politicians committed to local public works projects prevailed. In 1979 Congress, in a rider to the annual public works appropriation bill, exempted Tellico from the Endangered Species Act, and the project was completed. A last-ditch effort by the Cherokee Indians, who argued that the destruction of the ancestral remains by the project violated the First Amendment, failed.[37]

Tellico is a prime example of the use of courts by public interest constituencies to gain information, to broaden traditional avenues of agency decision making, and to delay agency decisions in order to permit full-blown ventilation by other political branches of the merits of agency choices. From the start, TVA stood firm in its resolve to complete the project as it saw fit. It vigorously resisted any intrusion into its methods and only reluctantly surfaced its complete justification for Tellico. Throughout the controversy the agency used its formidable ability to marshal and disseminate supporting technical data to mold the controversy into a clash between economic progress versus rabid environmentalism. To the end, the agency did not acknowledge the deficient economic justification for Tellico, as found by the Endangered Species Committee.[38]

Tellico represented the first of a number of episodes in which TVA's version of the public interest was usurped by public constituencies resorting to the courts to enforce congressional mandates that required changes in TVA's traditional method of decision making. Using proven strategies, TVA adroitly managed to package its promotion of the dam in the language of democracy—focusing on continuing congressional support for the project—at a time when pork-barrel politics was increasingly being criticized as economically and socially bankrupt.[39]

In 1947 TVA's general counsel, in a review of TVA litigation, observed: "TVA, on its part, has regarded cooperation with State and local agencies as a *sine qua non* to the successful conduct of a regional development program. As a result, relatively few intergovernmental difficulties involving TVA-State relationships have arisen." This feature of TVA's role as a decentralized national agency changed markedly in the 1970s, when TVA and various Valley states clashed over TVA policies. The reasons for this shift paralleled the increased willingness of public and private interest groups to challenge TVA's authority.[40] Three reasons stand out. First, for many years TVA exercised enormous control over state policies affecting the agency. The agency's technical and scientific expertise overwhelmed the meager commitment of state resources to such areas as natural resources planning, environmental protection, and economic development. Hence the agency easily influenced legislation and regulations impinging on TVA's discretion. Second, states were reluctant to attack an agency that could claim so persuasively that its policies were in the public interest and promoted the regional good, rather than the parochial interests of each state. Finally, as an arm of the federal government, TVA was clothed with sovereign immunity, a doctrine that protected it from interference by state authorities.

The first important confrontation with a state occurred in the Tellico controversy. In 1970 the governor of Tennessee, Winfield Dunn, communicated to TVA his administration's position that, because of its adverse environmental and social impacts, the Tellico project should be abandoned. TVA politely responded by reiterating its justifications for Tellico and indicating firmly that it would not change its mind. After this rebuff the state withdrew from active opposition and except for providing limited technical assistance, left the fight to the private opposition.

The major confrontation in TVA-state relationships revolved around Kentucky's efforts to regulate air pollution from TVA's coal-fired steam plants. Kentucky was the site of two large TVA steam plants—Paradise and Shawnee. Over the years each plant was responsible for sizable crop damages caused by sulfur dioxide (SO_2) emissions. After the passage of the Clean Air Act of 1970, which created for the first time a meaningful federal-state regulatory program, Kentucky and other Valley states attempted to enforce the new statute to require compliance from large stationary sources of pollution.[41]

Following the act's scheme, in 1972 the Kentucky Air Pollution Control Commission devised a plan for reducing air pollution to acceptable limits. At the heart of the enforcement of this plan was a permit system. Initially, an applicant for a permit was required to supply the commission with specific information regarding its pollution output. Following receipt of this information, the commission was empowered to hold public hearings and to deny a permit if the applicant failed to supply the requested information. Once issued, a permit could be revoked or modified if the source failed to comply with permit conditions.

When requested to apply for a permit, TVA and other federal facilities in Kentucky refused, claiming Kentucky could not compel federal agencies to yield to Kentucky's regulatory authority. TVA and the other agencies did agree to supply the data requested on the standard application form. EPA encouraged TVA to supply this information but agreed that federal facilities were not required to apply for state operating permits.

In 1973 Kentucky filed suit against TVA, the Army, and the Atomic Energy Commission seeking an interpretation of Section 118 of the Clean Air Act that would require these facilities to submit to state permit requirements. Section 118 stated in its relevant part: "Each department, agency, and instrumentality of the executive, legislative, and judicial branches of the Federal Government . . . engaged in any activity resulting, or which may result in the discharge of air pollutants, shall comply with Federal, State, interstate, and local requirements respecting control and abatement of air pollution to the same extent that any person is subject to such requirements." Based on this language, Kentucky argued that TVA was required to obtain a permit because otherwise the states could not enforce the substantive limits contained in their approved plans.[42]

The U.S. Supreme Court rejected Kentucky's argument. In reading the act, the Court believed that Congress meant to differentiate between "emission standards and compliance schedules—those requirements which unless met work an actual reduction of air pollution discharge—differently from administrative enforcement methods and devices. . . ." The court did not believe that Congress had intended to waive the federal government's sovereign immunity but instead had "fashioned a compromise which, while requiring federal installations to abate their pollution to the same extent as any other air contamination source and under standards which the States have prescribed, stopped short of subjecting federal installations to state control." In concluding, the Court noted that Congress need only amend the act to make its intention clear.[43]

Hancock v. Train represented a pyrrhic victory for TVA. By far the worst polluter of all federal facilities in the Valley states, TVA had the most at stake of any of the involved federal facilities. Not only were there a dozen major sources in the TVA system but each of these plants was far from compliance with state standards. Full compliance would mean large expenditures and modestly increased rates.

TVA lobbied in the deliberations over the 1977 amendments to the Clean Air Act to avert congressional repudiation of *Hancock v. Train*. The agency's efforts, however, were futile. TVA was in the forefront of Congress's thinking when Section 118 of the act was finally amended in 1977 to require federal facilities to comply with state permit requirements. TVA was prominently cited as one of a number of federal agencies that "continue to try to evade the mandate of Federal law to comply with all State and local requirements. Instead of playing the leadership role envisioned by Public Law 91-604, many federal agencies and facilities have been laggard or have obstinately refused to obtain required permits, to submit required reports, to conduct required monitoring, to permit on-site inspections, and even to meet compliance schedules and emission limits."[44]

The 1977 amendments represented a moral blow to TVA's intransigence regarding clean air compliance. The new Section 118 altered the balance of power between TVA and state enforcers. Had the permit issue not meant much to TVA, it is difficult to imagine why the agency resisted so long and risked its substantial good will with state authorities. The only rational conclusion is that *Hancock v. Train* represented more than a battle over federal-state principles. Instead, for TVA the controversy implicated the historical autonomy of the agency in the day-to-day conduct of its operations.

Not unexpectedly, the issue of TVA autonomy from state regulation did not die with Congress's action in 1977. In 1982 TVA contested the state of Tennessee's authority under the Clean Water Act to require the agency to obtain a permit for a project on the Ocoee River in Tennessee that would divert river water for electrical generation. The project was bitterly opposed by white-water canoe and rafting organizations who prized the Ocoee for its white-water recreational qualities.

Under the Tennessee Water Quality Control Act, the Tennessee commissioner of public health requested that TVA obtain a permit because its proposed diversion would constitute an "alteration" of the properties of the water. Taking the affirmative, TVA filed suit in federal court and persuaded the court that, in spite of Congress's explicit actions in 1977, TVA did not fall within the purview of Tennessee's authority. Interestingly, the TVA board was divided two to one on this legal interpretation. The dissenting board member, S. David Freeman, took the unprecedented step of communicating his legal opinion to the commissioner. The case is on appeal, a decision being expected in 1983.[45]

The issues of federalism and the strategic intervention of the courts stand out in these episodes. TVA has not hesitated to challenge state authority when the agency perceives an encroachment on its autonomy, real or in principle. The agency also has not hesitated to litigate to the bitter end these issues of principle. In *Hancock v. Train*, and Congress's subsequent action, it would appear that this strategy of resistance backfired. But, as the *Ocoee* controversy illustrates, the dogma of TVA autonomy remains alive.

TVA's relationships with other federal agencies normalized following its early conflicts with the Departments of Interior and Agriculture. But with the growth of intragovernmental regulation in the late 1960s and 1970s, TVA's overriding goal of providing low-cost electricity collided with the federal government's commitment to pollution control. The agency charged with enforcing federal law in the environmental area, the Environmental Protection Agency, possessed resources unlike any entity TVA had faced in modern times. EPA's scientific and technical resources closely rivaled those of TVA. No longer would TVA be able to deploy its exclusive expertise to overwhelm state and local regulatory authorities with data, computer modeling, and personnel.[46]

The emergence of active environmental groups accompanied the creation of EPA. In the Tennessee Valley few public interest advocacy organizations existed in the early 1970s. The state chapters of national organizations, such as the Sierra Club, concentrated more on local issues, such as wilderness designations, than on issues with statewide or regional implications, such as air pollution. With the availability of new expertise from the national level, however, certain organizations, like the League of Women Voters, reached beyond their traditional compass to tackle broader issues and institutions. TVA was a logical focus.

The subject of the ensuing dispute was SO_2 emissions from TVA's coal-fired power plants. In 1973 TVA plants produced approximately 53 percent of all SO_2 emissions in the Southeast and 14 percent nationwide. To deal with this problem, in the late 1960s TVA devised a monitoring system—anomalously called SDEL (sulfur dioxide emission limitation)—to ensure that concentrations of SO_2 did not exceed permissible ground-level concentrations. The agency also constructed tall stacks (up to 1,000 feet) at selected plants to enhance the dispersal of SO_2 emissions. Based on the scientific information available in the late 1960s concerning the effects of SO_2 emissions, TVA's intermittent-control system represented a state-of-the-art technological approach to the problem of local SO_2 emissions. The flaw in TVA's SDEL approach was its fallibility (crop burns continued), its inability to affect the problem of long-distance transport of SO_2 emissions, and its disregard of the intent of Congress in enacting Section 110 of the Clean Air Act in 1970.[47]

TVA's commitment to a low-cost air pollution control strategy makes sense when put in an institutional context. By the late 1960s TVA was commited to its next great transition in power generation: from coal to nuclear. Nuclear power, in TVA's opinion, represented the best approach to providing electricity in the future at the lowest feasible cost. In addition, several of TVA's coal-fired plants were aging rapidly, and the replacement of these plants with nuclear units seemed an attractive option. Under this replacement scheme investments in pollution control at TVA's coal-fired plants represented wasted resources. If TVA could delay compliance with the 1970 Clean Air Act until its nuclear units were on line, its problems would be solved and its strategy vindicated. This is the context that EPA inherited in the early 1970s.

TVA's major line of defense in the SO_2 controversy was legal. TVA took the position that Section 110 of the Clean Air Act, requiring source-by-source emission limitations, did not require continuous emission controls but rather permitted intermittent measures so long as ambient standards were protected. For a number of years EPA vacillated over its position on this question. By 1974, however, EPA made clear that it would only accept continuous controls—low-sulfur coal, washed coal, or flue-gas desulfurization, or combinations of these—as acceptable compliance measures.

As early as 1972, TVA and EPA were at loggerheads. The technical staffs of the two agencies distrusted each other, and neither believed the other was acting faithfully to the interests of either the Clean Air Act or the public. On one level, it is surprising that these institutions did not accommodate comfortably to each other in this controversy. It would have been very easy for EPA to accept TVA's halting steps toward SO_2 reductions and not challenge TVA's expertise in pollution control. Such an accommodation, which would have averted the bitterness of later years, was never a real alternative because of the conflicting ideologies on both sides. EPA represented a bureaucracy primarily interested in pollution control; TVA wanted to run its power system as free as possible from the confines the EPA threatened.[48]

Another factor contributing to the friction was the continuous presence of public interest groups in the public arenas where the controversy was aired. As early as 1972, in testimony before the Tennessee Air Pollution Control Board on Tennessee's State Implementation Plan (SIP), the Tennessee League of Women Voters testified in favor of imposing strict continuous emission limitations on TVA plants and prohibiting TVA's intermittent-control and tall-stack strategies. Before this time the Valley's public interest organizations could hardly match TVA's expertise in air pollution control. Beginning in 1972, groups such as the league began to draw on data from Washington organizations and EPA to confront TVA with principled alternative policies. The league, long known for its concern over good government, also helped convert the controversy from a forbidding technical dispute to a struggle over government compliance with environmental laws.[49]

In 1974 EPA and TVA attempted to resolve the dispute through the creation of a joint task force. The task force report, issued in January, 1975, reflected the profound differences between the two agencies on the legal, technological, and scientific issues involved in the dispute. For example, the EPA representatives, most of whom were drawn from EPA Region IV, contended that TVA's tall-stack strategy exacerbated health problems in a wide geographical area. TVA vigorously disputed this contention, arguing there was insufficient evidence of adverse health effects. Similar conflicts exised on most major issues considered by the task force.[50]

In the middle of the task force's deliberations, TVA filed suit to obtain a binding interpretation on the legality of intermittent controls. The petition for review, filed in the U.S. Court of Appeals for the Sixth Circuit, challenged the authority of the EPA administrator to disapprove portions of Kentucky's SIP permitting the use of intermittent controls at TVA plants. It should be emphasized that under each state SIP, TVA was scheduled to be in compliance with the applicable SO_2 limits by mid-1975. Kentucky granted TVA a two-year extension to mid-1977. TVA's legal action virtually ensured that the agency would fail to comply by the relevant dates.

In September, 1975, the Sixth Circuit upheld EPA's disapproval of the Kentucky plan. Although the decision accorded with the results reached by other circuits on the tall-stack question, TVA sought review of the Sixth Circuit decision in the U.S. Supreme Court. This move froze the controversy until April, 1976, when the Supreme Court refused to consider the case. At this juncture TVA's strategy of delay seemed to be doomed. But the agency had one more card to play: Congress was initiating a mid-course correction of the Clean Air Act. TVA seized on this final opportunity to modify the law in its favor.[51]

In order to present the issue to Congress, TVA had to stall for more time. The agency accomplished this objective by sparring with EPA over the interpretation of EPA's tall-stack guidelines. It was not until November, 1976, that EPA took a step that it had long delayed. It issued notices of violation against ten TVA steam plants under Section 113 of the Clean Air Act, the enforcement section of the act.

Part of the reason for EPA's delay in issuing enforcement orders against TVA was the unprecedented action of one federal agency suing another for enforcement of administrative orders. Assuming that Congress intended in the Clean Air Act to authorize EPA to sue TVA, an assumption not shared by TVA, such a suit might not have presented a justifiable controversy in the courts. The rationale for this claim lay in the nature of the president's control over the two agencies. If the president had the authority to direct TVA to comply with the Clean Air Act through an executive order, then the courts might find that no real controversy existed between these arms of the executive branch. This unresolved legal issue was the source of much consternation within EPA and the Department of Justice as the crisis escalated.[52]

Following EPA's issuance of the notices of violations in November, 1976, TVA continued to contest EPA guidelines governing tall stacks. Finally, in March, 1977, TVA submitted plans for systemwide compliance with SO_2 limits without reliance on tall stacks. Significantly, in submitting this proposal, TVA refused to enter into a formal consent order with EPA because of its continuing unwillingness to acknowledge EPA's enforcement power. Despite TVA's abandonment of its reliance on tall stacks, three major issues remained. One was whether Congress would amend the Clean Air Act in 1977 to adopt TVA's position. A second was the posture of the citizens' organizations interested in the controversy. Finally, the acceptability of the content of TVA's compliance program—the crucial methods and timetables—remained in doubt.

It became plain in the spring of 1977 that TVA's strategy of delay was directed ultimately at Congress. Working with TVA lobbyists, Senator Baker of Tennessee introduced a measure that would have exempted four of TVA's worst-polluting plants from compliance with constant emission controls by permitting credit for the tall stacks at these plants. The original Baker amendment was ultimately defeated, with critics citing the inequity of exempting TVA—the government's own utility—

from requirements of the Clean Air Act that many other private utilities had met on time. In its final form the Baker amendment—Section 123 of the act—permitted only the Kingston steam plant to include credit for its tall stacks in its emission modeling. TVA's failure on this front dashed its hopes of escaping compliance with constant controls.

At the same time TVA was seeking relief in Congress, public interest organizations in the Valley were organizing to litigate over TVA's continuing failure to comply with the requirement of constant emission controls. An unusual Valley-wide coalition was formed to serve as plaintiffs. The organizations included traditional environmental groups (e.g. Sierra Club), organizations devoted to public health issues (e.g. Alabama Lung Association), a good-government group (Tennessee League of Women Voters), a consumer-energy organization (Save Our Cumberland Mountains), and a national public interest environmental law firm (Natural Resources Defense Council, NRDC). This coalition, drawing on expertise from the Washington-based NRDC, filed suit against TVA in June, 1977, under the citizen suit sections of the Clean Air Act. The suit sought the expeditious implementation of an environmentally sound, systemwide compliance plan to reduce SO_2 emissions. At almost the same time suits were filed by the states of Alabama and Kentucky seeking substantially the same relief.[53]

The initiation of litigation by the private organizations, the change in leadership in EPA, and the appointment of S. David Freeman to the TVA board in the summer of 1977 broke the stalemate that had existed between TVA and EPA. By the middle of the summer all parties were committed to fashioning an acceptable compliance plan, and negotiations toward this complex goal began.

Numerous technical and policy issues faced the parties during the negotiations. They can be broken down into two broad categories: (1) the methods and degree of control required at each facility and (2) the enforceability of the plan. The first category involved, for example, whether TVA would purchase western or eastern complying coal or construct SO_2 scrubbers or coal-washing plants, whether the emission limitations at each plant were supported by the 1977 Clean Air Act amendments and by modeling, and whether TVA was committed to implementing a compliance plan as rapidly as possibly through outside contractors. The second category included procedures for dealing with scrubber malfunctions and coal variability, requirements for reporting, and provisions for TVA's failure to meet agreed-upon milestones. It took nearly nine months for the parties to negotiate a consent agreement. TVA's negotiating team was led by S. David Freeman, the plaintiffs' team by EPA's assistant administrator for enforcement, Marvin Durning, and Richard Ayres of Natural Resources Defense Council, co-counsel for the private citizens' organizations. If massive litigation was to be avoided, each party to the negotiations had to support the final consent agreement.

When agreement finally was reached in March, 1978, the parties expected rapid approval by the respective courts, the U.S. District Court for the Middle District of Tennessee in Nashville and the Northern District of Alabama in Birmingham. But such approval was derailed by a series of events that symbolized the significance of this controversy. In April, 1978, TVA Director William Jenkins resigned, citing the encroachment on TVA's autonomy by federal agencies such as EPA. In May, 1978, on the final day of his term, Aubrey Wagner refused to sign the settlement agreement, claiming that the costs of the settlement were too high and burdensome on TVA consumers. In January, 1979, after the settlement had been approved by Richard Freeman, the newly appointed second TVA board member, the court in Nashville ordered the parties to file an "economic impact statement" justifying the settlement. This unusual procedure was ostensibly precipitated by a letter drafted by the director of the President's Council on Wage and Price Stability criticizing the costs of the settlement. Finally, in April, 1979, a group of rural electric and municipal cooperatives intervened in the settlement approval process, arguing that the settlement unnecessarily required TVA to exceed the minimum requirements of the Clean Air Act.[54]

The consent decree submitted to the court called for TVA to reduce its SO_2 emissions by approximately 1 million tons by the end of 1982. The reductions were to be achieved on a plant-by-plant basis by a combination of strategies—large-scale purchases of eastern low-sulfur coal, coal washing, and scrubbing. The total cost of the agreement was estimated at close to $750 million. It was estimated that this investment would result in a $2–3 per month increase in an average consumer's electric bill. The agreement also: (1) specified a rigid timetable during which TVA would reduce emissions on an interim basis until final compliance was achieved; (2) provided for a monetary penalty of $260 million (this penalty, rather than being paid into the federal treasury, would be used by TVA to construct a scrubber at its Cumberland steam plant in anticipation of future requirements to reduce SO_2 there); and (3) created an implementation committee composed of representatives of all the parties to the litigation to monitor the progress of the compliance program.[55]

The utility cooperatives that intervened in the case cited the costs and uncertainties of scrubbers and the large civil penalty as their primary objections. They sought to persuade the court that the settlement was a disservice to TVA consumers; at the same time, TVA, EPA, Kentucky, Alabama, and the private citizens' organizations cited the benefits of the agreement to public health and the environment. The court best captured the unusual nature of the controversy in the following dialogue:

THE COURT: I understand, but Mr. Ayres, you purport to represent the public?
MR. AYRES: Certainly, that is true.
THE COURT: And E.P.A. purports to represent the public?
MR. AYRES: Yes, sir.
THE COURT: And the Department of Justice represents the public, and the T.V.A. is a public agency. The Tennessee Cooperative Association represents the public users of power in the Tennessee Valley. All of you tell me where the real adversity is. It is citizen against citizen here, and they are the same people. That is why I am saying this is not a normal type of adversarial relationship.[56]

Two unforeseen developments led to approval of the decree in December, 1980. The first was the discovery by TVA of a computer error that led to an overestimation of the future pollution reduction required at the Cumberland steam plant, where TVA was building scrubbers in lieu of paying the $260 million civil penalty. Upon discovery of this error, the original parties to the case agreed to drop the request for civil penalties and the scrubber requirement at Cumberland. The second development was an agreement among the original parties to modify the compliance strategy at the Johnsonville steam plant by substituting low-sulfur coal for scrubbers. This modification was based on new projections by TVA indicating that, owing to lower power demand, the Johnsonville plant would not be producing at full power in future years. These modifications to the decree satisfied all parties. The implementation of the decree, which began as early as 1978, proceeded with few major problems. Those problems that did arise were resolved by the implementation committee without further resort to the courts.

The air pollution litigation represented the deepest incursion on TVA autonomy in its history. Through the litigation TVA was compelled to relinquish its sole control over its air pollution control policy and share decision making with federal, state, and even public representatives. The episode marked one of the few occasions in which TVA's view of the public interest was challenged by competent, informed opponents who marshaled public opinion and preferences to their side. TVA's monopoly on information governing complex technical and scientific issues and their impact on the public was exposed.

In the end, the agency responded to the challenge quite skillfully. It portrayed the consent decree as promoting the broader public interest by reciting the health and environmental benefits of the compliance program and predicting how the required SO_2 reductions would ameliorate acid-rain damage in the Northeast. TVA's conversion on air pollution policy saw it become one of the few utilities in the country that, in 1982, supported congressional legislation designed to solve the problem of acid rain. TVA also cooperated fully with the implementation committee created by the decree.[57]

In dealing with the issue of air pollution, TVA's early policy positions coincided with those taken by most private utilities; namely, until damage was proven, the costs of pollution control were not justified. As more data about the costs and benefits of air pollution control began to appear in the 1970s, TVA vigorously adhered to its early posture of resistance. Such a stand undoubtedly affected the utility industry's general perception about the prudence of prompt compliance with the Clean Air Act. By 1982 TVA had reversed itself so dramatically that environmental organizations pointed to its clean-up effort as a model for other utilities.

In the end, the question remains whether the air pollution controversy was an aberration or a harbinger of greater use of litigation to channel TVA policies. Whether TVA will, in the future, avoid aligning its policy positions so totally with the private sector remains an open question. Only by acting like a progressive governmental enterprise will TVA avoid the intrusion on its policy making represented by the air pollution controversy.[58]

A final area where heightened public concern has translated into judicial recourse involves TVA's rate-making activities. With the enactment of the 1959 self-financing amendment to the TVA Act, TVA no longer was dependent on congressional appropriations to fund its power system. In enacting this measure, Congress relinquished a major rationale for strict legislative oversight of TVA's future power activities.

Unlike the overwhelming majority of utilities in the country, TVA is not subject to any regulatory control over its rate-making activities. Neither the respective state public utility commissions nor the Federal Energy Regulatory Commission (FERC) possesses any jurisdiction over TVA power activities. TVA's claim to unfettered discretion over its rates flows from the broad grant of authority accorded the agency in its statute. The only potentially meaningful review of TVA rate-making activities comes through infrequent congressional oversight hearings. But even Congress, unless it significantly amends the TVA charter, a course it has been unwilling to take since the agency's creation, has no formal control over TVA's power program.

Given the absence of formal avenues of review, aggrieved consumers of TVA power have turned to the courts seeking review of TVA rate-making activities. To date, three serious challenges have been mounted. In *Mobil Oil Corporation v. TVA*, Mobil Oil, seeking to invalidate the minimum-bill provision of its power availability contract with TVA, called into question TVA's discretion in formulating industrial rates. Although it relieved Mobil of a late payment penalty sought by TVA, the court found that the power availability contract was part and parcel of TVA's rate-making function and therefore was within the unreviewable discretion of TVA. The decision observed that "the fixing of rates which will balance and achieve all these different objectives (set out in the TVA Act) is a matter which Congress has entrusted to the TVA Board, and which involves the clearest sort of commitment to agency discretion."[59]

As TVA rates continued to climb, another industrial customer sought to enjoin a systemwide rate increase, claiming that the procedures employed by TVA in reaching its decision to raise rates were defective under the Administrative Procedures Act and the due-process clause of the Fifth Amendment. The court, in *Consolidated Aluminum Corporation v. TVA*, rejected Consolidated's claim, noting that TVA's procedures were adequate given the discretion accorded TVA to fix rates. In reaching this conclusion, the court stated that although TVA's fixing of rates was quasi-legislative in nature and constituted informal rule making, the informal rule-making provisions of the APA did not apply because of the exemption for matters relating to public property, in this case, the sale of TVA power.[60]

The third attempt to penetrate TVA's autonomy over its rate-making activities saw industrial customers align with residential consumers in a challenge to TVA's policy of charging present-day TVA consumers interest costs on construction of generating facilities that would not be producing electricity for many years. In *Tennessee Valley Energy Coalition v. TVA*, an organization representing low- and moderate-income consumers, joined by the Tennessee Valley Industrial Committee, representing TVA's largest industrial customers, claimed that TVA erroneously interpreted its statute and bond resolution to require the inclusion of interest costs—amounting to $1.8 billion in 1981 alone—in present-day rates, rather than deferring these charges to a time when the plants would be providing electricity to the system. The plaintiffs, relying on the contrary practices of a clear majority of the state public utility commissions and FERC, sought to remand the issues to TVA for formal, plenary reconsideration of its position. TVA asserted that, in reality, the plaintiffs were indirectly seeking review of its rates. Joined by its bond trustee, Bankers Trust Company of New York, TVA contended that its treatment of its interest charges was necessary to retain a sound financial footing should it be required to borrow money from the private bond market. Since 1974 TVA had borrowed approximately $14 billion from the Federal Financing Bank (FFB) to support its nuclear construction program, but the Reagan administration's Office of Management and Budget had criticized TVA's massive use of its privilege to borrow from the FFB at below-market rates.[61]

The last filings in this case before the Middle Tennessee district court were in March 1982. At this writing, no decision has yet been rendered by the court. TVA's decision in August, 1982, to cancel four of its planned seventeen reactors and to defer four others, however, may so reduce the amount of money borrowed by TVA that substantially more capitalization of interest would be permitted under the TVA statute. This major policy decision by TVA therefore may blunt the purpose of the *TVEC* litigation.

The emergence of an industrial-residential consumer coalition portends unique problems for TVA. In the face of claims similar to those raised in the *TVEC* litigation, it rings paternalistic for TVA to claim that it alone possesses the ability to determine what is in the best interests of its customers. Sophisticated consumer advocates might well formulate better policy options than TVA's own staff, given the dynamic context of utility decision making. On the other hand, perhaps only TVA is in the best position to make the kinds of intergenerational trade-offs called for in utility policy making. Certainly the agency cannot cave in to all self-interested demands by consumers—particularly industrial—seeking to gain marginal competitive advantages.

These are difficult questions that currently are being fought out in the crucible of public utility and court hearings nationwide. It is difficult to justify exempting TVA from this debate unless the agency can demonstrate that its procedures and processes ensure robust consideration of all issues affecting rate making. If the past is a guide, TVA would have difficulty carrying such a burden. For example, its board meetings were first opened to the public in 1974, only after insistent protest by members of the press. The agency, moreover, has failed to adopt plenary procedures for policy making that are now required of most federal agencies. The only real input into TVA decision making comes from the informal connections TVA maintains with its distributors and large industrial customers. The agency's attempts to hold listening sessions, provide a toll-free phone line, or publish newsletters have been more cosmetic than substantive. If rate making continues as a politically charged issue through the 1980s, it would be surprising if the courts did not respond to claims to TVA autonomy by reviewing TVA rate-making practices in some depth. The "hard look" at agency policy is a staple for courts that regularly deal with federal administrative agencies. Against a background of dubious calculations in its nuclear program, protests by TVA consumers, and reluctance by Congress formally to control TVA policies, the judiciary may be the best, and only, institution for ensuring fairness and rationality in TVA's power functions.[62]

The vigilance with which TVA has guarded its autonomy shows no meaningful signs of diminishing. Whether such autonomy is justified is the central question that TVA theorists must face. If the agency is able to become a living example of a progressive democratic institution, as it aspired to be in its early rhetoric, it deserves broad latitude to control its own affairs and to make the trade-offs inherent in its policies. At the first sign of retreat from this goal, when it conducts its affairs simply like a private power company, the agency loses its claim to special insulation from outside scrutiny.

Haltingly, the agency is attempting to recapture its liberal democratic roots. The creation of minimal mechanisms for public involvement, the more balanced content in its dissemination of information to the public, and the attempts to develop substantive programs (in the solar area, for example) are commendable examples of innovation by the agency. Yet to escape the increasing criticism leveled at its policy making, TVA may have to do more. What may be required is a reconceptualization of this "experiment" in democracy in an era of new technology and politics. Creative experiments, designed to prove that the agency is in the forefront of responsive government, need to be conceived. For example, TVA could conduct referenda on important policy decisions, using cable television as a mechanism for delivering solid information and registering votes. The agency could permit a check-off on consumers' electric bills designating a small portion of the rates paid to be used for technological innovation. Through such check-offs, it could also fund public organizations to monitor portions of TVA operations. Who could deny, for example, that power-demand forecasting could not benefit from independent scrutiny outside the agency? On a more abstract level, the agency could recast its mission to become the moral broker among competing interests and ideologies in the region. Rather than coalescing around a discrete, instrumental mission, such as providing abundant power, the agency might, for example, hold itself out as the arbiter of environmental conflicts in the region or the stimulator of decentralized grass-roots democracy. Pursuing such missions could rekindle the transformative fervor of the agency's early years.[63]

Unless the agency redefines its mission consistent with progressive currents, it will not escape the mounting criticism it has faced in recent years. Rather, it is likely to face continuing struggles in which opponents chink away at its discretion and independence. TVA may choose this course. In a perverse way it seems to thrive when it is beleaguered, a legacy perhaps of its old days.

No matter which course it chooses, there is little doubt that Congress will continue to evince heightened interest in TVA affairs. More oversight hearings have been held and General Accounting Office investigations conducted in the years since 1975 than in all previous years combined. But, paradoxically, Congress has displayed an unwillingness to open the TVA charter to change, motivated by the apprehensions of the Valley congressional delegations that a re-examination of the TVA charter would rob the agency of its exclusive Valley focus.

If reform is to come, and the agency fails to take the initiative, the courts are the most likely progenitors of change. Despite their lack of expertise, courts have displayed a remarkable predisposition to intervene in the affairs of complex institutions in response to claims that the public interest is not being served. The course of modern administrative law suggests that, in the 1980s, administrative agency decisions will be subject to exacting scrutiny by reviewing courts. Motivated by an orthodoxy that all constituencies deserve adequate representation in the administrative process, courts have refashioned administrative law to reflect the pluralism of the political process.[64]

It is doubtful that TVA can escape the corrective impulses of public law courts. As recounted earlier in this chapter, there has been significant accretion in the past decade in TVA's invincibility in the courts. Just one decision forthrightly rejecting TVA's traditional defenses will open a new era for the agency. Whether this era will usher in new forms of responsiveness or legal quagmires is difficult to predict. In the end, the choice belongs to TVA and the people of the Valley.[65]

NOTES

The author was attorney for the plaintiffs in three of the cases discussed in the article: *Save Our Cumberland Mountains v. TVA*, *Tennessee Thoracic Society v. Freeman*, and *Tennessee Valley Energy Coalition v. TVA*. This article benefited from incisive readings by John Gaventa, Neil McBride, and Richard Wirtz and the careful editing of Nicole Russler and Susan Kovac.

1. This tension was keenly recognized by the early TVA leadership. David E. Lilienthal and Robert Marquis, "The Conduct of Business Enterprises by the Federal Government," *Harvard Law Review*, 54 (Feb., 1941): 568–86. For a legal analysis of the TVA charter, see Richard Wirtz, "The Legal Framework of the Tennessee Valley Authority," *Tennessee Law Review*, 43 (Summer, 1976): 573.

2. See Bruce A. Ackerman and William T. Hassler, *Clean Coal/Dirty Air* (New Haven, Conn.: Yale University Press, 1981), pp. 4–7; Guido Calabresi, *A Common Law for the Age of Statutes* (Cambridge, Mass.: Harvard University Press, 1982), pp. 44–58; Paul Sabatier, "Social Movements and Regulatory Agencies: Toward a More Adequate—and Less Pessimistic—Theory of 'Clientele Capture,'" *Policy Sciences*, 6 (1975): 301–9; Richard B. Stewart, "The Reformation of American Administrative Law," *Harvard Law Review* 88 (June, 1975): 1676–81.

3. This is not to suggest that in its early years TVA was immune from congressional oversight. Comprehensive studies of TVA's practices were conducted by GAO and congressional committees. See Senate Document 56, 76th Cong., 1st sess. TVA was more insulated than other agencies, however, because of the broad permanent funding authorization contained in its charter. See generally Arnold R. Jones, "The Financing of TVA," *Law and Contemporary Problems*, 26 (Autumn, 1961): 725–37.

4. See generally David E. Lilienthal, *TVA: Democracy on the March* (New York: Harper and Brothers, 1944); Thomas K. McCraw, *TVA and the Power Fight, 1933–39* (Philadelphia: J. B. Lippincott, 1971); Marguerite Owen, *The Tennessee Valley Authority* (New York: Praeger, 1973); North Callahan, *TVA: Bridge over Troubled Water* (South Brunswick, N.J.: A. S. Barnes, 1980). Technical expertise and professionalism are hallmarks of a model of governmental institutions called by one commentator the "administrative efficiency" model. Douglas Yates, *Bureaucratic Democracy* (Cambridge, Mass.: Harvard University Press, 1982), pp. 20–32.

5. David E. Lilienthal, *The Journals of David Lilienthal*, vol. 1, *The TVA Years, 1939–45* (New York: Harper and Row, 1964), pp. 126–38. TVA's aversion to regulation by other federal agencies was revealingly expressed by David Lilienthal and Robert Marquis, a member of TVA's legal staff and TVA's general counsel from 1967 to 1975: "The usual justification for the regulation of private businesses by administrative agencies is the necessity of ensuring that their operations shall not conflict with the public interest. In the case of a public business, however, such an enterprise itself is no less obligated to serve the public interest in accordance with law than is the regulatory agency; hence the effect of such regulation is almost certain to be simply to duplicate management and dilute responsibility." Lilienthal and Marquis, "The Conduct of Business Enterprises," p. 575.

6. Rexford G. Tugwell and E. C. Banfield, "Grass Roots Democracy—Myth or Reality?" *Public Administration Review*, 10 (Winter, 1950): 49; also see Philip Selznick, *TVA and the Grass Roots: A Study in the Sociology of Formal Organization* (Berkeley: University of California Press, 1949). One study of TVA's relations with the states during its first twenty years of existence concluded: "The pattern of intergovernmental relations which

emerges from these events is not one of partnership, nor of continuing interaction between levels of government in working out joint policy, nor of shared responsibility. It is a pattern of firm federal control of basic programs under accountability to the Executive and the Congress, with intermittent attempts to make common cause with state agencies concerning fringe issues." Elliott Roberts, *One River—Seven States: TVA-State Relations in the Development of the Tennessee River* (Knoxville: University of Tennessee, Bureau of Public Administration, 1955), p. 90.

7. The utilitarian underpinnings of TVA policy provided the agency with a powerful moral justification for its actions. See generally J. J. C. Smart and Bernard Williams, *Utilitarianism: For and Against* (Cambridge: Cambridge University Press, 1973).

8. These models of how policy is made are drawn from Colin S. Diver, "Policymaking Paradigms in Administrative Law," *Harvard Law Review*, 95 (Dec., 1981): 393–434. See also William Ophuls, *Ecology and the Politics of Scarcity: Prologue to a Political Theory of the Steady State* (San Francisco: W. H. Freeman, 1977), pp. 184–99.

9. *Ibid.*, p. 400.

10. One populist commentator noted the almost arrogant quality of early TVA decision making: "Within its own domain, however, TVA was established and seemingly impregnable. What the nation might think about TVA or the TVA idea was for the nation to decide. That was a privilege that the Tennessee Valley had not had with respect to TVA. The agitations of a few men and the long deliberations of Congress had decided it all. . . . In other days, if you were discontented with a power company, you could appeal to the government. If you were discontented with TVA, to whom did you appeal? TVA was the government. In the Tennessee Valley there was nothing above it." Donald Davidson, *The Tennessee* (New York: Rinehart, 1948), pp. 323–33.

11. 297 U.S. 288, 291 (1966).

12. *Ibid.*, p. 319.

13. 306 U.S. 118 (1939). See also Joseph C. Swidler and Robert Marquis, "TVA in Court: A Study of TVA's Constitutional Litigation," *Iowa Law Review*, 32 2 (Jan., 1947): 296–326. For a critical examination of the important role lawyers played during the New Deal, see Peter H. Irons, *The New Deal Lawyers* (Princeton, N.J.: Princeton University Press, 1982).

14. 115 F.2d 990 (6th Cir. 1940).

15. It is important to note that TVA's power program was part of the national defense effort from approximately 1939 to 1955. Electricity from TVA dams and later steam plants assisted the war effort in World War II and the Korean War and supplied power to Atomic Energy Commission facilities. TVA's national defense role helps explain the powerful consensus that sustained it during these years.

16. See Marc J. Roberts and Jeremy S. Blum, *The Choices of Power* (Cambridge, Mass.: Harvard University Press, 1981), pp. 102–7, which chronicles TVA's approach to air pollution control.

17. Tugwell and Banfield, "Grass Roots Democracy." Also see James Branscome, "TVA—It Ain't What It Used To Be," *American Heritage* (Nov., 1977), pp. 69–75.

18. For example, in 1979 the agency commissioned a study from a multidisciplined group of scholars entitled the 1979 Summer Policy Study of the Role of TVA in Regional Development. According to TVA, the study was an attempt to provide fresh perspectives for agency policy makers. The results of the study were used by TVA to develop a new set of agency goals. TVA, Office of Planning and Budget, *Strategies for the 1980's: A TVA Statement of Corporate Purpose and Direction* (Knoxville, Tenn., Jan., 1981).

19. See generally James O. Freedman, *Crisis and Legitimacy: The Administrative*

Process and American Government (Cambridge: Cambridge University Press, 1978); Richard B. Stewart, "The Reformation of American Administrative Law," *Harvard Law Review*, 88 (June, 1975): 1667–1813.

20. See Charles E. Lindblom, *Markets and Politics* (New York: Basic Books, 1977), pp. 201–13; see also Jerome Rothenberg, "Welfare Comparisons and Changes in Tastes," *American Economic Review*, 43 (Mar., 1953): 885–90; Carl Christian Von Weizsacker, "Notes on Endogenous Change of Tastes," *Journal of Economic Theory*, 3 (Dec., 1971): 345–72; Roberts and Blum, *Choices of Power*, pp. 329–30; Charles A. Reich, "The Law of the Planned Society," *Yale Law Journal*, 75 (July, 1966): 1227ff.

21. 390 U.S. 1 (1968).

22. 606 F.2d 143 (6th Cir. 1979); 636 F.2d 1061 (5th Cir. 1981). In opposing claims in court, TVA has adroitly manipulated the protean nature of the TVA Act. If a particular agency policy is challenged and the act is quite specific on a particular point—such as the location of TVA headquarters in Muscle Shoals, 16 U.S.C. Section 831g(a)—the agency invariably will point to other relevant sections of the act and TVA's continuing, accepted practice to justify its policy. A recent example of this strategy occurred in the agency's abortive attempt in 1981 to raise salaries of TVA top management above the salaries received by the board of directors, despite a clear statutory prohibition to the contrary, 16 U.S.C. Section 831(b). Litigation over this issue filed by a Tennessee Republican senatorial aspirant, Robin Beard, was mooted after TVA withdrew its "bonus plan." On the other hand, the agency's lawyers have relied on express provisions of the act and resisted resort to competing interpretations when the express language of the act supported the agency's legal position. See *Tennessee Valley Energy Coalition v. Tennessee Valley Authority*, no. 81-1069 (M.D. Tenn. filed Oct. 8, 1981).

23. See Harry Caudill, *A Darkness at Dawn: Appalachian Kentucky and the Future* (Lexington: University Press of Kentucky, 1976); Bruce Daniel Rogers, "Public Policy and Pollution Abatement: TVA and Strip-Mining" (Ph.D. dissertation, Indiana University, 1973).

24. This was a classic example of the need for and obstacles to collective action. No one person suffered enough damage to initiate action, and the price of organizing a group effort was quite high. Through subsistence foundation grants, SOCM managed to conduct the organizing and education necessary to stimulate action. See Mancur Olson, *The Logic of Collective Action: Public Goods and the Theory of Groups* (Cambridge, Mass.: Harvard University Press, 1965). In 1908 Arthur Bentley described a closely analogous situation:

"It is common for cities to prescribe the width of wagon-wheel tires in proportion to the load carried, so as to save the pavements from the injury caused by narrow tires and heavy loads. In a city in which such a regulation does not exist, but where conditions make it important, a movement for it is begun. Some of the taxpayers will organize. They will lead the others. These others, however, although actually suffering in equal degree will be indifferent, and often really ignorant of the fact that any such movement is under way. Common speech will say they do not 'know' their own interests. Success will not be easy to achieve, for the team-owners will strenuously resist the adoption of the regulation. Nevertheless the movement, or some substitute for it, is bound to win after a greater or less time. It will win because the organization that leads it genuinely represents the mass of indifferent taxpayers. It will win because it will be clear that those indifferent taxpayers are potentially comprised in the group activity. There is a tendency to action among them. If sufficiently goaded they will certainly come to 'know' their own interest. The movement will win before all taxpayers are enrolled in it—long before then—and it will win in part by the strength of the unenrolled.

"There is no essential difference between the leadership of group by a person or persons. The strength of the cause rests inevitably in the underlying group, and nowhere else. The group cannot be called into life by clamor. The clamor, instead, gets its significance only from the group. The leader gets his strength from the group. The group merely expresses itself through its leadership." Arthur Fisher Bentley, *The Process of Government* (Bloomington, Ind.: Principia Press, 1908).

25. Enforcing the weight limit was admittedly a difficult task for state officials. For example, narrow coalfield roads made spot detention and weighing of coal trucks with portable scales a dangerous job. The state claimed, however, that it did not possess the resources necessary to station an enforcer regularly at Kingston.

26. SOCM's other options were: (1) file an action—in the nature of *mandamus*—against the state enforcers claiming that they were failing to carry out their duty to conduct minimal enforcement efforts; (2) sue the individual truck operators pursuant to an unusual Tennessee citizen suit provision; T.C.A. Section 59-1112; or (3) file a petition with the Federal Highway Administration seeking to force it to penalize Tennessee for failing to protect federally funded roads; see 356 U.S. 30, 34–35 (1958).

27. Underlying TVA's arguments was its emphasis on its private, corporate character. This subtle shifting of roles is a strategy TVA also has employed over the years. When TVA believes its public agency character would better protect its prerogatives, it has heavily emphasized this role. *Hancock v. Train*, 426 U.S. 167 (1976), is an example of TVA asserting its public role over its private one.

28. This support was expressed in communications between state enforcement officials and counsel for the plaintiffs. An official of the state was subpoenaed to testify at the hearing, but the judge permitted only oral argument by counsel for SOCM and TVA. The case is reported in 374 F. Supp. 846 (E.D. Tenn. 1972).

29. In 1976 SOCM sued four of the largest coal truck companies in a citizens' suit. *Bradley v. WACO, Inc.*, no. 9521 (Roane County, Tenn., Chancery Court). The case was mooted by TVA's subsequent change in policy. Memo from Leon Ring, TVA general manager, June 11, 1979, Tennessee Valley Authority Archives.

30. SOCM and other environmental organizations failed in an attempt to compel TVA under the National Environmental Policy Act of 1969 to prepare environmental impact statements for each major coal contract let by the agency. The agency successfully argued that such a requirement would undermine its coal-purchasing practices. *NRDC v. TVA*, 367 F. Supp. 128 (E.D. Tenn. 1973), aff'd, 502 F.2d 852 (6th Cir. 1974).

31. See Chapter 7 of this volume.

32. For a critique of the use of economic theory in environmental decision making, see Mark Sagoff, "Economic Theory and Environmental Law," *Michigan Law Review*, 79 (June, 1981): 1393–1419.

33. *Environmental Defense Fund v. TVA*, 339 F. Supp. 806 (E.D. Tenn. 1972); *Environmental Defense Fund v. TVA*, 468 F.2d 1164 (6th Cir. 1972).

34. *Ibid.*, pp. 1172–73.

35. *Environmental Defense Fund v. TVA*, 371 F. Supp. 1004 (E.D. Tenn. 1973).

36. *Environmental Defense Fund v. TVA*, 492 F.2d 466 (6th Cir. 1974); 16 U.S.C. Section 1536 (1976); 437 U.S. 153 (1978); Endangered Species Act amendments of 1978, 16 U.S.C. Sections 1531–36, 1538–40, 1542 (Supp. 1979). This legislation was spearheaded by Senator Howard Baker of Tennessee.

37. *Sequoyah v. TVA*, 620 F.2d 1159 (6th Cir. 1980).

38. For an account by its lead lawyer of the Tellico litigation, see Zygmunt J. B. Plater, "Reflected in a River: Agency Accountability and the TVA Tellico Dam Case," *Tennessee*

Law Review, 49 (Summer, 1982): 747–87. See also John H. Gibbons, Holly Gwin, and William Chandler, "The Efficacy of Federal Environmental Legislation: The TVA Experience with Endangered Species and Clean Air," *Utah Law Review,* 1979 (1979): 701–18.

39. Pork-barrel politics has been subject to critique from both left and right of the political spectrum. Environmental organizations have questioned the validity of the methods used to justify questionable projects. See generally Daniel Swartzman, Richard A. Liroff, and Kevin G. Croke, eds., *Cost Benefit Analysis and Environmental Regulations* (Washington, D.C.: Conservation Foundation, 1982). Conservative politicians, seeking to reduce federal expenditures, have also assailed selected projects.

40. Swidler and Marquis, "TVA in Court," pp. 320–21.

41. 42 U.S.C. Sections 7401 *et seq.*

42. *Hancock v. Train,* 426 U.S. 167 (1976).

43. *Ibid.,* pp. 185–86, 198–99.

44. House Report 95-294, 95th Cong., 1st sess., p. 199.

45. T.C.A. Sections 70-330(b) and 70-366; *United States ex Rel. Tennessee Valley Authority v. Tennessee Water Quality Control Board,* no. 82-3030 (M.D. Tenn. filed Apr. 9, 1982); S. David Freeman to Dr. Eugene Fowinkle, Jan. 14, 1982, Tennessee Department of Public Health, Nashville.

46. See generally James O. Wilson and Patricia Rachal, "Can the Government Regulate Itself?" *Public Interest,* no. 46 (Winter, 1977). This account has benefited from Robert F. Durant, Michael R. Fitzgerald, and Larry W. Thomas, "When Government Regulates Itself: The EPA-TVA Air Pollution Experience" (University of Tennessee Bureau of Public Administration Working Paper 1, 1980), in which the authors interviewed a number of key participants in the controversy. For a more detailed account of the litigation, see Keith Casto, "Public Law and Public Power: The TVA Air Pollution Conflict," *Tennessee Law Review,* 49 (Summer, 1982): 789–841; Dean Hill Rivkin, "The TVA Air Pollution Conflict: The Dynamics of Public Law Advocacy," *Tennessee Law Review,* 49 (Summer, 1982): 843–83.

47. SDEL was a system resting not on emission limitations but rather on dispersion of air pollutants into the atmosphere. See generally Richard E. Ayres, "Enforcement of Air Pollution Controls on Stationary Sources under the Clean Air Amendments of 1970," *Ecology Law Quarterly,* 4 (1975): 441–78.

48. As large institutions that were aware they would be dealing with each other for years, EPA and TVA could have developed "informal bilateral controls" to avoid controversy and litigation. See Marc Galanter, "Why the 'Haves' Come Out Ahead: Speculations on the Limits of Legal Change," *Law and Society Review,* 9 (Fall, 1974): 95–160.

49. Each state was required to develop and implement an SIP designating the amount of emission reduction required by each source in the state. For a study of the complexities of this process, see Marc J. Roberts and Susan O. Farrell, "The Political Economy of Implementation: The Clean Air Act and Stationary Sources," in Ann F. Friedlander, ed., *Approaches to Controlling Air Pollution* (Cambridge, Mass.: MIT Press, 1978).

50. EPA and TVA, "Preliminary Assessment of Alternative Sulfur Oxide Control Strategies for TVA Steam Plants" (1975).

51. *Big Rivers Electric Corp. v. EPA,* 523 F.2d 16 (6th Cir. 1975); *Kennecott Copper Corp. v. Train,* 526 F.2d 1149 (9th Cir. 1975); *NRDC v. EPA,* 489 F.2d 390 (5th Cir. 1974).

52. See Larry Hammond, deputy assistant attorney general, Office of Legal Counsel, Department of Justice, to Douglas Costle, administrator, EPA, Aug. 22, 1977, on file with author.

53. The suits were filed under Section 304 of the Clean Air Act, the citizen suit provi-

sion. See generally Jerry L. Mashaw, "Private Enforcement of Public Regulatory Provisions: The 'Citizen Suit,'" *Class Action Reports*, 4 (Jan.–Feb., 1975): 29–43. Because Section 304 required that the suit be brought in the federal judicial district where the plant was located, five separate suits in three states were commenced. The suits were consolidated before district courts in Birmingham, Ala., and Nashville, Tenn.

54. Barry Bosworth to E. G. Chavez, Consolidated Aluminum Company, Jan. 10, 1979. In Mar., 1979, the Carter administration affirmed its support of the consent decree in a letter from Michael Egan, associate attorney general, to Sanford Sagalkin, deputy assistant attorney general, Lands and Natural Resources Division, Department of Justice, Mar. 9, 1979, in *Hearings* . . . (see above), p. 477, reprinted in Hearings on Executive Branch Review of Environmental Regulations before the Subcommittee on Environmental Pollution of the Senate Committee on Environment and Public Works, 96th Congress, 1st sess., p. 173. The letter stated that "the President has reviewed this matter carefully and believes that entry of the consent decree is in the public interest and consistent with the President's policies."

55. The penalty was assessed pursuant to Section 120 of the Clean Air Act. This provision was designed to recapture from polluters the economic advantages gained from noncompliance. See Michael Levinson, "Deterring Air Polluters through Economically Efficient Sanctions: A Proposal for Amending the Clean Air Act," *Stanford Law Review*, 32 (Apr., 1980): 807–26. In TVA's case EPA's computer model showed that TVA gained approximately $260 million from failing to take the steps necessary to comply with the respective state requirements.

56. Official Transcript of Proceedings, *Tennessee Thoracic Society v. Freeman*, no. 77-3286 and consolidated cases (M.D. Tenn.) (July 31, 1979).

57. See letter and report from C. H. Dean, Jr., chairman, TVA, to Senator Robert Stafford, chairman, Senate Environment and Public Works Committee, July 24, 1981, reprinted in *Impact—TVA Natural Resources and the Environment*, 4, (Nov., 1981): 1–11.

58. TVA's relations with other federal regulatory agencies remain problematic. For example, TVA has objected to Nuclear Regulatory Commission proposals designed to expand a utility's duty to analyze the social impact of nuclear plant construction. In addition, TVA has contested policies of the Federal Office of Contract Compliance governing equal employment opportunity. These disputes, however, have not gained substantial press or public attention.

59. 387 F. Supp. 498, 506 (N.D. Ala. 1974).

60. 462 F. Supp. 464 (M.D. Tenn. 1978).

61. No. 81-1069 (M.D. Tenn. filed Oct. 2, 1981); see Senate Environment and Public Works Committee, *Hearings on Increasing the TVA Bond Ceiling*, 96th Cong., 1st sess.

62. The Valley press has been criticized for its superficial and unquestioning coverage of TVA activities. Neil G. McBride, "TVA and the Press," *Intermediary*, 1 (Jan., 1977). This factor also contributes to the heavy reliance placed on TVA's own data on major policy issues. See generally Richard B. Stewart and Cass R. Sunstein, "Public Programs and Private Rights," *Harvard Law Review*, 95 (Apr., 1982): 1193–1322.

63. For an elaboration of theories designed to revitalize traditional democratic institutions, see Jane J. Mansbridge, *Beyond Adversary Democracy* (New York: Basic Books, 1980); Robert A. Dahl, *Dilemmas of Pluralist Democracy* (New Haven, Conn.: Yale University Press, 1982). Tugwell and Banfield foreshadowed the need for new strategies by TVA in a review in *Public Administration Review* 9 (1949): 47.

"The alternative to the grassroots approach is not less participation by citizens; it is, on the contrary, more meaningful participation—participation not through kept committees or through organizations which themselves stand in the relation of manipulator to mass, but from the play of political pressure from a variety of publics upon a government which has power commensurate with its tasks. . . . The wider the issue, the wider must be the public that decides it; but to the extent that an issue is local, authority to deal with it must be brought to bear upon it. This is surely a most delicate and intricate operation in administration, but it is in this way that real and responsible publics will be brought into existence." Tugwell and Banfield, "Grass Roots Democracy."

Also see TVA, Office of Planning and Budget, *Strategies for the 1980's.*

64. The literature on institutional reform litigation has burgeoned in recent years, reflecting the intensified use of courts to affect public policy issues. See, e.g., Abram Chayes, "The Role of the Judge in Public Law Litigation," *Harvard Law Review*, 89 (May, 1976): 1281–1316; Theodore Eisenberg and Stephen C. Yeazell, "The Ordinary and the Extraordinary in Institutional Litigation," *Harvard Law Review*, 93 (Jan., 1980): 465–517; Symposium, "Court-Ordered Change in Social Institutions," *Law and Human Behavior*, 6 (1982): 97–189; Robert E. Buckholz, Jr., *et al.*, "The Remedial Process in Institutional Reform Litigation," *Columbia Law Review*, 78 (May, 1978): 784–929; Robert A. Katzmann, "Judicial Intervention and Organization Theory: Changing Bureaucratic Behavior and Policy," *Yale Law Journal*, 89 (Jan., 1980): 513–37; Martin Shapiro, "On Predicting the Future of Administrative Law," *Regulation*, 6 (May/June, 1982): 18–25.

65. Judicial review of important TVA activities must be carefully calibrated to have both symbolic and substantive impact on the lives of TVA consumers. At best, this impact will be "incremental, gradualist, and moderate." Joel F. Handler, *Social Movements and the Legal System: A Theory of Law Reform and Social Change* (New York: Academic Press, 1978), p. 233. It would be unwise for social reform groups in the Valley to rely too heavily on law reform actions, for public advocacy itself embodies an ideology that could be inimical to long-term reform of social and economic conditions. See David M. Trubeck, "Public Advocacy: Administrative Government and the Representation of Diffuse Interests," in Mauro Cappelletti and Bryant Garth, *Access to Justice*, vol. 3, *Emerging Issues and Perspectives* (Milan, Italy: Dott A. Giuffre Editore, 1979), pp. 490–94.

9 Richard A. Couto

New Seeds at the Grass Roots: The Politics of the TVA Power Program since World War II

THERE is a symbiotic relationship between TVA's missions and the various forms of support it has received during its fifty years of operation. The formation of new coalitions to support the goals of TVA is a central factor in its survival and is key to an understanding of changes in its goals over time. The end of World War II, for example, renewed the need to justify and defend TVA's power program. This need, in turn, required a new political coalition. The distributors of TVA formed that coalition and forged a consensus on TVA's power program that prevailed until 1978 and had unanticipated consequences on TVA's mission. This paper will trace the emergence of the distributors as an active element of TVA's political environment and the consequent modification of its mission. The distributors were, of course, only one element of the political environment that sustained TVA's power program after World War II. But the details of their influence help explain some of the other changes in TVA's support and some of the later conflicts between its power program and its mission of natural resource management. In addition, the role of the distributors in TVA's power program since World War II facilitates comparison with developments in the Rural Electrification Administration during the same time.[1]

Missions and Coalitions

Initially, Democrats from the seven TVA states, New Deal Democrats, and progressive Republicans—most notably, Senator George Norris of Nebraska—provided TVA with its support. The consensus of this group evolved about TVA's role as "yardstick," a public measure of the performance of private electric utilities to keep costs down and to serve all markets, not merely the most profitable ones. In addition, resource management for regional recovery and for the integrated development of a natural unit, a river valley, provided other foci for consensus. TVA's record up to World War II was impressive. TVA construction crews regularly completed dams sooner than projected and under the estimated costs. The architecture was innovative and judged as symbolic of an enterprise of imagination and democratic determination.[2] But as the river projects neared completion, congressional support waned. Appropriations for new dam construction were increasingly difficult to gain from Congress by 1940.

TVA needed another mission and World War II provided it. Power was needed for manufacturing aluminum for airplanes during the war. Likewise TVA, along with other suppliers, provided power for the Manhattan Project, which developed enriched uranium for the atomic bombs dropped on Japan. TVA provided to this project at Oak Ridge an amount of power equal to New York City's total use at this time. These national needs removed the obstacles that had impeded appropriations from Congress for new construction, and TVA responded with style. Construction went on twenty-four hours a day, seven days a week, on new dams, most notably Fontana and Douglas.

But by 1945 the war was over, the river projects were complete, there seemed no clear national mission for TVA, and previous congressional support was gone. Most important, in 1947 TVA faced Republican majorities in both the House and the Senate. These factors guaranteed a reexamination of this New Deal program. As Aaron Wildavsky observed, "TVA required a new national consensus on the terms under which it would continue to operate."[3] The clearest indication of this need came in 1947 when the House did not approve appropriations for a coal-fired steam plant that TVA proposed to build at New Johnsonville, Tennessee. A request for a new coal-fired plant again raised major issues

TVA had faced before: its size, its encroachment upon service areas of private utilities, and the propriety of providing federal funds to a regional electric supplier. On this latter point a wag observed, "The Tennessee is the only river which flows through seven states but drains the other forty-one."

These questions were shelved temporarily when Democratic majorities returned to Congress and appropriated funds for seven new coal-fired steam plants between 1949 and 1952. But in 1953 a Republican president, Dwight D. Eisenhower, and a Republican-controlled Congress shut off new plant construction appropriations. Eisenhower was determined that TVA would not expand with federal funding during his administration. The Republican Congress of 1953 concurred and denied appropriations in the budget prepared by the former Truman administration for a proposed TVA coal-fired steam plant at Fulton, Tennessee. This plant was intended to serve the power needs of nearby Memphis. Eisenhower intervened personally in the issue and proposed a convoluted arrangement whereby private utilities in Arkansas would indirectly provided electrical power to that city. This arrangement and the ensuing controversy became known as Dixon-Yates. The controversy was redirected when Democratic Senator Lister Hill of Alabama leveled conflict-of-interest charges at members of the administration involved in the arrangement, and it ended when Memphis resolved to build its own plant.

The Dixon-Yates controversy did not resolve the issues related to TVA's future. It made clear, however, that TVA's opponents did not have the strength to dismantle the agency; on the other hand, TVA's proponents did not have the strength to win further appropriations from Congress for new plant construction. The resolution of the issues involved came in 1959 with passage of the Revenue Bond Act. This act stipulated that TVA would finance new construction with up to $750 million raised through bonds. In addition, the service area boundaries were permanently set, thus relieving the concerns of private utility supporters about TVA's apparently limitless capacity for expansion. Finally, TVA was required to continue to pay back annually to the federal treasury a portion of past appropriations, with interest.[4]

These events are familiar to many social scientists, but their significance in terms of goal displacement is often understated. Wildavsky, for example, used the controversy to extol pluralism as a process to determine "policy outcomes most satisfactory to the widest range of interested parties."[5] But part of this new consensus was a change in TVA's mission, as Omega Ruth McQuown astutely observed in her dissertation. McQuown concluded that by 1961 TVA had become a regional institution in a double sense. First, TVA was an important part of the way of life in the region; second, "effective control over its goals and politics has passed to regional interests." This change, she suggested approvingly, was a solution to the difficulties of gaining national consensus on a social policy and was perhaps inevitable where there was a void of national goals.[6]

One set of regional interests that influenced TVA's goals and policies after 1959 was the members and managers of the distributor boards of TVA power and the organizations they formed. They were in a position to exercise influence because the members of the distributor boards, by the terms of their TVA contracts, were chosen for their status and business success. Distributor board members and managers were an elite within the TVA service area and emerged after the postwar controversies as the best-organized constituency for TVA's clear and increasingly central mission: cheap and abundant electricity for the development of the region. The influence of the distributors was a consequence of three functions they performed in TVA's changing political environment from 1945 to 1959. They created regional associations and interest groups to defend TVA's power program. They established ties with Congress and state government that aided TVA. And they fostered and implemented the dramatically increased use of electricity in the Valley. We will examine each of these changes and the unanticipated consequences they had for TVA's later policies.

New Seeds: Regional Support and Indentification

After the war every major action to change or threaten TVA seemed to bring a reaction within the Valley. Gordon C. Clapp, then TVA's general manager, informed the TVA board of the early plans to start an association of distributors in 1946. Clapp declared that "TVA has purposely had little to do with the development of a Valley-wide association; the staff has neither encouraged nor discouraged the idea."[7] But when the Republicans gained control of Congress the following year, they turned down appropriations for the New Johnsonville steam plant, and TVA warmed up to the idea of an areawide association of distributors. Chairman Clapp was the main speaker at the first meeting of the Tennessee Valley Public Power Association (TVPPA) in March, 1947. TVA's general manager wrote with enthusiasm about the prospects of TVPPA and expressed his belief that TVPPA displayed a vitality and purpose which promised great things for the people of the Tennessee

Valley.[8] TVPPA opened an office in Washington in 1948 to allow communication among the distributors about legislative matters affecting TVA and to facilitate testimony from the grass roots to congressional committees. The Washington office was soon busy with battles over appropriations for New Johnsonville and other steam plants. By 1950 TVA provided small sums in financial support for TVPPA's efforts to promote electricity's use. TVA also provided information and ideas for TVPPA's research and publications about private utilities and the TVA.[9]

When a new Republican Congress denied appropriations for the Fulton steam plant in 1953, another voluntary association, Citizens for TVA, Inc. (CTVA), was a response. The links between CTVA and the distributors were evident. J. Wiley Bowers, executive secretary of TVPPA, was also the first executive director of CTVA and later served as secretary-treasurer of this organization. Other representatives of the distributors served as officers as well. TVA distributors, collectively and individually, raised more than $26,000 for CTVA by the end of 1953 and later solicited individual customers on behalf of CTVA.

CTVA had a broader membership than TVPPA, however. It enlisted mayors, judges, labor leaders, newspaper editors, as well as distributors and the customers of distributors, to engage in the major controversies of the fifties, specifically Dixon-Yates and self-financing. It claimed 35,000 members in 1954[10] and conveyed the impression of broad regional support for TVA. For example, in 1958 CTVA took out a full-page ad in several Washington papers to urge approval of the self-financing bill. The editors of eighty-three Valley newspapers endorsed the ad.

In time CTVA saw threats to TVA from within as well as from outside the agency. Specifically, when President Eisenhower named Herbert D. Vogel, retired brigadier general of the Army Corps of Engineers, as the new TVA chairman in September, 1954, CTVA viewed him as another step back from Eisenhower's campaign promise to operate and maintain TVA at maximum efficiency. CTVA conflicted with Vogel regularly over proposed self-financing bills before supporting such measures. CTVA's conflict with Vogel was at heart a difference over who represented the interest of TVA. Vogel criticized CTVA as "a political front organization" thwarting self-financing bills so as to "make it appear that the administration seeks to destroy TVA."[11] This charge brought a rejoinder from Leonard Beard, president of CTVA and mayor of Sheffield, Alabama: "Vogel is revealing his true attitude—that he is not for TVA. We have known his wishes were counter to the best interest of TVA and this is another step to prove it. . . . Vogel dislikes our organization because we have gotten in his way when he has tried to weaken and curtail

TVA."[12] Both CTVA and TVPPA worked to keep Vogel a minority board member and blocked confirmation of Eisenhower's next appointee, Arnold Jones, for more than a year.[13]

While TVPPA and CTVA frequently acted in concert, they also had differences. CTVA's executive directors chided TVPPA's president for public criticism of TVA over leasing arrangements for municipally constructed plants such as the one in Memphis. CTVA sought a united front within the Valley and was more determined than TVPPA to hold out longer for the best possible financial arrangement for future TVA construction. CTVA was concerned that the resolution of the Dixon-Yates controversy, a separate Memphis plant, could mean the "balkanization of TVA." CTVA was most concerned to reintegrate Memphis into the TVA system and to maintain an integrated system that would benefit everyone. Distributors within TVPPA, on the other hand, were reacting to projected shortfalls in power supply and were discussing a variety of self-financing mechanisms, including one to build new plants with local public funds as Memphis did, and to lease the plants to TVA for operation. TVA, under Chairman Vogel, was not receptive to the idea. The two citizens' groups differed on the focus of their discontent; for CTVA it was "the enemies of TVA," but for TVPPA it was the stubborn shortsightedness of TVA.[14]

Vogel recalled TVPPA as being collaborative and CTVA as being much more partisan. Other observers felt that the genius of CTVA was to polarize the conflicts in the form of public versus private power, us against them. Time and time again CTVA ferreted out the alleged machinations of the private utilities. They portrayed the lobbyist of the private utilities, Purcell Smith, for example, as a latter-day Samuel Insull, the notorious private utility head and financier of the 1920s. Likewise, CTVA countered the private utilities' and anti-TVA efforts vigorously. In one such successful counteraction CTVA gained an IRS ruling that the anti-TVA ads of the private utilities were political actions whose cost could neither be deducted from taxes nor passed on to customers.

Another regional group to defend TVA organized when the National Chamber of Commerce renewed its attack on TVA. The Chamber of Commerce suggested in 1958 that any legislation enabling TVA to continue or to expand should contain a set of amendments that would have substantially changed the agency.[15] In response, thirty-one chambers of commerce in the Tennessee Valley withdrew from the national association on November 10, 1958, in Pulaski, Tennessee, and began the Associated Tennessee Valley Chambers of Commerce. Barrett Shelton, editor of the *Decatur Daily*, was elected as its first president.

The significant aspect of these developments is that some groups within the Valley—businessmen, local officials, newspaper editors, and other influential citizens—saw their interests as coinciding with the interests of TVA. These groups organized to defend themselves and TVA both from those outside the Valley who would have changed the agency substantially and, upon occasion, from those within the agency who were suspected of the same intentions. The TVPPA identified with TVA and to this day interprets Dixon-Yates as "a frontal attack on the Tennessee Valley . . . by the private power companies and others."[16] Paul Tidwell, general manager of Meriwether Lewis Cooperative at this time, recalled, "We were then beginning to think as a unit and not as individual distributors. We saw this (Dixon-Yates) as a threat to break up TVA. We had become interested in rural electrification and we didn't want it broken up."*It should be kept in mind that in 1953, when developments on the national level threatened TVA, it had only recently completed rural electrification and the benefits of electric power were just being realized.

New Seeds: Political Liaison

An important feature of this regional support and identification with TVA was the belief that TVA was not in a position to defend itself. This was an impression the agency fostered. David E. Lilienthal, an original TVA board member, had asserted that "rivers have no politics" and that it was "good politics" to keep politics out of TVA.[17] He said this while exercising some of the keenest political skills of any twentieth-century American public official. Nevertheless, these assertions became hallowed symbols within TVA. In 1953 Gordon Clapp offered another reason for refraining from the fray of congressional battles. In a letter to George Dempter, president of CTVA, Clapp explained, "Even if TVA had a financial resource to combat this campaign of misrepresentation (Dixon-Yates), it would not be appropriate for us to take time from our assigned tasks to do so."[18] Barrett Shelton, who was prominent in several fights on behalf of TVA, admitted feeling protective of TVA because of his belief that as a federal agency it could not speak for itself.

TVA's desire to stay above the political fray left a vacuum that regional voluntary associations quickly filled. In 1944 the rural co-ops in Tennessee formed the Tennessee Rural Electrical Cooperative Association (TECA), which later encouraged every co-op to send a lobbyist to

---

*Quotes used without citations came from interviews conducted in 1980 and 1981.

the state legislature. Today they make up 30 percent of all registered lobbyists in Tennessee. Similar developments occurred in other states with extensive TVA power service. These groups and their leaders established ties with congressional representatives from the region as well. For example, CTVA polled all candidates for Congress on their views on Dixon-Yates. Sam O'Neal, Washington lobbyist for TVPPA, prepared a survey of the Eighty-third Congress that identified supporters and opponents of public power and some senators and congressmen whose positions were unknown. In addition to establishing new ties with Congress, the CTVA also tried presidential politics. They met with President Eisenhower in 1954 but with little apparent success. They recommended the renomination of Gordon Clapp as chairman, but he was not reappointed. In addition, the president and the group differed over what transpired at the meeting. Eisenhower reported that the group had expressed the opinion that a municipal plant in Memphis was not feasible. The members of CTVA denied this and reported that their comments were that TVA was an integrated system and new plants built to serve concentrated, urban populations like Memphis would ultimately mean diseconomies of scale within the region and higher rates for rural, dispersed populations.[19]

Neither Wildavsky nor Marguerite Owen give TVPPA or CTVA much credit for influence in the Dixon-Yates struggle or the efforts to gain passage of the Revenue Bond Act.[20] On the other hand, both TVPPA and CTVA claimed extensive influence in the stand-off that occurred in the Dixon-Yates controversy. Both groups demonstrated their ability to marshal a wide and impressive array of leaders and politicians within the Valley on behalf of TVA. They represented the fulcrum on which electoral and legislative efforts rise or fall: organization. Mayors, county judges, and governors joined one association or another. The governors of Tennessee and Alabama, as well as mayors and county judges, contributed tax revenues to support CTVA. Governor Frank Clement also issued a pamphlet with his signature defending TVA.[21] CTVA had editorial support of the major newspapers within the TVA service area that had traditionally supported TVA. Individual consumers contributed more than $26,000 in the first year of CTVA.[22] TVPPA, meanwhile, could deliver phone calls, letters, petitions, and contributions on behalf of legislative efforts. Bowers, TVPPA executive director, estimated that he could produce twenty TVA supporters in Washington from among the distributors with twenty-four hours' notice.

At the very least these groups contributed to the emerging consensus about TVA's future by exhibiting an organized determination within the TVA service area that it would continue its mission of cheap and abundant power. In this sense TVPPA's assessment is probably accurate: "TVPPA's vigorous role against this threat will be recognized as a turning point in the fight for continuation of the successful power program in the Tennessee Valley."[23] TVPPA's effort and that of the other groups were turning points in another sense. TVPPA's links with key congressional leaders made for influence within Congress and within TVA. House leaders included Democrats Bob Jones of Alabama and Joe L. Evins of Tennessee, chairmen of the Public Works Committee and the Appropriations Committee's Public Works Subcommittee respectively. Senators from the Valley states were equally prominent, including Hill, Sparkman, Stennis, Eastland, Kefauver, Gore, and, later, Howard Baker. Fred Key, the retired general manager of the Middle Tennessee Electric Cooperative, recalled "that after McKellar and up until 1967, no politician in the area dared to go against TVA. It was like motherhood."

New Seeds: Increased Utilization of Power

The use of electricity increased dramatically after World War II. Both Lilienthal and Clapp spoke of electric use as a central mission of TVA. Lilienthal wrote of TVA's generating capacity as 12 billion genii, and measured democracy in terms of kilowatt-hours. As Lilienthal stated late in his life, in an interview with the author for the film *The Electric Valley* (a documentary produced by the James Agee Film project in 1983): "Electricity happens to coincide more than almost any other service with a change in the standard of living. Refrigeration could change the diets of people more than a dietician could. (Electricity) had a profound social effect. In many respects it is the charge that makes for social change." Managers among the distributors shared Lilienthal's view of low-cost power as the fruit of the democratic process, a measure of equity between sections of American society and the building blocks of a social revolution. TVA's policies had beneficial influences beyond the Valley as well, in Clapp's estimation. He pointed out that TVA's promotional rates, i.e. decreased costs for increased electrical use, provided the stimulus for electric use in the Valley, improved services from private utilities across the country, and ultimately lowered their rates. "With few exceptions, the load building effectiveness of lower rates had to be demonstrated to the industry by publicly-owned systems."[24]

TVA had active and eager partners in this demonstration. Clapp suggested at the founding meeting of TVPPA in 1947 that "the tremendous progress already made could be surpassed easily in the future."[25] But this would require that demand for electricity exceed TVA's generating capacity and that residential and commercial users dramatically increase their use from the levels prior to and during the war. Co-ops and municipal distributors accounted for only 21 percent of TVA power sold in 1940.[26] Similarly, in 1945 only 27 percent of the farms in the Valley had electricity.[27] Fred Key recalled:

In 1940 you spent your time convincing rural people to take electricity; they could afford it; and that the poles would not ruin their farms. I spent most of my days and nights in one-teacher school buildings convincing people they could use it.

The war made the difference in a lot of the people's attitudes. Men came back to the Valley from the war wanting the things they discovered on the outside. Demand just took off; hundreds of applications; we were working seven days a week. Money and material were the only limits we had.

By 1950, 83 percent of the Valley's farms had electricity.[28] Two percent loans from the Rural Electrification Administration were available to TVA co-ops on the condition they promised to achieve coverage to all parts of the area they served.

Having reached tens of thousands of new customers, it was now necessary to educate them, as well as established urban customers, in the use of their electric power. Beginning in 1950, the TVPPA undertook two decades of effort to promote electrical use. In 1950 and 1951 TVPPA, with TVA assistance, sponsored the Home and Farm Electrical Expositon, which traveled to ninety-seven different locations within the TVA service area and reached 700,000 people, despite frequently inclement weather. The exposition covered five acres with tents, trucks, and trailers. "It brought the story of electrical living to many thousands of people who had had electric power only a short time," according to Arthur L. Dow, TVPPA president in 1950.[29] The *Nashville Tennessean* displayed some of the enthusiasm engendered at the exposition in its report on the heat pump displayed there: "This revolutionary device offers an insight into the constantly amplified blessings in store for the housewife and, for that matter, the whole family who are lucky enough to be located where they can enjoy cheap, TVA rates."[30] The exposition featured a walking-talking refrigerator from General Electric, mynah birds from Westinghouse named Acey and Decee, and of course numerous opportunities to win electrical appliances. Jennings Perry, executive director of CTVA in the late fifties, recalled that he could always tell when he had reached air space over the Valley on night flights from Washington. Electric lights left on at night were a signal testimony of TVA's low rates and a phenomenal load-building success.

There is no doubt that the load-building efforts had TVA support. G. O. Wessenauer, long-time manager of power for TVA, identified demonstrations of the use of power as the new role of the distributors: "We feel that the transfer of the (Home and Farm) Exposition and the responsibilities for a load development program are in line with TVA's policy of transferring to local agencies the responsibility for and management of activities that can be handled on a local level. We are very hopeful that by using the Exposition funds and equipment the Association can build a load promotion program which will release TVA's energies for other activities."[31] Similarly, Clapp solemnly congratulated Mark C. Stewart upon his election as president of TVPPA in 1952, citing "his serious responsibility" to maintain "the growth that the Valley has gained in its electric development."[32]

But TVA offered criticism as well as encouragement. Wessenauer chided the distributors in 1959 for not doing more to increase electric consumption. In the case of a dozen or so distributors the selling job had been outstanding, but for most of the rest, he suggested, much more could be done: ". . . Growth won't happen automatically. . . . We must show the people how our service can make it possible, and it will take hard work and it will give us aches and pains. But it will be worthwhile. We need that growth if we are to live as electric suppliers."[33]

Despite this dissatisfaction, the record of growth was impressive. In 1945 the average annual residential use was 1,754 kilowatt-hours. By 1959 that average increased by almost 450 percent to 7,863 kilowatt-hours. Nationwide use also increased but not nearly so dramatically. In 1945 average residential use nationally was 1,186 killowatt-hours; in 1959 that average was 3,450 killowatt-hours. This was an increase of slightly less than 290 percent. Utilization was greater because costs were lower. In 1959 the average residential rate within the Valley was only 40 percent of the national average; as a consequence, residential use in the TVA service area was more than double the residential use in the rest of the country.[34]

In addition to this growth in residential use of electric power, other users generated even more demand on the TVA system. Federal installations used 54 per cent of TVA's power in 1959. Industries and businesses, served directly by TVA or by its distributors, used twice as much power as residents in 1959. Stefan H. Roback, chief of TVA's Industrial Economics Branch, expressed TVA's concern with increased commercial use when he asked the distributors in a 1953 address, "Are the distributors ready for the job ahead in continued industrialization of the Valley?"[35] The distributors demonstrated their readiness by establishing staff positions to recruit industry to their areas. In addition, in the mid-fifties the distributors and co-ops of TVA power formed and supported industrial development associations to encourage the location of new industry in the Valley. Industrial and commercial use increased within the Valley from approximately 6.1 billion killowatt-hours in 1948 to approximately 14.5 billion killowatt-hours in 1959. These amounts represented 71 and 56 percent of TVA's total output, excluding sales of federal customers, in these respective years.

The fifties were years of increased electric consumption based upon the TVA expansion financed by appropriations from the Truman years. As the decade closed, demand within TVA's service area was close to the capacity of its generating system, and this produced additional pressure for some form of compromise measure to finance additional power.

Changes at the Grass Roots

It is clear that the Revenue Bond Act was the compromise measure by which the TVA power program could continue. But clarity in mission implies a sound political environment, and the political environment of TVA's power program had changed substantially. In particular, the distributor boards no longer functioned within TVA as Lilienthal and others had described them previously. It was as if the functions of the distributors and related groups were the seeds of a new relationship with TVA sown at the grass roots. Lilienthal had described the distributor boards as "the most far-reaching instance of grass roots partnership between local agencies and the TVA," and a lesson of the wisdom of "putting electricity distribution in the hands of non-political boards made up largely of men with business experience."[36] But one member of the TVA Washington office during the fifties observed, "Prior to the war there had been no real pressure for local leadership. TVPPA represented the desire of well-qualified people to assume leadership which was not just an adjunct to TVA." Since the claims of Lilienthal, the distributor boards have become much more active on behalf of TVA. From 1947 to 1959 they had organized and identified with TVA power issues; they had established ties with state legislatures and Congress and had used those ties; and they had aggressively promoted increased use of electricity, which built up TVA's load factor.

These activities met what Charles Perrow has identified as essential needs of TVA or any organization;[37] hence the distributors, through the organizations and elites they could mobilize, became a more important part of TVA's political environment. They were important because of their ability to gain sufficient capital for TVA to operate, to secure local support and hence legitimacy for TVA, and to coordinate the relations of TVA with the consumers of electric power. Perrow suggests that when any group conducts these essential activities for an organization, the background characteristics of the members of such a group will shape the operational goals of the organization. Given that Lilienthal sought a homogeneous background for distributor members, "men with business experience," it is understandable how the operative goal of TVA became cheap and abundant power as a means of regional development.

Ironically, it was Vogel, who had been suspected of attempting to destroy TVA, who offered a concise statment of TVA's new operative goal in March, 1961:

TVA's experience has demonstrated, and the TVA Act assumes, that provision of power at the lowest feasible cost to consumers is a vitally important means of encouraging the establishment of new job-producing industry and furnishes a lasting base for improvement of the economic opportunities of the people. . . .

We are convinced that the TVA power system can make its greatest contribution to the development of industry and the alleviation of unemployment by maintaining its power rates at the lowest possible level.[38]

Vogel wrote in response to a request from President John F. Kennedy that TVA consider "relevant human factors" in addition to engineering factors in determining new plant locations.[39] An important aspect of this exchange was that the president had requested information on site location before a final board decision, but Vogel's response informed the president of the board's decision and its reasons. Vogel pointed out that the new plant, Bull Run, would not use congressionally appropriated funds, thus implying that there was no need for presidential input into the site location decision.[40]

The political environment of TVA at this time demonstrated far less volatility. TVA's relations with Congress up to 1967 were especially notable for a lack of controversy over the power program. Presidential appointments were made, the debt ceiling was increased in 1966, and, most notably, TVA's expansion into nuclear-generated steam plants went by almost without comment.[41] TVA's dealings with Congress on its power program became so placid that the seeds of the new relationship of TVA and the distributors were dormant. Some of the groups in the Valley formed to defend TVA declined in membership. CTVA had a last flurry of activity during the presidential election of 1964 in reaction to Barry Goldwater's comment that he would consider selling TVA. The Associated Valley Chambers of Commerce passed from the scene more quietly. Eventually both groups merged with the Tennessee River Valley Association (TRVA) in 1971. The TRVA was also the successor of the Tennessee River and Tributaries Association, which promoted development on the tributaries of the Tennessee River.

During this era of calm the distributors, through the TVPPA, continued in their new functions. They exceeded the promotional activities started in the early fifties, for example. TVPPA began a Gold Medallion Home Program in 1960 to encourage the all-electric home within the Valley, and began promoting the all-electric school. Distributors worked to increase summer power demands by promoting air conditioning. In addition, there were numerous efforts to contribute to the load factor. These included appliance jamborees, promotion of electric clothes dryers, outdoor lighting programs, kitchen spectaculars, and in 1965 trading stamps were awarded with the purchase of a major appliance. TVPPA also worked at capital formation and lobbied for a higher debt ceiling in 1966 to permit TVA expansion. They also defended TVA against external threats like President Richard M. Nixon's plan to sell to private industry the gaseous diffusion facilities used to enrich uranium. Such a plan would have had consequences for the demand for TVA power and perhaps would have introduced a new supplier of electricity to the Valley, presumably a private utility. Hence this arrangement was seen as another Dixon-Yates.

TVPPA's opposition to this measure was expressed in conjunction with two other organizations, the National Rural Electric Cooperative Association (NRECA) and the American Public Power Association (APPA). TVPPA had forged links with these groups in the fifties. Two managers of TVA co-ops served as president and as officers of NRECA after 1960. Likewise, TVPPA drew closer to APPA, and its Washington representative eventually served as deputy associate executive director of APPA. Insofar as TVA was the flagship of public power in this country, these national organizations often participated in conflicts related to TVA. These alliances and working relations with national organizations marked a change in the influence of the TVA distributors.

Some of their functions brought the distributors into conflict with TVA even at this time of calm. Specifically, customer relations sparked a feud between leaders of the distributors and the TVA board. There was a strong expression of anger mixed with disappointment over the manner in which the TVA board announced rate changes in 1961. The new schedule of retail rates in 1961 was lower than previous rates and was established to commemorate the centennial anniversary of the birth of Senator George W. Norris. Wesley M. Jackson, president of TVPPA, wrote Vogel of his organization's view that "TVA was grossly inconsiderate of the Distributors" in publicly announcing lower retail rates that only two of the 155 distributors would be able to implement. TVA had not lowered its wholesale rate, and only two distributors could afford to offer the new lower retail rates that TVA instituted and yet still achieve operating costs. But TVA had created an areawide anticipation of lower rates. Jackson expressed TVPPA's view that "it appears that our 'partnership' arrangement has deteriorated measurably." Despite these feelings, Jackson assured Vogel that TVPPA would keep its anger to itself, fully confident "that our differences can be satisfactorily resolved privately and without third-party participation."[42]

The Tennessee Rural Electric Cooperative Association went further at its 1961 annual meeting and censured TVA for "the inconsiderate manner in which the Norris Centennial rate schedule was announced." TECA requested that TVA return to the "full practice of cooperation with its distributors."[43] But there was conciliation as well as criticism, and TECA President J. W. Jellicorse described TECA as TVA's loyal opposition: "We all want TVA to talk with us about important rate changes. But the power companies will find our ranks closed tight, where there is an attack on TVA from the outside."[44]

The furor over the Norris centennial rates indicated a consistent sore point between TVA and the distributors: relations with the electric bill payers of the service area. The distributors were the first to get the reaction of their customers when TVA changed policies, as with the centennial rates. After 1967 TVA increased rates often without warning. This aspect of TVA policy making forced the distributors to bear the wrath of consumers over higher rates and would eventually disrupt relations between TVA and the distributors. But up until 1967 relations were calm. Revenues from bonds paid for new plants, and congressional appropriations paid for new dams. There was peace in Congress over the Valley, and peace in the Valley as well. For instance, Vogel became the head of the Tennessee River and Tributary Association for a brief period immediately after leaving TVA. This group originally opposed him for his unwillingness to seek federal funds for new development on the tributary rivers. Despite his earlier differences with TRTA, CTVA, and TVPPA, he had won acceptance and some admiration by 1962. Barrett Shelton expressed general approval of Vogel, which indicated the new harmony within TVA's political environment.

TVA's external environment was so secure, in fact, that the distributors began to fight among themselves for want of a common enemy. New conflicts occurred among the distributors and between them and TVA over questions of operation, especially about competition for the urban-fringe service areas with denser populations and lower operating costs. Thus rural co-ops resented municipal distributors expanding into suburbs or servicing malls in rural areas and leaving them with the more sparsely populated and costly electric markets. But by and large, by 1959 and the passage of the Revenue Bond Act, "the questions that bugged everyone were settled," as Vogel put it.

Old Missions and New Questions

The political environment of TVA was to become far more volatile in 1967 when TVA began raising its rates. When rates began to rise, the unanticipated consequences of change at the grass roots became more evident. For one thing, TVA was far more conciliatory to the distributors at the time of its first rate increase than it had been earlier. After the flap over the Norris centennial rates, the boards of TVA and TVPPA began to meet annually to improve communication. At the fifth annual meeting in 1967 the TVA staff presented the cost and income figures that dictated its first rate increase in twenty-seven years. TVA and TVPPA officials reviewed and approved procedures for notification to the distributors and customers of TVA power. But as rate increase followed rate increase, the relations between TVA and the distributors became strained. In February, 1973, J. C. Hundley, executive director of TECA, wrote Aubrey J. Wagner, chairman of TVA's board, complaining of the frequency of TVA rate increases and their timing. From the first increase in 1967 until 1973, retail rates to residential customers had increased by 62 percent in six increments. These increases brought a "deluge of high bill and rate complaints" from which TVA was almost completely insulated. At one point, Hundley complained, TVA had increased rates four times in nineteen months, guaranteeing that customer furor over one rate increase would not even abate before starting again because of another rate increase. The increase announced for January, 1973, hit people in the peak bill period owing to home heating costs and was a public relations blunder in Hundley's estimation. Hundley requested that TVA adopt a "larger–less often" policy of announcing major rate increases that would cover its costs over a longer period of time.[45]

Hundley was not alone in his concern. The manager of the Knoxville Utility Board, now TVA Chairman Charles H. ("Chili") Dean, Jr., also wrote Wagner for suggestions on "how to better formulate our plans for survival in an unfriendly environment."[46] This environment included consumer protest and plans for the take-over of the utility board, according to Dean. The battles with customers were far more unpleasant than the previous battles of the fifties with private utilities and the external enemies of TVA, according to Paul Tidwell, a rural co-op manager and past president of NRECA. "When we were selling electricity for less than a penny a kilowatt-hour, we were 'the golden boys,' but when prices went up, we became public enemy number one." The wrath of their customers gave the distributors incentive to encourage TVA in its policies of lowest possible rates, and they were still the best organized constituency in TVA's political environment.

The distributors expressed loyalty to TVA time and again, despite their continuing problems over the handling of rate increases. Hundley, for example, offered Wagner space in the TECA magazine to explain to retail customers the reasons for rate increases. Moreover, he defended TVA against such critics as Republican Congressman Robin Beard of Tennessee, to whom he wrote, "We strongly urge you to refrain from abusing the Federal agency that has been responsible for the development of the Tennessee Valley region."[47] The distributors defended TVA from other encroachments as well, such as the transfer of AEC gaseous diffusion plants, which might have had negative consequences for TVA. They also initially opposed the Federal Financing Bank (FFB) because of the mandatory requirement that TVA use it. The distributors saw in that requirement another attempt by other parts of the federal government to curb the autonomy of TVA. Eventually, the bill passed without the requirement that TVA use FFB.

In addition to this function of defense, the distributors continued to provide for the other needs of TVA. They lobbied for higher debt ceilings in 1970 and 1975, bringing the allowable ceiling to $15 billion.

There was also an effort to renew TVA's legitimacy in the face of increasing rates. In 1970 Barrett Shelton pulled together a coalition of TVPPA and TVRA to form an Emergency Committee for the Valley. This committee investigated the increased purchases of coal and uranium resources by oil companies and pushed for a Justice Department investigation into price fixing and manipulation of coal supplies. None of these actions brought the cost of electricity down, but they did couch TVA's problems in terms of external forces plotting against TVA and the public. Once again there was an element of "us against them."

The chairman of TVA from 1962 to 1977, Aubrey J. Wagner, indirectly fostered good relations with the distributors. Wagner clearly supported the goal of cheap and abundant power for regional development, and the distributors had little reason to fear opposition to this operative goal from within TVA. Wagner had joined TVA in 1934 and worked his way up the ranks. He became assistant general manager in 1951 and was general manager while Vogel was chairman. In 1961 President Kennedy appointed him to the board and a year later named him chairman. Wagner shared TVA's past achievements and struggles with the distributors and spoke in their terms: "If there needs to be an example anywhere of what you can do with low cost energy to develop a region and to help a people grow, the TVA is that example." Despite their differences, the distributors trusted Wagner to do all in his power to keep rates low.

Wagner's task was difficult, especially because a new set of critics emerged during the sixties to offer a substantial and articulate challenge to TVA's mission of cheap and abundant power for regional development. The grounds for their criticism were TVA's coal policies, from its purchase to the emissions coming from its combustion. Harry Caudill attributed the decline in unionized coal mines and the development of destructive surface mining in eastern Kentucky to TVA's purchasing practices, which centered on the lowest possible price for coal. He castigated TVA as "an immense government-owned electric power corporation" with "even less interest in the land affected by their far-flung operations than their compatriots in the investor-owned companies."[48] Caudill's criticism was echoed by many others and represented a change in the opposition to TVA. These were not the displaced homeowners that TVA had always had to contend with or the private monied interests that Lilienthal had railed against. This was criticism from people who, in the thirties, would have been called the "grass roots."[49] The environmental critics pointed out that integrated development, as a mission of TVA, seemed to conflict with its goal of low-cost power—at least in eastern Kentucky. TVPPA editorialized on the irony of a multi-purpose agency now scourged by environmentalists and defending itself before Congress:

So, on two consecutive days, the Chairman of the TVA Board—chairman of an agency that is "more than a power utility"—found himself defending the agency's policies on strip mining, air pollution, and water pollution.

Surely, the founders of TVA—who view the agency as a multipurpose resource development agency—would have been confounded, nearly forty years later, to find the "resources" agency attacked on all sides as anti-resource development.[50]

There was other evidence within TVA's experience of the conflict between its coal policies and its broader goals. In 1971 sulfur emissions from TVA's Shawnee plant damaged crops in the immediate area. TVA began the practice of compensating farmers for crop damage. Similarly, in 1967 the one hundred or so citizens of Paradise, Kentucky, culminated several years of complaining about particulate matter and sulfur dioxides emitted from the stacks of the TVA plant with a petition for requesting cleaner emissions. This plant had been the first financed with bond revenues and the first in TVA's expansion of the sixties. TVA's response was to exercise its power of eminent domain, to purchase the community and level it to the ground. Years later Frank Smith, who was a TVA director at the time of this decision, would suggest, "There was only one responsible solution, do away with Paradise. Get them out of the way."

These incidents are offered as evidence of observed conflict among the goals of TVA and a corresponding change in its political environment. The technology to control emissions was costly and would have increased rates, thus undermining the goal of lowest costs. Likewise, adequate reclamation would have driven up the cost of strip-mined coal. TVA did make some effort to abate emissions and promote reclamation, but it also opposed efforts to attain more stringent emission controls or elimination of strip mining. Consequently, the new critics persisted in their demands. But its old support remained firm. The TVPPA provided legitimacy for TVA's coal policies. It not only defended the agency but arranged for APPA representatives to come to the region and inspect TVA's coal policies. The APPA found them satisfactory. TVA had thus become a yardstick of environmental externalities in the pursuit of low-cost power. Its reluctance to conform to the compliance with the law demanded by the Environmental Protection Agency is illustrative of the new features in TVA's political environment, including the influence of the distributors.

TVA's successful past expansion into coal-fired plants now posed a problem. TVA had sixty-three coal generating units in twelve plants in Kentucky, Tennessee, and Alabama in 1970 when the Clean Air Act amendments were passed. By these amendments the EPA was invested with the authority to formulate and enforce national ambient air quality standards. States were given opportunities to devise their own standards and enforcement plans on the condition they exceed the federal standards. By 1972 the seven TVA states had standards with which the TVA plants were far out of compliance. Figures for 1973 showed that TVA power plants emitted 2.37 million tons of sulfur dioxide, 14 percent of the national amount and 53 percent of emissions from electrical generators in the Southeast.[51]

TVA chose to measure emissions immediately proximate to the plant and proposed an intermittent control system (ICS). The idea behind the ICS, coupled with much taller stacks, was to release the same quality of emissions but with proper atmospheric conditions to ensure wide dispersal of pollutants and thus conformity with ambient standards at ground level near the plant. This was unacceptable to EPA, which insisted, along with the states, that pollutants be eliminated at their source and that emissions be made cleaner before being released. All of TVA's plants were in noncompliance with the emissions standards of EPA and the states.

The distributors supported TVA's position. Barrett Shelton had told a United Nations Scientific Conference on the Conservation and Utilization of Resources in 1948 of the marvelous developments in Decatur, Alabama, that TVA fostered. Now, in 1973, he traveled to the Alabama Air Pollution Control Committee to tell them: "When the Tennessee Valley Authority tells you something, you can count on it. They are qualified people. They are people with integrity. They are not down here for the purpose of escaping responsibility. They are as interested in clean air as you are."[52]

Similarly, TVPPA worked for a reprieve from the stringent standards of 1970. They lobbied hard for an amendment in 1973 to the National Energy Act that would have sanctioned TVA's use of the ICS. This amendment would have permitted a saving of $200 million annually, according to TVPPA. Although this amendment was not passed, the act itself required a review of regulations and standards. This review permitted TVA more negotiating room with the EPA and additional time to come into compliance. In the meantime, a concerted effort was undertaken to help defray TVA's expense in complying with air quality standards.

This effort began in the office of Congressman Jones, but before long it demonstrated the extent of support for TVA's goal of low-cost electric power. Jones proposed a bill to permit TVA to apply the interest payments it owed the federal treasury to the cost of constructing environmental facilities for its plants. These payments had become major expenditures as the interest rates grew beyond those anticipated in 1959. In 1974 the annual payments would come to $63 million; total payments on interests since 1959 came to $686 million. Republican Howard Baker of Tennessee sponsored the bill in the Senate and chaired the hearings. He identified the intent of the legislation: ". . . to distribute equitably among the people of the nation and the Tennessee Valley the costs of capital improvements required to meet environmental objectives."

Shelton, writing on behalf of TRVA and the Emergency Committee, also explained the bill in terms of equity and as a measure to create parity with private utilities. Congress, through a series of tax measures, he explained, was subsidizing pollution devices of private utilities in the form of foregone revenue. At the same time Congress not only offered no financial incentives to TVA to install pollution devices but also maintained its requirement that TVA make payments at interest rates no one had anticipated in 1959.[53] Also testifying on behalf of TVA were the president of TVPPA; Joseph Ives, of NRECA; and Alex Radin, executive director of APPA. Radin testified that as long as Congress had permitted private utilities to recoup some of the costs, TVA should also have incentives. Senator Edmund Muskie asked Radin whether or not TVA's request would be followed by a similar request from other publicly owned electrical utilities, in much the same manner as a camel's nose is followed by its body. Radin responded, only half-assuringly, "The camel doesn't exist at the present time."[54]

The hearings offered new evidence of the make-up of TVA's support. Clearly this was a measure by which TVA could save money and presumably pass it along to ratepayers. The interests of TVA and the distributors were linked together and coalesced with the interests of public power nationally. This generated a volume of support and a degree of unanimity that had not been seen in a long while. The Valley congressional delegation also flexed its muscle. Jones shepherded the bill through the House with the support of Evins. The measure won by a margin of nine votes. Howard Baker won approval for the measure in the Senate. The measure was defeated at the point where TVA and public power traditionally had the least support: the Republican White House. Gerald Ford vetoed the measure.

TVPPA interpreted this defeat in terms of the traditional opponents of TVA.

Who did President Ford listen to? As his veto message puts it, his "environmental advisers as well as my economic advisers." That means the long-time TVA foe, the Office of Management and Budget; the Treasury Department; and the Environmental Protection Agency.

The private power companies reverted to their old, narrow pattern, and strongly opposed the bill. Lest the lesson be forgotten: the private power companies seem as determined as ever to cripple and hurt TVA, and to remove it from the national scene. The private power companies, for all of their "cooperation," still would like to see TVA vanish. The companies resent the lower rates, and indeed, the very existence of TVA. Cooperation with the power companies means cooperation that benefits them.[55]

The impasse between TVA and EPA began to break up on June 22, 1977, when nine citizen groups, including the Sierra Club and the League of Women Voters, and the states of Kentucky and Alabama filed suit in federal court to force TVA to comply with federal air pollution standards. At this point TVA was in compliance about 16 percent of the time, while national utilities were in compliance 74 percent of the time. On July 13, 1977, the EPA also brought suit against TVA.

New Missions and Old Coalitions

When S. David Freeman was named to the TVA board in 1977, he took steps to bring TVA into compliance. Freeman recalled that at the Senate hearings on his nomination,

Senator Muskie looked at me and his eyes glared. He said, "Dave, I'll vote for you if you go down there and obey the law. Those people down there are defying my air quality law."

TVA was in serious trouble with leaders in the Congress. There was a feeling TVA had cheap rates because it was evading air standards and reclamation.

It was obvious to many that TVA's standoff with EPA could not continue. With lawsuits pending against TVA, Freeman moved quickly to negotiate a settlement. The settlement exceeded a billion dollars and was an unprecedented TVA expenditure, not only in size but by category. It internalized a portion of the health and environmental costs that had previously been externalized. The settlement was so expensive that William Jenkins resigned as TVA director rather than act on the settlement, and Aubrey Wagner refused to vote for it prior to his retirement. Wagner preferred to let the cost that TVA customers would have to bear be set by the courts than by a compliant TVA board. Left as chairman and the only board member, Freeman was unable to act until Richard Freeman, no relation, joined the board and voted for the settlement.

In effect, what these developments signified was not only a change in the TVA board but also a consequent reinterpretation of TVA's mission. Freeman was outspoken on this. He suggested that the "energy world was turned upside down: but yet TVA seemed to continue with the same bag of tricks." TVA's historical pattern of growth—doubling capacity every decade or so—needed to be altered. "I believe that if TVA leads this Valley down that road for the rest of the century, it will be leading the Valley down a dead end, and it will be making a fundamental mistake that will make Franklin Roosevelt turn over in his grave."[56]

When the new chairman showed ambiguity toward low-cost power, the distributors reacted to this threat within TVA somewhat as they had with Vogel. They objected not only to Freeman's clean air settlement but also to rate increases, surprise announcements, new direct approaches fron TVA to customers that bypassed distributors, and a host of cost-increasing management and alternative energy policies. Behind all these measures was Freeman's belief that TVA could revive a national mission. At various times he offered conservation, solar energy, the electric car, and nuclear safety as a national mission for TVA. But there was no organized constituency for these missions. On the other hand, Freeman was faced with a set of powerful interest groups within the Valley, the distributors, who were used to lowest-cost policies for regional development. They had provided TVA with legitimacy, client relations, and capital formation. In a sense Freeman's position was similar to that which faced TVA's early agricultural program. An organized constituency for established policies stood ready to defend itself and those policies against TVA.[57] In turn, TVA needed the services this constituency could provide and could secure them nowhere else. An important difference between the early TVA agricultural program and Freeman's position, however, was that TVA had created the groups Freeman now confronted.

The immediate response of the distributors to the clean air settlement was to defend TVA's traditional operative goal of cheap and abundant electricity as the means of regional development. In an unprecedented action TECA and a number of municipal distributors sought a court injunction to halt the implementation of the clean air settlement that Freeman had negotiated. Frank Perkins, executive director of TECA, said that his organization had to convince TVA "that we were not just whistling Dixie" when his membership objected "that TVA was spending more of its ratepayers' money than it needed to, to obey the law."[58] TECA reverted to the sharp criticism of TVA directors that it had leveled against Vogel. At the 1980 annual meeting TECA expressed its "extreme disappointment that these men (David and Richard Freeman), who have had placed in them such a great trust by the consumers of the Valley, have failed the consumers in this matter," and resolved "to continue our fight in the courts in behalf of the ratepayers that justice may be done." TVA later discovered some misconceptions in its estimates, the EPA allowed TVA to apply the fines to the cost of equipment, and thus the settlement was reduced and enacted.

The essential point is that TVA could not control the distributors when they felt TVA was violating an operative goal which they had defended. When the new TVA board changed its position toward EPA, it traveled alone. TECA's organized opposition to the negotiated settlement was evidence of some distributors' willingness to defend the traditional goal of cheap and abundant power against the policies of the new board.

At about this time TVPPA achieved a new level of activity. The 1978 TVPPA annual meeting was the best attended in its history, and Jerry Campbell, executive director of TVPPA, stated, "Freeman gave us dozens of reasons to unify more than in the past. He made us look for influence and forced us to find our effectiveness. Our staff has grown during his time from three to ten."

TVPPA fought with TVA over Freeman's initiatives to spend power revenues on research and development of alternative energy sources. TVPPA also differed with TVA over the standards of the Public Utility Regulatory Act (PURA). This act required utility regulatory commissions to examine standards of service and rate making of electric utilities. TVA assumed the function of such a commission vis-à-vis the distributors and in effect reviewed and revised parts of the contract it had with each distributor. TVPPA spoke on behalf of all distributors and expressed particular concern that TVA do all that it could to provide incentives for new industries. For example, TVPPA opposed the TVA recommendation of increased preferential rates for residential users; under this plan TVA residential users would get a block of electric service at a low cost and then pay higher cost for larger amounts. This inverted rate was seasonally adjusted to make sure that home heating needs in winter would be met with cheaper electric rates. Although the

TVA charter required it to give residential users preference in the use of electricity, TVPPA suggested that excessive preference would conflict with TVA's other goal of regional economic development. That is, a "subsidy" to residential customers would require other electric users to pay higher rates.[59] The conflict TVPPA saw between preferred rates and TVA's other responsibility of regional development implied a concept of regional development that was tied clearly to the interests of commercial and industrial users.[60] In a conciliatory action that recognized the power of the distributors, TVA set up joint committees of TVA staff and members of TVPPA to negotiate the final terms to implement standards under PURA.

As in previous times, TVPPA could fight for some TVA policies even as it opposed others. TVPPA lobbied for a higher debt ceiling of $30 billion in 1980 and in 1981, and defended TVA against President Reagan's transition team's report on TVA. In response to a suggestion to expand the TVA board, TVPPA and many other distributors argued that the fundamental structure of the board was sound and that no structural changes in the agency were necessary. They suggested that President Reagan could make all the changes necessary by his appointment of a new TVA director.[61] Unlike Vogel, Freeman did not have the national political resources to sustain himself in the face of an erosion of traditional support for the TVA chairman. In an unprecedented move President Reagan, at Senator Baker's suggestion, demoted an active board member from the chairmanship and named Charles H. Dean, Jr., to be the new director and to succeed S. David Freeman as chairman of TVA. Significantly, Dean's previous experience included serving as the general manager of the Knoxville Utility Board and as president of TVPPA from 1976 to 1978. He was the first distributor ever to be appointed to the board. Baker, in recommending Dean to President Reagan, specifically referred to Dean's ability to better represent the "viewpoints of both the consumers and the distributors."[62] The appointment of Dean, the modification of Freeman's agenda for change, and the influence of the distributors in Baker's oversight hearings in 1981 indicated to TVPPA Executive Director Campbell that the distributors had entered "a new era of influence."

New Missions and New Coalitions

Dean's appointment clearly indicated TVA's volatile political environment after 1978. A new TVA board had broken ranks with the distributors and other constituent groups. Together they had defended a policy of abundant power at the lowest feasible cost in the face of environmental and congressional critics, even after this policy clearly negated the original resource management role of TVA. Freeman made clear that the realities of energy production would mean ever-increasing rates and dropped some of TVA's resistance to internalizing environmental costs in energy production. This modification in mission reinvigorated the allies of TVA's former operative goals, who influenced Freeman's removal as chairman.

Dean's earliest comments suggested deference to the distributors' preferred policies. He indicated the board would have less to do with the day-to-day operation of TVA. He showed less enthusiasm for solar energy than Freeman had and suggested that the promise of solar energy lay in the too-distant future. He suggested a method to complete the nuclear plants, which the Freemans had deferred. Congress, he thought, should appropriate funds to finish the deferred plants. These plants could then be placed in a strategic energy reserve as a hedge against an interruption in the import of foreign oil. Dean, like Freeman, examined the possibility of selling surplus TVA power to surrounding utilities, especially those that used oil. Such roles would reduce anticipated power surpluses resulting from TVA's nuclear construction program and restore a national mission to TVA.

The distributors welcomed Dean's new initiatves. Many of the distributors remembered life before electricity; they presumed a relationship of electric power and the creation of jobs and they consequently had a stake in "keeping the lights on."[63] Many prepared to make the TVA region "an oasis of energy in an energy-parched land" even if it meant higher rates. They believed there would always be buyers for electric power at any price and that the electric future belonged to those with sufficient supplies rather than low prices. Freeman himself subscribed to these beliefs and for a while maintained a united front with the distributors against GAO reports, the report of the Reagan transition team, and the congressional hearings, all of which suggested that TVA was overbuilding. The distributors once again legitimized TVA in their position by expressing a demand from the "grass roots" for TVA's construction program. Further, the distributors proposed public power authorities that would provide capital at lower interest rates and reduce costs.

However, when the criticisms of TVA's nuclear power were incorporated in the figures of TVA's own staff, it also became evident that a new chairman was not enough to restore a stable political environment.[64] The myriad factors affecting TVA's nuclear program—higher marginal

costs and interest rates, safety and waste disposal questions, rate increases, uncertain demand forecasts—guaranteed conflicts with the
dominant operative goals of TVA since World War II and ensured a continuing volatile enviroment. The consensus created by the Revenue
Bond Act in 1959 dissipated in the face of the new demands of nuclear
power. TVA could not continue to provide abundant power at the lowest
feasible cost because new nuclear plants were more expensive than several other options before TVA. The new board shaped a new issue for
TVA, abundant power or the lowest feasible cost.

This choice implies a modified mission, and the history of TVA suggests that the complexities of the nuclear issue will require some change
in TVA's political environment to resolve them. The distributors have
been the best organized constituency for TVA's power program since
World War II because of functions they performed. Their support for a
modified mission of TVA may be a major factor in its ability to undertake new activity. Clearly, the traditional constituents of TVA may make
minimal modifications of TVA's power program, or new coalitions of
constituents may emerge for more substantial change. In any event, the
symbiotic relationship of TVA's mission and its form of support will be
evident once again.

NOTES

1. Philip J. Funigiello, *Toward a National Power Policy: The New Deal and the Elec-
tric Utility Industry, 1933–41* (Pittsburgh: University of Pittsburgh Press, 1973); Marquis
Williams Childs, *The Farmer Takes a Hand: The Electric Power Revolution in America*
(Garden City, N.Y.: Doubleday, 1952); Louise B. Young, *Power over People* (New York: Ox-
ford University Press, 1973); Vic Reinemeir and Jack Doyle, *Lines across the Land—Rural
Electric Cooperatives: The Changing Politics of Energy in Rural America* (Washington,
D.C.: Environmental Policy Institute, 1979).

2. See Harry Wiersma, "The River Control System," in Roscoe C. Martin, ed., *TVA:
The First Twenty Years: A Staff Report* (University: University of Alabama Press; Knoxville: University of Tennessee Press, 1956), pp. 77–94. Lewis Mumford reviewed an exhibit of photographs of TVA projects at the Museum of Modern Art in very appreciative
terms: "These structures are as close to perfection as our age has come. There is something in the mere cant of a dam, when seen from below, that makes one think of the Pyramids of Egypt. Both pyramid and dam represent an architecture of power. But the difference is notable, too, and should make one prouder of being an American. The first
grew out of slavery and celebrated death. Our was produced by free labor to create energy
and life for the people of the United States." "The Architecture of Power," *The New Yorker*
(June 7, 1941), p. 58. See also a series of highly complimentary articles by James Agee,
"TVA I: Work in the Valley" and "TVA II: The Power Issue," *Fortune,* 50 (May, 1935):
93–98, 153, and 98, 154–70.

3. Aaron Wildavsky, *Dixon-Yates: A Study in Power Politics* (New Haven, Conn.: Yale University Press, 1962), p. 323.

4. See Aaron Wildavsky, "TVA and Power Politics," *American Political Science Review*, 55 (Sept., 1961): 576–90.

5. Wildavsky, *Dixon-Yates*, p. 325.

6. Omega Ruth McQuown, "From National Agency to Regional Institution: A Study of TVA in the Political Process" (Ph.D. dissertation (University of Florida, 1961), pp. 58–59.

7. Memo, Gordon R. Clapp to TVA board of directors, Mar. 13, 1946, TVA Archives, Knoxville, Tenn.

8. George F. Gant to States Rights Finley, Mar. 18, 1947, TVA Archives.

9. G. O. Wessenauer met with the public information officer of TVPPA and suggested that it counter some of the information of the Edison Electric Institute. Specifically, TVPPA could emphasize TVA's vast difference from private utilities in power distribution. In addition, TVPPA could compare public managers with private managers in measures of use, cost, rural electrification, appliance sales, rate of business activity, etc. Memo, G. O. Wessenauer to George F. Gant, May 11, 1950; see also memo, Wessenauer to Gant, Mar. 21, 1950, both in TVA Archives.

10. The most complete files I have found belong to the Cumberland Electric Membership Corporation, Clarkesville, Tenn. For newspaper accounts, see *Chattanooga News–Free Press*, Feb. 25, 1954; *Memphis Press Scimitar*, Jan. 30, 1954; and *Memphis Commercial Appeal*, Jan. 31, 1954, copies in TVA Technical Library, Knoxville Tenn.

11. Interview, Nov. 3, 1981. See also Herbert D. Vogel speech at Clinton, Tenn., May 4, 1955, copy in TVA Technical Library.

12. Reported in *Nashville Tennessean*, Nov. 4, 1956, copy in TVA Technical Library.

13. Jones was nominated in Sept. 1957, but confirmed only in July, 1958. Opponents to his nomination came to respect and admire him and offered to support his reappointment in 1966. Jones's response was to inquire, "Will you work as hard for me as you did against me?"

14. William Sturdivant, executive director of CTVA, to Ken Whitaker, information officer of TVPPA, July 15 and 19, 1955, Citizens for TVA Files, Cumberland Electric Membership Corporation.

15. U.S. Chamber of Commerce, *TVA: What's Next?* (Washington, D.C., 1958).

16. Tennessee Valley Public Power Association, *TVPPA: A History of Service in the Tennessee Valley* (Chattanooga, Tenn., 1980), unpaged, references made chronologically, emphasis added.

17. David E. Lilienthal, *TVA: Democracy on the March* (New York: Harper and Row, 1944), pp. 179, 187.

18. Reported in *Knoxville News-Sentinel*, Sept. 12, 1953, copy in TVA Technical Library.

19. *Knoxville News-Sentinel*, Mar. 16, 1954, copy in TVA Technical Library.

20. Wildavsky, *Dixon-Yates*, pp. 126, 235, refers to the TVPPA as the Tennessee Public Power Association. Owen does not mention it at all—but then Owen managed to write a history of TVA without mentioning Estes Kefauver or Albert Gore either: *The Tennessee Valley Authority* (New York: Praeger, 1973).

21. Frank G. Clement, *TVA and You: A Message from the People of Tennessee*, available through TVA Technical Library. This pamphlet was intended for nationwide distribution. Clement also wrote a pamphlet printed by Citizens for TVA: *A Report to the*

President of the United States on the Tennessee Valley Authority from the Governor of Tennessee.

22. "Financial Report of the Citizens for TVA September 1–December 31, 1953," in the files of Cumberland Electric Membership Corporation. Further evidence of the relationship of the distributors and co-ops with Citizens for TVA is that J. C. Hundley, executive director of the Tennessee Electric Cooperative Association, was finance chairman for Citizens for TVA. He was succeeded by J. Wiley Bowers, executive director of TVPPA. Nat Caldwell, a newspaper reporter active in Citizens for TVA, offered this assessment: "The distributors were Citizens for TVA and Citizens for TVA were the distributors."

23. TVPPA, *History of Service*, 1955 ed., unpaged.

24. Gordon R. Clapp, *The TVA: An Approach to the Development of a Region* (Chicago: University of Chicago Press, 1955), p. 107. Selznick commented on the distributors' role in power use. He cited a TVA official who lamented the lack of education programs for the co-ops, which would make "the load building program . . . easier and more sensible." Selznick viewed this as another compromise of the voluntary association with the formal organization's need to get things done. Philip Selznick, *TVA and the Grass Roots: A Study in the Sociology of Formal Organization* (New York: Harper and Row, 1966), p. 241.

25. Cited in "TVPPA Gets Going," *Public Power* (May, 1947), p. 11.

26. David E. Lilienthal to George W. Norris, Feb. 14, 1940, TVA Archives.

27. TVPPA, *1950 TVPPA Home and Farm Electrical Exposition* (Chattanooga, Tenn., 1950), p. 2.

28. *Ibid.* For a detailed view of rural electrification in the Tennessee Valley up to 1952, see memo, R. A. Kampmeier, assistant manager of power, to Manager's Files, Dec. 17, 1951, TVA Archives.

29. Reported in *Nashville Tennessean*, July 7, 1950, copy in TVA Technical Library.

30. *Ibid.*, May 21, 1950.

31. G. O. Wessenauer to John Oliver, Feb. 20, 1953, TVA Archives.

32. Gordon R. Clapp to Mark C. Stewart, May 6, 1952, TVA Archives.

33. Cited in Victor C. Hobday, *Sparks at the Grassroots: Municipal Distribution of TVA Electricity in Tennessee* (Knoxville: University of Tennessee Press, 1969), p. 104.

34. *Electricity Sales Reports and Power Program Summary*, TVA Technical Library. See also Thomas K. McCraw, "Triumph and Irony—The TVA," *Proceedings of the Institute of Electrical and Electronic Engineers*, (Sept. 1976): 1372–80.

35. Stefan H. Robock, address to annual meeting of TVPPA, Apr. 7, 1953, copy in TVA Archives.

36. Lilienthal, *TVA*, p. 136.

37. Charles Perrow, "The Analysis of Goals in Complex Organizations," *American Sociological Review*, 26 (Dec., 1961): 854-66.

38. Herbert D. Vogel to President Kennedy, Mar. 17, 1961, TVA Technical Library.

39. President Kennedy to Herbert D. Vogel, Mar. 8, 1961, TVA Technical Library.

40. Vogel to Kennedy, Mar. 17, 1961, TVA Technical Library.

41. For an examination of TVA's interaction with its political environment, see George E. Rawson, "The Process of Program Development: The Case of TVA's Power Program" (Ph.D. dissertation, University of Tennessee, 1979). See pp. 99–104 for TVA's congressional relations from about 1960 to 1967.

42. Wesley M. Jackson to TVA board of directors, Aug. 9, 1961, TVA Archives.

43. Letter and attachments of William M. Roberts to L. J. Van Mol, Dec. 22, 1961, TVA Archives.

44. *Ibid.*

45. J. C. Hundley to Aubrey J. Wagner, Feb. 22, 1973, TVA Archives.

46. Charles H. Dean to Aubrey J. Wagner, Feb. 24, 1974, TVA Archives.

47. J. C. Hundley to Robin Beard, Dec. 5, 1974, TVA Archives.

48. Harry M. Caudill, *A Darkness at Dawn: Appalachian Kentucky and the Future* (Lexington: University Press of Kentucky, 1976), p. 27.

49. Interestingly, Selznick in his preface to the 1964 edition of *TVA and the Grass Roots* cited critics of TVA's strip-mine policies as further evidence that TVA was influenced by the right wing, as he had suggested in his study of TVA's agricultural policies.

50. *TVPPA News* (Apr., 1972), p. 2.

51. David Ross-Stevens, *Tennessee Valley Authority and Air Quality Control,* (Nashville: Tennessee Environmental Council, 1976).

52. Reported in the *Decatur Daily,* Apr. 17, 1973.

53. Senate Public Works Committee, 93d Cong., 2d sess., *Granting Financial Incentives to the Tennessee Valley Authority for Construction Costs of Environmental Facilities* (June 19, 1974) (hereafter referred to as *Hearings*), pp. 57ff.

54. *Ibid.*

55. *TVPPA News* (Jan., 1975), p. 2; *ibid.* (Mar., 1975), p. 2.

56. S. David Freeman, "TVA's Role in Industrial Growth," remarks at a symposium on "TVA and the Environment," Tennessee Environmental Council, Nashville, 1976.

57. The Rural Electrification Administration also witnessed a similar development of the rural co-ops. See Reinemeir and Doyle, *Lines across the Land,* esp. pp. 134–50 on environmental positions.

58. *Nashville Tennessean,* Dec. 11, 1980.

59. TVPPA, *Response of Tennessee Valley Public Power Association Concerning Proposed Determination by TVA on Six Rate Standards* . . . (Chattanooga, Tenn., 1980), p. 12.

60. "Testimony at Hearings of the Senate Public Works Committee on TVA," Section VI: Economic Development of the TVA Region (Mar., 1981). "As of October 1980 . . . of the five large southeastern utilities, only Alabama Power has higher rates than TVA industrial rates, while Georgia Power Company, Duke Power Company, and Carolina Power and Light Company all have lower industrial rates." Note the use of private industry as a "yardstick" for TVA.

61. *Ibid.,* Section X: Advisability of Amendments to TVA Act. It should be noted that TVPPA and several other groups of distributors successfully opposed David Stockman, director of the Office of Management and Budget, in his efforts to curtail the operations of the Federal Financing Bank. The FFB provides loans to government programs including TVA and REA at costs slightly lower than private market interest rates.

62. *Nashville Tennessean,* Apr. 29, 1981.

63. Managers of the rural co-ops speak of participation in "the largest public works program in human history" and of the satisfaction of spending a life in public service. This set of leaders, with their unique experiences in electrification and development, is changing quickly: in 1973 it was estimated that 70 percent of rural co-op managers would retire or be replaced by 1983. *TVPPA News* (May, 1973), p. 2. Other people who shared this faith in electricity are gone from TVA. Wagner is now retired but was cited with approval in a speech explaining the promotion of electricity: "We live in a high energy civilization. The progress of men and nations is directly related to the amount of energy available to them." *TVPPA News* (Dec., 1971), p. 2. Bob Jones is gone from Congress. TVPPA wrote of his belief in public power:

"There will not be another Bob Jones in the congress. When he departs from congress next January, he will take with him the awareness and understanding and historical perspective and fierce dedication to the Tennessee Valley's electric power program that only one who has fought for it for three decades can have.

"Bob Jones is of the school of believers of public power for the benefit of people. He is disdainful of those who unjustly harp at and criticize public servants in a non-profit Federal municipal and rural co-op electric system as if they were attempting to rip off the consumers."

64. TVA, *Review of the TVA Load Growth/Plant Construction Situation* (Knoxville, Tenn., 1982).

PART FOUR

TVA and American
Democracy

10

Craufurd D. Goodwin

The Valley Authority Idea—The Fading of a National Vision

THE American people emerged from World War II with a sense of foreboding about the state of the union. The economy had performed abysmally during the 1930s and the polity seemed ready to unravel in consequence. Failure was everywhere. Most important, the system demonstrated that it was unable to generate enough jobs for the people. Closely related was the incapacity to grow steadily—to produce more goods and services, which would permit an increase in living standards and a surplus for large national projects. Some diagnosed this condition as "secular stagnation," a malaise associated with the closing of the frontier. The United States in the 1930s also seemed distressingly far from the economists' dream of competitive markets. Reports from the Temporary National Economic Committee and other inquiries suggested that monopolies were widespread and unrestrained by legislation and public agencies. Finally, many people were convinced that the sufferings of the 1930s were distributed unevenly. In particular, they thought, farmers, organized labor, and certain regions such as the South and West experienced greater unemployment, income decline, and "exploitation" by monopolies than other parts.

But where could disgruntled Americans turn for reform? The concept of a heavily concentrated corporate state with balance and cooperation among the parts had been discredited by experience with NRA and fascist leaders such as Mussolini. On the other hand, a move toward a truly free-price system in which all markets would "clear" automatically and incentives would be provided naturally sounded like what had been attempted unsuccessfully in the 1920s. Indeed, the Sherman and Clayton acts to restrain or eliminate monopolies had been on the books for decades, but little control of monopolies had been accomplished. Centralized planning and allocation also could be rejected on several grounds. They smacked of the socialist experiment in the U.S.S.R. and had a frightening and alien ring. Moreover, planning, with rationing and price and wage control, were experienced during World War II and left distinctly bad memories. The image of a monolithic bureaucracy, seeming to make problems worse instead of better, made it difficult for anyone to argue for central planning at war's end.

As it turned out, America accepted national policies that combined "Keynesian" manipulation of macroeconomic aggregates to maintain full employment and stimulate growth, with an increasing array of redistributive programs to correct inequities among regions, classes, racial groups, and other categories of citizens. But this solution was not yet clear by the middle 1940s, when few people yet understood the principles of modern macroeconomics and most doubted that major redistribution would ever take place so long as those in control would lose by it.

The valley authority promised solutions to these economic and political problems worrying the American people. A valley authority, it was argued, could respond to all the needs of a region. It could provide employment, stimulate growth, attend to those who suffered most, and have the strength to resist the power of monopolies. And it was a distinctively American creation. It grew out of the immensity of America and the prevailing American distrust of centralized bureaucracy. It had been tried in TVA and, in the eyes of some observers at least, had been a success.

This paper examines extension of the valley authority idea beyond TVA, mainly during the period 1945–50. Ultimately the idea was rejected. This may have been because the national goals for which the valley authority was designed were supplanted by concern over inflation and national mobilization to cope with a worldwide communist conspiracy or because an alternative Keynesian approach to national economic problems grew steadily in popularity.

The debate over valley authorities was one of the few wide-ranging explorations into the structure of the American economy during the last forty years. It was an inquiry into large issues in what is now called "political economy." It generated creative thought, eloquence, and much unscrupulous politics. It was led largely by intellectuals *within* the federal bureaucracy. Participants in Congress, the press, universities, and the populace at large generally had subsidiary roles. Today, when a solution to economic problems may require reforms as revolutionary as the valley authority, it is instructive to observe the accomplishments and failures of this debate.

The desire for valley authorities was a presage of two movements in the political affairs of all advanced industrial countries in the last half of the twentieth century: one for regional devolution of power (represented by pressures for renegotiation of terms of the Canadian constitution, a "free" Wales and Scotland, and independence for the Basque region); second, a revolt against centralized bureaucracy, a demand to return to local authority and responsibility—symbolized in the United States by the appeal to "get Washington off our backs."

Germination

Just as the federal bureaucracy in the 1930s and 1940s, swollen with bright and energetic persons, was the rich soil in which Keynesian ideas took root and grew, so too the valley authority idea began and had its early life in the public sector.[1] But whereas Keynesian ideas flourished first in parts of the Bureau of the Budget and in the federal treasury, with the support of some members of Congress and their staffs, the valley authority grew out of the Department of Interior and its component bureaus and agencies, in association with sympathetic senators and congressmen. The idea arose out of two strands of thought within Interior. The first reflected frustration with and distaste for conflict and disorganization among programs to advance development. The second strand was sheer admiration for the accomplishments of TVA—in part the increasing prosperity of the region, but also the style and joie de vivre of the operation. Proposals for replication of TVA began almost the day it was born. President Roosevelt sent Congress a message in 1937 that suggested seven regional authorities to cover the nation, and at a news conference on November 14, 1944, he reaffirmed the suggestion and said he could draw a map of the regions blindfolded.[2] Since, among other things, valley authorities promised more pork in the barrel, there were calls from politicians for extension to the Arkansas, central Colorado, Columbia, Missouri, and St. Lawrence valleys, among others.

The demise of the National Resources Planning Board in 1943, a victim of its enemies and of wartime pressures, provided a sharp stimulus for creative thinking about planning. Serious reflection came from Stephen Raushenbush, chief of the Branch of Economics and Statistics in Interior and the "house intellectual," a close adviser to Secretary Ickes. Raushenbush had begun to worry about postwar resource planning as early as 1942 while on the staff of the War Resources Council. The war effort, he said, made urgent the best use of scarce means and demonstrated that this could not come about through existing governmental structures.[3] Later, in 1944, with the war still far from won, Raushenbush observed that it was none too early to start preparing for peace. In particular, "A whole series of national resource decisions will come up within the next few years. They will cover many of the basic elements of our economy: land, fuels, new industries, regions, water." Raushenbush feared that postwar planning would be seriously constrained by demobilization and the plethora of relief and assistance programs that remained from the Depression. A vigorous and imaginative approach was needed to achieve efficiency and equity in the face of this legacy. He identified five large questions of national policy to be answered if rising productivity were to prevail:

1. How much new land shall be brought into cultivation through Government aid? Should aid for new land be made conditional on the nongrowing of crops in surplus and already subsidized? . . .

2. What is the place of the mineral industry in our national economy? Neglect of the problems involved here may produce higher tariffs and adversely affect our exports of manufactured goods. It may load us up with useless and costly stock piles or increase our relief load. . . .

3. Can a sensible fuel policy be devised? The new pipe lines have again brought the coal interests into conflict with natural gas and oil expansion, but they are still unready to compete with their own gas through the pipe lines, or over the wires with super power energy. . . .

4. What are the best industrial bases for regional expansion? This expansion may become the equivalent of the automobile boom in the 20s. It represents a highly desirable decentralization of additional plant and equipment. Low-cost energy, and new chemical developments in both wood and petroleum use, may pull industry west and southward. Yet there are certain conditions for successful expansion of underdeveloped regions. . . .

5. What are the best combinations of water use in certain key areas? (Missouri, Arkansas, Colorado and Columbia River basins and the Central Valley region of California.) . . .

Raushenbush pointed out that unfortunately

. . . neither the Congress nor the Administration are presently organized to consider . . . (major resource problems) either on a broad national level or on a level of disinterested weighing of economic costs and advantages. Every measure comes up as a special commodity interest measure, is handled by a special interest agency, and goes before special interest committees of Congress. The ground-clearing work of the National Resources Planning Board is ignored. The Bureau of the Budget has not been allowed funds sufficient to coordinate even the planning of post-war public construction work. Even when rival agencies agree on a program, there is no certainty that the best public interest has been met.

Equally important is the fact that every misuse or parasitic use of our resources makes it more difficult for us to attain and maintain a high national income. Subsidies for cotton and gold mining both have the same effect, that of diverting part of the income from more useful production. . . .

The rethinking and restatement of our resource problems should be against this background. It should be very specific, and be put in terms of dollars and cents. It should avoid the over-generalized approach which the NRPB felt constrained to take. It should be in terms of: How much? At what cost? What benefits? Who gets help? Who gets hurt? How much?[4]

Raushenbush's own views, and those of some colleagues, were that a national growth policy would be devised most effectively by converting Interior into a Department of Natural Resources and then organizing it "regionally" rather than by the centralized functional bureaus as at present. Washington-based personnel would retain only "staff" functions. Some young reformers within Interior turned to the example of TVA, not merely for a model of how to organize one valley but for a wider conception of economic planning on a disaggregated basis and for an exciting vision of the future. The prospect of achieving wonders of social progress in the postwar world seemed not very bright under the chaotic regime of the Interior Department. The autonomous valley authority was a beacon of promise.

Interior Secretary Harold Ickes could not bring himself to endorse wholeheartedly any move such as this, which would substantially reduce his power and weaken the structure with which he had become comfortable. Moreover, the bureaus and agencies, with their congressional supporters, were not about to give up the power and influence required by this plan. Yet Interior officials were not blind to the mounting sentiment for regionalization. So they gave nominal support to the notion, redefined as the "coordination" of agencies and bureaus within a region, while in fact defending the status quo.

By 1944 the valley authority idea was rapidly gaining both adherents and specificity inside and outside Interior. President Roosevelt's endorsement of additional valley authorities gave encouragement to supporters and some measure of protection to those within the bureaucracy who pursued the idea. Senior officers of Interior felt the hot breath of the critics on their necks, and in December, 1944, they anxiously prepared a specific blocking alternative. They concluded that they might have only "a year or two at the most to accomplish such regionalization before the (valley) authority legislation would be enacted."[5] In fact, in Congress there was a near stampede to introduce valley authority legislation. To create a Missouri Valley Authority during the Seventy-eighth Congress alone, bills were presented in the House by Congressmen Gillette, Rankin, and Cochran, and in the Senate by Senator Murray. Within the Interior Department Raushenbush had swung toward the multiplication of valley authorities from his unsuccessful scheme for full-scale regionalization. The hotbed of agitation moved for a time from Washington to the Northwest, where the Bonneville Power Administration, an agency of the Interior Department, perceived itself as the most promising candidate for elevation. At BPA several staff members developed and expounded the conception of a valley authority with vigor and imagination. Moreover, they stayed with it tenaciously for more than five years. The most influential was C. Girard ("Jebby") Davidson, a young lawyer from Louisiana who had pursued graduate study at Yale and worked on the legal staff of TVA before becoming general counsel at BPA.[6] Ivan Bloch, son of the composer Ernst Bloch, worked closely with Davidson, on the staff of BPA and later as a consultant. Together these two, with several close associates, provided much of the case for valley authorities. Bloch could have spoken for the group when he wrote in 1944: "This whole problem of regional development is my passion, my vocation, and my avocation."[7]

Quickly, a network grew up among adherents to the valley authority idea, and it became difficult to disentangle the origins of strands of thought. Advocates included Interior staff members like Davidson and Bloch; congressmen and senators like Mitchell, Murray, and Jackson; members of the general public committed to the principle in their own regions (mainly the Columbia and Missouri valleys); and journalists captivated by the idea or anxious to present it to their audiences. All depended to some degree on the "TVA experience," evident in the formal published data and set forth in popular works by David Lilienthal and Robert Duffus. TVA staff did not play a vigorous proselytizing role in gathering converts or calling for application of "their" idea elsewhere.

It is interesting to examine the expressions of the valley authority idea in the years before the end of World War II. First, the proponents expected the new structures to provide jobs for returning servicemen and warworkers, many of whom had been unemployed during the Depression. It was not clear why regional agencies could accomplish these tasks more effectively than national ones, but direct access to capital markets and the capacity of local people to identify marketable goods were mentioned. As Davidson told the master of the Oregon State Grange: "Instead of having 'leaf-raking projects' of the old WPA, time and money could be better spent if plans are prepared on a regional basis for the development of the nation's resources."[8]

Second, and closely related to the short-run problem of employment, was the long-run need for economic development. The people had come to expect rapid growth, and social upheavals would occur if a new western frontier were not created. But growth could not be stimulated successfully from Washington. Only through regional planning bodies would the people experience the growth they demanded. In Bloch's words:

> All the latent opportunities for real economic expansion are here: land, forest, water, minerals, and a vigorous people. But with divided authority, conflicting interests of its government authorities, it will be a long-pull proposition with the "Principle of Uncertainty" the guiding role.
>
> The problem is a critical one for the nation. For, emotionally, as well as materially, the West can give an outlet for the restless spirit of our people. It can stave off what appears to be a rising murmur of impatience in the slower increases of democracy.[9]

A regional approach to planning was endorsed at this time by such distinguished economists as Alvin Hansen and Harvey Perloff.

Third, valley authorities would provide for systematic public discussion of communal objectives at a level where implementation would take place. Several objectives were incompatible, such as conservation and unconstrained development, and the public must make choices. They had to select among such goals as flood control, navigation, land reclamation, power development, resource conservation, and national defense. Valley authorities could determine paths of "unified development" and reconcile conflicting objectives in the most efficient fashion.

Fourth, after unemployment and stagnation, the greatest danger to the American economy after World War II appeared to be domination of key markets by monopolies. Valley authorities were a novel weapon against monopolies. They could exert influence over evil doers indirectly by establishing "yardsticks" for performance, and they could enter markets directly. Monopolies in the past had been able to gain market control through technical means and political subversion. Neither the Federal Trade Commission nor the Justice Department had been effective restraints. The valley authority might constrain monopolies through their control over power, irrigation, land reclamation, and improvements in navigation.

Finally, the valley authorities would be consistent with, and an improvement over, the several layers of government provided in the American federal system. Indeed, the American federal structure as much as the economy had proved inadequate to deal with the problems of the mid-twentieth century. Yet the system preserved values that were extremely precious and should not be imperiled lightly, including personal liberty, the sanctity of private property, and the diffusion of power. The valley authority was a nonthreatening innovation and safer than central planning, especially as it had a working prototype in TVA. Citizens around the country would welcome the innovation and work within it if the enemies were prevented from misrepresenting and confusing the issues. Again, in Bloch's words:

> The people of this region would accept a Columbia Valley Authority of the same measure as the T.V.A. if they were given a real chance to think it through. The voices of reason are weak in comparison with those of the Electric Bond and Share group or vested bureaucracy of certain Federal agencies. I am afraid that only a lengthy dose of unemployment and a resurgence of vigorous progressivism in the Federal government can bring about a realization of what's missing. . . . Our efforts to work from the bottom up will thus always be cursed until enough time elapses to show that we are truly an expression of the region's needs.[10]

In the midst of war, advocates of valley authorities were quick to admit that they did not see precisely the form that new policies, practices, and structures should take. They conceded that there remained problems of how to reconcile local and national objectives, how not to destroy the tax bases of governments by converting private to public property, and how to maintain an efficient staff within the constraints of the federal Civil Service. But proponents retained faith that these problems could be overcome.[11] Regional decentralization seemed the only way for a nation of America's vastness to restore a sense of scale. Waldemar Kaempffert, science editor of the New York Times, made this point succinctly when, in a letter to Bloch, he reflected on the analogy between TVA and what was contemplated for the Columbia Valley. "TVA is to me one of the finest socially conceived projects to the credit of Congress. Everything from industry to the electrification of farming, from navigation and flood control to forestation seems to be embraced. As a result TVA becomes much more than a purveyor of power. It is actually a social agency for the development of a region, which though rich in resources, has not nearly the potentialities of the undeveloped northwest."[12]

Two discussions of the valley authority idea around the end of World War II give a sense of its form and substance. A round-table discussion on NBC radio, organized by the University of Chicago, brought together Senators James E. Murray and Joseph C. O'Mahoney with U.S. Circuit Court Judge Jerome M. Frank and political scientist C. Herman Pritchett. In the introduction the "seven new TVAs" proposed by Roosevelt were described as "the boldest suggestion for the human control of nature ever made—the most imaginative plan for the use of natural resources ever devised."[13] Senator Murray saw it as the means to gain a "balanced economy," and O'Mahoney hoped it would help to achieve "full employment after the war" and "to substitute production for peace for production for war." With respect to flood control, Frank said, "Great rivers are giants, and all the Lilliputians must cooperate to tie these giants down. It will not do for a few pigmies to tackle a giant leg, and another few to tackle a giant arm. A flood of public opinion is eroding opposition to intelligent river control."[14]

In June, 1945, a series of three articles in *The Nation* by Carey McWilliams dealt with the national defense aspects of valley authorities. On the one hand, McWilliams argued, the war might not have been won without the foresight that led to construction of the Bonneville and Grand Coulee dams. These dams supplied crucial defense industries in the Northwest, especially aluminum smelting. On the other hand, the defense buildup exposed the West to serious postwar dangers. "Since its resources are largely undeveloped, an enormous investment program is required. And since the economy is already out of balance, there must be unified regional development. Both requirements demand a plan and a planning agency. Yet there was no organization responsible for the prompt and efficient execution of either the transitional or the long-range part of this program." Instead a cacophony of federal voices could be heard on the future of the Northwest. "It is fantastic to assume that these various agencies, with a little gentle compulsion, can prepare a master-plan for the region or that they could jointly execute a plan if one were prepared." To McWilliams the answer was obvious—a CVA.[15]

The politics of valley authorities were in flux during the last years of the war. In the two regions where experiments might be undertaken— the Columbia and the Missouri valleys—citizen groups were formed and political contests begun. Bills to create an MVA were submitted in the Senate (S. 55, by Senator James M. Murray of Montana) and in the House (H.R. 2203, by Congressman John J. Cochran of Missouri). They emphasized above all the need for management of "an uncontrolled river." But in addition, by effective resource management and reduced power rates, an MVA could accomplish "the transformation of a declining agriculturally-based economy into a healthy, balanced and prosperous industrial agricultural economy." In the short run the MVA would "offer assurance of economic security to many thousands of returning servicemen and demobilized war workers."[16] The MVA proposal inspired serious reflective thought within the region,[17] as well as some proselytizing efforts outside it.

The bill to create a CVA (S. 460) came from Senator Hugh Mitchell of Washington. A major difference from the MVA movement was that leadership came from a federal agency. Bonneville had a hand in drafting the bill; it provided Mitchell with speeches and articles, and various BPA officials took directly to the hustings.[18] BPA Administrator Paul J. Raver set down his views on the proposal in February, 1945, in an address entitled "Valley Development and the National Economy." He argued that "planning" had become essential to achieve goals as diverse as a national highway system and world peace: "However, the country is too large for implementing nation-wide plans as a unit. . . . On the other hand, the states are too small. . . ." Regional planning was the intermediate step that worked. "We have had a number of plans. Some of them, such as the NRA and 'pump priming' have not succeeded. Some of them, like TVA, have achieved a recognized success." A principal obstacle to regional planning was the use of unfair "bogey words" like "fascism and socialism." Raver pictured BPA converted into a valley authority, anticipating markets and responding to them in the public interest by determining rates for power, irrigation, and other services.[19]

Senator Mitchell set out in April, 1945, to explain the CVA idea in a series of short articles.[20] He pictured the regional "authority" as a political conception that began with the Port Authority of New York and New Jersey and continued with TVA. It coped with problems of the twentieth century by supplementing structures set up in the eighteenth. Communication and transportation were still not sufficiently developed to permit effective nationwide coordination in a country of continental proportions. The challenges consisted of "immediate post-war problems" and "our long-range future." He worried lest the word "authority" conjure up images of totalitarian control; he preferred "commission." He emphasized that an "authority" would coordinate the parts of government rather than supplant them. An important distinction between TVA and his proposed CVA was that the former was concerned with "rebuilding a devastated area" while the latter would develop "an unspoiled and rich country." A regional agency, he said, could guarantee full employment to workers and buoyant markets to farmers, two conditions the free market had not supplied before the war. He played upon traditional fears of westerners and insisted that "the region cannot be allowed to relapse into a mere agricultural colony of the industrialized East. Electric power, the 'white coal' of the west, if used as an effective development tool (including research on regional products), would allow for a real redistribution of economic power in the U.S." To those who worried that valley authorities would balkanize America, Mitchell suggested a National River Basin Development Board made up of cabinet members, the heads of valley authorities, and other interested parties.

In contrast to the Missouri Valley, where the legislative sponsors and local enthusiasts for a valley authority were disorganized, in the Northwest the staff of BPA, especially Davidson, kept Mitchell well supplied with ideas and advice. In a speech in Seattle in May, 1945, Davidson gave precision to the argument made by Mitchell that the CVA was needed to assure both full employment and growth.[21] He estimated that in order to retain the population attracted by war industries, 2,300,000 new jobs would have to be generated in peacetime. These workers, if suitably employed, could produce goods and services worth $7–8 billion per year. This level of economic activity, in turn, would require annual net investment of $1.5 billion. Private sources would generate savings of only $700–900 million. The balance of about $500–700 million would have to come from public investment. State and local governments could take care of $100–200 million, leaving $400–500 million per year to be provided by the federal government. Yet at least twenty different federal agencies operated in the Columbia Valley, and it was impossible to imagine them collectively providing just this right amount. The CVA could do so.

The Mitchell bill attracted support from various parts of the citizenry. Organized labor was enthusiastic about the prospect of more jobs. Farmers hoped for markets for their products. Public utility commissioners approved any stimulus to development.[22] However, opposition appeared as well. Foresters agreed that a "blue print" was necessary for power development and flood control but wanted only "a strengthening and expansion of the New Deal farm program, plus a new national forestry program." Private power companies, coal producers, and coal-carrying railwaymen all condemned what they claimed would be a public subsidy for their competitors. They used a network of "reclamation associations" (ostensibly groups of irrigation farmers) to carry out a negative "educational campaign."[23] State legislatures and some local newspapers joined in the criticism.

Ironically, despite presidential approval of valley authorities, the most vociferous and effective opposition came from the federal government itself, from a range of agencies that felt directly threatened. In their attacks the agencies reflected a legacy of conflict with TVA going right back to the act of 1933, which had failed to provide for effective coordination of federal activities in the Valley. The Corps of Engineers was the only agency truly displaced by TVA, but the others were forced into direct competition that sometimes became bitter and acrimonious, especially in the field of agriculture. Despite various accommodations worked out in practice, the theory behind the valley authority did not permit long-term solutions to the conflict.[24]

Opposition from the federal agencies to this new specter of competition took various forms. The most straightforward was outright condemnation. For example, Paul Raver gave the following account to Secretary Ickes of comments made at a public meeting in Montana by Colonel C. P. Hardy of the U.S. Army Corps of Engineers:

"I will say in the beginning," said the Colonel, "I am against authorities. We have too much government already; why create more?" Referring to a young sergeant, winner of a Congressional Medal of Honor, who had been introduced a short time before, Colonel Hardy said: "We saw here today a soldier who was fighting the fascists. While our young men are giving their lives in this fight, are we going to let fascism be set up right in this country? Although river authorities are not fascist in name, they are fascist in character."[25]

The Department of Agriculture was only slightly less hostile because of the threat to the agricutural extension services, the U.S. Forest Service, the Soil Conservation Service, and the Farm Security Administration.

Opposition from the Bureau of Reclamation was less overt but, in the words of one observer in BPA, "we would have had to be deaf, dumb, and blind not to know that it has existed and has been effective."[26] This staff member found that "the attitude of Bureau of Reclamation toward valley authorities . . . has been a record of forceful, if undercover, opposition to valley authorities as such. Nowhere can I find a public statement by an official of the Bureau of Reclamation which endorses valley authorities, even in principle. Considering the frequent opportunities given Bureau officials to speak at meetings of the Reclamation Associations and kindred groups, this is a remarkable record." It was not hard to see why the bureau was so concerned; valley authorities would destroy their long-standing relationships with constituencies, including congressional committees. As Marquis Childs told readers of the *New York Post*, "TVA's may knock slats out of the Old Pork Barrel."

Others in Interior were not much more enthusiastic. Ickes was often contradictory, at least in public. Perhaps in deference to presidential doctrine, he would begin public statements with something like "I am in favor of these river valley authorities. I have been for a long time. It is a natural development and one that will mean a great deal for the country."[27] But then he would stress the need for "coordination" of the authorities by Interior and conclude that "the Department of the Interior is the natural coordinator of their activities—is has the experience, the personnel and the broad national outlook on conservation matters." Testifying before the Senate Commerce Committee on S. 555, to establish a Missouri Valley Authority, Ickes said: "At a time when many Senators say, and responsible students of governments agree, that there must be fewer independent agencies to bewilder and annoy the citizenry, S. 555 steps right out and establishes the first of a flock of new ones." He continued: "It is not too much to say that one of the most important lessons which we have learned from the T.V.A. experiment is that time, money, and manpower can be saved if future authority legislation incorporates some element of compulsion to insure efficient collaboration between authorities and the rest of the Federal Government."[28] Such immersion in Interior would, of course, have been in sharp contrast with TVA practice and valley authority principle.

Other officials of Interior endorsed the goals of valley authorities but argued that these were already the objectives of the bureaus and agencies. Before a departmental "institute" in November, 1945, organized to plot the department's postwar path, William Warne examined the functions proposed for a valley authority and concluded that several were not performed effectively at present by the department. But he drew from this the message not that authorities should be established but that the department should be reorganized and granted powers held at present by other parts of government such as the Department of Agriculture. Failing that, he had hope for better coordination through such bodies as the Federal Inter-Agency River Basin Committee. Following Ickes's lead, he concluded, "There would be no question as to the tremendous advantages that would accrue if the regional development agencies were placed in the Department of the Interior."[29]

Warne was answered eloquently at the institute by BPA staff member D. L. Marlett, who complained that Warne thought only of "the big job" of public works construction. Valley authorities would aim at transforming an entire region, recognizing "their hopes and aspirations, their culture, their economic conditions, and their heritage in the river basin and all that composes it." He said:

> It seems to me that in the Federal Government generally, we have developed an institution of central office experts who are too far removed from the dynamic problems of the region, who traffic in too abstract and often inaccurate information, whose human capacities are too limited to understand and do the job that must be done in each region, who hold things up because of these limitations and their fear to take action, and who constitute a formidable vested-interest class in opposition to true regional administration. . . . In fact, a major advantage of the regional authority is its complete break with traditions and inhibitions of the past so that true regional administration will have an opportunity to function, leaving to the future the acknowledged problem of working out a new-type relationship consistent with the executive responsibility of the President and his Cabinet.[30]

Commenting sarcastically on Warne's proposal for "coordination" as a response to postwar problems, Stephen Raushenbush complained to the department's solicitor that the "Department's top brains" were putting all of their energy "into the lubrication of creaking machinery." He continued: "What this Department needs more than grease is the energy and unity that might come from a few ideas; industrial programs, coal, mineral and oil programs, a plan for dealing with the Army Engineers on the rivers, an atomic energy program, etc. Your concentration on coordination unfortunately becomes exclusive of other things. Your appeal to the womanly housekeeping urges of the bureaucrats becomes sedative."[31]

Valley Authorities in the Postwar World

In 1945 a new president complicated the maneuvering within Interior and other parts of government. Ickes moved quickly to mold the views of Truman. In August he submitted a draft letter for the president's signature to the chairman of the Missouri Committee for MVA suggesting that valley authorities be lodged in the Interior Department. White House aide Sam Rosenman advised Truman that this was Ickes's "favorite proposal, and one to which I think he had persuaded President Roosevelt." He reported that "I have discussed this matter with David Lilienthal of TVA at great length. He feels most strongly that it would be very detrimental to TVA to place it under Interior, and that the other authorities would start under a handicap if they were placed in Interior." Truman wrote to Ickes, "I don't agree on this proposition," and he took Rosenman's advice not to sign.[32]

In fact, Harry Truman brought to the presidency an exceptional interest in valley authorities and an unusual depth of experience. Only a few days before President Roosevelt's death, as vice-president, he addressed a long letter on the subject to a Cleveland salesman who had written to inquire about the fate of MVA: "As far as the MVA Bill is concerned, I think I am more thoroughly familiar with it than anyone who has been raising so much fuss over it. It was I who first got the concrete plan started to get the peculiar situations in the Missouri River Valley worked out."[33] Truman went on to describe the peculiarities of the Missouri River basin: the involvement of nine states, the fact that most valley residents were interested in one object of the MVA but not several, the difficulty of dam construction, and the limited markets in prewar years for farm products. In short, "the Missouri River cannot be handled in the same manner as the Tennessee, or the Columbia, or the Colorado Rivers. It is an entirely different proposition from any of them." Truman did not comment directly on specific plans for an MVA, but implicitly he was critical of the current euphoria surrounding the Norris bill: "the matter can't be worked out in the crackpot press, and it isn't a matter for a ten-day newspaper campaign. I have been working on it for twelve years and we have some prospects now of getting the plans worked out."

President Truman was not to be given long in office to contemplate quietly the question of valley authorities. At his very first news conference he was asked how he "felt about MVA." He replied, "I think I made a speech in New Orleans (in 1944) endorsing the Missouri Valley Authority. I advise you to read that speech."[34] But in fact he had always been qualified in his endorsement, and so he stayed. He was much more supportive of an authority for the Columbia basin, a region he thought well suited for an autonomous unit like TVA. When asked his views about the Mitchell bill for a CVA, he said, "I am for it."[35] On a memorandum from Ickes again advocating coordination with Interior, Truman wrote: "applies more to Missouri Valley than to Columbia. Columbia is parallel to Tenn. Val."[36] Davidson informed Ickes in October that the president had told Senator Mitchell and Congressman Jackson that "he was in favor of a Columbia Valley Authority and agreed that entirely different problems were presented in the Pacific Northwest than in the Missouri Valley area." The president also indicated that he favored "an autonomous authority set up along the lines of the Tennessee Valley Authority."[37]

In a "special message to the Congress presenting a 21 point program for the reconversion period" on September 6, 1945, Truman kept his options open. He paid his respects to "the example of the Tennessee Valley Authority, which has inspired regional resource development throughout the entire world." He urged Congress to "proceed as rapidly as possible to authorize the regional development of the natural resources of our great river valleys."[38] But he stopped short of saying how this regional development should be accomplished.

Truman made his first major public statement on valley authorities at the dedication of TVA's Kentucky Dam on October 10, 1945.[39] He said that as a senator he "was always a strong supporter of TVA." Then he described TVA in terms that David Lilienthal had made famous: "It is more than dams and locks and chemical plants and power lines. It is an important experiment in democracy. In it, administrative methods have been devised which bring the people and their Federal Government closer together—not in Washington, but right where the people live." Then he added a characteristic Truman touch: "TVA is just plain commonsense. It is commonsense hitched up to modern science and good management. And that's about all there is to it." He suggested that "most of these commonsense principles can be applied to other valleys." Lest anyone take this as a blanket endorsement, he added, "No two valleys are exactly alike, of course. For that reason, the details of just how this region or that region should be developed are matters that require study and judgment in each particular case." To a worried critic of valley authorities, he wrote in similar vein a few weeks later that there were undoubtedly many ways to achieve "regional resource development" and his mind was not closed to them. "TVA has demonstrated successfully one way in which this can be done. Another experiment in which four Federal agencies are participating—The War Department, Department of the Interior, Department of Agriculture, and the Federal Power Commission—is now making another demonstration" (in the Missouri Valley).[40]

The role of TVA in the discussion of new valley authorities was complex. The advocates continued to depend heavily on the TVA staff for data and testimony, both of which were freely given. They visited TVA sites as if they were the Mother Church. In some cases TVA officials even entered the controversies of the other regions, issuing public statements and correcting false information in the press.[41] But this was a time when TVA was itself under attack, not only from its competitors and from those ideologically opposed in the private sector but also from federal bureaucrats who were either jealous of its privileged status or genuinely affronted by its degree of autonomy and limited accountability.[42] There is indirect evidence, at least, that while publicly supportive of new authorities, in private Lilienthal and others at TVA were more cautious. The draft of a message to Congress on valley authorities in 1945 has written on it "From Fortas, Lilienthal opposed."[43] Oscar Chapman, assistant secretary of interior in 1945 and 1946, has suggested that Lilienthal's opposition was the most important reason why CVA was not pressed at that time. Lilienthal, Chapman said, thought that if CVA were established, "they both would be put under the Secretary of Interior."[44]

Early in 1946 the movement for valley authorities began to lose steam. Moreover, the forces in opposition within and without government were mobilizing. The president, while formally supportive, had many more crucial matters to attend, and he declined to give the movement leadership. The advocates at Bonneville began to feel seriously threatened and some expected to receive their "walking papers" at any time. These almost came at a meeting to which they were summoned in Secretary Ickes's office in Washington, apparently instigated by Commissioner Straus of the Bureau of Reclamation. Davidson told of the meeting years later:

We were on trial. We were accused of taking all of this jurisdiction away from Interior, and giving it to an independent agency. There must have been twenty people sitting around this big room that Secretary Ickes used. Under Secretary Fortas was there and was helpful to our point of view. There was a good deal of discussion as to whether the CVA would report to the President through the Secretary of the Interior. Ickes would have bought this but those believing in the Valley Authority principle felt it must be independent.

It is not a matter of public record, but what happened at that discussion was that Raver and I talked fast enough and around the subject enough so that the old man took it under advisement.[45]

In February, 1946, within two weeks of this meeting, Ickes was out of office, over a dispute with the president concerning confirmation of an appointee. In his place by March was Julius "Cap" Krug, an engineer who had worked at TVA. Suddenly a valley authority man was in the secretary's chair, and he brought Davidson from Bonneville to Washington as assistant secretary.

Valley Authorities on Hold

The years 1946 through 1948 were hard for the Democratic party. It lost the Congress in 1946, and there was a prevailing belief that Truman would serve only his one abbreviated term. Advocates of liberal reforms, especially those that appeared to be extensions of New Deal philosophy and programs, were compelled to bide their time. Supporters of valley authorities organized themselves into leagues and societies, but they were on the defensive.[46] In public the president was with them—but in a largely perfunctory fashion. He talked generally about "these great development projects," which "will open the frontiers of agriculture, industry, and commerce,"[47] but there was no mention of new legislation.

In both the Columbia and the Missouri valleys, 1946 brought a sense of gloom. One of Davidson's former colleagues at BPA wrote to him that despite strenuous efforts by BPA staff "the CVA program . . . has bogged down." Senator Mitchell, he said, had begun to show "complete lack of direction and coordination in the handling of the campaign," while "the League for CVA is in much the same confused situation."[48]

The MVA advocates were buoyed up by major floods along that river in 1947 and they counted still on gaining unqualified presidential endorsement, but this was never forthcoming. Proponents came to believe that Truman was deeply influenced against the MVA by General Pick of the Corps of Engineers. Benton Stong, chairman of the Regional Committee for an MVA, wrote in June, 1948:

. . . I became completely disgusted with the White House operation in regard to MVA a year ago and classified Truman as a foe and not even a potential ally.

. . . At the time of the flood a year ago, the President's operations were so completely dominated by his friend General Pick that he offended nearly everyone else in this Administration. . . . As late as six months ago, Truman told Jim Patton that he would support a Columbia Valley Authority, but not a Missouri Valley Authority. He is obviously too much of a Pendergast operator to permit the needs of the valley interfere with his personal friendship and operations.[49]

One of the strongest arguments used by advocates of an MVA as early as 1941 was that the Corps of Engineers, with its characteristic orientation toward river transportation, and the Bureau of Reclamation, led by Commissioner Sloan, with its concern for irrigation, failed to co-operate and were often in open conflict. The result was lack of concern for such objectives as flood control and electric power generation and the adoption of inconsistent practices. However, in 1945 Truman enforced an entente between the two warring agencies that led to the "Pick-Sloan plan" for development of the Missouri Valley. The advocates of MVA called this a "shot-gun marriage" of no real consequence. But for a while the wind was out of the MVA sails.[50]

Like a religous sect facing persecution and the prospect of time in the wilderness, the advocates of valley authorities gathered in July, 1947, at a sort of revival or camp meeting entitled "The First Valley Authority Conference," held in Washington.[51] The meeting was organized by Morris Llewellyn Cooke, a "management engineer" and former president of the Rural Electrification Administration. The 400 persons who "attended at their own expense representing various parts of the country" heard testimony from familiar spokesmen of the two major regions as well as from representatives of farm groups and labor and even a few converts from the heathen (such as a colonel in the Corps of Engineers). The tone of the proceedings was strongly evangelical. The chairman said that the papers "constitute something approaching a rebellion against the present neglect and mismanagement of our river valleys, and open a crusade for their sound planning and democratic management." The challenge was to carry forward the "great experiment" of TVA in the face of "Congressional placidity, except in negative action." Those assembled heard appeals again for an end to the "colonial status" of the West, accounts of the venality of special interests opposing valley authorities, and description of the pervasive good effects of TVA throughout the states it touched.

There was much stirring rhetoric at the conference. For example, Senator Lister Hill of Alabama said, "You are enlisted in a great cause in the battle for these authorities. You are fighting for America. You are fighting to preserve our nation and to save our civilization." And there was much discrediting of the opposition: Benton Stong, representing the National Farmers Union, said, "Assigning the United States Army Engineers to the job of controlling floods in a river is precisely like sending Typhoid Mary to stop a typhoid epidemic." A delegate from the Union of South Africa reported that, ironically, the valley authority principle might end up having more influence outside America than within. Senator Murray of Montana declared optimistically, "It is my expectation that this conference will provide the acceleration necessary to bring a strong, regional development movement into being, with the certain ultimate result of establishing valley development authorities in many areas of the country." A resolution was passed unanimously by the conference calling for a "National Institute for River Valley Development." Nothing seems to have come of this proposal.

No one gave Harry Truman much chance in the 1948 elections except some of his close advisers and he himself. His tactics were simple. He proclaimed that America had a vision of freedom, equity, and efficiency, and it had the will and capacity to make the vision reality. The major impediments were the Republican party and the Congress it controlled. Increasingly he specified an extension of TVA as an important means to accomplish the national vision. In his State of the Union Message in January, 1948, he said: "We can learn much from our Tennessee Valley experience. We should no longer delay in applying the lessons of that vast undertaking to our other great river basins."[52] With respect to "large multipurpose dams and accompanying watershed programs . . . such integrated programs should be stepped up, as soon as economic conditions permit."[53] And what had been the Republicans' position on such matters? "They had been obstructionists," he told a group of Young Democrats. "They were against TVA."[54]

On a whistle-stop trip through the Northwest in June, 1948, Truman saw for the first time how well the valley authority idea actually played in Pocatello and Spokane, Ephrata and Wenatchee, Skyomish and Portland. He told audiences that the Interior Department had provided him with a report on the Columbia River basin that he had got up early in the morning to read. He agreed that public power was the means to achieve development for all. "I want to see the development out here and in every other section of the country carried out for the welfare of the people as a whole, and not for a few who want to exploit the people."[55] A serious flood on the Columbia shortly before his arrival contributed to the receptive environment Truman found for discussions of river basin management. But he was still rather short on details. He told the Washington State Press Club on June 10: "What we have done in the Tennessee Valley, we can do elsewhere." And "I have urged time and time again that the experience of the TVA shows the way in which we should move in other great river basins."[56] He still did not endorse the CVA in so many words. The 1948 platform of the Democratic party included a regional development plan but no mention of valley authorities.[57] Truman was waiting for the voters to give their verdict.

The Big Campaign

The voters, of course, gave President Truman a resounding victory, and the advocates of valley authorities came out of hibernation. Only a week after the election one BPA staff member proposed a work program that would yield "a respectable body of facts and analyses on federal river system engineering-economics that would comprise a bible for Federal power policy. . . . Basically, the supporters of Federal hydro have relied on unrelated arguments—the abuses of the utility holding companies, high utility rates, need for a Federal yardstick or club, power shortages, need for reclamation, or flood control." He proposed eleven studies, drawing on the experience of TVA and BPA, which would provide the basis for a "complete rationale."[58]

President Truman determined soon after the election to push ahead with a CVA. Budget Bureau Director James Webb recommended that White House aide Charles Murphy be assigned responsibility for preparing draft legislation and executive branch recommendations. The responsibility could not be placed with Interior because "the question as to whether such an Authority should be located within the Department of the Interior or should be separate, in the pattern of the TVA, is one of the important issues which must be solved."[59]

The discussion of a plan for CVA in 1949 was very different from 1945. Supporters were still at work in BPA, but now the leadership of Interior was largely behind the idea, notably three TVA veterans, Secretary Krug, Assistant Secretary Davidson, and Walton Seymour, director of a new analytical unit called the program staff. But the problems of reconversion from war, for which CVA had originally been proposed, were now past and almost forgotten. The threatened recession had not materialized and economic growth had continued at rates unprecedented in peacetime. Market concentration had still not been much reduced, but somehow monopolies did not seem a pressing threat. A new problem for which valley authorities had no obvious answer was inflation. Moreover, to help manage the economy, a new institution was on the scene, the Council of Economic Advisers. It was perceived as a kind of attendant physician to a patient, regularly (quarterly) measuring the vital signs and prescribing fiscal medicine. Although the council would not take issue directly with a program endorsed by the president, the idea of decentralized regional administration could not easily be reconciled with the principle of centralized macroeconomic management.

President Truman promised in the State of the Union Address on

January 5, 1949, to "apply the lessons of our Tennessee Valley experience to our other great river basins."[60] In the budget message five days later he said the nation "should apply the lessons of our Tennessee Valley experience without delay wherever they offer promise of improvement."[61] On January 13 he announced plans to explore the creation of a CVA. Then on January 25 he directed five cabinet-level officers (Interior, Agriculture, Commerce, Budget, CEA) to draw up legislation "taking into account the characteristic needs of the region, the interest of all parts of the executive branch and lessons of our prior experience with the kinds of operations which will be involved."[62]

Over the next several months the valley authority idea received careful professional scrutiny and public attention in a way that had not been equaled since the early days of TVA. The political forces in the Northwest were not very different from what they had been in 1945, although the cast of characters had changed. Hugh Mitchell, sponsor of the 1945 bill, was now in the House rather than the Senate. This time both he and Congressman Henry Jackson sponsored draft legislation. The Republican governors of the three main affected states (Washington, Oregon, Idaho) were opposed, while the legislatures and the press were divided. In public discussion the best-formulated arguments in favor came still from the Interior Department (especially Assistant Secretary Davidson and his staff), from farm groups, and from organized labor.[63] Nationwide, old friends of the idea were exhilarated at the prospect of going into battle. David Lilienthal, now at the Atomic Energy Commission, greeted the president's announcement with a "whoop of gratification."[64] Opponents were still the private power interests and (indirectly) those parts of the federal bureaucracy that were most threatened. Friends of the proposal warned of an unscrupulous campaign ahead. Former Senator Rufus Holman of Oregon wrote to President Truman that in former campaigns, "Twice my home has been forcibly entered during the absence of my family and every letter and paper read with nothing stolen."[65] What was different in this period was that the analytical powers in the Executive Office of the president were trained on the idea and searched for problems and inconsistencies. This time it really looked as if a CVA might happen and the proposal had to be taken seriously.

The task of preparing the CVA draft legislation and related chores, which had been assigned to Charles Murphy, was passed on to White House aide David Bell, an economist who had worked on economic policy in the White House for several years. The questions and issues that Bell discovered grew out of the CVA proposals were both large and small in their implications.[66] Among the large questions were, first, should CVA be a "planning, coordinating, and directing" agency, or should it "conduct operations," in some cases inevitably in competition with other parts of the government? TVA was perceived to do largely the latter. Could a single organ perform both kinds of functions satisfactorily at the same time?

Second, "to what extent and in what manner should the States and localities participate in plans and operations?" One of the frequent claims for a CVA was that it would respond to local interests. Former Senator Clarence Dill wrote to Truman that "because it would be under regional control," CVA would be "devoted to the development of this area by men who have lived here and know the conditions of the Pacific Northwest."[67] But, state and local governments asked, did this description not apply to them as well?

Third, "there is a knotty question as to how the regional programs and policies of the Authority are to be properly related to national programs and policies covering the same resources." If taxpayers in Maine and Vermont were to be asked to pay for part of CVA, it was necessary to identify the "national benefits to be derived from the maximum development of regional resources."

Fourth, how could arguments for decentralization of economic development be separated from a larger case for federal devolution? If resource management was handled badly from Washington, "the same criticism could be applied to any Federal activity." After listening to all the arguments about just what a valley authority should cover, Bell made the pragmatic proposal that the authority work out "practical agreements" with each functional agency. Then, "if and when experience demonstrated that any functions should be transferred to the CVA, the President could do so." But he conceded to Murphy, "These arrangements . . . are open to challenge on the ground that they provide overlapping authority, and are intended to permit the CVA eventually to become a baby Federal Government in the Columbia region."[68] Both the Commerce and Agriculture departments said the answer to this question lay in confining CVA to the planning and management of water resources exclusively.[69] But, of course, this would have changed the spirit of the proposal.

Fifth, what was to prevent new authorities from becoming ever more powerful para-governments, unconstrained by the usual constitutional checks and balances? Wilbert Fritz of the Bureau of the Budget warned,

"A compound regional authority can easily grow into a form of super-state beyond the practical possibilities of national control."[70] Philip Fleming, administrator of the Federal Works Agency, asked what would happen to the rest of the federal government, left, as it were, to operate in the areas between the holes of the Swiss cheese: "The old-line departments and agencies will be thoroughly emasculated and they will be left to function only in widely separated areas not within the boundaries of any of the established regions . . . to have both types of organization (geographical and functional) operating side by side throughout the Nation, would result in great confusion and inefficiency."[71]

Sixth, if CVA was to be an operating agency, what price should it pay for operating capital? The CVA proposal specified average rates paid on government securities. But was this arrangement wise and fair? If the authority was intended to produce a yardstick for private firms, in a range of markets it would have a decided advantage and in risky or speculative markets it might produce a yardstick that was several inches too short. Private firms entering the capital markets would have to pay an interest premium in proportion to the risk predicted for the investment. On this basis private firms simply could not compete and would be driven out of business.

Seventh, how could compensatory fiscal policy, to maintain full employment and growth, be undertaken if autonomous regional authorities each responded to their own imperatives in creating effective demand? Fritz in the Budget Bureau, where Keynesian ideas had become established early, told David Bell unequivocally: "Creation of an autonomous program in the Columbia Basin and the setting of such a pattern for other valley authorities could adversely affect economic stability."[72] Such a charge was especially damaging at a time when concerns for full employment were still very prominent and when, with four years of fair success in hand, it seemed that government might accomplish the goal. It may have been unfortunate for CVA that the Spence bill, or Economic Stability Act (H.R. 2756), was before Congress at the same time.[73]

Among the smaller questions about CVA were, first, how should a new agency of this type, if it were one of many, be financed so that accountability was assured and subsidy levels were consistent with the preservation of free enterprise and efficiency in markets where the agencies competed? Most economists were unpersuaded that long-run market prices should be different from minimum average cost of the competitive firm unless specific externalities were identified. Wilbert Fritz wrote: "The balanced national development of resources is much more important than the concentrated development of the resources of a particular region by arbitrary subsidization."[74]

Second, the Executive Office of the president, with its small staff, was already overworked. How could it realistically monitor a new set of complex regional organs? Agriculture Secretary Charles Brannan insisted "there must be separate Presidential staff machinery in Washington to accomplish this."[75] Brannan thought this problem would be solved by making an authority "primarily a planning, coordinating and supervising agency which function it would not be able to properly discharge if it were to duplicate and compete with the work of the operating agencies." He provided an alternate bill to have this effect. A member of Brannan's staff also called for a new natural resources unit within the White House: "In answer to those who may say that the Tennessee Valley experience disproves the need for a Presidential resource staff, the answer is (1) that full realization of a truly comprehensive resources program has not yet been achieved in the Tennessee Valley and (2) that the experience to date, cited above in other river basins is as important, and probably more so, than experience in the Tennessee Valley."[76]

Third, the word "authority" grated on many ears. Was there an acceptable alternative? A variety of substitutes were proposed, with "administration" ultimately being accepted.

Fourth, how was it possible to guard the interests of "fringe states" in a system of valley authorities, in the case of CVA, Montana, Wyoming, Utah, and Nevada? It was not in the nature of river systems to conform precisely to political boundaries, or even to begin unambiguously at some geographical point. Yet arbitrariness conflicted with the notion of system.

Fifth, on what principles should interactivity subsidies take place? It was common practice in multiple-purpose river projects to subsidize irrigation from power rates, but for what reasons, except possibly political ones, was not clear. One Budget Bureau staff member remarked: "This practice of hiding the irrigation subsidy is bound to make good planning of resource development difficult and bad planning easier and thus have a damaging long-run effect upon the wise use of our resources." Similarly fertilizer production (attractive to rural voters) was often mentioned as a desirable activity deserving of encouragement, but a persuasive rationale for so doing was not presented to the skeptics. Implicit in both these subsidies, of course, was the principle that agricultural development was preferable to industrialization. A detached observer might ask why.

Sixth, were there not alternative procedures to achieve the advantages claimed for valley authorities? For example, one skeptic asked, "Is it practicable to do the whole job of integration at the Budget Bureau level?"

Seventh, just what was meant by the repeated reference to "plan"? "Is a resource development plan a static or dynamic thing?" If the latter, how would adjustments be made? The Jackson bill (H.R. 427) required the Authority to submit to Congress an integrated plan for the control and use of water in the basin within two years of passage of the act. Advocates thought this an effective means of preserving political control over the "plan." Skeptics had their doubts.

Most of the efforts to answer these and other questions about the proposed CVA came from within Interior: from Assistant Secretary Davidson and his staff, from the program staff headed by Walton Seymour, from the Pacific Northwest Field Committee located in Portland, and from the BPA. But since most of the questions were of a substantial, almost constitutional, character, they could not readily be answered in the heat of preparing draft legislation and mobilizing the political forces necessary for it to be enacted. The questions reflected the climate of cold-eyed analysis that had grown up in the executive branch of government since World War II. The questioners were typically social scientists, unpersuaded by sentiment or rhetoric.

The "special message to Congress recommending establishment of a Columbia Valley Administration" was delivered on April 13, 1949.[77] It avoided the rough questions that had arisen during the prior three months of exploration. The goals specified were still growth, employment, and "unified" or "integrated" approaches to these problems. A Columbia Valley Administration (rather than Authority) was proposed, and was described as a "consolidation" of activities currently performed by the Bureau of Reclamation, BPA, and the Corps of Engineers. No other "Federal activities" were included, and there was no mention of a further extension of the model. In fact, the president said: "We have not found—nor do I expect that we shall find—a single organizational pattern that will fit perfectly the resource problems in the many diverse areas of the country." The message emphasized the need for consultation at every level of government and with Canada, which had a piece of the basin. Within the federal government itself the administration's "activities should harmonize, and not conflict, with Federal policies concerning agriculture, commerce, labor, and the other broad areas of national interest." In effect the CVA proposal presented in April was a timid rendition of the original idea. In form and content it was very different from the visionary statements of 1944.

Conclusion: A Whimper, Not a Bang

Shortly after President Truman's message to Congress in April, 1949, a series of bills was introduced into Congress more or less faithful to his proposals. Hearings were held in the Senate from May through August and in the House from June through August.[78] None of the bills ever came out of committee. The advocates kept pressing for some action for more than a year, but to no avail. Evidently as a means to still the disappointed advocates, President Truman in 1950 appointed a Water Resources Policy Commission, headed by the old valley authority advocate Morris Cooke. Until its report the White House could and did say that the subject was once again receiving a good hard look. But by this time the Korean War had distracted everyone's attention from such large questions as structural reform in government. By the time peace returned, a Republican president was in the White House and the valley authority idea was dead, probably forever.

A variety of circumstantial explanations can be given for the ultimate failure of the valley authority movement. First of all, a series of political mischances seriously weakened its friends and strengthened its foes. Above all, Cap Krug resigned as interior secretary in 1949 and was replaced by the undersecretary, Oscar Chapman, an oldtimer in the department and a lukewarm supporter of valley authorities at best. Chapman, for reasons that seem to have been both personal and ideological, moved Assistant Secretary Davidson away from his long-standing public power interests and ultimately drove him in frustration back into private life.[79] By mid-1950, then, CVA was again without friends at the top in Interior. It was not quite a return to the Ickes days, but close to it.

In Congress CVA in 1948 effectively lost one of its staunchest advocates, Senator Glen Taylor of Idaho, who ran as Henry Wallace's running mate in the presidential elections. Thereafter Taylor was anathema to the Democratic party leadership. But CVA retained its most vigorous enemy in the other senator from Idaho, Henry Dworshak. In 1950 friends of CVA joined with others to defeat Dworshak for re-election, but his successor died in office only a few weeks later. When Dworshak was then appointed to the vacant seat by the Idaho governor, it simply took much of the ginger out of the CVA movement.

In addition to these political misfortunes, the energy and adroitness of the various foes of CVA were impressive. Enemies in the private sector again and again deplored the road to serfdom along which they pictured CVA as a major milestone. Moreover, they were quick to characterize the advocates as unwilling dupes of socialism, "professional vote seekers, self-styled labor leaders or habitual do-gooders."[80] In the federal bureaucracy the two agencies that stood to lose the most, the Bureau of Reclamation and the Corps of Engineers, announced that they had reached "agreement on principles and responsibilities for the plan of development" for the Columbia River basin, thus in effect removing the argument that these two giants would not cooperate. Supporters of CVA insisted that this "Pick-Straus plan" would simply make it easier to move to a basinwide administration under CVA. But critics replied that, with this plan in effect, there was little more that a CVA could contribute.

Most important of all, it seems, was that by 1949, in contrast to five years earlier, the CVA was no longer a powerful vision of a new future, a plausible solution to problems of various kinds that frightened the populace. Over these five years both the national problems and the alternative solutions had changed. This was clearly reflected in the national mood; it was not a vintage year for visions. The valley authority idea could still get a hearing, but now it was treated with skepticism by bureaucrats in government and by many concerned citizens outside.

Two environmental conditions were very much against the valley authority advocates: the intellectual climate and the political and social milieu. The valley authority was to be an instrument of economic, political, and social development. Advocates may have been right, but they lacked the well-developed theoretical arguments and analytical equipment to make the case persuasively. Within the discipline of economics, and reflected in those parts of government that used the economists' tools, the theory of economic development consisted more and more of "the neoclassical synthesis"; according to this theory, growth would occur optimally if full employment and price stability were maintained through provision of just the right amount of aggregate effective demand, and if the economic system were made up of free markets, or markets that acted as if they were free. Some of the speculations of the earlier American Institutionalist economists, or the German Historical School, about the nature of human motivation and the interaction among social and political structures and economic performance might have provided support for regional authorities, but these ideas were still undeveloped and were by now well outside the mainstream of the economics profession. Certainly they were seldom reflected in the probing questions about CVA posed by the critics.

The late 1940s were a conservative era in the understanding of political development. Unlike the 1930s, when it appeared that the American political system might burst asunder, the war and contact with authoritarian regimes made many political thinkers in the United States conclude that perhaps, after all, they had the best political system yet devised, and possibly that ever could be devised. In this environment revolutionary suggestions like that for regional autonomy were not particularly welcome. This was also an era of decolonization around the world, when dozens of new nations were coming into existence; the American attitude was that out of generosity the American political model, with its federal system, tripartite division of powers, and checks and balances, should be displayed for emulation and adoption by these nations if they were so enlightened. There was little sense that for America this too should be a time of change, of political experiment. Behind the mood of political conservatism, of course, was the sense that increasingly America was in a worldwide struggle for political survival with an adversary whose political system was diametrically different. Surely while locked in such a struggle it was awkward, if not treasonous, to talk of modifying structurally what was being defended.

In social thought the late 1940s were years before America came to recognize that it was far from being the homogeneous melting pot some had imagined it to be. The one great regional conflict in American history, the Civil War, had been a searing experience that many wished to forget and all were determined not to repeat. It had pitted one region against another and emphasized their differences. It would be going too far to suggest that Americans saw in valley authorities a vestige of the forces that led to civil war. But it is fair to observe that regional distinctions and pressures for heterogeneity and autonomy generated uneasiness in Americans, both directly and unconsciously.

The ultimate failure of CVA was foretold quite early. Evidence came in quickly that interest simply was not strong enough in the various constituencies. Skepticism could be detected not only in the Budget Bureau and the Council of Economic Advisers but among the White House staff who were charged with carrying the ball. An official interviewer was dispatched in February, 1949, to sample elite public opinion. He "talked with more than 40 persons in the Pacific Northwest, representing just about every shade of opinion, including labor, farm organization, public and private power, banks, chambers of commerce, Governors of Washington and Oregon, publishers, educators, Federal agency officials, ordinary individuals, etc."[81] He summarized his findings as follows: "Strongest views of majority respondents representing all interests seem to be (a) against word authority, Columbia Valley Corporation generally acceptable, (b) for specific provisions for local voice or directorate, (c) against TVA type of device as not applicable to huge Columbia River system, (d) for some kind of corporate coordinative device with large number feeling such device should use existing agencies in carrying out program." Murphy and Bell toured the Northwest in March, 1949, and returned with no sense of profound support among the masses. Ivan Bloch reported sadly in August of the League for CVA that "the organization is in bad shape, and doesn't seem to have any success raising funds."[82]

It would be wrong to suggest that by the fall of 1949 the valley authority idea had been decisively defeated. Many strong advocates remained, among them, with some qualifications, the president. But during several months of intense discussion and probing inquiry the advocates were not able to make enough converts. Politically the idea remained alive throughout the remainder of President Truman's second term. He continued to endorse the concept broadly and CVA specifically, especially during political tours in the West.[83] (Interestingly, on the hustings he tended to slip back into the old phraseology of Columbia Valley *Authority*.) Moreover, cabinet members like Chapman, Brannan, and Sawyer, who opposed the whole notion, continued to be admonished if they spoke out in public against it. But one gets the clear sense that by late 1949 few astute observers thought seriously anymore that a brave new valley authority structure would come into being. Various compromise measures were explored, including a "Basin Account," which would permit integrated, multipurpose programs to be undertaken by whichever government agency was most appropriate.[84] Another proposal was to merge the Bureau of Reclamation and the Corps of Engineers into one large development agency. Neither of these suggestions was taken up. The valley authority concept persisted in the rhetoric of the Democratic party for some time. Adlai Stevenson included it in his lists of desiderata in 1952. But its great trial had come and gone in 1949. It was the victim of changing times, of new goals and new problems, and of new ways of understanding and dealing with them.

NOTES

1. The progress of Keynesian ideas within the federal government has been well documented. See, for example, Donald Winch, *Economics and Policy* (New York: Walker, 1970).

2. Stephen Raushenbush, memo for the secretary, June 6, 1942, Regionalization (Spe-

cial Assignment) file, Branch of Economics and Statistics Files, Records of the Department of the Interior, Record Group 48, National Archives (hereafter RG 48, NA).

3. "National Resource Problems and Programs," Mineral Policy—1944 file, Branch of Economics and Statistics Files, RG 48, NA. Evidently this was a document prepared by Raushenbush for discussion within the department.

4. Stephen Raushenbush, memo for the undersecretary (Fortas), Jan. 13, 1945, Regionalization file, Branch of Economics and Statistics Files, RG 48, NA. Raushenbush listed the principal documents in the discussion of regionalization, from 1942 to 1946, in a memo for Mr. Wolfsohn, special assistant to the secretary, Apr. 4, 1946, Regionalization (Special Assignment) file, Branch of Economics and Statistics Files, RG 48, NA.

5. William E. Warne, memo regarding a centralized research, planning, and coordinating agency in the Department of the Interior, n.d. (attached to "Memo for Mike Straus," dated Jan. 7, 1943), Planning and Coordinating Division file, Branch of Economics and Statistics Files, RG 48, NA.

6. Davidson set forth the issues to be addressed by BPA in looking forward to a western regional authority, in a letter to Arthur C. Jacquot, Aug. 8, 1945, Subject File CVA Memoranda 1944–50, C. Girard Davidson Papers, Harry S. Truman Library, Independence, Mo.

7. Bloch to Waldemar Kaempffert, June 25, 1944, Subject File CVA Memoranda 1944–50, Davidson Papers.

8. Davidson to Morton Tompkins, Dec. 28, 1944, Subject File CVA Legislation Nov., 1944–June, 1948, Davidson Papers.

9. Bloch to Kaempffert.

10. Ibid.

11. R. F. Bessey, a staff member of BPA, attempted in 1944 (with charts) to sort out the problems of relating the valley authorities to each other and concluded rather vaguely that "the national coordination set-up should be limited to that necessary for harmony in policy and program formation and administration, and for facilitating the Valley programs themselves." Bessey, memo to Paul J. Raver on "Valley authorities, Relationships," Nov. 27, 1944, Subject File CVA Legislation, Davidson Papers. A document, probably prepared by Raushenbush in 1944 or 1945, speculated about new political devices, including a Popular Advisory Council with representation from "a cross section of the entire population, Indian, Spanish-American, and Anglo-American. Representation could be functional, representing the different population and economic groups in different parts of the region." The paper's author proceeded from the principle that "the Authority type of regional government needs to get rooted democratically in the local people and their institutions." The untitled document is contained in Regionalization file, Branch of Economics and Statistics Files, RG 48, NA.

12. Waldemar Kaempffert to Ivan Bloch, June 13, 1944, Subject File CVA Memoranda 1944–50, Davidson Papers.

13. The University of Chicago Round Table: Seven New TVA's? (Dec. 3, 1944), p. 1.

14. Ibid., p. 21.

15. Carey McWilliams, "The Northwest Needs a CVA," The Nation (June 2, 1945), pp. 622–23. See also "Power Is the Banker," ibid. (June 9, 1945), pp. 645–47.

16. "Resolution on the Establishment of a Missouri Valley Authority," of a conference in Jefferson City, Mo., May 11 and 12, 1945, OF 201A, Truman Library.

17. See, for example, a thoughtful paper by a lawyer, Taylor Sandison, on the subject in MVA Addresses File, Jerome Walsh Papers, Truman Library.

18. Ivan Bloch described the efforts of BPA on behalf of a CVA in a letter to his colleague Samuel Moment, Oct. 16, 1945, Subject File CVA Memoranda 1944–50, Davidson Papers. The background of the CVA movement is described in a Bureau of the Budget report entitled "Organizing for the Development of the Columbia Valley," CVA-S.J.S. W. H. Assignment File, Stephen Spingarn Files, Truman Library.

19. Paul J. Raver, "Valley Development and the National Economy," Subject File CVA Legislation Nov., 1944–June, 1945, Davidson Papers.

20. Typed copies of these twelve articles are in Publications by Hugh Mitchell File, Davidson Papers.

21. C. Girard Davidson, "A Columbia Valley Authority," speech delivered in Seattle, May 19, 1945, Subject File CVA Legislation Nov., 1944–June, 1945, Davidson Papers.

22. E.g. Ellery Foster, director, research and education, IWA-CIO, to Anthony Wayne Smith, assistant director, Industrial Union Councils, CIO, Nov. 27, 1945, Subject File CVA Legislation Jan.–Apr., 1946, Davidson Papers; G. A. Peters, president, Southwest Washington Utility Districts Association, to president Truman, Jan. 28, 1945, OF 360, Truman Library. Davidson described the support from agriculture in a letter to Senator Mitchell, May 15, 1945, Subject File CVA Memoranda 1944–50, Davidson Papers.

23. Paul J. Raver described the growing opposition in a letter to Secretary Ickes, Apr. 5, 1945, Subject File CVA Legislation Jan.–Apr., 1946, Davidson Papers.

24. See Martha Derthick, *Between State and Nation* (Washington, D.C.: Brookings Institution, 1974), pp. 28–32.

25. Paul J. Raver to Harold L. Ickes, Jan. 11, 1945, Subject File CVA Legislation Jan.–Apr. 1946, Davidson Papers.

26. George Sundborg, memo to Paul J. Raver on "The Bureau of Reclamation and Public Power," Jan. 24, 1946, Subject File CVA Memoranda 1944–50, Davidson Papers.

27. "Ickes Backing Rivers Control," stand on valley authorities given to F. A. Banks, Dec. 20, 1944. Subject File CVA Legislation Nov., 1944–June, 1945, Davidson Papers.

28. Statement of Harold L. Ickes, Hearings before the Senate Commerce Committee, 79th Cong. (1945), to consider a bill to establish a Missouri Valley Authority, S. 555, Apr. 18, 1945, Subject File CVA Background Material, Davidson Papers.

29. William E. Warne, "What Can the Department of the Interior do for Regional Development Better Than an Independent Authority Can Do?" Post-War Resources Institute, Washington, D.C., May 5–9, 1945, Subject File CVA July–Dec., 1945, Davidson Papers.

30. D. L. Marlett, comments on Warne paper, Subject File CVA July–Dec., 1945, Davidson Papers.

31. Stephen Raushenbush, memo for the solicitor, May 18, 1946, Regionalization (Special Assignment) file, Branch of Economics and Statistics Files, RG 48, NA.

32. Truman to Ickes, Aug. 15, 1945; this and related correspondence is in OF 201A, Truman Library.

33. Truman to E. L. Clary, Mar. 30, 1945; this and subsequent correspondence with Clary is in SV 112, Truman Library.

34. *Public Papers of the Presidents: Harry S. Truman* (hereafter *Public Papers*), 1945, p. 10.

35. *Ibid.*, p. 133.

36. Ickes to Truman, Nov. 23, 1945, OF 360-A, Truman Library.

37. Davidson to Ickes, Oct. 1, 1945, Subject File CVA July–Dec., 1945, Davidson Papers.

38. *Public Papers*, 1945, pp. 301–2.

39. *Ibid.*, pp. 389–94.

40. Truman to Ora Bundy, president, National Reclamation Association, Nov. 10, 1945, Columbia Valley Authority file, Charles Murphy Files, Truman Library.

41. The relationship of TVA to the advocates of valley authorities elsewhere can be found in the following documents: Hugh B. Mitchell to David E. Lilienthal, Oct. 31, 1945, and Lilienthal to Mitchell, Nov. 13, 1945, Subject File CVA Legislation (S. 460 draft of Oct. 30, 1945), Davidson Papers; C. Girard Davidson to Joseph C. Swidler, Jan. 9, 1946, Subject File CVA Legislation (S. 1716) Jan.–Apr., 1946, Davidson Papers; David E. Lilienthal, "TVA Answers the Doubters of MVA" (n.d., 1945?), MVA-Addresses by D. E. Lilienthal File, Walsh Papers; Swidler to Davidson, Apr. 12, 1946, Subject File CVA Legislation (S. 1716), Jan.–Apr. 1946, Davidson Papers; and W. L. Sturdevant, director of information, TVA, to the Editor, *Kansas City Star*, Feb. 28, 1945, MVA Debate File, Walsh Papers.

42. See, for example, "draft for president's signature," presumably by Clark Clifford, of letter to James E. Webb raising "the question of the general relationship of TVA to the rest of the Government," and Gordon R. Clapp to Clark M. Clifford, Dec. 18, 1946, both in Tennessee Valley Authority file, Clark M. Clifford Files, Truman Library. The general skepticism of TVA in the Budget Bureau is set forth in F. J. Lawton to Clifford, Nov. 8, 1946, *ibid.*

43. Subject File 1945: River and Regional Development, Samuel Rosenman Papers, Truman Library.

44. Chapman Oral History, p. 468, Truman Library.

45. Davidson Oral History, p. 14, Truman Library.

46. E.g., *Public Papers*, 1946, pp. 60–61, and 1947, pp. 334–38.

47. E.g., minutes of organization meeting, League for CVA, held at Portland, Ore., Dec. 22, 1945, Subject File CVA General Memoranda 1944–50, Davidson Papers.

48. J. Kenneth Kaseberg to C. Girard Davidson, Apr. 10, 1946, Subject File CVA General Memoranda 1944–50, Davidson Papers.

49. Benton J. Stong to Jerome Walsh, June 18, 1948, MVA Correspondence File, Walsh Papers.

50. E.g., see Benton J. Stong to members of working committee, Regional Committee for an MVA, July 7, 1947, MVA Correspondence File, Walsh Papers.

51. A typed account of the conference proceedings is in the MVA–Valley Authority Conference File, Walsh Papers.

52. *Public Papers*, 1948, p. 5.

53. *Ibid.*, p. 78.

54. *Ibid.*, p. 260.

55. *Ibid.*, pp. 300–301.

56. *Ibid.*, pp. 320–22.

57. A copy of the platform is in Subject File CVA Background Material, Davidson Papers.

58. S. Moment, "B.P.A. Program—1949–52—Some Proposals" (Nov. 12, 1948), Program Staff Power–Bonneville Power Administration file, Office Files of Walton Seymour, RG 48, NA.

59. James E. Webb, memo for the president, Dec. 30, 1948, Truman Library.

60. *Public Papers*, 1949, p. 5.

61. *Ibid.*, pp. 83.

62. *New York Times*, Jan. 25 and 28, 1949.

63. E.g., Congress of Industrial Organizations, Policy Directives in Legislation for a Columbia Valley Authority, Jan. 28, 1949, Murphy Files.

64. Lilienthal to Matthew J. Connelly, Jan. 17, 1949, OF 360A, Truman Library.

65. Holman to Truman, Jan. 25, 1949, OF 360A, Truman Library.

66. Documents that reveal the evolving White House investigation of issues raised by the CVA proposal are: D. E. Bell, memo to Charles Murphy on "Framework of the Columbia Valley Authority," Feb. 1, 1949, Columbia Valley Authority file, Murphy Files; [Bell], "Notes on Interdepartmental Meeting on CVA," Feb. 4, 1949, Columbia Valley Administration file, David E. Bell Files, Truman Library; Bell, memo to Charles Murphy on "Relation of CVA to Departments of Agriculture and Commerce," Feb. 15, 1949, Columbia Valley Authority file, Murphy Files; Wilbert G. Fritz (Bureau of the Budget), memo to Bell on "Suggested additional items for consideration in the Columbia Valley Authority Bill," Feb. 16, 1949, Columbia Valley Administration file, Bell Files; Bell, memo for Mr. Murphy, June 29, 1949, Columbia Valley Administration file, Bell Files; Charles F. Luce to Bell, July 14, 1949, Subject File CVA Unclassified Material, Davidson Papers.

67. Dill to Truman, Feb. 17, 1949, OF 360A, Truman Library.

68. Bell, memo to Murphy, Feb. 15, 1949.

69. Ralph R. Will, U.S. Department of Agriculture, to Bell, Feb. 9, 1949, and William R. Davlin, Department of Commerce, to Bell, Feb. 11, 1949, Columbia Valley Authority file, Murphy Files.

70. Fritz to Elmer B. Staats and Roger W. Jones, Mar. 16, 1949, CVA Bill File, Records of the Bureau of the Budget, RG 51, NA. This Budget Bureau Bill File contains abundant skeptical testimony on the valley authority idea.

71. Fleming to Elmer B. Staats, Mar. 15, 1949, CVA Bill File, RG 51, NA.

72. Fritz, memo to Bell, Feb. 16, 1949.

73. For evidence of enthusiasm for the Spence bill by advocates of CVA, see Economic Stabilization Act of 1949–Spence Act File, Office Files of C. G. Davidson, RG 48, NA.

74. Fritz to Staats and Jones, March 16, 1949.

75. Charles Brannan to Frank Pace, Jr., Mar. 14, 1949, CVA Bill File, RG 51, NA.

76. Will to Bell, Feb. 9, 1949.

77. *Public Papers*, 1949, pp. 208–13.

78. Hearings before the Senate Public Works Committee, 81st Cong., 1st sess., on S. 1595, S. 1631, S. 1632, and S. 1645; and Hearings before the House Public Works Committee, 81st Cong., 1st sess., on H.R. 4286 and H.R. 4287.

79. Davidson Oral History, p. 157, Truman Library.

80. "Business of West Is Opposed to a CVA," *New York Times*, Mar. 30, 1949.

81. J. Otis Garber, series of teletype messages, Feb., 1949, contained in CVA Bill File, RG 51, NA.

82. Bloch to Paul Unger, Aug. 29, 1949, Subject File Ivan Bloch Correspondence, Davidson Papers.

83. E.g., *Public Papers*, 1950, pp. 8, 28, 90, 345, 351, 352, 357, 373, 429, 430.

84. David Bell, memo to Charles Murphy on Columbia River "Basin Account" legislation, Nov. 13, 1950, Columbia Valley Authority file, Murphy Files.

11

William C. Havard, Jr.

Images of TVA:
The Clash over Values

N 1944, when David Lilienthal published the story of his
personal romance with the Tennessee Valley Authority,[1] he
was barely in his mid-forties. He had served as one of the
three directors of the agency since its organization in 1933, been its
chairman since 1941, and had done more than anyone else to set its policy directions since the mid-thirties. Lilienthal was to serve as chairman from 1941 to 1946, when he left to take charge of the emerging
Atomic Energy Commission. But his influence on TVA did not end with
his departure from a regional to a more central arena of power, since
his successor as chairman, Gordon Clapp, had been general manager
throughout Lilienthal's chairmanship and generally followed the course
set by Lilienthal. Thus no single figure in TVA's history did so much to
fabricate the image of the agency from the perspective of the insider as
Lilienthal. And no available portrayal is more appropriate than his as
an ideal against which one might assess TVA's political performance.
The heroic dimensions and the bright optimism of its tones are best
conveyed in Lilienthal's own words:

This book is being written in the valley of a great American river, the Tennessee. It is about the river, and that valley; about the soil of its farms, the white
oak and pine on its mountain slopes, the ores and minerals that lie buried in its
hills. It is about the rain that falls so violently upon its fields, and the course the
water follows as it seeks out first the streams and then the river itself. This book
is about the people of this valley region, the men who work the land, the men

297

who roll the silver sheets of aluminum, who run the cotton gins, and stand behind the counter in the general stores. It is about the women who tend the spindles or stir the kettles or teach the children in the schools.

This is the story of a great change. It is an account of what has happened in this valley in the past ten years, since Congress set the Tennessee Valley Authority to the task of developing the resources of this region. It is a tale of a wandering and inconstant river now become a chain of broad and lovely lakes which people enjoy, and on which they can depend in all seasons, for the movement of the barges of commerce that now nourish their business enterprises. It is a story of how waters once wasted and destructive have been controlled and now work, night and day, creating electric energy to lighten the burden of human drudgery. Here is a tale of fields grown old and barren with the years, which now are vigorous with new fertility, lying green to the sun; of forests that were hacked and despoiled, now protected and refreshed with strong young trees just starting on their slow road to maturity. It is a story of the people and how they have worked to create a new valley. . . .

The Tennessee River had always been an idle giant and a destructive one. Today, after ten years of TVA's work, at last its boundless energy works for the people who live in this valley. . . .

Today it is builders and technicians that we turn to: men armed not with the ax, rifle, and bowie knife, but with the Diesel engine, the bulldozer, the giant electric shovel, the retort—and most of all, with an emerging kind of skill, a modern knack of organization and execution. . . .

Such are the things that have happened in the Tennessee Valley in the past ten years. Here men and science and organizing skills applied to the resources of waters, land, forests, and minerals have yielded great benefits for the people. . . .

This hour, moreover, is the right time for telling of such things. . . . Seeing the reality of things they had never dreamed could happen, men have been deeply stirred; now almost nothing seems impossible. . . . They seem no longer greatly moved and lifted by abstractions. Their thinking is less complicated but closer to life than that of the intellectual on the lecture platform or the political leader drafting a manifesto.[2]

While David Lilienthal was actively engaged in the political and technological effort he perceived as necessary to translate this image fully into concrete reality, a literary artist was creating another—quite different—image of TVA. This artist was a close observer of man and nature rather than a practitioner of sociotechnocratic crafts. Donald Davidson, professor of English at Vanderbilt University, was a member of the Nashville Fugitives and Agrarians of the 1920s and early 1930s. He developed his image of the TVA in the larger context of his two-volume history of the Tennessee River and its environs, a work of epic proportions that is at once romantic and realistic in its rich blending of melodrama, tragedy, and bitter comic irony.[3] Although he focuses on the TVA throughout the latter half of the second volume, the first volume opens with a transformational theme that, on the surface at least, recalls Lilienthal's melodramatic beginning:

Down the valley of the Tennessee two rivers flow—two rivers blended indistinguishably where for centuries there was only one. They slant southwest, then west, then north, in the wide curve that marks the course of the Tennessee. One of these, uppermost and immensely obvious, is the new Tennessee, a man-made river, the product of engineering operations of such calculated daring that the imagination is daunted to find precedent for them. A unique modern contrivance, designed and finished in a little over a decade, it is less a river than a chain of lakes, formed by the impounding of river waters behind great dams that stand athwart the valley in Egyptian impassivity. It is one of the best-advertised rivers in the world, and has been visited and studied by the emissaries of many foreign governments as well as by ever-increasing throngs of American tourists. With reason, it is an object of supreme interest to all who want to learn how to control the waters of a river valley and how to convert their force into electrical energy, while achieving at the same time material benefits which are thought not to be readily attainable by other means. This shining, modern thing, so new that its concrete structures have not had time to weather, is the river of the TVA.

Beneath the giant stairs of great lakes, merged with them and all but lost in them, flows another river—the old Tennessee, the river of the Cherokee Indians and of their Creek and Chickasaw neighbors. . . .

Many times it has been at the center of the conflicts and decisions that have shaped the American republic. But it has not been well advertised, and therefore is not well known to the modern generation. Historians have neglected it. Even the natives of its valley have somehow lost acquaintance with it.[4]

In the last part of volume 2 of *The Tennessee* Davidson develops his saga of the Valley's transformation at the hands of TVA. And it is a vastly different story from that told by Lilienthal. While fully acknowledging the impressive technical achievements of TVA, and even paying some tribute to the contributions made by the agency to improvements in navigation, agricultural efficiency, and some of the other aspects of economic life in the Tennessee Valley, Davidson is concerned with the costs of the transformation, and he finds them high indeed. It was not the reckoning of monetary costs against the returns that bothered him, although he raised serious questions about these. (The notion of cost-benefit ratios that later became a major standard for justifying public works projects would have struck Davidson as another form of de-culturation fostered by an advancing technocracy—both social and physical—with its implementary power vested in large-scale, centralized, industrial and governmental bureaucracies.) In Davidson's view the costs were ultimately unassessable in monetary or any other quantifiable terms because they involved those unmeasurable qualities of man, nature, and society as they exist in symbiotic wholeness.

Thus to every claim advanced on behalf of TVA's accomplishments by Lilienthal, Davidson enters a caveat: the massive conquest of nature was attended by at least as much destruction as reconstruction. Thousands of acres of the best bottom lands were taken out of agricultural production, hasty clearance of reservoir basins denuded rich hardwood forests, and overacquisition of peripheral lands produced greed and exploitation by a few at the expense of the many. The past was so mortgaged to promises of the future that a proud historical culture was giving way to a dehumanized urban-industrial society. Throughout, Davidson stresses the primacy given the electric power program over all other TVA activities, and points up the inequitable relative benefits of that program to various groups in society, including the TVA "interest" itself. Furthermore, his interpretation indicates that a steady diminution of individual and community self-determination occurred despite TVA's continuing emphasis on devolutionary democracy. The land acquisition program displaced individuals, families, and whole communities in the name of comprehensive regional development, and the controlling decisions about the region's future were centralized in TVA, with a subsequent reduction of the influence of private groups and traditional state and local government units on the economics, politics, and culture of the area.[5]

The titles of Davidson's chapters on TVA in *The Tennessee* convey in aphoristic, double-edged phrases the stages of agency development. They also reveal Davidson's corrosive skepticism about its origins and early operations: Chapter XI—"The Uneasy Reign of King Kilowatt I" (the efforts of those of the progressive "New South" persuasion to "enthrone" electric power as a great vendable commodity through traditional incremental techniques that combined the generation and distribution activities of private power companies and governmental internal improvement projects designed to enhance navigation on inland waterways and control flooding); Chapter XII—"Trials by Jury and Otherwise" (Davidson's view of the imperialist assault of the dominant American urban-industrial culture on the "backward" mid-South in the effort to impose progress externally on a people too benighted to know what was good for them, much less capable of utilizing means appropriate to the realization of developmental objectives); Chapter XIII—"At Last! The Kingdom Really Comes!" (the expansive origins of TVA);

Chapter XIV—"The T.V.A. Makes a New River" (the ambivalent results of radical alterations of nature); Chapter XV—"The Workings of T.V.A." (a summary of the aspirations and varied activities of "The Great Leviathan"); Chapter XVI—"Navigation, New Style" (the promise and performance of TVA in river transportation); Chapter XVII—"Green Lands and Great Waters" (floods, fertilizer, agriculture—"improvement" and its price); and Chapter XVIII—"The Battles of T.V.A." (how TVA survived its internal battles, prevailed in its struggles with private power interests, and overcame opposition from those adversely affected by its programs and its political opponents alike).[6]

Davidson's conclusion is a sardonic recapitulation of his view of TVA as a march, not toward democracy but to an unchallengeable position as the central political and economic power in the Valley:

Within its own domain . . . TVA was established and seemingly impregnable. What the nation might think about TVA or the TVA idea was for the nation to decide. That was a privilege that the Tennessee Valley had not had with respect to TVA. The agitations of a few men and the long deliberations of Congress had decided all. Outside of a handful of responsible parties, the most ardent enthusiast for TVA within the valley had as little to do with its origin, maintenance, and continuance as had TVA's most bitter opponent. Whether TVA's power program, or any other of its programs, was right or wrong, cheap or costly, fair or unfair, it had to be accepted in the valley. One might hold that TVA as a power enterprise existed primarily for the benefit of urban areas and big industry and that therefore, in principle, it had violated the law and deceived the people. Or one might hold the opposite. It made no difference. It was nothing that either critic or defender could do anything about.

Accordingly, when Mr. Clapp moved up into Mr. Lilienthal's place, there was about the same amount of concern in the valley as when, during the Middle Ages, the peasant learned that a new king had been crowned at a distant city. All that anybody could do was to hope and pray that Mr. Clapp would be a good king and would behave kindly toward his subjects. If he should turn out to be a bad king, there was still not much that anybody could do. In other days, if you were discontented with a power company, you could appeal to the government. If you were discontented with TVA, to whom did you appeal? TVA was the government. In the Tennessee Valley there was nothing above it.[7]

What, one may ask, is the point of this lengthy excursion through two such polar conceptions of the meaning of TVA? The immediate answer is that several points, rather than a single one, can be made about the nature and content of the issues that divided Lilienthal and Davidson, all of which provide a broader cultural context for a comprehensive examination of the origins and subsequent history of TVA.

The first point is that neither Lilienthal nor Davidson hesitates to cast TVA in a cosmic role. They both treat it in the setting of a comprehensive "world-view" rather than as a complex governmental agency among many others, thus comprehendable as part of the American constitutional arrangements and historical experience in the application of those arrangements to the problems arising in the practice of American politics. Both regard TVA's meaning as one that can be grasped only if it is approached from the perspective of a coherent view of nature, man, and society. That is to say, they present TVA as having its foundation and impetus to action in conceptions that have more generic ontological, metaphysical, ethical, and historical implications than its more prosaic political origins and operations indicate. These larger philosophical concerns are less fully and explicitly developed in Lilienthal's writings than in Davidson's. But in both instances the consequence is to elevate TVA to the level of a generic social and political institution—a major force, whether positive or negative, in the human effort not only to comprehend but to realize, as far as the limits of existence will allow, the good life, i.e. one grounded in the basic values of truth, beauty, and justice. Even in terms of these weighty abstractions, they see TVA as more than an organization developed out of experience with, and in response to, the problems of a particular local, regional, or national body politic. It was available as a potential development model of global application; in the language of Hegelian idealism it was a concrete universal.

As already noted, both Lilienthal and Davidson perceived TVA as an instrument of transformation in the three ontic elements—nature, man, and society—and their interrelations. In Lilienthal's conception, science, technology, and organizational skills (social science's version of technology) united to enable man to control nature for his material benefit and thus free him from many of the seemingly inevitable burdens of mundane existence—poverty, drudgery, disease, filth, floods, and physical exhaustion. The language is often that of Faustian metaphysics; at other times it suggests a secular religion: "There is almost nothing, however fantastic, that (given competent organization) a team of engineers, scientists, and administrators cannot do today." "In the desperation of a fight to survive, miracles have been wrought in laboratories and with machines." "When these men [builders and technicians] have imagination and faith, they can move mountains." To these instrumental powers must be added a moral purpose, which is that the instruments be used for the "benefit of the people" if they are to prove "a blessing and not a curse." And two other "principles" must be added: "resource development must be governed by the unity of nature herself" and "the people must participate actively in that development." In brief, Lilienthal sets his image of TVA against a world-view that comes directly out of the eighteenth-century enlightened *Philosophe*. As such, it looks to a progressively unfolding future in which the evils of the past will be largely overcome, and the possibility will be opened to ". . . a way of life new to this world."[8]

By contrast, Davidson's world-view is grounded in a pre-Enlightenment or "pre-modern" conception of nature, man, and society. In this view it is not for the mind and will of man to assert complete control over nature for his own benefit, because man, too, is part of nature and thus subject to the laws of nature and of nature's God. Although the qualities of mind and spirit that are uniquely human may be part of the structure of being that places man closer to divine reality than any other form of existence, the eternal mysteries will never be fully vouchsafed to man in his finite condition. Indeed, to claim completeness of knowledge and to assert the total dominion of man (even "democratic" man) over nature and society in the name of that knowledge is the ultimate form of *hubris* because it purports to transmogrify man (or, collectively, "mankind") into God. And to take that step is to defy the limits of existence in the assertion of limitless access to power for the ostensible purpose of perfecting man and society.

For Davidson the transformation effected by TVA was destructive in two senses. In the deeper sense it overstepped the claims of both knowledge and the uses of power as instruments of change, thus contributing to what Davidson clearly considered the distorted conception of the nature of man and society characteristic of modernity. The more immediate and direct effect was the displacement of a traditional society in the name of rehabilitating a land and people by an external imposition of ideas and structural alterations. These, despite all talk about the march of democracy, effectively forestalled any form of local self-determination either by local decisions about the relation between the preservation of old cultural values and the adoption of new ones or by a choice of incrementalism in opposition to total alteration as a means to effect change. Davidson, of course, viewed society historically, or as a syncretic result of past experience rather than the product of man's ingenuity in creating abstract rational structures and then finding the instrumental means of reifying them. The destruction of a traditional society involves the abandonment of history as an open-ended story of man's cultural development, and giving in to the claim of various prophets who have no means of fulfilling their promises.[9]

These ontological positions are, at the least, intrinsically interesting. They also had the effect of elevating TVA to cosmic status in the minds of the generic makers of its images. But other considerations that follow from them, or are directly or indirectly related to them, have had major consequences for the way various people have perceived TVA, whether they were within the organization, part of the general public, or in the agencies of government (at all levels) with which TVA had mandated or voluntary cooperative relations. For one thing, the images projected by Lilienthal and Davidson were so comprehensive and so diametrically opposed in every essential aspect that practically all subsequent interpretations of TVA, whether laudatory or critical, appear derivative from one or the other of these protagonists. Their respective images have also played a part in shaping the internal organization of TVA, the way it went about formulating its policies, the balance among its various activities at a given time, its intergovernmental relations, the organized support it has been able to utilize to sustain itself, and the political conditions of both expansiveness and constraint over time. In short, symbols are important: practical political success and political images tend to become inextricably mingled.

Lilienthal's influence has been more direct, and in many ways easier to document, than Davidson's. He not only had a key part in developing the agency's self-image, but through his unquestionable skills in public relations and political maneuver he played a major role in spreading that favorable image through the news media, in magazines and books, and in public appearances. In turn, Lilienthal used the esteem TVA enjoyed in intellectual circles, in the Valley other than in those areas (especially in east Tennessee) where the relocation of rural residents generated hostility, and in most other parts of the United States and abroad to support the consolidation of TVA's programmatic successes and move into new or altered services or methods of operation.

Timing, of course, played a major part in the earliest days. While TVA struggled to establish both an identity and a mode of operation appropriate to its mission, Lilienthal enjoyed all the popularity of Roosevelt's early New Deal. In this atmosphere, with the positive central government now able to attain political and legal acceptance for new or broadened activities, it was easy to view TVA as one of the brightest jewels in the New Deal crown. It is not possible to say whether TVA could have maintained this image apart from its massive contributions to World War II through its expanded power production (a fivefold increase during the war years), and through the conversion of its fertilizer plants to production of ammonium nitrate for munitions. But the war and the postwar transition to a peacetime use of its expanded power resources enabled TVA to attain a stability not achieved prior to the war, and ensured that it would not be curtailed or dismantled in the way that a number of New Deal agencies were.

TVA continued into the immediate postwar years with its image shining more brightly than before. Yet it was now bereft of the glamor of its New Deal origins. It also lost its distinction as a governmental agency that claimed to have reinvigorated an economically stagnant geographical area. The impetus for economic development, both locally and nationally, now came from a complex variety of sources, as the United States embarked on a decade of unprecedented economic expansion. The last of its innovative (if opinionated and contentious) original directors was soon to depart, and it was beginning to settle into a more routine bureaucratic mode. Some of its programs were so stable, or so little known beyond the relatively few persons or groups served directly by them, that they had no conspicuous place in the image of TVA perceived by the general public or in the larger circles of government. With the navigation and flood control projects virtually completed and largely taken for granted, the TVA power service area consolidated, and the demand for electric power seemingly unappeasable in the foreseeable future, TVA found itself in the position of being regarded more and more as another giant power company, with its favorable image among the general public largely dependent on its continuing to make electric power (the demand for which it had once worked so hard to stimulate) available at half the rates in the rest of the country.

But after its survival through many struggles had culminated in the phenomenal growth of its power program to a monopolistic dominance in the Valley, TVA was, somewhat ironically, to enter an era in which its general image gradually became closer to Davidson's projection than Lilienthal's. The "modernization" of the Tennessee Valley eventually brought to the region those problems of an urban-industrial society that had beset the older "developed" areas of the country by the end of the 1950s. In this changing socioeconomic environment its altered public image was eventually to play a part in generating new problems for the agency.

Davidson, of course, had little direct influence on the growth of a negative image of the TVA. The 1930s and 1940s were hardly propitious times for the rejection on broad cultural grounds of the contributions any institution offered for solving problems of sheer economic survival. Most of the opposition to TVA, though often stated in terms of principle, was based on real or perceived damage to the interests of individuals and special groups: the private power interests, those who were displaced from their farms and homesteads, those whose property it expropriated for less than the return demanded or hoped for, and, in larger numbers, the electricity ratepayers confronting the steadily increasing rates of the inflationary decade of the 1970s. But as problems associated with the "modern" urban-industrial society mounted and the quest enlarged for a "postindustrial society" (whatever meaning may be given that ambiguous term), Davidson's arguments (once widely scorned as reactionary) have gained substantial cogency, even though those who use them now may have no clue to who formulated them or at least adapted them to use in the earliest negative characterization of TVA. Today one finds Davidson's criticisms (without attribution to him) in newspapers, magazines, books, the electronic media, and the public forum by environmentalists of several persuasions (ecologists, conservationists, and nature preservationists), economic libertarians, aficionados of the "small-is-beautiful" cultural concept, self-identified urban reformers, advocates of the devolution of political power, and numerous intellectuals, both in and out of the universities.

So the clash of values—both fundamental and derivative, joined by Lilienthal's and Davidson's respective portrayals of TVA—continues in full force. Even though these views of the agency are, more often than not, expressed as practical concerns about particular economic and political issues they still bear traces of those larger questions over which Lilienthal and Davidson were so deeply divided.

The contending images of TVA, as drawn by Lilienthal and Davidson, have other implications that seem more closely related to the purposes of this book than the cosmic background against which the agency's transformation achievements or failures are set. The authors in this volume have attempted to analyze the policies of TVA over its entire history in the more practical context of the general arrangements by which the United States is governed. Within this practical legal and administrative setting the clashes over values are observable in action as well as in abstract expressions of ethical and political norms justifying those actions.

Much of the continuing interest in TVA as a distinctive subject for political analysis results from the widespread acceptance of it as unique within the American system. Although created by an act of Congress following long and varied attempts to address a series of problems in the Tennessee Valley, and subject to some of the general controls exercised by the president and Congress to assure accountability, it remains difficult to place TVA properly in any of the standard taxonomic arrangements of American governmental institutions. Although it may be classified as a federal agency, its autonomy in certain areas of finance and administration, as well as its broad discretionary authority with respect to programs, are assured by laws that more often resemble a constitutional charter than ordinary statutes. Although established as a public corporation and organized along the lines of a private business structure or governmental proprietary corporation, the assignment of multipurpose functions to it extends TVA's scope well beyond that of the usual corporation, public or private. Although conceived as a *regional* authority, with its area of operation defined loosely in terms of a "natural" geographical unit crossing a number of political boundaries, it received its mandate from the national government rather than through a compact among the states included in the area it serves. It is always open to the claim (or charge) that it is a semisovereign entity superseding the authority of the states in some or all of the broad functions it is empowered to carry out. Although considered a special, multipurpose agency rather than a general government, TVA has engaged in an independent, or semi-independent, way in all three of the main functions of general governments in the United States—direct service, regulation, and entrepreneurial activities. Given its extensive legal autonomy, vaguely defined geographic boundaries, and broad scope in the practice of intergovernmental relations, it is not surprising that much of the politics of TVA has been involved in trying to establish an appropriate range of authority and limits in developing programs and engaging in working relations with other governmental units and agencies at all levels in the pursuit of its varied activities.[10]

As a distinctive governmental entity TVA has, in the course of its origin and development, confronted in various degrees all the issues over sources of authority, the distribution, use, and abuse of political power, and the proper functions of government that have informed the history of the American polity. In this sense TVA may be said to have replicated the basic experience of American political history generally—a political cosmion, in effect, drawn out of the political cosmos of American government, within which the same kinds of clashes occurred over fundamental issues as those that took place in the cosmic sphere. And efforts similar to those that are characteristic of American government at large may be seen in the history of TVA, as the agency has sought to establish itself as an authoritative institution working toward realization of the public good through the use of principled means. That the end is never fully realized and the means are sometimes unprincipled are not sufficient reasons for abandoning either critical or constructive efforts to establish an institutional image which comports with the accepted standards of organizational legitimacy, authorizations of power to act, and limits on the way that power is exercised in carrying out its functions that are applicable to the established government at large.

The following general issues of legitimacy and governmental practice run through the entire history of TVA, just as they are continuing items on the agenda of American political debate: (1) a range of issues related to popular participation in government, including the allocation and limitations of powers, devolution versus centralization, pluralism, and effective general participation as contrasted with dominance through bureaucratic centralism; (2) those issues concerning the proper role of government, including the differentiation between what is public and what is private, planning as a form of control as opposed to the free play of the market, and individualism versus collectivism; (3) issues involving making and implementing public policy decisions, building popular and general governmental support for programs, responsiveness and accountability, and the related problems of organization and leadership in making and administering policy.

This book is mainly about what TVA became as a result of the decisions that came out of the latter struggles—the political, legal, administrative, organizational, and managerial ones. These issues, of course, have to do with the way we act in the conduct of our day-to-day lives. They are the palpable struggles that we follow in the media, and that we may be directly involved in because we have interests at stake and access (or lack of access) to various means of influencing outcomes. We witness these issues of practice as they originate in problems out of which conflict and cooperation are generated within an accepted structure, and we observe (and/or participate in) the process through which resolutions are reached or fail to be reached. In turn, we can analyze the effect that such struggles have on the institutional structures within which they are carried on.

The history of TVA is, in one sense, an assembly into some intelligible order of a number of "incidents" of decision making and implementation that took place within that agency. One such ordering device is simple chronology, although experience hardly presents itself to us in neat sequential packages. But behind the effort to narrate the events are questions of analysis that enter into the interpretive ordering of history, beginning with the separation of events into those that are more or less important in making the institution into what it has been over time. Screening for appropriate evidence in turn suggests questions about values that make TVA a worthy subject of historical study. This step, of course, takes us back to the starting point of this essay, for behind the instrumental values reflected in the struggles over practice (mainly questions of technique) are those larger philosophical issues of human purpose and the deeper meaning of TVA's activities for all those affected by them.

Thus it is that the outcome of the battle within the original TVA board between the chairman, Arthur Morgan, a puritan moralist, devotee of the Protestant work ethic, and communitarian, who seemed to regard the very practice of the political arts as ethically suspect, and David Lilienthal, a consummate political practitioner and thoroughly "modern" man, brought with it not just the characteristics of TVA identified with Lilienthal's operating values but also some of his larger views of social and political reality. And so it was with all the "big" events that shaped TVA: the development of a public power monopoly in the region, the expansion from hydro to steam-produced power (with vertical integration making TVA the biggest single coal producer and consumer in the country), and from there into nuclear power production, with its opportunities for expansion for a time seemingly limitless. After a while the activities no longer seemed to require justification in terms of those inchoate cultural values that gave meaning to all its instrumental activities, many of which were now self-moved by the technological and bureaucratic imperatives of a functioning and well-received (for a time almost sacrosanct) public institution.

But time knows no rest, and history has no perfect stopping place other than those reposing in the visionary imaginations of prophets. TVA now has a history where it once simply had a vision. From the retrospective of the immediate present it might appear that some of the prophets of doom had more prescience than the visionaries with regard to the larger values that informed TVA. Before pursuing that switchback in the historical road, however, it might be well to consider briefly another retrospective that had more positive value connotations for TVA, even though in it the original vision was somewhat blurred by the shaky course of historical reality.

Aubrey J. "Red" Wagner joined TVA in 1933 as a young engineer just out of the University of Wisconsin. He retired forty-four years later, having spent his entire career in the agency. From 1954 until 1961 he was general manager, and from 1962 until 1977 he was chairman of the board of directors, serving in that capacity longer than any previous chairman. He could certainly be considered a representative spokesman for the mature TVA. A man who rose to the top from within TVA management, he was also perceived by a great many observers in and out of the organization as a technician who embodied the agency's increasing focus on the power program as the great stimulus to economic development in the Valley. Some ten years before his retirement, Wagner wrote an assessment of TVA after nearly thirty-five years of its operations. That overview opened with the following statement:

The lifetime of TVA has almost spanned a generation. Many of those who in the early 1930's fought the battles leading to the creation of TVA—the conservationists, the "farm bloc," the political leaders—have passed from the national scene or are stepping aside one by one. Most of the men who shaped TVA's first operating policies, designed its first dams, and produced its first fertilizers have been supplanted by others. The young people of that earlier time—those who watched while a river was placed in harness, while gullies were healed with well-fertilized cover crops, while electricity marched on new, life-giving wires across the land—today these people are grown; to their offspring, the physical transformation of a river valley is a fact of history.

It seems an appropriate time to present an assessment of TVA, in some respects with relation to the past but more generally in terms of its impact on the future. This, in effect, means an assessment of the future of the Tennessee Valley, for TVA's task from the beginning has been to help build a brighter future for this region. To this end we might seek answers to questions such as these: What is the state of our natural resources in the Tennessee Valley after three decades and what should be done to make them more responsive to human needs? What kinds of life can we fashion from these resources? As we face the future, do we see a horizon of greater employment, improving business, expanding opportunity, and enlightened freedom?[11]

In this broad emphasis Wagner's assessment is, of course, reminiscent of Lilienthal's appraisal at the end of the first decade—the stress on the great achievements in construction to control nature for man's benefit, followed by a futuristic projection. But Wagner casts both the achievements of the past and the projections for the future along lines that are much more restrained than those of Lilienthal. The transformation theme is still there, but it is muted; there has been a *physical* transformation, but a radical alteration of the life of man and society is not even alluded to, let alone suggested as a real possibility. At best the potential for a good life has been enhanced by TVA's programs. In the case of nature, Wagner brings in Bacon's injunction that in order to be commanded nature must be obeyed, but, like Lilienthal, he makes little of the implications of that generalization. Wagner presents the accomplishments of TVA largely in quantitative terms, treating qualitative issues, if at all, in an elliptical way. TVA has simply made the Tennessee River and its Valley over into a mid-southern Great Lakes region, with its 10,000 miles of shoreline containing vast amounts of water-related land that is now open to development for a wide variety of balanced uses to be determined by *local* choice. The multifunctional nature of TVA's mission is still there. It continues to provide an identity for the agency, but TVA's achievements, while substantial, have hardly been miraculous, and are acknowledged to have opened up new problems out of the partial resolution of old ones. The limits and incremental nature of change are much clearer in Wagner's brief retrospective than they were in Lilienthal's more extended and largely eschatological perspective.

As for the future of the people in the region, Wagner's focus is much more on what needs to be done than on the teleological progressivism so apparent in Lilienthal. The needs themselves, as well as the expectations, are much more mundane than the virtually unlimited possibilities suggested in the earlier, and more idealized, image of TVA. Jobs are now the principal need, and the creation of jobs implies continuing growth—growth that TVA alone cannot assure, especially in a society which has already moved from a traditional rural-agricultural configuration to a predominantly urban-industrial one whose interdependencies increasingly require projections in quantitative terms and the interplay of many institutions and forces that cannot be centrally controlled. Thus Wagner places considerable emphasis on the further growth of business and on the development of human "resources" that would have the physical and psychological mobility and the skills needed to ensure that growth. The projections, in brief, were still basically optimistic, but the realism that comes only with maturity and recognition of limits of what one institution can do to solve the complex problems of a modern society had come to TVA. If entropy had thus set in, the agency had not altogether lost its strong sense of identity and purpose under the urge merely to survive. The later self-image, if less colorful than the earlier one, was still fairly bright, although much less visible to the external world.

If Wagner's assessment may be taken as a projection of the positive image of TVA in its recent years, and serves as a preserving or continuing successor to Lilienthal's glowing picture from the earlier period, no individual in the later era has provided the comprehensive critical (negative) image that Davidson did in relation to the formative years. But innumerable partial or piecemeal portraits of TVA are available for arrangement into a collage that forms a contemporary negative image, and most of these pieces may be said metaphorically to be assembled under Davidson's critical eye. At the time this essay was being written, the news media were full of reports of events in which TVA's role was portrayed in an extremely bad light. Those events and the critical way they were interpreted clearly mirror Davidson's negative attitude. In the interests of economy of space, the examples have to be treated briefly here.

The most noticeable and persisting of these negative images is produced by the mounting environmentalist attack on TVA for its dual assault on nature. One charge is directed at the profligate consumption of resources by TVA to meet increasing demands for power to serve unconstrained and imbalanced corporate growth. The critics first launched their attack on the use by TVA of coal (especially strip-mined coal) to fire its steam plants, and the assault was later extended to the nuclear part of the power program. In both cases, of course, environmental pollution added to the campaign heat, and no amount of effort on the part of the agency to take a lead in the development of standards and practices in restoration of strip-mined lands and in safety precautions in the construction and operation of atomic energy installations could effectively counter the attacks. During S. David Freeman's recent chairmanship a rather mixed group of strident critics systematically turned up at his public addresses, which is especially ironic because Freeman's main interest was energy conservation before he was compelled to spend most of his time on the self-impelled issue of power demands in relation to the mounting energy crisis. This Catch 22 dilemma was complicated by accelerating costs (some of which were affected by delays in construction of new generating facilities and other problems occasioned by environmental concerns) that not only led to loss of tacit popular support for TVA but caused additional scathing criticism of the agency on the part of ratepayers who were outraged at the 200 percent increase in electricity charges in the 1970s.

A recent illustration of the pertinence of Davidson's view of the destruction of traditional culture and its human costs is the complete expropriation of TVA of the Land Between the Lakes for use as a demonstration project in conservation and recreation, which involved the displacement (in some cases forcible) of some 3,000 people in settlements that dated from the American Revolutionary period. Although the acquisition was completed in the early 1970s, the resentment lingers on, as indicated by the poignant feature stories that still crop up in print from time to time. John Egerton, free-lance writer, former owner of land in the affected area, and in his own right a committed environmentalist, has forcefully summarized the reaction: "The Land Between the Lakes is a 'national demonstration' of the destructive consequences of bureaucratic insensitivity and greed, an example of cold and impersonal manipulation to create a controlled environment in which the past is obliterated and all human activity is regulated. It is a concept of urban renewal writ large across a rural landscape."[12]

A final illustration of negative portraiture is totally contemporary and involves the dual issues of the degree of autonomy of TVA and its relations with other political bodies generally. The directors announced in the late fall of 1981 that they intended to give bonuses (amounting to more than $36,000 in some cases) to their top managerial people in order to fend off the possibility of losing them to private utility industries. The reaction in Congress was immediate and heated. Although the involved members of Congress were not at all certain about their ability to prevent this action, strong statements were forthcoming from many of them, including several from the states in the Tennessee Valley, and a resolution was approved in the House expressing its opposition. The TVA board persisted in proclaiming its right and intent to distribute the bonuses. However, by adoption of a conference committee amendment proposed by Democratic Senator James Sasser of Tennessee to the energy and water appropriations bill, Congress found a way to make the issuance of these bonuses illegal.[13] This contretemps blotched the public image of TVA and, at least for the time being, damaged its relations with Congress.

In sum, the public has seldom seen TVA presented in a favorable light in the media in recent years. One regional magazine referred to "TVA's Traumatic Mid-Life Crisis," and presented the crisis (at least by implication) as one related to the image of TVA that arises out of its having been caught in the changed circumstances involving the larger crisis of the modern urban-industrial society.[14] Having had a part in the movement of a substantial subregion of the South from a traditional to a "modern" society, TVA now finds itself confronted by the values of that traditional society, by values that many now see as badly needed in the "modern" society, at least in coping with a further transition to a "postindustrial" society. Davidson and others expressed some of those values in so striking a manner during that period when modernization of the South was getting fully underway and TVA's positive image was so ascendant that one may conjecture that a delayed diffusion of the older culture's values has been taking place for more than a decade. TVA has become guilty by association for having been too much a part of modernization and not sufficiently solicitous for the preservation of the fundamental values of the old culture. That judgment may in a way be fair retribution for the condescending attitudes expressed toward the South by those harbingers of change to an industrialized society whose ideas and actions Davidson had so thoroughly deplored.

When contrary images of a political institution are strikingly presented, and are conceived out of fundamental conflicts of value, those competing images are likely to be exaggerated versions of reality. Even so, one of them may come closer than the other to providing an adequate interpretation of the purposes, functions, and effects of the institution at a given period in its history. At all times each of the conflicting images (and the values on which they are based) may need correction in the light of a critical perspective drawn from its opposite. Thus it might be said that there are no ideal institutions, only ideal *types*. Like all human institutions, TVA falls considerably short of the ideal, either in its purposes or its operations in pursuit of those purposes. As a character in one of Robert Penn Warren's novels once noted, history knows no leaps, except perhaps for the leap backward. TVA became established on the basis of perceived societal needs, and it can demonstrate major accomplishments in meeting those needs within the context of a working political tradition. It is solidly established because of those achievements, and because it did not violate the basic expectations embedded in the practice of American politics even when considered from the perspective of its presumed distinctiveness.

TVA is unlikely to be dismantled. But excesses of both thought and action were involved in its origin and early development, some of which now constitute serious obstacles to its adaptation to purposes and practices designed to meet changed or changing needs. If society is in transition, we can never be quite sure what it will become, even though we are constantly engaged in trying to affect both the direction and the mode of that transition. At the urging of President Carter and others, including several of the agency's leading executives, TVA moved in the direction of conservation and constrained growth in its own region (especially in its energy programs) rather than toward unlimited growth, and could perhaps become the national pacesetter in all areas of energy development. As the agency reaches its fiftieth anniversary, a negative public image has emerged to contest the previously widely accepted positive one, and the agency is again deemed to be highly controversial. But as Gordon Clapp has noted, if TVA ever ceases to be controversial, it will cease to exist.

NOTES

1. David E. Lilienthal, *TVA: Democracy on the March* (London: Penguin Books, 1944).

2. *Ibid.*, pp. 13–16.

3. Donald Davidson, *The Tennessee*, 2 vols. (New York: Rinehart, 1946 and 1948). Vol. 1 is subtitled *The Old River: Frontier to Secession*, vol. 2, *The New River: Civil War to TVA*. The book was originally published in Rinehart's impressive Rivers of America series; the University of Tennessee Press brought out a facsimile edition of vol. 1 in 1978.

4. *Ibid.*, 1:5.

5. Readers familiar with the Nashville Agrarians will recognize the continuity of the arguments advanced here with those of Davidson and others in *I'll Take My Stand: The South and the Agrarian Tradition*, by *Twelve Southerners* (New York: Harper and Brothers, 1930; Baton Rouge: Louisiana State University Press, 1977).

6. Davidson, *The Tennessee*, 2:176–333.

7. *Ibid.*, pp. 332–33.

8. All quotations from Lilienthal, *TVA*, ch. I.

9. The summary of Davidson's conceptions given here is much less literal than the preceding one on Lilienthal's views of TVA as an instrument of transformation. I have, therefore, drawn on other of Davidson's writings than *The Tennessee*, as well as on the ideas of others who were influenced in their thinking by Davidson or who obviously influenced him. Although further qualification of both sketches would be desirable—in Lilienthal's case to make his own sweeping phrases less simplistic than they appear, and in Davidson's to include more of the complexities and cohesion that are characteristic of him in the corpus of his work—I have made every effort to avoid distortions of either reduction or inflation in this context.

10. For a succinct review of the legislative history and contents of the TVA Act, see Joseph C. Swidler, "Legal Foundations," ch. 2 in Roscoe C. Martin, ed., *TVA: The First Twenty Years: A Staff Report* (University: University of Alabama Press; Knoxville: University of Tennessee Press, 1956), pp. 16–29. For a fuller discussion of the legislative efforts leading to the eventual passage of the act, see Chapter 1 of this volume. The most comprehensive treatment is Preston J. Hubbard, *Origins of the TVA: The Muscle Shoals Controversy, 1920–1932* (Nashville: Vanderbilt University Press, 1961).

11. Aubrey J. Wagner, "The Future of TVA," in John R. Moore, ed., *The Economic Impact of TVA* (Knoxville: University of Tennessee Press, 1967), p. 146.

12. John Egerton, *The Americanization of Dixie: The Southernization of America* (New York: Harper's Magazine Press, 1974), p. 60.

13. Among the continuing newspaper stories on TVA, see especially "House-Senate Panel Rejects TVA Bonuses," *Nashville Tennessean*, Nov. 19, 1981, p. 21.

14. Rudy Abramson, "TVA's Traumatic Mid-Life Crisis," *South Magazine* (July, 1980), pp. 32–35.

12 Dewey W. Grantham

TVA and the Ambiguity
of American Reform

EARLY interpreters of the Tennessee Valley Authority stressed the agency's reform role as well as its impressive accomplishments. Thus the English historian Denis W. Brogan, in a book published in 1950 on *The Era of Franklin D. Roosevelt*, entitled one of his chapters "The Dazzling TVA." This was not just another federal agency, Brogan wrote. It was "a great crusading enterprise whose success or failure would, it was thought, demonstrate the possibility of free, democratic planning in a world in which 'planning' had become a panacea, but a panacea whose effective use seemed confined to authoritarian states."[1] Although the aura of reform that surrounded TVA gradually disappeared and its reputation eventually suffered in liberal circles, the experiment would seem to qualify as an important reform institution in twentieth-century America.[2] To view the undertaking from this perspective may provide a useful dimension for an interpretation of its history. It is also possible that the Authority's origins and institutionalization, as well as the political and ideological controversies that have swirled around it, will throw light on the ambiguous character of modern American liberalism.

The essential chronology needs to be provided at the outset. The background of the enterprise is important, for the long controversy that preceded passage of the TVA Act in 1933 did much to determine the scope and direction of the new federal agency. The controversy focused

316

attention on significant new issues that were dealt with in the 1930s. By 1932 the regional focus and multiple-purpose approach to the development of the Tennessee River basin had gained strong support, many of the engineering problems had been solved, and southern leaders had come to view the Muscle Shoals project as a vehicle for regional development. The ravages of the Great Depression, the dramatic shift in the strength of the major political parties, and the support of Franklin D. Roosevelt cleared the way for the establishment of the Tennessee Valley Authority (see Chapter 1 of this volume).[3]

The years of the New Deal and World War II—the era of Franklin D. Roosevelt—proved to be the formative period in the history of the Authority. TVA's valley-wide jurisdiction and multipurpose function were made clear in the statute of 1933, and with a sympathetic chief executive and powerful friends in Congress, the agency was largely free to create its own identity and to translate a set of broad objectives into a structure of programs, relationships, and operations. There were, to be sure, a variety of obstacles confronting the first board of directors, and as Paul Conkin has remarked, "unanticipated events and conflicting personalities" helped mold the institution that began to take shape in the thirties (Chapter 1 of this volume, p. 3).

This period was dominated by the unfolding of TVA's great construction projects and by a series of challenges to the agency's effectiveness, indeed, to its very existence (see Chapter 2).[4] But after surviving the most serious threats to its autonomy, as well as the adverse effects of its own internal disarray and a thoroughgoing congressional investigation, TVA was free to move forward with greater unity and concentration. The experiences of the thirties clarified the agency's priorities and laid lasting foundations for most of its programs. The centrality of the power program in the Authority's congeries of undertakings had become apparent with the ascendancy of David E. Lilienthal among the directors. At the same time, Harcourt A. Morgan's dominant position in directing the course of TVA's various agricultural operations did much to develop an infrastructure based on local interest groups. In spite of the growing importance of its power program, the agency was immersed in a multiplicity of other tasks. This was a natural consequence of its broad legislative mandate and of its efforts to construct a carefully integrated system of dams and reservoirs. Navigation, flood control, and maximum production of hydroelectric power, centering in the great dams on the Tennessee and its tributaries, not only necessitated the coordination of three vital functions but also encompassed many related activities that touched the lives of the people in the Valley. The reservoirs created by the dams, for example, pointed to the need for erosion control, which called for improved farming methods, reforestation, and conservation measures.

The popular response to TVA during these formative years was extraordinary. "There seems to be something about the boldness and vigor of the whole enterprise," the writer Stuart Chase noted in 1936, "which fires the imagination and enlists enthusiastic support."[5] The Authority's projects received extensive coverage in American newspapers and magazines, and a steady stream of visitors, from the United States and abroad, moved through the Valley to witness the wonders of the new experiment in the South. "As the great Leviathan rushed its physical works to completion and developed its numerous co-ordinated applications of physical and social science," one chronicler later wrote somewhat sardonically, "it became evident that here in the Tennessee Valley, of all places, was emerging one of the marvels of the modern world."[6] Public support in the Valley was decidedly favorable, although in the beginning there seems to have been some suspicion of "Yankee meddling" and federal intervention.[7] As enthusiasm for TVA mounted, it was almost as if the region's inhabitants had discovered a new utopia. From its earliest settlement, one author remarked, "the Tennessee country had attracted utopians from afar and quickened utopian dreams among valley dwellers themselves."[8] There was much evidence, too, of a remarkable esprit de corps among TVA staff members and a conviction among its employees that the agency's work was unprecedented and important.[9]

World War II created an important new stage in TVA's evolution. It now appeared as a national agency devoted to defense as well as to power production, flood control, navigation, and conservation. Joining the mobilization drive, the Authority stepped up the pace of its dam construction projects, built its first steam plant, modified its fertilizer program to meet wartime needs, and contributed to a number of other war-related activities, including the secrecy-shrouded atomic energy program at Oak Ridge. But if the war strengthened TVA and helped justify it as a defense enterprise, it also reinforced the agency's growing emphasis upon its function as a power facility (see Chapter 3).[10] It was now assumed that TVA would provide electrical power for military research and development as well as for the civilian needs of the Tennessee Valley.

In the fall of 1945, not long after VJ-Day, President Harry Truman dedicated Kentucky Dam, the last of the main-river dams envisioned by the planners of the 1930s. The basic shape of the TVA structure had emerged by this time. It was hard to deny the technical success of the agency. The massive dams on the Tennessee and its tributaries had harnessed the river, largely solved the problem of the recurring, devastating floods in the Valley, and created a great inland waterway for commercial traffic and recreation. TVA had wrought a physical transformation in the Tennessee Valley. By mid-century the Authority had become the largest producer of electricity in the United States, had developed an integrated power service area, and through its promotional rates and efficient management had demonstrated how electrical power could improve the lives of the people in the Valley. Meanwhile, the agency's internal organization had been perfected, and it had established vital relationships with state and local governments, municipal power boards, rural cooperatives, agricultural colleges, farm organizations, and other federal agencies (see Chapter 5).

As TVA reached maturity following the war, it entered a period of consolidation and prolonged expansion, particularly in its power operations. The consumption of electricity in the Valley increased dramatically, reflecting both the economic buoyancy of the region and the vast amounts of power required by the Atomic Energy Commission's installations and by defense-related industries located in the area. The hydroelectric turbines in the Authority's dams, which produced about 80 percent of its power, could no longer keep up with the growing consumption of electricity. Having earlier established itself as sole supplier of electricity in the Tennessee Valley and having consistently proclaimed its determination to provide electrical energy at the lowest possible cost, the agency gradually defined its raison d'etre as that of producing all the power needed in its service area, no matter how large the amount might be. The solution devised by the board of directors was to supplement its hydroelectric system with steam plant generation. The board's decision was encouraged by the abundant coal reserves in the region and by recent improvements in the technology of coal-fired steam plants. By the mid-1960s more than three-fourths of the Authority's electricity was being generated by steam plants (see Chapter 3, pp. 77–78).[11]

The giant steam plants were expensive to build, and TVA was forced to go to Congress for sizable appropriations at a time when the legislators were increasingly resistant to further expansion of the agency. One reason for this congressional distrust was the powerful opposition of private utility companies, which were haunted by the specter of an expansive TVA moving beyond its existing service area on the basis of a dynamic steam plant program. The Eisenhower administration, responding to these pressures as well as a conservative ideology, formulated a plan to curb the Authority and possibly transform its function as a public power agency. The ensuing Dixon-Yates controversy undermined the administration's scheme but eventually led to a compromise embodied in the Revenue Bond Act of 1959. While this measure ended TVA's dependence upon Congress for appropriations to finance its power program, it confined the agency to its existing service area (Chapter 3, pp. 73–76).[12] Thereafter, as Erwin C. Hargrove observes, TVA "ceased to be a direct agent of national policy" (Chapter 4, p. 117).

For several years following the adoption of the self-financing act of 1959, TVA operated in a time of unaccustomed calm. The Authority was relatively free of congressional control, and a modus vivendi had smoothed its relations with private utilities in surrounding areas. Meanwhile, its power program was growing rapidly. But by the mid-1960s new problems were arising. The directors were no longer sure that they could meet the ever-mounting demands for power by relying on steam plants. The cost of coal rose sharply in the late 1960s, the Authority found itself under attack for using large quantities of strip-mined coal, and in 1967 the board reluctantly announced its first general rate increase. Hoping to solve these and other problems, the directors decided in 1966 to launch a nuclear power program. By the mid-1970s TVA had become the world's largest nuclear power operation, with seventeen units in service or in some stage of development[13] (Chapter 3, pp. 80–81).

Although TVA's generating capacity continued to increase at an impressive rate during the 1970s, the agency was soon mired in the quicksand of several painful dilemmas. The technological advantages of steam plant and nuclear power generation were not sufficient, given the Authority's commitment to power expansion, to prevent a series of rate increases. TVA's customers, after so many years of cheap electricity, could neither comprehend nor easily forgive such unnatural price hikes. Ironically, the self-financing act, while freeing TVA from dependence on congressional appropriations for its power additions, made it necessary for the ratepayers in the Valley to assume the burden of financing the continuing development of the power program. Critics also focused upon strip mining, thermal and air pollution, the hazards of nuclear energy, an unresponsive bureaucracy, and so on. TVA found itself in trouble with the Environmental Protection Agency in Washington, and it was involved in numerous court actions (Chapter 7, pp. 188–89; Chapter 8, pp. 200–220).[14] Still, the Authority's directors held to their course.

By 1980 the agency had developed a power-generating capacity of 30 million kilowatts, held more than $13 billion in assets, and operated 47 dams and a waterway 650 miles long. But if TVA had demonstrated "the workability of a unified system of federal regional management for river control and power supply" (Chapter 5, p. 140), its future seemed as uncertain in the early 1980s as it had during the drawn-out struggle of the 1920s.

Any attempt to evaluate the Tennessee Valley Authority as a reform organization must consider its intellectual and political roots. Many threads of development came together in the creation of the agency, and several of these strands reached back to prewar progressivism. Preston J. Hubbard concluded, for example, on the basis of a careful study of TVA's origins, that the Authority was "primarily the handiwork of a relatively small band of Progressives in Congress led by George W. Norris." Their motives, Hubbard wrote, sprang largely from "a desire to uphold Progressive principles regarding public welfare which called for planned mutiple-purpose development of the nation's water resources."[15] The progressives seized upon the Muscle Shoals issue as a means of restraining concentration in the dynamic private utilities field, of formulating a more equitable approach to the waterpower problem, and of advancing the cause of conservation and good resource management.

Although the reform origins of the TVA are broadly compatible with the liberal-progressive tradition in the United States, many of the elements of that tradition are ambiguous and at odds with one another. Characterizing American liberalism before the New Deal, Otis L. Graham has suggested that "one face of reform had been moralistic and emotional, nostalgic for small-town and small-business values. The other aspired to a more scientific and pragmatic approach to social problem-solving, was managerial by temperament, accepted large institutions as the inevitable framework in which progress must be pursued."[16] Neither side of this duality offers an adequate summary of the reformism that eventually produced TVA, though both sides of the tradition were reflected in the motivation of its founders.

Three themes are especially noteworthy in TVA's progressive background. One emphasized the role of regulation and the principle of protecting the "public interest," of safeguarding consumers and small entrepreneurs against high rates and unfair competition, of promoting what one historian has described as "economic justice and democracy in the handling of resources."[17] An important manifestation of this concern was the reaction to the problem of the "power trust" in the 1920s and the symbolic significance that this new evidence of monopolistic power had for American liberals, including Senator Norris. A second theme was the entrepreneurial strain that ran through progressivism. It constituted a primary component of southern progressivism in the early twentieth century. As Paul Conkin writes of certain protagonists in the Muscle Shoals controversy, "Here wandered various boosters of southern progress, from those who placed their hopes on the benefits of cheap fertilizer and improved agriculture to those still trying to attract northern capital and new manufacturing ventures" (Chapter 1, p. 12).[18] The third theme that linked TVA and progressivism was the concept of efficiency, an idea identified with the conservation movement, with multipurpose river development, with government corporations, and with social planning.[19] Senator Norris's proposal for the public operation of Muscle Shoals drew sustenance from all of these forces.

It is not surprising that these themes should have been prominent in the social thought of TVA's first board of directors. Arthur E. Morgan, the chairman, combined an engineer's faith in technology and efficiency with a commitment to the ideal of creating a cooperative society. While he regarded TVA as a broad, multipurpose undertaking, he was keenly interested in using it as a laboratory for social experimentation, as a scheme for a designed and planned social and economic order. He was, in short, "an idealist who desired a social revolution for the Tennessee Valley."[20] For Harcourt A. Morgan, the Authority loomed as an opportune instrument for the economic development of the region and especially for the modernization of southern agriculture. David E. Lilienthal, the third member of the original board, came to the new agency convinced of its need to develop a great public power program as a means both of breaking the stranglehold of the private utilities and of demonstrating the extraordinary benefits that could be derived from electric power. Seeking to create a political environment that would support technological goals, Lilienthal, in Erwin Hargrove's description, linked the embryo TVA program of electric power to the fight of public power against the private companies (Chapter 4).[21]

If TVA's roots were firmly fixed in the soil of progressivism, its development in the 1930s was profoundly affected by the milieu of the New Deal. Indeed, TVA's evolution as a reform endeavor was closely related to the broader reformism of the Roosevelt administration. As one of the president's favorite projects, the agency received invigorating assistance from Washington in the form of appropriations, public works loans, political support, and friendly counsel. At the same time the Tennessee Valley experiment was a source of strength and inspiration for Roosevelt and the New Deal. Its antimonopoly objectives and decentralization features appealed strongly to the disciples of Justice Louis D. Brandeis, and it mirrored several important aspects of New Deal liberalism. It contributed to the sharp ideological split between the major political parties. Furthermore, the Authority was one of the most successful of all New Deal ventures, and in later years it was perhaps the most visible legacy of the New Deal. It even won support from some of Franklin Roosevelt's opponents. One such advocate was the socialist Norman Thomas, whose deepening criticism of Roosevelt's presidency had gone so far by 1935 that he could approve only TVA, which he called "a beautiful flower in a garden of weeds."[22]

The word "planning" was often heard among reformers in the 1930s, and the Roosevelt administration's recovery experiments encouraged the belief that the New Deal would undertake a scheme of national planning. The administration's programs for agricultural production and industrial recovery represented a kind of planning, though not in any coherent or systematic way. Planning was more widely touted in the varied activities of TVA, and of all New Deal programs, it came closest to being a planning agency. Yet the Authority was never a genuine experiment in regional planning, and little attention was given to this function after Arthur Morgan's departure. The concept of multiple-purpose river development did require centralized direction and the reconciliation of competing uses by experts.[23] Although the TVA directors soon abandoned any definition of planning that "denoted a blueprint of targeted objectives or mandatory criteria," they embraced what one scholar describes as "a coordinated approach to resource problems, physical and human, mobilizing all available technical and social skills to advance the interests and welfare of the valley people" (Chapter 5, p. 139).[24]

In many respects TVA was the centerpiece of the New Deal's response to the economic and social plight of the South in the 1930s. The region's depressed agriculture and colonial economy certainly provided a great challenge to the New Deal's recovery programs and reform efforts. Against this background, TVA became what George B. Tindall has aptly termed "a massive monument of economic growth and development."[25] The engineering achievements alone were remarkable: within a decade the federal agency transformed an unruly river into an impressive waterway providing navigation, flood control, and vast amounts of hydroelectric power. These benefits undoubtedly contributed to the industrial expansion and economic diversification of the Tennessee Valley, though it is impossible to be precise in measuring the Authority's stimulative effects. New Energy poured into the Valley as a result of TVA's multipurpose activities: the electricity produced at the dams, the clearing of the rivers, the rebuilding of the forests, the re-plenishing of the soil, the improvement of agricultural methods, the development of recreation. But beyond this, as Arthur M. Schlesinger, Jr., has written, "there was something less tangible yet even more penetrating: the release of moral and human energy as the people of the Valley saw new vistas open up for themselves and for their children."[26]

Among the Roosevelt administration's reform objectives was the formulation of a national policy on electric energy. TVA was the first of the New Deal's power undertakings, and it was always at the center of the administration's quest for a comprehensive and effective power policy. Roosevelt's search resulted in the appointment of two national policy committees, enactment of the Public Utilities Holding Company Act of 1935, creation of the Rural Electrification Administration, completion of the Bonneville power project on the Columbia River, and the recommendation of seven "little TVAs" in 1937. But the most dramatic focus in this wide-ranging administration campaign was the bitter struggle in the Tennessee Valley between the public power and the private power traditions. TVA, along with the holding company act, represented the New Deal's principal offensive against the "power trust."[27] As it turned out, the administration was never able to develop a well-defined, coordinated policy in the field of electric power, "only a series of piecemeal, *ad hoc* arrangements."[28] TVA was a feature of these "arrangements," but it also became the nation's most successful public power project. Although the Authority failed to provide a workable "yardstick" with which to measure the rates of private power companies, it served as a pacesetter for the industry. The agency's pioneering role in reducing its rates and widening its market seemed to demonstrate the advantages of the public power approach.[29] No other venture contributed so much to the vitality of the public power tradition in the United States.

Within the context of New Deal reform, TVA also assumed a role of some importance in the conflict over economic policy during the 1930s. The Roosevelt administration's initiatives in this area, like its efforts in the field of electric power policy, were shifting and inconsistent. Yet TVA seemed to represent, in varying degrees, most of the major emphases in the New Deal's economic policies. It is true that TVA ran counter to the approach of the National Recovery Administration, though there were elements of economic planning, centralized control, and rationalization in both undertakings. TVA was more in tune with the New Deal's antitrust activities, with the antimonopoly campaign and the idea of enforcing competition. The agency's spokesmen lashed out at the perpetuators of the South's colonial economy and took part in the movement to equalize intersectional freight rates. TVA can also be regarded as a manifestation of the concept of "counterorganization," the idea of using the government to promote the organization of economically weak groups, restoring economic balance and developing an economy of "countervailing powers" capable of achieving the full utilization of resources.[30]

"One of the central problems of twentieth-century America," Ellis W. Hawley writes, "has revolved about the difficulty of reconciling a modern industrial order, necessarily based upon a high degree of collective organization, with democratic postulates, competitive ideals, and liberal individualistic traditions inherited from the nineteenth century."[31] TVA impressed many liberals in the thirties as both a means of resolving this dilemma and an innovation adaptation to federalism. Here was a novel instrumentality in the American system of government, a public corporation with unprecedented autonomy within the existing departmental structure and with relative freedom from supervision by presidential and congressional staff agencies (see Chapter 5). Some contemporaries described it as an American version of Sweden's "Middle Way." It suggested a way of bringing national power into harmony with local administration. It appeared to demonstrate the virtues of decentralization, which was at the heart of the neo-Brandeisian approach, and in a more general sense it seemed to reflect the new interest in regionalism and to manifest a heightened cultural nationalism.[32] Finally, TVA illuminates the reformism of the thirties because it was one of the most conspicuous and popular symbols of liberal idealism during that decade. The experiment captured the liberal imagination as an augury of progressive politics, social planning, regional development, and the entire panoply of New Deal reform. Thus began "the romance" of liberal intellectuals with the Tennessee Valley Authority. No other agency in the 1930s or since, William E. Leuchtenburg asserts, "has commanded the same kind of allegiance or has aroused similar emotions."[33] Reform in the Depression years was essentially *economic* reform; it tended to be tough-minded, practical, and "anti-utopian." Still, as Leuchtenburg remarks, the New Dealers had their "Heavenly City," most of all the Tennessee Valley, "with its model

town of Norris, the tall transmission towers, the white dams, the glis-
tening wire strands, the valley where 'a vision of villages and clean
small factories has been growing into the minds of thoughtful men.'"[34]

The TVA itself, sensitive to the importance of good public relations
and adept at publicizing its activities through newspapers and other
publications, contributed significantly to the creation of its image as an
efficient, innovative, and reform-minded institution. So assiduous were
TVA and its advocates in this endeavor that a mythology soon grew up
around the Authority's putative freedom from politics, "grass-roots democracy," and decentralization. David Lilienthal's popular account of
the agency, *TVA: Democracy on the March* (1944), quickly became a
text for the liberal creed. In a new edition of this work published a few
years later, Lilienthal suggested that TVA was "probably the best known
single demonstration of modern American democracy."[35] While the validity of this assertion is arguable, TVA did attract a great deal of favorable comment from foreigners, many of whom characterized it as a
democratic as well as a technological innovation. In the mid-1930s, for
example, Julian S. Huxley described the agency as "a major experiment
in social planning." Odette Keun, a French observer, considered it a
magnificent blueprint for liberalism.[36] Such encomiums enhanced TVA's
reputation among liberals in the United States.

In the Tennessee Valley TVA gave rise to a new vision of progress.
Southern liberals like George Fort Milton, editor of the *Chattanooga
News*, considered the Authority the pinnacle of the New Deal and the
hope of the New South. Milton championed the undertaking as a means
of developing the region, though he opposed any interference with the
cultural heritage of the Valley. As the Authority grew, he came to see it
as a power development and coordinating organization that might serve
as a catalyst for desirable economic and social changes in the region
(see Chapter 11).[37] TVA's popularity in the South was related to the conviction that the agency was promoting the section's industrialization
and economic development.[38] Southerners were stirred by the drama of
the Authority's political controversies and engineering feats. They applauded its accomplishments and savored its national recognition. Here
was a *southern* enterprise whose achievements were admired in other
parts of the country and whose "style and joie de vivre" nourished
the image of an extraordinary American institution (see Chapter 10,
p. 265).

After about 1940 TVA as a reform agency, like the New Deal, lost
much of its strength. This was true in part because the Authority had
narrowed its mission and increasingly concentrated its energies and re-

sources on the expansion of its power program. In the meantime, the agency's deference to local elites and conservative groups in developing its agricultural program had seemingly limited its rehabilitative efforts in conservation and rural life.[39] The imperatives of the war and its aftermath, as well as the changing social and political climate in the United States, also contributed to the general weakening of reform. In later years liberal critics of TVA called attention to its growing conservatism. One journalist reported in the early 1960s, for instance, that the agency was being run by two men who had lost "the aggressive, idealistic fervor of the early days." TVA was behaving like a giant utility company, emphasizing the production of cheap electric power at the expense of further development of the natural and human resources of the Valley.[40] There were some new nonpower programs in the postwar period, including the Tributary Area Development project and the Land Between the Lakes recreational area. But these initiatives were dwarfed by the gigantic power complex.

The movement for the extension of the valley authority idea following World War II showed how difficult it would be to reproduce an agency like TVA. Advocates of such authorities in the Missouri River and Columbia River valleys depended heavily upon the "TVA experience" (Chapter 10, pp. 268–70).[41] Thus President Truman, who sponsored the creation of a Columbia Valley Administration, invoked the example of TVA, which he declared had "inspired regional resource development throughout the entire world" (Chapter 10, p. 278). Despite support from the Truman administration, a goodly number of congressmen, and various elements in the two regions most affected, no additional valley authorities were established. There was determined opposition to such proposals: from the resurgent private utilities and other organized groups, from many congressmen, from within the executive bureaucracy, from agencies like the Army Corps of Engineers and the Bureau of Reclamation. The political mood, moreover, had become more conservative, and the prevailing attitude toward the nation's institutions and traditions now fostered an affirming rather than a reforming approach. The abortive campaign of the 1940s in behalf of more valley authorities pointed up the fact that TVA had originated in the struggle to resolve a singular problem—the disposition of the Muscle Shoals properties following World War I—and in a set of unusual conditions in the early 1930s. This combination of circumstances was not likely to reappear: by mid-century the valley authority idea had become a "fading vision" (Chapter 10, pp. 289–92).

As a matter of fact, TVA itself no longer enjoyed widespread national support. The Authority continued to symbolize the New Deal, and the valley concept still appeared in the campaign rhetoric of the Democratic party. TVA also provided an earnest, in some quarters, of national planning that might yet be realized, and it attracted foreign interest as a possible model for the development of backward economies. But it encountered increasing opposition in Congress, even among southern Democrats from districts outside the confines of the Tennessee Valley. In contrast to the response it had once elicited, the agency seemed to inspire mounting sectional suspicion and hostility after mid-century.[42] The declining vitality of liberalism, its more moderate ideological complexion, and its preoccupation with an ever-expanding capitalist economy also helped dissipate TVA's national image as a reform institution.[43] Although President Truman supported the expansion of the Authority's power program, he was ambivalent about the valley authority idea. The agency was a matter of only passing concern to John F. Kennedy and Lyndon B. Johnson, who occasionally extolled its virtues but for the most part seemed to view it as a legacy of the New Deal and earlier Democratic triumphs, on the one hand, and as an example of American ingenuity and a weapon in the Cold War, on the other. While Jimmy Carter spoke of TVA as a laboratory for the development of a national energy policy, neither he nor any other postwar Democratic president made it a constituent part of his reform agenda.

Many people in the Tennessee Valley, however, continued to regard TVA as an innovative and reform-oriented organization. If cheap electrical power, agricultural and industrial development, and a modern navigation channel from Paducah to Knoxville constituted "reform," then the agency was still involved in the reforming business. TVA enjoyed overwhelming popular support in its own area, and it continued for many years to serve as a rallying point for the region's liberals.[44] It was strongly backed by the Valley's major leaders and organizations as well as most voters. Political leaders vied with each other in the intensity of their loyalty to the Authority, and politicians with national ambitions, such as Governor Frank G. Clement and Senators Albert Gore and Estes Kefauver, saw in the issue an avenue to success in the arena of national politics.[45] Newspapers, chambers of commerce, and local organizations in the Valley were also powerful defenders of TVA. Distributors of TVA power organized the Tennessee Valley Public Power Association, Citizens for TVA, Inc., and other groups to support the agency. These pressure groups not only promoted the use of electrical power and industrial development but also exerted great influence in the state legislatures of the Valley and made their presence felt in Congress. They became, as Richard A. Couto has shown, an important part of TVA's political environment (see Chapter 9).

Nevertheless, by the 1970s TVA had lost much of its home support, was once again under attack in Congress, and was less and less often identified as a "reform" institution. With its central function—the production and distribution of electricity—now a bone of bitter contention, it was no longer implicitly accepted as a reliable means of regional development. Nor was it a unifying force for liberal politicians in the Valley. Even so, TVA was still in existence after almost half a century. It continued to stand for something. Indeed, as one scholar has recently observed, its very existence makes a philosophical statement.[46]

There is doubtless more shadow than substance in the reform claims of the Tennessee Valley Authority. An offspring of early twentieth-century progressivism, World War I preparedness, and reform politics in the 1920s and 1930s, TVA became an integral part of the New Deal. Yet aside from its progressive provenance and its brief experience as a highly publicized reform venture in the 1930s, its chief significance in the context of modern American reform is that of a lingering but luminous symbol of the New Deal. Despite Arthur E. Morgan's hopes, the agency has never been very important as an instrument of social reform. Indeed, the effect of its programs has often been to benefit influential and middle-class elements in the Valley rather than the poor and disadvantaged, at least in the short run. TVA never developed a comprehensive rural resources program. It neglected small farmers, black people, and the needs of some remote areas. Its grass-roots doctrine was misleading and disingenuous, however well it served TVA as a protective ideology.[47]

Still, one may well ask about the chances of achieving more extensive social reform in the South during the 1930s and 1940s. Given the strength of local elites, the influence of rural and small-town politicians, and the conservative and tenacious character of the region's cultural traditions, the prospects for such reform may not have been very bright. Working through local groups and institutions was in some measure a matter of practicability and realistic possibilities for the agency. It was also a calculated means of creating a favorable political climate. The Authority's success in popularizing the notion of grass-roots democracy may have assured its existence as an "independent agency permanently based in the Valley (Chapter 2, p. 57). The partnership approach reassured state and local governments and enabled TVA to encourage activities by those governments rather than trying to create institutions or cooperative enterprises on a regional scale.[48]

TVA's failure to launch a frontal attack on poverty, racial discrimination, and traditional social arrangements typified, rather than differed from, most New Deal undertakings. Whatever its hopes for more thoroughgoing social reform, the Roosevelt administration also found it necessary to come to terms with existing centers of political and economic power. The difficulties that confronted New Deal reformers are revealed in the experience of the Farm Security Administration, in the weakness of the New Deal community program, and in the administration's circumspect approach to the problem of race relations. Of course, many liberals were attracted to TVA because they viewed it as a social agency dedicated to the development of a backward section. Some liberals were probably disappointed in the Authority's preoccupation with the production of power, as well as its role in the development of the atomic bomb and as a bulwark in the postwar defense buildup. In any case, American liberals gradually lost their ardor for the agency, just as the love affair between liberal intellectuals and the workingman eventually cooled.[49]

The TVA, Philip Selznick reminds us, "suggested a model of a task force way of coordinating effort, a way of bringing together the energies of government and making those energies and those contributions highly visible and therefore making it possible for such an enterprise to mobilize the commitment of a people." In the early days, Selznick notes, TVA seemed to be committed to "people-centered values" and to the idea that "engineering technology would be only a means."[50] But with the passage of time there was a subtle shift in the Authority's nonpower programs, a shift from the language of resource development and management to the language of economic development. While this change should not be exaggerated, there was some basis for the emerging conception of the agency as undemocratic, bureaucratic, and insensitive to "people-centered values."[51]

On the other hand, TVA has been "a productive government enterprise" (Chapter 5, p. 142). It has also been a creative promoter of change in the South. It took the lead in creating a new landscape in the Tennessee Valley, a landscape of well-designed dams and buildings, improved agriculture, and scenic value based on a chain of lakes with clear blue water and large areas of green forest.[52] It functioned as a modernizing force in the region by providing an example of scientific, technical, and managerial capacity in its own organization and by serving as a clearinghouse for activities ranging from technical studies and research to vocational training and education. It encouraged the establishment of new agencies such as planning commissions and the introduction of new services by state and local governments.[53] No other institution, with the possible exception of the federal forces led by Generals Grant and Sherman, has had a greater impact upon the Tennessee Valley.

Regional development probably represents the agency's most important contribution to American reform. TVA's promotion of industrialization, agricultural efficiency, and the modernization of institutional life helped give reality to the old dream of regional rehabilitation and economic progress in the South. The Authority was an important factor in the redistribution of economic power in the United States. Its greatest success has been the production of low-cost electrical power, which seemed to constitute a prerequisite for the South's more rapid industrialization and economic diversification. The dynamic power program undertaken by the agency was itself a significant regional reform. The directors, displaying vision and determination, committed themselves to providing electricity more cheaply and more efficiently than the region's private utilities, and they boldly assumed that a vast demand for such energy was a realistic possibility (see Chapter 6).[54]

The Tennessee Valley Authority was conceived as a *national* agency with a *regional* focus. This strengthened the relationship between the South and the New Deal and encouraged the nationalization of southern politics. It also facilitated TVA's role as a modernizing institution. The blending of national and regional interests in the Authority provided an alluring prospect for many southerners. In practice the agency did a good deal to justify their faith. It was responsible for a large infusion of federal money into the region; it emphasized the virtues of efficiency and modernization, it demonstrated the feasibility of decentralization; it operated through local leaders and established institutions; and it devoted itself to a resourceful program of economic development. But if in this respect TVA expressed the most salient tenets of southern liberalism, it also revealed the limitations and ambiguities of modern American reform.

NOTES

1. Denis W. Brogan, *The Era of Franklin D. Roosevelt: A Chronicle of the New Deal and Global War* (New Haven, Conn.: Yale University Press, 1950), pp. 240–58; quotation on p. 246.

2. The concept of "reform" used in this essay refers to the broad range of political, economic, and social changes identified with mainstream American liberalism. It is best exemplified in the political coalitions, policies, and beliefs and commitments of reformers during the progressive era and the New Deal years.

3. See also Preston J. Hubbard, Origins of the TVA: The Muscle Shoals Controversy, 1920–1932 (Nashville, Tenn.: Vanderbilt University Press, 1961).

4. For these and other aspects of TVA's formative experience, see also Thomas K. Mc-Craw, TVA and the Power Fight, 1933–1939 (Philadelphia: J. B. Lippincott, 1971).

5. Stuart Chase, Rich Land, Poor Land: A Study of Waste in the Natural Resources of America (New York: McGraw Hill, 1936), p. 277.

6. Donald Davidson, The Tennessee, vol. 2, The New River: Civil War to TVA (New York: Rinehart, 1948), p. 251.

7. See, for example, Jonathan Daniels, A Southerner Discovers the South (New York: Macmillan, 1938), pp. 48–49, 57–59, 72.

8. Davidson, The Tennessee, 2:145.

9. John Gunther, who spent some time investigating TVA in the 1940s, wrote that "never in the United States or abroad have I encountered anything more striking than the faith its men have in their work." Quoted in Marguerite Owen, The Tennessee Valley Authority (New York: Praeger, 1973), p. 77.

10. See also Roscoe C. Martin, ed., TVA: The First Twenty Years: A Staff Report (University: University of Alabama Press; Knoxville: University of Tennessee Press, 1956); Wilmon H. Droze, High Dams and Slack Waters: TVA Rebuilds a River (Baton Rouge: Louisiana State University Press, 1965).

11. See also George E. Rawson, "The Process of Program Development: The Case of TVA's Power Program" (Ph.D. dissertation, University of Tennessee, 1979), pp. 2–3, 59–60, 158.

12. See also Aaron Wildavsky, "TVA and Power Politics," American Political Science Review, 55 (Sept., 1961): 576–90, and Dixon-Yates: A Study in Power Politics (New Haven, Conn.: Yale University Press, 1962).

13. Rawson, "Process of Program Development," pp. 2–3, 74, 160, 166; Victor C. Hobday, Sparks at the Grassroots: Municipal Distribution of TVA Electricity in Tennessee (Knoxville: University of Tennessee Press, 1969).

14. Rawson, "Process of Program Development," pp. 96–97, 102, 171; "A Second Spring Stirs the TVA," Business Week (Oct. 29, 1966), pp. 112–18; James Branscome, "Appalachia—Like the Flayed Back of a Man," New York Times Magazine (Dec. 12, 1971), pp. 107–8, 114–16; Peter Barnes, "TVA after 40 Years," New Republic, 169 (Nov. 10, 1973): 15–18.

15. Hubbard, Origins of the TVA, p. viii.

16. Otis L. Graham, Toward a Planned Society: From Roosevelt to Nixon (New York: Oxford University Press, 1976), p. 8.

17. J. Leonard Bates, "Fulfilling American Democracy: The Conservation Movement, 1907 to 1921," Mississippi Valley Historical Review, 44 (June, 1957): 31.

18. See also William A. Doran, "Early Hydroelectric Power in Tennessee," Tennessee Historical Quarterly, 27 (Spring, 1968): 72–82; George F. Milton, Jr., "The South and Muscle Shoals," Independent, 112 (Jan. 19, 1924): 39–41; "The Muscle Shoals Situation as Viewed in Mississippi," Manufacturers' Record, 87 (Feb. 19, 1925): 70–71.

19. See, for example, Samuel P. Hays, Conservation and the Gospel of Efficiency: The Progressive Conservation Movement, 1890–1920 (New York: Atheneum, 1969).

20. Roy Talbert, Jr., ed., "Arthur E. Morgan's Ethical Code for the Tennessee Valley

Authority," *East Tennessee Historical Society's Publications*, 40 (1968): 119–27; quotation on p. 119. See also Talbert, "Beyond Pragmatism: The Story of Arthur E. Morgan" (Ph.D. dissertation, Vanderbilt University, 1971).

21. See also Thomas K. McCraw, *Morgan vs. Lilienthal: The Feud within the TVA* (Chicago: Loyola University Press, 1970).

22. Arthur M. Schlesinger, Jr., *The Age of Roosevelt: The Politics of Upheaval* (Boston: Houghton Mifflin, 1960), p. 180. See also Schlesinger, *The Age of Roosevelt: The Coming of the New Deal* (Boston: Houghton Mifflin, 1958), p. 319, and William E. Leuchtenburg, *Franklin D. Roosevelt and the New Deal, 1932–1940* (New York: Harper and Row, 1963), p. 149.

23. See Samuel P. Hays, "Conservation and the Structure of American Politics: The Progressive Era," in Hays, *American Political History as Social Analysis* (Knoxville: University of Tennessee Press, 1980), p. 238. For planning and the New Deal, see Graham, *Toward a Planned Society*, pp. 1–68.

24. For a different perspective, see Nancy Grant, "Blacks, Regional Planning, and the TVA" (Ph.D. dissertation, University of Chicago, 1978), pp. 1–30, 101–49.

25. George B. Tindall, *The Emergence of the New South, 1913–1945* (Baton Rouge: Louisiana State University Press, 1967), p. 446; see pp. 391–539, 607–49, for a comprehensive treatment of New Deal programs in the South.

26. Schlesinger, *Coming of the New Deal*, pp. 333–34.

27. See McCraw, *TVA and the Power Fight*; Schlesinger, *Politics of Upheaval*, pp. 362–83; Leland Olds, "Yardsticks and Birch Rods," *Harper's Magazine*, 171 (Nov., 1935): 648–59; Morris Llewellyn Cooke, "The Early Days of the Rural Electrification Idea: 1914–1936," *American Political Science Review* 42 (June, 1948): 431–47; D. Clayton Brown, "Sam Rayburn and the Development of Public Power in the Southwest," *Southwestern Historical Quarterly*, 78 (Oct., 1974): 140–54.

28. Philip J. Funigiello, *Toward a National Power Policy: The New Deal and the Electric Utility Industry, 1933–41* (Pittsburgh: University of Pittsburgh Press, 1973), p. 260.

29. The use of electrical power was promoted, in the Tennessee Valley and elsewhere, by the Electric Home and Farm Authority. One writer has characterized this agency, which was established in 1934, as the "first clear-cut entrepreneurial excursion" by the federal government into the consumer credit business. See Joseph D. Coppock, "Government as Enterpriser-Competitor: The Case of the Electric Home and Farm Authority," *Explorations in Entrepreneurial History*, 2d ser., 1 (Winter, 1964): 187–206.

30. Ellis W. Hawley, *The New Deal and the Problem of Monopoly: A Study in Economic Ambivalence* (Princeton, N.J.: Princeton University Press, 1966), pp. 187–204.

31. *Ibid.*, p. vii.

32. See Gordon R. Clapp, "The Tennessee Valley Authority," in Merrill Jensen, ed., *Regionalism in America* (Madison: University of Wisconsin Press, 1951), pp. 317–29; Hawley, *New Deal and the Problem of Monopoly*, p. 289; Tindall, *Emergence of the New South*, pp. 575–606.

33. Leuchtenburg, commentary presented at Vanderbilt conference on TVA.

34. Leuchtenburg, *Franklin D. Roosevelt and the New Deal*, pp. 339–45; quotation on p. 345.

35. David E. Lilienthal, *TVA: Democracy on the March* (New York: Harper, 1953), pp. x–xi. Also see Lilienthal, "The TVA and Decentralization," *Survey Graphic*, 29 (June, 1940): 335–37, 363, 365–67.

36. Huxley, "The T.V.A.: A Great American Experiment," *Times* (London), May 21, 22, 1935; Keun, *A Foreigner Looks at the TVA* (Toronto: Longmans, Green, 1937), p. 89.

37. James A. Hodges, "George Fort Milton and the New Deal," *Tennessee Historical Quarterly*, 36 (Fall, 1977): 383–409, esp. pp. 405–8. See also North Callahan, *TVA: Bridge over Troubled Waters* (South Brunswick, N.J., and New York: A. S. Barnes, 1980) pp. 129–31. Donald Davidson entitled one of the chapters in his history of the Tennessee River "At Last! The Kingdom Really Comes!" Davidson wrote that the establishment of TVA was viewed, in and out of the region, as a means of overcoming the South's image as a backward and barbarous section—as a way "to wipe all sins away." Davidson, *The Tennessee*, 2:211–18.

38. See, for example, Ted Leitzell, "Uncle Sam, Peddler of Electric Gadgets," *New Outlook*, 164 (Aug., 1934): 50–53, 63.

39. See Philip Selznick, *TVA and the Grass Roots: A Study in the Sociology of Formal Organization* (Berkeley: University of California Press, 1949), for an elaboration of this theme.

40. John Ed Pearce, "The Creeping Conservatism of TVA," *Reporter*, 26 (Jan. 4, 1962): 31–35.

41. See also Hermann Herrey, "TVA's of the Future," *American Scholar*, 14 (Autumn, 1945): 488–93.

42. See Wildavsky, "TVA and Power Politics," pp. 383–90.

43. For postwar liberalism, see Alonzo L. Hamby, *Beyond the New Deal: Harry S. Truman and American Liberalism* (New York: Columbia University Press, 1973), and Edward A. Purcell, Jr., *The Crisis of Democratic Theory: Scientific Naturalism & the Problem of Value* (Lexington: University of Kentucky Press, 1973), pp. 235, 239, 254–56, 265–69.

44. For examples of many favorable appraisals of the agency, see Bill Wolf, "These Southerners Just Love Yankees," *Saturday Evening Post*, 226 (Sept. 5, 1953): 22–23, 42, 47–49; Stanley J. Folmsbee, Robert E. Corlew, and Enoch L. Mitchell, "A New Era in Tennessee: TVA," in *History of Tennessee*, 2 (New York: Lewis Historical Pub. Co., 1960): 307–20; Robert Sherrill, "More Power and Energy to the People," *Lithopinion*, 8 (Summer, 1973): 8–19.

45. See, for example, James B. Gardner, "Political Leadership in a Period of Transition: Frank G. Clement, Albert Gore, Estes Kefauver, and Tennessee Politics, 1948–1956" (Ph.D. dissertation, Vanderbilt University, 1978).

46. Francis E. Rourke, commentary presented at Vanderbilt conference on TVA.

47. See, for example, Grant, "Blacks, Regional Planning, and the TVA," pp. 150–317, and Selznick, *TVA and the Grass Roots*.

48. Martha Derthick, *Between State and Nation: Regional Organizations of the United States* (Washington, D.C.: Brookings Institution, 1974), p. 189.

49. See, for example, Jerome M. Mileur, ed., *The Liberal Tradition in Crisis: American Politics in the Sixties* (Lexington, Mass.: Heath, 1974), esp. p. 5.

50. Selznick, commentary presented at Vanderbilt conference on TVA.

51. It is interesting to note that most of the contemporary criticism of TVA has come from within its own region, including the questioning of economic growth, the expression of concern about the environment, and the protest against nuclear hazards. This was a South, "of all things, with a Sierra Club!" See Otis L. Graham, commentary presented at Vanderbilt conference on TVA.

52. See, for example, Brian Hackett, "TVA: Creator of Landscape,: *Journal of the Town Planning Institute*, 37 (Nov., 1950): 7–14.

53. M. H. Satterfield, "TVA-State-Local Relationships," *American Political Science Review*, 40 (Oct., 1946): 935–49; Gordon R. Clapp, "Public Administration in an Advanc-

ing South," *Public Administration Review*, 8 (Summer, 1948): 169–75; Albert Lepawsky, "Government Planning in the South," *Journal of Politics*, 10 (Aug., 1948): 536–67; Lawrence L. Durisch, "Southern Regional Planning and Development," *ibid.*, 26 (Feb., 1964): 41–59.

54. This point was made in the suggestive commentary by Philip Selznick, presented at the Vanderbilt conference on TVA. See also John P. Ferris, "The TVA Approach," *University of Tennessee Record*, Extension Series 26 (May, 1950): 72–83; B. U. Ratchford, "Government Action or Private Enterprise in River Valley Development: An Economist's View," *American Economic Review*, 41 (May, 1951): 299–306; Norman I. Wengert, *Valley of Tomorrow: The TVA and Agriculture* (Knoxville: University of Tennessee, Bureau of Public Administration, 1952); Wilmon H. Droze, "TVA and the Ordinary Farmer," *Agricultural History*, 53 (Jan., 1979): 188–202; John R. Moore, ed., *The Economic Impact of TVA* (Knoxville, University of Tennessee Press, 1967).

CONTRIBUTORS

PAUL K. CONKIN is distinguished professor of history at Vanderbilt University. He is the author or editor of nine previous books, including *FDR and the Origins of the Welfare State* (1967, 1975) and *Prophets of Prosperity: America's First Political Economists* (1980).

RICHARD A. COUTO is director of the Center for Health Services at Vanderbilt University, an assistant professor in the department of Medical Administration, and a lecturer in the Department of Political Science. He is the author of *Poverty, Politics and Health Care: An Appalachian Experience* (1975) and *Streams of Idealism and Health Care Innovation: An Assessment of Service-Learning and Community Mobilization* (1982).

WILMON H. DROZE is executive director of the Georgia Agrirama. His publications include *High Dams and Slack Waters: TVA Rebuilds a River* (1965).

CRAUFURD D. GOODWIN is James B. Duke Professor of Economics at Duke University and dean of the Graduate School. He is author or editor of nine books including *Exhortation and Controls: The Search for a Wage-Price Policy, 1945–71* (1975) and *Energy Policy in Perspective: Today's Problems, Yesterday's Solutions* (1981).

DEWEY W. GRANTHAM is Holland N. McTyeire Professor of History at Vanderbilt University. His books include *Hoke Smith and the Politics of the New South* (1958, 1967) and *The Regional Imagination: The South and Recent American History* (1979).

ERWIN C. HARGROVE is professor of political science and director of the Institute for Public Policy Studies at Vanderbilt University. He is the author of *Presidential Leadership, Personality and Political Style* (1966) and *The Power of the Modern Presidency* (1974) and co-author of *Presidents, Politics and Policy* (1984).

WILLIAM C. HAVARD, JR., is chairman of the Department of Political Science at Vanderbilt University. His numerous publications include *The Changing Politics of the South* (editor; 1972) and *A Band of Prophets: The Vanderbilt Agrarians after Fifty Years* (co-editor; 1972).

AVERY LEISERSON, a former president of the American Political Science Association, is professor emeritus of political science at Vanderbilt University. His publications include *Administrative Regulation: A Study in Representation of Interests* (1942) and *Parties and Politics* (1958).

RICHARD LOWITT is chairman of the Department of History at Iowa State University. He is author of a three-volume biography of George W. Norris and is co-editor of *One Third of a Nation: Lorena Hickok Reports on the Great Depression* (1981).

MICHAEL J. McDONALD is associate professor of history at the University of Tennessee, Knoxville. He is co-author of *T.V.A. and the Dispossessed* (1982) and *The New South Comes to Appalachia: A History of Knoxville, Tennessee* (1983).

DEAN HILL RIVKIN is associate professor of law at the University of Tennessee, Knoxville. He is the author of *Clinical Legal Education and the Promotion of National Goals* (1978).

VERNON W. RUTTAN is professor of economics and of agricultural and applied economics at the University of Minnesota. His publications include *Induced Innovation: Technology, Institutions and Development* (co-author; 1978) and *Agricultural Research Policy* (1982).

WILLIAM BRUCE WHEELER is associate professor of history at the University of Tennessee, Knoxville. He is co-author of *The New South Comes to Appalachia: A History of Knoxville, Tennessee* (1983).

INDEX